85424 7008   WIT   £96-50

Local Plans in British Land Use Planning

Local Plans in British Land Use Planning

by

PATSY HEALEY
Oxford Polytechnic, UK

PERGAMON PRESS

OXFORD · NEW YORK · TORONTO · SYDNEY · PARIS · FRANKFURT

U.K.	Pergamon Press Ltd., Headington Hill Hall, Oxford OX3 0BW, England
U.S.A.	Pergamon Press Inc., Maxwell House, Fairview Park, Elmsford, New York 10523, U.S.A.
CANADA	Pergamon Press Canada Ltd., Suite 104, 150 Consumers Road, Willowdale, Ontario M2J 1P9, Canada
AUSTRALIA	Pergamon Press (Aust.) Pty. Ltd., P.O. Box 544, Potts Point, N.S.W. 2011, Australia
FRANCE	Pergamon Press SARL, 24 rue des Ecoles, 75240 Paris, Cedex 05, France
FEDERAL REPUBLIC OF GERMANY	Pergamon Press GmbH, Hammerweg 6, D-6242 Kronberg-Taunus, Federal Republic of Germany

First edition 1983

Library of Congress Cataloging in Publication Data
Healey, Patsy.
Local plans in British land use planning.
(Urban and regional planning series; v. 31)
Includes bibliographical references and index.
1. Land use — Great Britain — Planning. 2. Regional planning — Great Britain. I. Title. II. Series.
HD593.H4 1983 333.73'17'0941 82-25958

British Library Cataloguing in Publication Data
Healey, Patsy
Local plans in British land use planning. — (Urban and regional planning series; v. 31)
1. Real estate development — Great Britain — History
2. Regional planning — Great Britain — History
I.Title II. Series
333.3'8 HD1390
ISBN 0-08-025242-7

In order to make this volume available as economically and as rapidly as possible the typescript has been reproduced in its original form. This method unfortunately has its typographical limitations but it is hoped that they in no way distract the reader.

Printed and bound in Great Britain by William Clowes Limited, Beccles and London

IN MEMORIAM
D.R.H.

Acknowledgements

The author would like to thank the following for permission to reproduce material:

School of Advanced Urban Studies, Bristol
Her Majesty's Stationery Office
Bolton Metropolitan Borough Council
St Helen's Metropolitan Borough Council
London Borough of Islington
Horsham District Council
Ordnance Survey
Hampshire County Council
North West Leicestershire District Council
Gloucester City Council
London Borough of Lambeth
Faber and Faber Ltd

Contents

List of Tables

List of Diagrams

Introduction

In 1965 I joined the planning department of one of the newly-created London Boroughs to work in the Development Plan team. I had then no formal training in planning, and until this time, I had thought in a vague unformulated way that planning was something to do with public intervention to distribute resources more fairly than the market could achieve. It was difficult to discern any connection between this general political idea and the tasks of the Development Plan team of which I became a member. These included collecting large amounts of information - about numbers of dwellings and their condition, about how many people worked in what jobs in what locations, about how many health centres were needed and where these should go. Somehow this information was supposed to produce a Development Plan, but what the nature and purpose of this document might be was never made clear.

Meanwhile, as we worked away collecting a variety of facts, the economic and social life of this part of inner London was affected by substantial factory closures and major comprehensive redevelopment schemes. Ugly multistorey system-built blocks of flats emerged on the skyline while dereliction spread at ground level. Our work in the Development Plan team was in no way able to account for the processes of technological change which were producing factory closures. Nor did it offer any comment on the value and consequences of high-density high-rise redevelopment. I was no clearer at the end of my three years in this Borough as to the purpose of this sort of planning and the role of development plans within it than I was at the beginning. The information we collected has probably had only marginal and temporary uses for any one. Efforts to prepare a development plan have continued in a desultory way, though after 1972 this no longer became a task required of the Borough by statute. Even when its preparation became discretionary, no-one seemed to inquire in any serious way into what sort of a tool and what sort of a statement a development plan was.

My experience was not untypical of many of those who came into planning in the 1960s. The demand for our services had increased significantly because of the greatly increased scale of public and private urban development and renewal during this period. Many of us were social science graduates, often, as I was, untrained in planning. We learnt the ethos of planning, such as it was, from our colleagues and from the planning schools we attended. At this time, both practitioners and planning schools were under attack for a longstanding habit of treating the physical structures of cities as if they were somehow separable from social and economic processes. Young geographers like myself did little to redress the balance, since we were similarly deficient in skills in relating social processes to spatial structures, and none in grasping the role within social processes of the activities of the government agencies of which we were a part. We had, in effect, joined the enterprise of British town and country planning at a time of paradigm shift, when people had lost confidence in traditional approaches but were in the main unaware of the emergence of new ones. We thus were offered no concepts with which to understand the work context in which we found ourselves. So I remained unenlightened about the nature and purpose of development plans even though at this time a major review of the development plan system was underway.

The vacuum of ideas about planning which followed the toppling of the physical design tradition in planning was soon filled. Borrowing ideas from the United States, some planners and several of the planning schools turned with enthusiasm to notions of planning as a societal scientific decision-making process. This was of course not a new idea, having been advocated in the 1940s by Karl Mannheim and others. But it was revived having been washed clean of its ideological associations with socialism. A characteristic of such ideas, known these days as procedural planning theory, was that social and economic processes were little inquired into, since the aim of planning was to change the *effects* produced by these processes, while the institutional procedures by which such planning would operate were treated as elements to be created as appropriate to the task in hand. Functional efficiency to achieve societal goals was the aim. Little attention was given to the procedures of the British planning system as they actually operated. Development plans were considered only as the opportunity to define strategies.

Roughly contemporaneously, British planners were attracted to American notions of social planning, which encouraged the recognition that some groups in society were not necessarily gaining from the drive for economic growth, and which legitimized attempts by planners at devising policies of positive discrimination in favour of these disadvantaged groups. Such ideas were particularly attractive to those working in inner city situations where the evidence of social disadvantage was difficult to avoid. Planners here began to conceive of their role as developing general community welfare strategies which would in particular alleviate such disadvantage. Development plans became for them a format to be filled with appropriate policies. Plans were thus considered as an unproblematic and neutral tool, readily transferable, not only between different parts of the same country, but from one country to another.

However, as planners in the early 1970s became involved in the preparation of structure and local plans, the two types of development plan introduced in 1968, it soon became clear that these new paradigms were themselves seriously flawed, both as normative frameworks to guide the practice of planning and as explanations of that practice. Exercises in societal decision-making confronted methodological problems of information-overload, and political and organizational problems over who should define and develop policy options. Emphasizing the needs of the disadvantaged related uneasily with a long-unquestioned belief that planning was somehow in the public interest, or a process of balancing competing interests. And the attempt to escape from the preoccupation with physical structures was jolted by central government's insistence that development plans should be concerned primarily with land use and development policies and proposals. Thus the new paradigms

of the late 1960s and early 1970s brought few advances in understanding the
nature and purpose of development plans. Yet there were undoubtedly more
planners involved in their production in 1975 than there were in 1965. Few
were likely to be any clearer as to their nature and purpose than I was ten
years previously.[1]

This book is an analysis of the nature, purpose and operation of development
plans in British planning practice, focusing on the local plan. To
undertake such an analysis, I have followed yet another paradigm shift
within planning thought. My emphasis will be on development plans as
procedural tools used by government agencies as an element in programmes for
intervening in the way land is used and developed. Although the term
"development plan" may appear to refer to a general tool which can be used
in any situation, it says little about the form which such a plan may take
and the purposes to which it ought to be put. My argument is that the form
of development plans as procedural tools is something which is evolved in
specific social-historical contexts, which in turn affects the content of
plans and of the policies and proposals which it may contain.

To understand the nature and purpose of development plans, we therefore have
to examine their distinctive form and content and how this has evolved. To
evaluate their role and function, we have to examine how they relate to
programmes of intervention in land use and development as a whole, to the
outcomes of these programmes, to who controls the content of the programmes
and to who benefits from the outcomes. The British planning system is often
claimed to determine "the public interest" in the way land is used and
developed, and development plans are portrayed as a vehicle within which
what constitutes the articulation of this interest may be expressed. My
contention is that the definition of what constitutes the public interest
within the planning system is not a neutral process, and that we must
therefore examine carefully not only the content of policies and proposals
and the outcomes of the actions of planning authorities but the extent to
which procedures and the way they are used constrain or allow possible
interpretations of the public interest.

Through such an examination of the British local plan, in its varying
definitions and in the way it has been used, I hope to provide not only an
account of a much-neglected area of British planning practice, but to
highlight significant characteristics of the British planning system as a
whole. My concern with institutional procedures, as opposed to the
principles of town design or the methodology of strategic choice, is itself
a different way of thinking about planning than the dominant articulate
traditions of planning thought until the mid-1970s. It is, however, a
concern which has always been a vital consideration in the practice of the
British planning system. In developing my account, I have drawn not only
on the reality of actual planning practice, but on three areas of recent
academic discussion which, though so far largely separate, in my view need
to confront each other if we are to advance our understanding of land use
planning.

The first is the broad set of theoretical perspectives currently dignified
with the title of the political economy of public intervention, and of
urban and regional development; I discuss this body of work in Chapter 9.
Its important contribution has been to focus our attention on the way the

---

[1] These comments are expanded later, particularly in Chapter 2, where sources
are provided.

interests created by economic production interrelate with the political
articulation of these interests, and the manner in which this
interrelationship infuses government operations at every level. The second
area of discussion is the international concern with urban land policy,
though this so far arises more from consultancy experience than academic
development. This field, to which I refer in Chapter 1, reflects a
perception that the achievement of more efficient and equitable
distributions of activities and resources within urban areas is affected
more fundamentally than had previously been appreciated by the way land is
made available for development. The literature here is primarily
prescriptive in emphasis, but does focus our attention on the variety of
mechanisms which have been used to intervene in the way land is used and
developed. It thus encourages us to consider why in Britain we have the
particular set of mechanisms that we do.

The third field I have drawn upon is the body of ideas associated with the
recent interest in interorganizational relations and "implementation".
These ideas stem largely from the realization that policies are not simply
articulated and then followed through by the agencies appointed to carry
them out. These agencies themselves have to be understood as political
entities interacting within and between each other. To understand the
operation of any public programme therefore requires close observation of
the practices of those public agencies involved in carrying it out. As I
have argued elsewhere (Healey 1982c), in my own view the insights gained
from this type of investigation need to be absorbed and reinterpreted in
the terms of the structural explanations being put forward by the "political
economists". Chapter 9 indicates some ways in which this is already being
done. However, a great deal more work is required before we have available
any satisfactory way of understanding how the British planning system works
which takes account of the dimensions which these three areas of discussion
raise. These could be summarized as the impact of general political and
economic relations on the form and content of particular government
programmes; the precise formal characteristics of these programmes in
relation to the outcomes sought from intervention; and the detailed
operational practices which develop as formal programmes are absorbed and
interpreted within specific instances of political and economic relations.

This book is primarily a contribution to the analysis of land and land use
planning, or government programmes of intervention in the way land is used
and developed. As such, I hope it will be of value to those interested in
the British planning system and more generally, in the analysis of public
programmes. I also offer it as an approach to understanding land use
planning as it is evolving in other countries, and as a warning against the
facile transfer of tools evolved in the distinctive conditions which apply
in Britain to other parts of the world. This is *not* primarily a book about
"how to do local planning". Yet I have included within it a discussion of
several of the methodological points which those engaged in the practice of
local plan production currently face. I hope also that practitioners will
find the approach and the examples I have used of some assistance to them.
However, I cannot avoid the conclusion that the "local plan" as enshrined in
legislation and as currently used in local authorities is not the most
appropriate tool for the uses to which it is being put in the 1980s. I
therefore conclude, in Chapter 10, with what I intend as a contribution .to
the debate about the future form of the British planning system, and about
the sorts of tools which might be appropriate for the purposes for which
local plans are now used.

The organization of the book falls into three parts. In Part I I review the
context and background to the practice of local plan production and use. In

Chapter 1, I consider the reasons why governments may intervene in the way land is owned, used and developed, the sorts of mechanisms they may use for this and the development plan as a particular mechanism or tool. Chapter 2 provides a brief history of the British planning system since the war, and the place of development plans within it. Chapters 3 and 4 look at the evolving definition of two types of development plan which are currently in use in Britain, structure and local plans. Part II describes local plan practice, in detail, drawing on my own review of local plans as well as such published material as exists. Chapter 5 examines why local plans have been prepared and Chapter 6 investigates the way they have been prepared. In Chapter 7 I look at the product, the content of plans in terms of their policies as well as the form of their expression and the nature of the plans as documents. Chapter 8 reviews how local plans once produced have actually been used. The content of Part III has already been indicated. Chapter 9 attempts an explanation of the practice described in Part II and Chapter 10 considers the ways in which we might think about changing the planning system and consequently the nature and form of plans. In view of the disparate nature of the literature on this whole subject area, I have provided a full collection of references, as well as an index to the plans I refer to in the text.

This book is one outcome of several years of thinking and researching the detailed operation of the British planning system. During this time I have worked closely with colleagues at Oxford Polytechnic, particularly Martin Elson and Paul McNamara; and at the School of Advanced Studies, Bristol, notably Jacky Underwood, Colin Fudge, Sue Barrett and Robin Hambleton. Over this time, I must adknowledge particularly the stimulation, criticism and moral support of Martin Elson and Jacky Underwood. In addition, the following have made very helpful comments on individual sections of the book as it developed, especially Jacky Underwood, Liz Hill and Paul McNamara, as well as Michael Hebbert (Chapter 2), and Paul McNamara, Eric Reade, Richard Farnell, John Montgomery and Peter Saunders (all on Chapter 9). The errors and inadequacies of the book are, of course, entirely mine. I must also thank Oxford Polytechnic for giving me a term's leave of absence in Autumn 1980; SAUS, Bristol, for putting me up during that period; and the SSRC and DoE for financing empirical research which has contributed to my general understanding of the detailed operation of the planning system. Heather helped with the filing, and John, Liz, Vince and Dave with the index. Finally, Joan Minter's capacity to translate my handwriting into typed text has been an enormous help as those who know my handwriting will testify.

Crowmarsh   Patsy Healey

PART I

CHAPTER 1

Land Policy, Land Use Planning and Development Plans

Local plans in Britain are one of two forms which a "development plan" can take as defined in British town and country planning legislation. They are also whatever anyone chooses to define them as. The conflicts this leads to will be discussed in later chapters. The purpose of this chapter is to raise general issues about any exercise in land use planning, the term I shall use to describe what in Britain is referred to as town and country planning. Section 1 considers the nature of land and land use as a concern of public policy. Section 2 examines the purposes of land use planning, relating these to different notions of the role of the state. In Section 3 I raise the question of the relation of institutional arrangements and procedures in a particular area of public policy to purposes and interests, concluding with comments on the implications for the discussion of development plans of the issues raised in this chapter.

1. LAND POLICY AND LAND USE PLANNING

One of the characteristics of British "town and country planning" is an endemic confusion among those involved in it not only about its purpose, but about its object of concern. A long list of apparent synonyms can be found in the literature - physical planning, land use planning, town planning, town and country planning, environmental planning, spatial planning, urban planning, urban policy and urban design. This multiplicity of terms is not confined to Britain, but is repeated in many countries.

One could treat this terminological proliferation as unimportant, but it is not just an issue in semantics. The terms tend to cover a different "set" of objects of concern. Thus urban policy may refer to resource allocation without an explicit spatial dimension, while physical planning may focus on urban physical development with very little relation to social and economic policies. Some argue that the terminological confusion is deliberate, that the lack of specificity about what "town and country planning" is and does is functional to the state's needs to legitimate its activities (Scott and Roweis 1977 p.1114, Castells 1977 p.76). Some clarification of the terms to be used in this book is therefore necessary, although the real world has a habit of escaping the academic's efforts at precision, and this seems particularly so in the field of land policy for reasons which will be suggested below.

3

My starting point is that in referring to "land policy" and "land use planning" we are discussing the purpose and operation of government intervention in the way land is owned, used and developed. The British statutory local plan is a particular tool created in legislation to pursue certain aspects of *government land policy*. In this book, I am therefore explaining how this tool came to be devised, within the context of evolving government land policy, and how it has subsequently been interpreted in practice.

The term *land policy* has been used in recent years, particularly in the international literature, to distinguish policies about land - its ownership, allocation, use and development - from social or economic policy. Thus Lichfield and Darin-Drabkin (1980) present land policy as a subset of development policy. These authors, and Dunkerley *et al.* (1978), use the term *land policy* to cover questions of land ownership and transfer, land costs, the allocation of surplus land values, as well as the control of urban land use (Dunkerley 1978).[2] In Britain, where in recent years there has been a tendency to discuss land use policy separately from issues of land ownership and land values, the term "land policy" has been used by Ratcliffe (1976) who makes an attempt to bring the two areas together. I will do likewise.

Some will argue that it is invalid to identify an area of land policy separately from the social and economic forces which generate the forms of ownership, allocation, use and development of land. The logic following from this argument would be that issues relating to land and its development should be treated as a part of, for example education policy, of housing policy or of industrial policy. The problem here is that there are mechanisms of land allocation, such as land and property markets, which interrelate generators of activities in land. The case for distinguishing land policy as a category of discussion lies partly in this phenomenon, that land issues cut across the "sectoral" subdivisions into which government policy is commonly divided. It can also be argued that as land is a distinctive resource (compared to labour and capital), policy about its ownership, allocation and use should be discussed as a distinct category.

There is no need to make too much of the validity of separating out particular areas of public policy for examination. All policy "areas" are interrelated. Even the categories "social" and "economic" are difficult to disaggregate into distinct areas of policy. Yet both in government organizations and in academic work, some subdivision of "all government activity" is necessary in order to cope with detailed operations or detailed analysis. The important point is to remember that all such subdivisions are to some extent artificial. Thus any studies within a "policy area" should take account of the wider forces which structure events within that area and relationships with other policy areas. There will therefore be tendencies to stray across organizational and analytical boundaries. The tendency to widen the area of concern of town and country planning noted above arises partly because land policy cuts across sectoral divisions which are firmly entrenched politically and organizationally. In Britain, there are also other factors encouraging this tendency, such as the

---

[2] This discussion emanates from UN seminars on urban land use (United Nations 1973) and the Habitat debates (Koenigsberger and Groak 1980).

professionalization of the personnel who administer town and country
planning. However, the land policies in operation in a country are not
necessarily *government* policies. As McAuslan (1975) has reminded us,
British statutory planning exists in conjunction with a long-standing
tradition of private law governing land ownership, allocation, use and
development. In countries in the developing world today, "traditional"
mechanisms for acquiring rights in land may persist in the same way.
Examples are the *mulk, miri* and *waqf* land tenures in Muslim countries
(Hamdani 1980), or the allocation of "stool" lands in the Ashanti region of
Ghana (Avis 1976). Land allocation through inheritance, though governed by
private law and often modified by taxes, is still of importance in Britain.[3]
And in most countries which operate on a capitalist basis, land and property
markets have a major role in determining how land is owned, exchanged, used
and developed.

I will now use a distinction borrowed from Townsend's discussion of social
policy (Townsend 1975 p.6). He notes that all societies have "social
policies" although these are not necessarily preferred by government or
involve government action. By not having an explicit policy, government is
acknowledging that the family and/or the market are adequately managing
social affairs. Similarly, a government could take a position that common
law, inheritance, and the market secure an adequate system for the ownership,
allocation, use and development of land. However, explicit government
programmes in respect of land have become a common feature of the older
industrialized countries since the late nineteenth century, and more
recently in developing countries, firstly in respect of rural land and more
recently with increasing urbanization in respect of urban land.[4] This raises
the issue of why governments decide to act in the area of land policy (or to
use the conventional terminology, why they *intervene*) and how such activity
is organized.

To conclude, I am arguing that an adequate analysis of British land use
planning must take account of firstly, the interrelation of government
policies about land with other policy concerns; and secondly, the
interrelation between what government does and other societal mechanisms for
allocating the same resources. This leads us into consideration of the role
of the state in social and economic development about which there has been
so much recent discussion.

It will be noted that I have so far carefully avoided any reference to
planning. It is common practice to refer to British "land use planning".
Is this a synonym for "land use policy" or does the word "planning" have a
distinct connotation? On the one hand it has been argued convincingly that
"planning" is not a phenomenon which exists independently of what is being
planned (Scott and Roweis 1977, Thomas 1979, Healey *et al*. 1982a). On the
other, the notion of planning symbolizes end-directed, forward-looking,
co-ordinated activities as opposed to the short term marginal adjustments
and atomized decision-making commonly associated with incrementalism, a
heroic rather than a humdrum approach, to quote Hayward (1975). Government
planning may also symbolize the dominance of some version of the public
interest in an area of resource allocation, and/or efficiency in government.

---

[3]See the recent discussion on the importance of inheriting houses, given
widespread owner-occupation, in wealth accumulation in this country (Murie
and Forrest 1980, Saunders 1978).

[4]Hence the work of Darin-Drabkin, Dunkerley *et al*., Lichfield and the United
Nations already referred to.

As I will demonstrate at several points in this book, planning as the
guidance of change by frameworks produced with rational-technical methods by
experts is embodied in the British system as one possible "mode of
operation". What has to be explained is why it is so embodied and the
circumstances in which the way land is used and developed is actually arrived
at by the use of such a mode of operation. I return to this question in
Chapter 9.

And finally, what about *development plans*? There is no reason to suppose
that the existence of such a plan necessarily has any association with
planning, either symbolically or in practice, though it may well do. Since
this section has been about definitions, at this stage it is sufficient to
identify the sort of plan I am referring to. The term development plan is
of course used in the literature on economic and social development. The
development plans I will be referring to are in a special category, perhaps
best distinguished by the term "physical development" plan. They are plans
which either visually, or verbally and numerically, or both, indicate (with
varying degrees of precision) where physical development is to be located
and the principles governing the way land in a specific area is to be used
and developed. They may exist in the form of a broad framework (as in the
British structure plan) or a very specific site development and programming
map (as in areas where a new development project is being undertaken). The
British local plan may be described in a general way as a site-specific
development guidance framework. Chapter 2 describes how these two types of
development plan - structure and local plans - have been developed in
British land use planning. I now turn to the debates about the purpose and
form which government land policy should take.

2. THE PURPOSES OF GOVERNMENT INTERVENTION IN LAND AND DEVELOPMENT

This book sets out to analyse the interpretation and use of a particular
legislative tool, the British local plan, one of the measures available to
government when intervening in land. However, I have argued in the previous
section that any such analysis must be located within an understanding of
why the state is engaged in such intervention. In this section I consider
the variety of arguments put forward for government land policies. In
Section 3 I examine the relationship between the discussion of *purposes* and
the discussion of *means*, as policy measures, institutional arrangements and
modes of operation. I do not at this stage provide a systematic theoretical
framework within which to conduct an analysis. This section suggests a
variety of theoretical possibilities and issues to focus on in the detailed
examination of local plans in practice which forms Part II. In Chapter 9 I
reconsider the problem of explaining this practice and at this stage suggest
a direction which theorizing could take.

A review of the literature on British land use planning reveals as great a
poliferation of potential purposes for government intervention in land as
the proliferation of terms already referred to. This is the result partly
of confusion as to exactly what land use planning is about. A degree of
vagueness was also helpful in obtaining and maintaining support for planning
(Foley 1960). A further reason why justifications for land use planning, or
for any aspect of government policy, may vary is that commentators make
different assumptions about what government is for and about the nature of
the activities on which it should act. Behind these assumptions lie often
implicit views about the nature of society and the role of the state within
it.

A typical assumption among planners is that the purpose of land use planning is to serve the general community interest, meeting "social needs" which the unfettered market does not do. Urban conditions of the nineteenth century and urban sprawl in the twentieth century are referred to as evidence of market inadequacy. Thus Keeble in his famous textbook defines "Town and Country Planning" as the "art and science of ordering the use of land and the character and siting of buildings and communication routes so as to secure the maximum practicable degree of economy, convenience and beauty". Keeble comments that the nineteenth century town is an example of piecemeal (and bad) planning - "there was no co-ordination between individual projects and no consideration of the social needs of the inhabitants or of the eventual overall pattern of the town" (Keeble 1969 p.1[5]). Fogarty states that the "aim of town planning is to create communities fully equipped with the physical means needed for satisfactory social life", but goes on: "The free play of private initiative may produce a great deal of social chaos - how much disgruntlement of these individuals is necessary for efficient town planning?" (Fogarty 1948 pp.72, 76).

Foley has pointed out that the expressed ideology of "British town planning" contained propositions which "while not too openly in conflict were not completely congruent" (Foley 1960 pp.85-86[6]). Town Planning at one and the same time was an arbiter and co-ordinator, reconciling competing claims for the use of limited land so as to provide a consistent, balanced and orderly arrangement of land uses (p.76); it was to provide a "good ... physical environment ... for the formation of a healthy and civilized life" (p.77) and to provide "the physical basis for better urban community life" (p.28). Implicit in these statements is a belief that society has common basic values and goals, that a general public interest can be identified, and that government can act in such an interest.

Many British planners were attracted in the 1960s to a more coherent and ambitious statement of this model of "planning in the general interest in a consensus society". The principles of systems theory were seen to provide not only an explanation of how society worked, but a distinct role for planning, as guiding or managing society in the collective interest (see McLoughlin 1969, Chadwick 1971). Society was to be seen as a set of interlocking systems seeking a dynamic equilibrium, an essentially functionalist and consensus model. Planning became a cybernetic societal guidance mechanism. The specifics of land use planning were soon lost in this approach, as planners' interest shifted to the wider task of societal guidance, or more humbly, urban governance (CES Working Party 1973). Even the operations of markets was given little attention, the emphasis being on the design of strategies and mechanisms for managing them (e.g. Friend and Jessop 1969. Friend, Power and Yewlett 1974).

The model used in conceptualizing such management is the systems one of stimulus-response. Government reacts to stimuli from society (the environment) by designing suitable responses, monitoring subsequent stimuli to check the correctness of its performance. Despite many criticisms of this view of planning (see Dimitriou et al. 1972, Bailey 1975, Scott and Roweis 1977, Thomas 1979), it still persists in professional thought. It dominated a discussion paper on *Planning and the Future* produced by the planners' professional institute in 1976 (RTPI 1976) and is evident in the following

---

[5]first published in 1951

[6]the page numbers are as in Faludi (ed.) 1973.

quotations, both by professors of planning in British planning schools:

> "the problem is that of social control of change in the environment, and how that process can best be managed in the interests of a wider society and a local community". (Davies 1980 p.14, writing on development control.)

> "town and regional planning must ... be viewed as a form of urban management whose objective is to develop the capability necessary to guide technological development and social change at the local and regional levels" (Masser 1980 p.39.)

The systems approach in British planning is part of a wider interest in efficient government management of society, a set of ideas which has had considerable impact in British central and local government since the mid-1960s (see Cockburn 1977, Hambleton 1978 and Dearlove 1979). A recent development of this managerial interest has left the holistic ground of systems theory for an approach which emphasizes the politics of organizational behaviour and the social-psychology of interpersonal relations.[7]

Because of the generality of this view of planning and its "contentless" quality (Thomas 1979), whether in its systems or behavioural form, it is difficult to discern what the role of government intervention in land ownership, allocation, use and development might be and might involve. It is this approach, backed by procedural planning theory, which has in particular attracted Scott and Roweis' criticism of deliberate mystification (Scott and Roweis 1977). But it can also be attacked by all those fearful of what they discern as an increasingly corporate state, since it implies extensive, co-ordinated, government action. There is an obvious link between the kind of thinking described above, and both the ideology and practice which can be associated with the notion of corporatism. By this is meant the alliance of the state, in its various agencies, with incorporated business and organized labour. Normally these powerful alliances are portrayed as operating at the national level, with major economic interests working closely with central government and large parastatal organizations. However, the term has also been applied to a similar style of elite groupings which could operate at the level of local government, as suggested by Simmie (1981) in his analysis of the operation of planning policy in Oxford.

There is another line of argument of the planning-in-the-community-interest variety which directly opposes this corporatist-managerial view of planning. In this it is argued that land policy, and land use planning, should seek to promote the community interest, as opposed to the bastions of private interest and of national government. McAuslan (1980) presents a very convincing analysis of why this has not happened in British land use planning, clearly implying that it should. Davidoff, writing in the United States, has promoted the notion of "advocacy planning" in which different interests are encouraged to debate alternative policies and plans for an area (Davidoff 1965). Davidoff and McAuslan are both referring to an ideal model of participatory democracy, in which the state should be some form of benevolent arbiter, allowing and encouraging open informed debate about issues as seen from different viewpoints.

---

[7] See, for example, the development of Friend's work 1969 to Friend, Power and Yewlett 1974, and Friend, Norris and Carter 1978.

Davidoff also argues that compensatory action is needed to ensure that those groups with fewer resources with which to participate are enabled to do so. Here he shares with another American, Gans (1968), and with Eversley (1973) a view that market resource allocation is inherently unequal and must be compensated for. For both Gans and Eversley, a major role of government intervention is to redress these inequalities. A different "compensatory" case can also be made for government intervention in land - to redress the market's incapacity to value adequately long-term resources and environmental heritage (Buchanan 1972, Allison 1975).

The above arguments for government action have taken as their starting point the needs of society as a whole or particular sections of the community. Noeclassical economists, on the other hand, typically argue for more or less government action on the basis of analyses of the operation of markets. Thus two recent accounts of urban land economics (Harrison 1977, Hallett 1979) both argue that some form of government action is needed to correct market failures, the land and property market being particularly subject to such failures due to the "peculiar" nature of land and buildings (Hallett 1979 p.36).

The "market for real property is subject to essentially the same principles of price formation as other markets. It is, however, complicated by the long life of the product" (Hallett 1979 p.63). Harrison, who takes a more objective view of the adequacy of markets, cites the following failures to which land and property markets are particularly subject: the imposition by one firm or person of harmful externality "effects" on others; the failure to supply certain goods (such as urban parks); failure in pricing adjustment (as in the case of high value vacant inner city land); imperfect information and failures of co-ordination (Harrison cites improvement areas as an example here); and finally the failure of markets to distribute goods to those who need them (Harrison 1977 chapter 4). Empirical support for the inefficiency of the unfettered market in allocating land into urban use can be found in Clawson's major study of suburban expansion in the United States (Clawson 1971), and in a more recent US study on the costs of urban sprawl (Real Estate Research Corporation 1975). Both Hallett and Harrison present a case for government intervention to support the market by correcting for failures, although Harrison would allow a "community interest" case not only in respect of dealing with externality effects but also to counteract the inequitable distributional effects of market allocations. Whatever views are taken of the desirability of the way land and property markets operate in Britain, this approach to government intervention at least focusses attention on specific analysis of the likely effects of the use of a plot-ratio, or minimum standards, or land use zoning in particular situations (see Harrison 1977 part 2).

The neoclassical economists' case for government intervention to correct for market failure, "reluctant collectivism", to use George and Wilding's phrase (George and Wilding 1976), receives support from those whose view of capitalist markets is essentially critical. Thus Ambrose and Colenutt 1975, and Saunders 1980, both illustrate in detailed case studies how local authority involvement in urban land development has facilitated the activities of major commercial interests although claiming to be acting in the public interest. These authors assume that the activities of the market lead to results which are in conflict with the interests of large sections of the community. In other words they challenge the consensus assumption of those who claim that land policy can be carried out by government in the general public interest, and those (such as Hallett) who believe that the market (suitably corrected) produces outcomes which are in the general interest. Broadbent summarizes the contradictory position that British

land use planning finds itself in if market operations and community
interests cannot readily be reconciled:

> "In superficial terms (planning) co-operates with business, smoothing
> the path of private development and regulating competition by providing
> some degree of certainty for developers. But it aspires (at least
> by implication) to achieve a socially optimum allocation of land
> uses, which often conflicts with the present system of allocation
> by the market" (Broadbent 1977 p.142).

This contradictory position is given a coherent theoretical explanation (if
not necessarily detailed support from analysis of actual practices) by
recent Marxist work on urban planning and land. This rests on a historical
materialist analysis of the economy as structured by the "capitalist mode of
production" in which owners of the means of production ("capitalists") seek
to extract "surplus value" from the direct producers ("labour"), in order to
accumulate capital. Not only does this involve a fundamental contradiction
between the interests of capital and labour, but lesser contradictions
between short term capital accumulation and long term reproduction of
capital. Thus "fractions" of capital may be in conflict over access to land
(see Nizard 1975, Lamarche 1976, Massey and Catalano 1978). The role of the
state is presented as primarily supporting the interests of capital, though
there are arguments about the degree to which the mode of production
determines the activities of government. In this analysis, the state must
both assist the process of capital accumulation and ensure the continuity of
the capitalist mode of production. Thus, and here I am following Gough
(1979) and O'Connor (1973), the state supports capital by investing in
"projects and services that increase the productivity of labour", ("social
investment") and by investing in "projects and services that lower the
reproduction costs of labour power" ("social consumption"). It also
provides "projects and services which are required to maintain social
harmony" ("social expenses")[8]. Thus Broadbent's contradiction is
reinterpreted as one between the needs of social capital and social expenses,
and within social capital, between social investment and social consumption.

This discussion has illustrated the way different rationales for government
intervention in land and development may be derived from different notions
of the role of the state. However, much of the literature I have cited
fails to specify with any precision how the role being allocated to "urban
planning" is realized in terms of a land policy. To conclude this section,
I summarize four broad types of purpose which government land policies may
be required to achieve, relating these to political philosophies concerning
the role of the state.

2.1 *To Provide a Neighbourhood Protection Service*

Given that individuals on the whole know best what to do with their land
and property, and the market is a reasonably successful system for
allocating land and property among individuals; all that is needed from
government is a minimum of regulations to protect individual owners from
actions by their neighbours which could harm their own property interest.
Such a minimal amount of intervention is consistent with the classic
liberal view of the state. This is likely to be protected already to some

---

[8]The phrases in quotation marks are from Gough (1979) p.51, though the
terminology is O'Connor's.

extent by common law, and often exists solely in the form of building regulations, rather than the elaborate land use planning legislation which is found in the U.K. Probably some regulation of this sort exists in most societies, but societies vary in the value placed on individual ownership of land and property. The problem of small scale adverse externality effects is obviously much greater as urbanization takes place. That some limitation of individual rights is desirable in urban areas can be illustrated by a case from Caracas, Venezuela. A developer excavating for the foundations of his own office block undermined the foundations of his neighbour's, which collapsed. However, there is current debate in Britain about how far the provision of this service is really a matter for government regulation or for the law.

2.2 *Government Intervenes to Support the Land and Property Market, by Correcting for Market Failures*

The sorts of failures to which land and property markets are subject have already been mentioned. The role of government here is to put the collective interest before individual interest when dealing with externality effects, to provide an information service (such as indicating which land is suitable for development and what other investors are proposing to do), to provide goods which the market fails to provide well, such as roads, water and drainage, as well as a range of social facilities, and to regulate prices where these create problems for the operation of land and property markets as a whole (as in speculative booms, see Harrison 1977 chapter 6). One of the major areas of discussion here, drawing on welfare economics, is the capacity of government to determine the collective interest, to provide more certain information than market analysis, to provide public goods efficiently and to regulate prices without inhibiting market operations. The amount of government intervention advocated depends on the view taken about the capacity of government and the degree of market failure. To some, government should provide basic services and a general development framework (so long as it allocates the "right" land for development (Denman 1974, Hallett 1979)). To others, government has a more developmental and managerial role (see Roberts (ed.) 1977 and Lefcoe 1978). It engages in entrepreneurial activities such as industrial promotion or the encouragement of comprehensive town centre redevelopment. It assembles land and makes it available for development. It engages in partnership with the private sector in development schemes. Such activities require sophisticated government personnel, who are capable of exercising considerable discretion in negotiating with private sector agents. Extensive government intervention of this kind involves in effect government management of markets *in their own interest*, which could be considered a form of "corporatism".

The above is a form of Keynesian economic management. Supporters of such a strategy argue over the mechanisms to further it (e.g. regulatory versus fiscal measures). To Marxists, however, intervention of this kind is characterized as part of the state's broad function of securing the "reproduction of the status quo" (Nizard 1975). "A city's control over the planning and equipping of its territory is more or less limited to the creation of the situational advantages (transport, facilities, public buildings absorption of costs due to land speculation etc.) on which part of the profits of property capital are based.... It is as if the role of the city was to clear and plough its own land in order for others to sow and harvest the best fruit" (Lamarche 1976 pp.103-4). The central point here is that both the state and the land and property market are part (in a

less or more determinist way depending on one's position within Marxist debate)
of a larger structure which results from the forces of production and
relations of production which make up the capitalist mode of production.
Cheap housing for the labour force helps to keep down labour costs with a
similar result. On the other hand, finance capital, which is important for
reinvestment in productive activities, benefits from high land and property
costs. Government land policy may attempt to provide cheap serviced land
and cheap housing, but be caught on the dilemma of the high cost of land. In
addition to this land policy role in relation to social "investment" and
"consumption", the state must maintain social harmony and its activities must
be seen as legitimate. It therefore has to expend time and effort in
presenting policies as if they were in the public interest, as in the
production and public discussion of development plans (Castells 1977 p.76).

There is much common ground between the neoclassical economists' view of
managed land and property markets and current Marxist analysis. The
difference lies in the Marxist view of the desirability of managed
capitalism and what government (as part of the state) is actually doing. Is
it managing capitalism, is capitalism managing it or are government
programmes merely reflecting more fundamental and contradictory economic
forces?

2.3 *Government Intervenes to Ensure that Land is Allocated, Used and Developed in the General Interest*

As already suggested, the general interest, or public interest, is a
nebulous concept capable of several interpretations (see Mitnick 1976). The
assumption here is that government can and should act above individual
interest on behalf of the general interest (even if it does not always so
act). It can provide a framework of rules and information. It can provide
public goods, directly undertake development activities and arbitrate
between different interests. Three variants of this justification can be
identified, each placing the emphasis of government activity in a different
sphere.

Firstly, government can act as an *arbiter*, balancing competing interests in
the use and development of land as in Foley's first ideology (Foley 1960).
Its main activity would be to consider proposals for development, with
inquiries being an important vehicle for determining the general interest.
The present interest in Environmental Impact Statements can be partially
linked to this role. As a development of this, government can provide the
arenas for open discussion among citizens about development proposals and
about the future use and development of land. In this *participatory* variant,
participation in the production of development plans for areas is as
important as the use of open inquiries. Here government does not assume
that it can define the general interest. It listens to definitions and
arguments and, finally, resolves fairly any conflicts which result. McAuslan
(1980) and Davidoff (1965) would both appear to be arguing for an approach
to land use planning of this kind.

The third, *managerial* variant, has similarities with the more interventionist
market support arguments. Government officials, formally accountable to
central and local politicians, are key agents in ensuring the general
interest. To do this they must be given considerable administrative autonomy
to interpret the general interest and to carry out activities in pursuance of
it. Such activities could involve the whole spectrum from land use
regulation and infrastructure provision to price regulation and land
acquisition. Government in effect engages in management of the urban and

rural estate according to its interpretation of the general interest. The differences between these three variants lie in assumptions about how the "public interest" can best be defined and how possible it is to establish principles which express the public interest in advance of making specific decisions about particular developments.

2.4 Government Intervenes to Counteract the Market to Ensure that Land is Used in the Interests of the Community, or Major Sections of it

Here, the land and property market is deliberately contained, regulated and possibly replaced in order to maximize alternative interests and values. The assumption is that government can act independently of market interests to promote these other values. This justification has similarities with the British Fabian or social democratic tradition. Government acts to promote social welfare, and particularly a society in which resources are more equally distributed. Gans and Eversley have already been mentioned as developing this argument in part in relation to land use policy, and it is a recurrent theme in the debate on land values (see Davies and Hall (ed.) 1978 chapter 1 and McKay and Cox 1979 chapter 3). Government action is aimed to provide for social needs, and might involve regulation of land prices; the collection through taxes of community created development value; substantial public sector landownership to structure the market, or even land nationalization; major development activities in infrastructure provision; social facilities, housing, industrial and commercial development. The regulation of private land use becomes a minor supporting activity.

However, there is an alternative set of values in the land policy area which government is asked to promote, namely those of the protection of amenity, and the conservation of environmental resources, including urban and rural landscape. This involves not only promoting these values over those of private individuals and firms in the discussion of development proposals, but protecting certain areas which have some specific quality (Conservation Areas, Areas of Outstanding Natural Beauty, Sites of Special Scientific Interest), engaging in land purchase to protect them (as in the purchase of green belt land by the London County Council) and managing the use of such land (as in management agreements). Harrison (1972) and McAuslan (1980) note the support given to the dominance of amenity considerations in British land use planning, and Allison (1975) provides a political-philosophical case for the promotion of these values. The problem is that even if governments can effectively limit the market to ensure greater social equality and environmental conservation, the two sets of values are not necessarily compatible (see Stretton 1976 and O'Riordan 1977).

These broad rationales for government intervention in land and development reflect different political philosophies, as I have suggested. However, they may co-exist when realized into policy measures and institutional arrangements since actual interventions may be the product of political compromises. Or arrangements made in an earlier period may be adapted for different purposes. The typology I have provided here does not as such offer any explanation of why the state at a particular point in time does adopt particular measures in the land and development field. In Chapter 9 I attempt to develop such an explanatory basis, using this in Chapter 10 to suggest scenarios for future land policy programmes. Here I continue this introduction by considering the relationship between purposes and mechanisms for intervention.

3. POLICY MEASURES AND INSTITUTIONAL ARRANGEMENTS IN THE LAND POLICY FIELD

In a simple world, purposes for government intervention in the land and development field would be defined and appropriate legislative instruments and institutional arrangements created. Programmes would then be developed to further the general strategy implicit or explicit in these institutional and procedural arrangements. However, such linear sequences from policy to action are rarely found in practice (Barrett and Fudge (ed.) 1981). Purposes may not be clearly articulated. Legislative tools and institutions developed with one set of purposes in mind may be deflected over time to serve other purposes. There may be conflicts between central government and the institutions it has created over what the purpose of the arrangements actually is. And the tools and institutions may in one way or another be inadequate for the purpose intended. Thus there is no necessary correlation between expressed purposes of government land policy and the means available for furthering that policy. Nor are the expressed intentions of land policy necessarily the purposes which are actually served by the policy in practice.

Such discrepancies in relation to local plans will be evident in Part II and I consider how far it is possible to generalize about the purposes expressed in the practice of local plan production in Chapter 9. Here I draw attention to the types of mechanisms that are commonly used when governments seek to intervene in land and development. The very fact that it is possible to generalize about land policy *measures* illustrates the degree to which it is possible to separate ends from means in this field. In this context it is important to assess how far a *local plan* as we understand it currently in Britain is a tool which can be transferred from one context to another, and how far its form and nature as a tool is specific to the particular historical circumstances in which it has evolved.

The international land policy literature has given considerable attention to land policy measures, which provides a more neutral ground than the discussion of purposes. A tripartite classification of measures is common. Neutze (1975) refers to land use planning, tax measures, and government involvement as landowner and developer. Roweis and Scott (1978) cite the following "(a) ... the application of a variety of fixed measures; (b) ... legally restricting private rights to use urban land in certain way; (c) direct physical undertaking of urban development (and/or redevelopment) programmes". Darin-Drabkin elaborates Neutze's classification into (1) legal measures influencing private land use decisions; (2) taxation methods influencing private land use decisions; and (3) direct action by public authorities (Darin-Drabkin 1977 p.186). In these classifications, certain measures are often omitted, notably building regulations, inquiries, impact statements and land nationalization. They tend to concentrate on the package of measures which a government intervening in a "managerial" way in a market economy might adopt. Thus we might see several of these measures adopted and actively operated where the purpose of intervention was to support market operations, or to manage land and development in the public interest. A government attempting to oppose the market to achieve social welfare or environmentalist values might also adopt many of these measures, although both values could lead to a case for land nationalization. Where arbitration or participatory discussion was adopted as the key to resolving conflicting interests in land, much greater emphasis on inquiries might be expected. Where a good neighbour role was the only one sought, we might find little more than building regulations.

Thus although there is a broad association between the kinds of policy measures which might be adopted and the purposes of intervention, different arguments could lead to the adoption of the same measure, such as zoning or taxation on land profits, or the carrying out of infrastructure works, or land acquisition. This is one of the reasons why the measures contained in the British 1947 Town and Country Planning Act appeared to have such broad support. Such a conclusion has two implications, however. Firstly we must look in detail at the specific form of any policy measure to see if we get any indication of the precise intention of those who designed it. Secondly we must observe the use to which the measure is put in practice since it could be directed towards quite a different purpose. I hope to follow these two precepts when I come to the discussion of local plans.

The same conclusion applies to institutional arrangements. By these I mean the organizations, procedures, personnel and ways of operating which are developed to implement land policy programmes. As with the policy measures summarized above, it is possible to arrive at a set of dimensions with which to describe the variety of institutional arrangements which might be encountered in a land policy programme.

1. Policy content centrally determined - locally determined;

2. Legal in format - administrative in format - participatory in format;

3. Rule-bound - discretionary;

4. Requiring specialist personnel - administration by non-specialists, or by laymen;

5. Emphasis on a planning (or rational-technical) mode of operating - on consultative or participatory modes;

6. Emphasis on common arrangements for all situations in the whole country (universality) - emphasis on selectivity for particular situations.

Obviously these dimensions are not discrete. A planning mode would involve an administrative, discretionary form, which in turn would require specialist personnel. Nor are they isolatable from the general ways in which government programmes are organized.

Can we relate positions on the dimensions to purposes of intervention? We may infer that the managerial justifications might all lead to institutional arrangements which involved considerable administrative power, the exercise of discretion by specialist personnel, selectivity in application, with different measures for different situations, and a planning rather than incremental mode (at least in principle). By contrast, a government interested only in a good neighbour role might pass universal legislation and administer it locally (a common situation with building regulations), or through legal remedy only. If the aim was to promote greater social equality by restraint on the land market, we might see universal legislation, *centrally* administered (to give it greater strength), with limitations on the discretion of officials to interpret rules. Yet similar institutional arrangements may result from different arguments for intervention and, though established by one interest (or more usually a coalition) for one purpose, be deflected in practice to serve other interests. I illustrate this in Chapter 2 when discussing the policy measures and institutional arrangements which constitute British land use planning.

These dimensions may help us to describe the variety of institutional arrangements we may encounter when looking at different government land policy programmes. If there is no necessary correlation between purposes, policy measures and institutional arrangements, such lists do not provide us with a way of explaining the variety. To understand what is in effect the public administration of government land policy, we would have to examine the particular evolution of land policy programmes in a given context and the relation between these and the evolution of public administration in general in that context. In Chapter 2 I provide an account of the historical development of British land policy since the 1940s to illustrate the particular institutional arrangements within which the tool of a local plan has evolved. I then look in more detail in Chapters 3 and 4 at the evolution of the two types of "development plan" used within the British planning system. To conclude the present chapter, some comments on this distinctive tool of land policy are in order.

From the discussion so far, it is evident that a physical development plan could be employed in connection with a number of land policy measures. It could provide a co-ordinative framework; it could indicate the principles upon which government might base its decisions about land use and development; it might illustrate the precise meaning of building regulations; it could provide an arena for public discussion about the future of an area; it might provide a public agency with a programming map to direct its activities; or constitute the basis for establishing land values on public acquisition or property taxation. Thus the potential for reinterpretation and dispute about what development plans are for is even greater than with most policy measures or institutional arrangements in the land policy field.

As we shall see in Chapters 2, 3 and 4, there is a great deal of current criticism about British development plans. They are said to be irrelevant; backed by inadequate powers; distorted by local government reorganization; related to too narrow a range of issues; inadequately linked to government resource allocation; inappropriate for expressing a community's views about its future; too closely related to the control of development; too little related to the control of development; the procedures for preparing plans are too cumbersome; the form of expression of policies in them is confusing; they cover the wrong timescale; there is too much public participation; there is far too little; they are vacuous because no-one is interested in them; they are vacuous because interest conflicts could not be resolved; central government is allowing far too much local discretion in the preparation of plans; central government is interfering far too much in the preparation of plans - and this is but a *selection* of the criticisms made.

Much of the current debate about development plans in British land use planning argues that for one reason or another development plans in general, or in the form in which they currently exist, or in the way they are being used, are irrelevant to or not consistent with the current nature of British land policy. In other words, it is argued that a development plan is not the right tool for the job in hand, or development plans as presently constituted in Britain are not the right tool. There is no dobut that this is an important area of debate.

However, this chapter has reiterated the point that there are different arguments to be made to justify government intervention in land. Those promoting these arguments may agree in general terms about the desirability of adopting certain policy measures and institutional arrangements, and on the value of development plans, broadly conceived. But they are likely to disagree about the specific uses to which measures, arrangements and tools such as a development plan should be put. Thus in examining the way local plans are used, it will be important to consider not only their relevance to "the job in hand", but the nature of the "job in hand" in the first place. What interests are promoting it? Who is hoping to gain from it? How could this gain be realized? How will the preparation of a local plan promote this realization? It is as easy to be deceived into thinking that a development plan is irrelevant as to imagine that it actually charts the future course of events.

To refute both tendencies, and by way of conclusion, I will quote first from Castells, writing on the "social effects of urban planning":

> "It was found that master plans, which appear to be the veritable embodiment of schemes for urban development, whatever their scale, have an underlying social and political logic, which varies for each plan in exact correspondence with the situation of political hegemony within the institutional apparatus on which the planning agency in question depends. This hypothesis turned out to be so precise that plans drawn up in indecisive political situations took the form of "question mark plans", while other plans underwent substantial changes as changes took place in the political parties controlling the planning apparatus. But, in addition to this observation, which is in the nature of things, what was significant was the importance of the ideological role of urban planning, since for such an ideology to be particularly effective in the realization of the social interests it embodies, the legitimation-recognition effect characteristic of all ideologies must accommodate itself to the specific means of expression which is urban planning. Plans stamp all individual schemes with a double character: on the one hand, they come to be seen as "reasonable", rational technical solutions to the problems posed and, on the other, they appear to bring about a convergence of the various social groups and urban functions" (Castells 1977 p.76).

Secondly, I will report a phenomenon I encountered in Kumasi, Ghana. This city of 600 000 people, in a country short not only of food but of modern building materials such as cement, was provided in 1963 with a Master Plan in the British style, a radial ring-road structure, carefully zoned by uses. Following the British tradition of excessive concern for the preservation of farmland and the environment, areas are zoned for agriculture and nature reserves, and for industry, commerce, transport and residential purposes in parts of the town, and surprisingly, urban development has followed the plan reasonably faithfully. It is in the location of housing development that the plan and events part company. The residential zones are mainly farmed while the farmland[9] and nature reserves are increasingly settled. The reasons for this curious phenomenon - a plan implemented in reverse - are to be found in the effect of the plan on access to land, an issue probably not considered when the plan was produced but no doubt well-appreciated by those still interested in keeping the plan in operation.

---

[9] Open farmland is tribal land allocated by chiefs for the maximum low income families can be persuaded to afford, on which dwellings are built out of traditional materials. Residential land is subject to building regulations which "guarantee" that modern building materials are used. Mortgages for development can then be raised, and land and property exchanged in a market form. As in most capitalist and semi-capitalist countries, urban land and property is an extremely good investment - so long as you can keep low income families off it except as rent-paying tenants. See Healey (1973) for a slightly different example of the use of development plans to defend property interests in Cali, Colombia.

CHAPTER 2

British Land Policy and Land Use Planning

1. LAND POLICY IN BRITAIN

A visitor to Britain interested in comparative land policy would be struck,
as Neutze (1975) was, by the sophistication of the public control of land
use and development, with its professionalized local planning service
regulating development backed by development plans, and by the dominance of
the private land and property market. A brief review of current discussions
about land policy would reveal that the spread of those with a stake in the
private market was increasing (through the rise of owner-occupation). At
the same time, the extent of publicly-owned land, particularly in the
depressed industrial regions, the inner areas and outer fringes of cities
was considerable (Harrison, Tranter and Gibbs 1977, Massey and Catalano 1978
p.51, Burrows 1978). The reviewer would also note that although common law
provides remedies for disputes over injurious effects caused by one owner or
user of land to another, government regulation is looked to in preference to
law for protection against bad neighbours because of the cost and cumbersome
nature of legal proceedings. He might also discover some discussion of what
voluntary groups could do to improve their local environment and manage
local land resources, but would find very little evidence of this in
practice. Much criticism of government "land use planning" would be noted,
planners meanwhile being preoccupied with detailed land management
questions and the promotion of local development of various kinds.

Currently, government land policy in Britain is predominantly concerned with
land use matters rather than land values. The periodic attempts to extend
intervention to regulate private financial gain from land development have
all foundered, debates on this issue being much more overtly politicized
than those on land use policy. The latter, on the contrary, has until
recently been seen as an area of apparent political consensus. The
objectives of land use policy from 1947 onwards, according to Hall's study,
have been the containment of urban development, the protection of the
countryside and natural resources, the creation of self-contained and
balanced communities, supplemented by the prevention of scattered
development, building up strong service centres, improving accessibility
and providing a high quality social and physical environment (Hall *et al.*
1973 p.39). On the face of it (but not on further investigation, as Hall's
study shows), these seem objectives likely to be acceptable to all except a
few land speculators; a classic "public interest" formulation of the

objectives of intervention. However, when he examined the planning system
in the late 1950s, Foley was able to identify potentially conflicting
objectives within the apparent consensus on the purpose of planning (Foley
1960), while Haar as early as 1951 noted that the protection and enhancement
of *amenity* in practice had a strong influence on the practice of planning
(Haar 1951). The continuity of this emphasis was demonstrated twenty years
later by Harrison (1972). The 1947 Act, the only comprehensive land policy
legislation in this country, provided comprehensive powers to regulate how
land was used and developed. It was clearly appreciated in contemporary
debates that the exercise of such powers, given that a market in land would
still exist, would have a major impact on land values by concentrating
potential gains from urban land conversion onto specific sites. To use
current American terminology, some people would make "windfall" gains, others
would suffer "wipeouts" (Hagman and Misczynski 1978). This creates the
appearance of arbitrary injustice - to those who suffer from "wipeouts", or
do not get "windfalls", and to the community, whose plans create these
windfall gains but who do not collect them.

However, the ability of government in Britain to do more than ignore
"wipeouts" (except those caused by the blighting effects of public
development) and from time to time tax "windfalls" has been limited by the
strong value put on private land ownership and the freedom of the owner to
do what he likes with his property. This reflects the historical evolution
of land allocation mechanisms in Britain from feudal arrangements to highly
developed land and property markets. Roberts, an American observer, notes
the strength of these values in referring to the "cognitive lenses through
which the Englishman looks at land". These are, he claims, the "garden
mentality", the appreciation that land is limited, the "belief that every
citizen has a right to a pleasant home", and the belief that property
owners should have a major role in determining how land and property is
developed (Roberts 1976 pp.4-6). The form of government land policy in
Britain is thus influenced by two contradictory ideological stands. On the
one hand, there is widespread appreciation that land use and development
should be managed in the public interest, given the small land area of the
country. On the other is an equally widespread appreciation, often held by
the same people, that land and property should be privately owned and
individuals free to make private gains out of its use and development. At
issue here is the question of who should bear the social costs of individual
developments and who should reap the benefits (Scott 1980).

How have these essentially cultural values related to economic forces?
Somewhat surprisingly, there have been very few studies which relate
government land policy to the changing structure of investment, or the land,
labour and infrastructure needs of firms, despite current interest among
planners in "the local economy". The most notable exception to this
generalization is Massey and Catalano (1978)[10]. Connections to the economy
are more commonly made at the level of broad generalities. The immediate
postwar imperative which spawned popular support for land planning was the
demand for social and physical reconstruction of bombed cities. In the
1960s, with population growth, economic expansion, increasing affluence and
an expectation that all these would continue until the year 2000, urban
expansion was seen to need regulation, growth needed "accommodating" and
cities needed "renewal" to make them suitable for modern life. Currently,
with economic stagnation, the emphasis is on encouragement to industry and
the removal of the most visible signs of economic decline (such as derelict
and vacant land).

[10]but see also Dunleavy 1977, Backwell and Dickens 1978, Newby 1979.

Whatever the relation between economic forces, political pressures and government land policy (an area which requires more and deeper investigation than it has been given up to now), debates about *land* - its ownership, allocation, use and development - have been significant *political* issues in Britain, if not always evidently so in party or parliamentary discussion. This relates firstly to its relative scarcity in Britain, secondly to its role in production (the availability of serviced land for firms) and accommodation (housing land); thirdly its investment value, participating in inflationary conditions; and fourthly, its ideological role in sustaining the image of Britain as a property-owning democracy.

The purpose of this chapter is to provide a brief account of the policy measures and institutional arrangements which constitute the most visible elements of government intervention in land, its ownership, allocation, use and development, in Britain. The measures and arrangements currently in use originated in the 1947 Town and Country Planning Act and related legislation, although as I will argue, the present "land use planning system" is more properly considered as a partially-modified remnant of a much broader conception of government land policy.

There are several accounts of British town and country planning, ranging from the descriptive (Cullingworth 1972, 1975, 1980; Cherry 1974, McAuslan 1975), the analytic (Hall *et al.* 1973, Hebbert 1977, McKay and Cox 1979), to the prescriptive and the polemic (e.g. Ratcliffe 1976). My aim in this chapter is not to provide a definitive account, but to draw on the material presented by these authors to illustrate the issues raised in the previous chapter. After some general comments on land policy, I outline the conception of government land policy contained in the 1947 Act and associated legislation. I then examine the changes that have modified (some would say, dismantled) this conception since 1950, and attempt an assessment of the characteristics of government land policy in 1980. I conclude by summarizing what are claimed to be the main effects of British land use planning since the war. In attempting to do this, I have been struck by the lack of systematic empirically-based reviews and evaluative studies in this field. The work of Hall *et al.* (1973), Cullingworth (1975, 1980), and Hebbert (1977) stand out as rare exceptions, complemented by a number of case studies of types of development situation and of particular instruments[11a].

2. TOWN AND COUNTRY PLANNING: THE "REVOLUTIONARY" APPROACH OF 1947

The Town and Country Planning Act 1947, one of the many legislative achievements of a Labour government committed to a major extension of government social welfare programmes, introduced a comprehensive set of measures to deal with land use and development[11b]. In conception and in the powers embodied in the legislation, this Act can be considered revolutionary, both in relation to the previous history of local town

---

[11a]These latter are most common in the rural policy field: see Blacksell and Gilg 1977, Preece 1981 on AONBs; Cloke 1979 and Martin and Voorhees 1981 on rural settlement policies; Mandelker 1962 and Thomas 1970 on greenbelt policies; and more recently Shucksmith 1981 on local housing needs policies in areas of development restrain.

[11b]Certain elements, including the control of development and the creation of a Minister for Town and Country Planning, had already been enacted during the war, see Cullingworth 1975.

planning schemes in Britain, and in terms of precedents in other parts of
the capitalist world. To some overseas commentators, it was a 'catastrophe'
(Dunham 1964). By contrast, C. M. Haar, the American planning lawyer,
wrote:

> "only now ... for the first time are sufficient powers conferred
> upon planners to shape an efficient material environment that
> will secure the best possible use of the limited land resources
> of what is after all a small island. The numerous and conflicting
> demands on this, its rarest commodity, have called forth the new
> technique of land planning.... It puts Britain in the lead of
> democratic planning for land" (Haar 1951 pp.156-171).

Land use planning in Britain is however *not* as conceived in the 1947 Act.
It is based on what is left of the Act after firstly, the removal of the
land value elements, and secondly, adjustments to the development plan
provisions (1968 Act), to the land compensation elements (1961 Act), and to
institutional arrangements consequent upon local government reorganization
(1972 Local Government Act in particular)[12].

The control of land use, as elaborated in the discussions which led up to the
1947 Act and informed by the famous Barlow, Scott and Uthwatt reports, was
seen to be necessary as part of the broader programme of postwar national
reconstruction. This conception is well illustrated in an often quoted
passage from the White Paper of 1944 on *The Control of Land Use*:

> "Provision for the right use of land, in accordance with a considered
> policy, is an essential requirement of the Government's programme of
> post-war reconstruction. New houses, whether of permanent or
> emergency construction; the new layout of areas devastated by enemy
> action or blighted by reason of age or bad living conditions; the
> new schools which will be required under the Education Bill now
> before Parliament; the balanced distribution of industry which the
> Government's recently published proposals for maintaining active
> employment envisage; the requirements of sound nutrition and of a
> healthy and well-balanced agriculture; the preservation of land for
> national parks and forests, and the assurance to the people of
> enjoyment of the sea and countryside in times of leisure; a new
> and safer highway system better adapted to modern industrial and
> other needs; the proper provision of airfields - all these related
> parts of a single reconstruction programme involve the use of land,
> and it is essential that their various claims on land should be so
> harmonized as to ensure for the people of this country the greatest
> possible measure of individual well-being and national prosperity".
> (Quoted from Cullingworth 1972 p.31.)

In effect, land use "planning" was to be part of a national exercise in
social and economic planning. Although support for extensive government
intervention came from both the left of centre (Fabian social democrats) and
right of centre (Keynesian "reluctant collectivists"), the coalition of
interests supporting intervention in land was even more widely based. Hall's
study attributes this to the temporary unification of urban and rural
interests, the county boroughs hoping to gain the release of land beyond
their boundaries for expansion purposes, the counties hoping to resist it
(Hall *et al.* 1973 especially vol. 2 chapters 1 and 2). Hebbert describes in
more detail the support given to the idea of town and country planning by

---

[12]See also the reorganization of London Government in 1963.

conservationists, agricultural interests, local authorities frustrated in
their development activities by the cost of land and the difficulty of
safeguarding it for future use, the postwar concern with providing adequate
housing, not to mention reformist groups of all kinds. Even industrialists
and property developers were prepared to give reluctant support, reflecting
their own difficulties at the time (Hebbert 1977 chapter 2)[13]. However, it
is unlikely that this substantial coalition would have occurred without the
national unity produced by the war, and the urgent need for reconstruction
produced by the widespread bomb damage in city centres.

The architect propagandists of the town and country planning movement were
particularly skilful in conveying a three-dimensional vision of a postwar
future, based though it was on naive links between social and economic
change and physical development programmes, and on highly-optimistic
assumptions about the capabilities of government. Some accounts of this
period put the credit (or the blame) for the conceptualization of town and
country planning which led to the 1947 Act and associated legislation on
these "charismatic" figures. Their well-publicized and tangible
illustrations of a new postwar future are said to have fired popular
imagination faced with the depression of war and the experience of blitzed
cities. It is also said that such image-building was convenient to
government at the time as a means of maintaining morale and deflecting
interest into a less contentious area of planning than that implied by
national social and economic planning (see Backwell and Dickens 1978). The
major opponents of the idea of land use planning emerge as Treasury civil
servants (Cullingworth 1975), and property speculators who had been buying
up areas of blitzed cities (Backwell and Dickens 1978).

Land use regulation was justified as necessary to achieve wider national
social and economic objectives. These were to be articulated in spatial
form via regional strategies and plans, expressing a major policy aim of
redistributing industry to revitalize the older industrial regions and
relieve congestion and expansion pressures in areas such as the South-East
and the West Midlands. Implementing this strategy required not only control
over the location of industrial development but of the use and development
of all land. This affected property interests at two levels. At the level
of the individual property owner, it was deemed necessary to give owners
whose interests were adversely affected by public control of land use a
right to register an objection, and, initially, to compensation. More
generally, there was the question of who should receive the financial
benefit from development. Both problems led to the discussion of
compensation and betterment (wipeouts and windfalls).

One solution to this problem was to nationalize all land and remove the
problem. Given the strength of the ideology of private ownership of land,
this never received significant political support. The Uthwatt Committee,
whose report is still one of the best British discussions on the issue,
recoiled from land nationalization on political and administrative grounds
(Uthwatt Report 1942). Instead, they recommended the nationalization of
development rights on undeveloped land. Land could not therefore be
developed without government permission. Uthwatt proposed that much of this
development land would be acquired by the state, and that the state would
engage in large scale purchase of urban land for redevelopment purposes.
This removed the need for future compensation, and a once-for-all system was
devised to compensate those with development expectations pre-dating the war.

---

[13]Backwell and Dickens (1978) support a similar conclusion, analysing the
contemporary interests of different fractions of capital.

Uthwatt had recommended differential treatment as between developed land and undeveloped land outside town areas. Such a two-tier system can be found currently in several developed and developing countries. Uthwatt saw two problems with this; firstly, distinguishing those areas within and outside two areas ("drawing the 'Uthwatt line'" - Cullingworth 1975 p.187); and secondly, the time it would take to prepare the necessary maps. Uthwatt therefore argued that all land in the country should be brought under a single scheme. This view prevailed, leading to the universal negative restriction to existing uses, (nationalization of development rights), one of the most distinctive characteristics of British land use policy. Where development value (betterment or windfalls) was realized, this was to be taxed by a development charge. Some thought this should be a flexible charge, but in the Act it was eventually fixed at 100%[14].

All private development therefore required government permission. Development was defined comprehensively as "the carrying out of building, engineering, mining and other operations in, on, over or under the land, or the making of any material change in the use of any buildings or other land" (1971 Act S22)[15]. Exemptions to this are provided for by a *General Development Order*, and changes of use are covered by a definition of uses known as a *Use Classes order*. The first set limits on the size and types of development which fell within the net of the planning system. Thus agricultural buildings and very small extensions have always been excluded. The second defines categories of uses within which land use change is automatically allowed. Both of these have been revised from time to time. To my knowledge, neither have been subjected to a systematic examination of their assumptions or effects, an exercise which is long overdue.

In making planning decisions, government may consider the provisions of a development plan and other "material considerations". The plan is intended to provide guiding principles as to the type, form and location of development. But built into the system is the notion that development proposals cannot be precisely predicted. Thus each case must be judged "on its merits". The plan is therefore in no way binding. If an applicant wishes to dispute a government decision, he can appeal, first to central government, and then to the courts (on matters of "procedure" but not "policy"). Thus the citizen (qua property owner) is provided with a "natural justice" right to object to government action which affects his interest and an opportunity for that objection to be heard. Nevertheless within the planning system there is substantial administrative discretion, subject to judicial review.

Although the 1947 Act contains very complex provisions in respect of these major restrictions on the land and property market, it was anticipated that the *public sector* would be the predominant developer. It would engage in extensive purchase of land using local authority powers and those of a Central Land Board. It would build houses, infrastructure, and social facilities. It would engage in a programme of constructing New Towns, and renewing the bombed areas and slums of old ones. It would also preserve areas of countryside and open such areas up to public access. Powers to do this were contained in the 1947 Act, and in the supporting New Towns Act

---

[14]Cullingworth suggests this was due to Treasury pressure (Cullingworth 1975 pp.244-8), a factor which may have accelerated the demise of the charge in the early 1950s.

[15]This definition has been carried through into all subsequent revisions of the 1947 Act.

1946 and the National Parks and Access to the Countryside Act 1949. Land values would not only be controlled by taxation, but by the dominance of the market by the public sector (as in urban development in Sweden and the Netherlands (Neutze 1975)).

All this provided government with extensive powers over how land was used and developed, and wide-ranging discretionary scope in interpreting how these powers should be used. This was necessary, it was argued, to allow government (in the form of the Minister for Town and Country Planning) to secure "consistency and continuity not only in the execution but also in the framing of national policy in regard to the use of land" (Cullingworth 1975 p.95). To assist in this, it was proposed in the discussions leading up to the 1947 Act that "outline plans" would be prepared "concerned with 'broad' features only", differing fundamentally from "the traditional planning map in which 'an assembly of complicated details' obscured the main concept of the plan" (Cullingworth 1975 p.94, quoting contemporary papers). It was suggested that such plans should be submitted to the Minister for approval and that there might be "'representations from responsible quarters' following extensive publicity" which the Minister would consider. This process would be more like a public discussion than a formal inquiry (Cullingworth 1975 pp.94-95). Detailed plans would perhaps not need an informal inquiry since the general principles would have already been agreed by the Minister in the outline plan. Thus the notion of two types of development plan, strategic and detailed, pre-dated the 1968 Act which created structure and local plans by at least twenty years.

In the 1947 Act, however, the two sorts of plan were merged into a single "development plan", subject to Ministerial approval, certain consultation requirements and system of objection and inquiry to provide for the "natural justice" right to be heard of those whose interests were affected by the plan. Thus the political and administrative power given to government in respect of land was marginally modified as a concession to private property interests. Cullingworth notes that some people at the time felt that flexible broad-brush development plans might not promote the clarity and certainty the private market would respond to (Cullingworth, p.97). However, the private market was expected to be operating on a very small scale. Probably more important in limiting the concept of a flexible strategic plan was the influence of lawyers concerned about the extent of administrative discretion this could imply[16].

Yet, in addition to extensive powers, enormous interpretive discretion was built into the system. In deciding how land should be used, government might engage in public discussion, while development plans provided an indication of general principles that public authorities would follow in promoting and regulating development. This discretion was unfettered by any requirement to stick rigidly to these principles. In the interests of a powerful and flexible policy-oriented planning system, no mechanisms other than political representation and central government overview were built in to ensure that these powers were not exercised arbitrarily. Similarly, no limitation was put on the range of matters which could be brought to bear on making decisions about future development. As we will see, this latitude has been both an opportunity and a disadvantage. In practice, the discretion in the system as created in 1947 has been progressively limited in *interpretation* by central government, local government, and the courts.

---

[16]My thanks to Michael Hebbert for suggesting this interpretation.

At the time, however, it was envisaged that central government would
exercise a major role in how the system developed, although many local
authorities which had been active in the 1930s were prepared to develop
their own approach. The Minister for Town and Country Planning was expected
to ensure policy consistency by approving plans, overseeing land purchase
and monitoring development control through appeals. However, as Haar noted,
the Ministry had

> "only a general mandate for securing consistency and continuity
> in the planning of land. And this vague direction gives the
> Minister no real field in which his is the last word, or for which
> he must bear responsibility. Indeed the only field which the
> Ministry for Town and Country Planning may mark out as its own is
> a source of weakness rather than strength", i.e. "amenity" (Haar
> 1951 p.30).

There was some debate on the type of authority which should exercise the
plan-making and regulating activities of the system as a whole. Some kind
of Land Use Commission was discussed during the war, its advantages being
flexibility, speed and policy continuity; less susceptibility to political
influence and more acceptability to the public because of its independence
and expertise. Others argued that local authorities should undertake the
work in the interests of democracy and because of their local knowledge
(see Cullingworth 1975 p.71). The local authorities themselves lobbied hard
to retain the activities they had been developing under the 1932 Town and
Country Planning Act. Apart from the creation of the Central Land Board,
the latter view prevailed, with Counties and County Boroughs becoming "local
planning authorities" in the 1947 Act. These then needed manning by staff
capable of exercising the discretion allocated to them. The Schuster report
on the education of planners (Schuster Report 1950), advocated multi-
disciplinary teams, with postgraduate training in planning, headed by
architects because of their skills in managing development projects.

This "elite corps" model proved too much for most local authorities. There
were very few trained planners around, and to carry out their functions as
local planning authorities, small sections were created in Architects,
Engineers or Surveyors Departments to carry out what became the immediate
priority, the exercise of development control functions. In many cases, the
preparation of development plans was farmed out to consultants, and only a
few authorities could call on the services of an architect-planner or
engineer-planner who understood either the thinking behind the legislation
or the ideas of the evangelist town planning movement. It is hardly
surprising that at this time many in central government doubted the capacity
of local authorities to undertake the task of implementing the land policy
programme, a suspicion which continues to the present day but with much less
justification. One consequence of the creation of a high manpower demand to
carry out planning functions was that a large number of staff were taken on
without an existing professional qualification. These then sought
independent professional status as town planners, seeing themselves as
distinct from but equal to the existing local authority professions, with
their own Town Planning Institute. Thus the 1947 Act in practice
encouraged the development of an occupational group of 'planners' who
evolved their own views on the nature and method of planning (Cherry 1974,
Healey 1982a).

Summarizing the policy measures and institutional arrangements of the
planning system as created by the 1947 Act in terms of the categories and
dimensions listed in Chapter 1, we find that these were *wide ranging in
scope,* covering land use control, taxation of private gain from development,

public land acquisition and the guidance of all this development effort by a central ministry through the means of development plans. Institutional arrangements were in theory highly *centralized*, particularly in respect of policy, with delegation of certain tasks, and primarily *administrative* in form. Local authorities were essentially to be agents, realizing central government policy. Administrative powers dominate, with appeal to the courts allowable only on the grounds that the Minister was acting beyond his powers. These powers were very wide in scope, requiring the exercise of considerable *discretion* in determining the issues to be considered in making administrative decisions and in the manner in which such decisions were made. This discretion and the scale of the operation in turn encouraged the development of a body of *specialized personnel*. Finally, there can be no doubt that the aim was to adopt a *"planning" mode* in considering land policy, with the emphasis on policy consistency and continuity.

In terms of purposes, it has already been noted that the introduction of such comprehensive town planning legislation was backed by a widely-based coalition of interests. It could in fact be marketed as satisfying almost any group except those doubtful of the value of more than marginal intervention in the market, who were at the time a small minority. Perhaps the conception could best be described as the managerial form of the third purpose listed in Chapter 1, with government intervening to ensure that land is allocated, used and developed in the general interest, as determined by government. Supporting this was an assumption that market-support (where necessary) could be combined with the protection and enhancement of the environment and the pursuit of social welfare for all. Hebbert notes that

> "the especial characteristic of the "planning ideal" was that it
> allowed reformists of quite different persuasions to unite in the
> demand for change, each assuming ... that a rational scheme of
> central direction would eliminate the checks of competing values
> and priorities against which they chafed in the existing order"
> (Hebbert 1977 p.244).

Hebbert then goes on to quote von Hayek: "But, of course, the adoption of the social planning for which they clamour can only bring out the concealed conflict between their aims" (von Hayek 1944 p.40). In other words, the apparent consensus could be sustained until the "general interest" required definition. Then the conflicts were likely to emerge.

Ten years later these conflicts still remained latent, as Foley (1960) and Glass (1959) note. This may have been because the definition of the general interest was undertaken by a large number of local authorities in development plans which were often little more than land allocation maps, and in decisions on individual development control cases. From the 1960s, however, with a booming property sector and growing concern for the environment, the consensus progressively disintegrated.

The comprehensive measures of the 1947 Act lasted for so short a period that no assessment of its effectiveness or the interests it might have served can be made. It was first undermined by central government's political priorities and administrative practices. On the former, Hebbert observes:

> "Town and country planning had to succeed within the interstices
> as it were of the three major priorities of home policy in the
> late '40s, economic recovery, full employment, and the housing
> drive" (Hebbert 1977 p.255).

Meanwhile, the Board of Trade rather than the Ministry of Town and Country
Planning administered industrial location policy. More generally, spending
departments were unprepared to be co-ordinated by the new Ministry, which
had little power to enforce such co-ordination. Unlike most Ministries,
Town and Country Planning's concern was with the manipulation of a resource,
required by many sectors, each represented by their own Ministries. Thus,
it was more comparable to the Treasury in its type of function, but with
less power than the main spending departments, rather than more. Local
authorities, as already noted, for their part had very limited staff
resources to deploy, and in the early years looked to the few planning
consultants for help. Finally, it became evident that government, for
political and financial reasons, would not after all be the main land
developer.

By way of conclusion, and to take us into subsequent developments, I repeat
here Hall's verdict.

> "Almost certainly the Labour Government, when it passed the 1947
> Planning Act, thought that it was replacing the modified *laissez-*
> *faire* system of the 1930s by another system, where most of the
> initiative came from the state and from its agents, the local
> authorities and the new town Development Corporations. Under
> this prescription ... the market was not required to work because
> it was strictly irrelevant ... the great bulk of all development
> would be carried through by public agencies. Regional plans,
> followed by county Development Plans and the operation of
> development control within the framework of these plans, would be
> necessary to ensure the broad framework of land uses and
> activities, within which the work of these public agencies would
> be carried on. But it does not seem to have been assumed that
> development control machinery would ever be needed for more than a
> small minority of the total development.
>
> In practice ... the situation has been quite different. Ever
> since the mid-1950s, private enterprise speculative building for
> sale has become the general rule for new building in the
> countryside; the exception for new and expanding towns. The
> change happened to be associated with the arrival in power of
> the 1951 Conservative government, which rapidly scrapped building
> licences and the financial provisions of the 1947 Act, all in a
> short period from 1951 to 1954. But this was more than a matter
> of party-political ideology: the intellectual tide against
> planning and control was running strongly after 1948, as witnessed
> by the 'bonfire of controls' in the latter days of the Labour
> government. And the change happened to coincide with the
> unexpected rise in the birthrate from 1955 onwards which might
> have compelled a change in emphasis even from a Labour Government.
> At any rate, it is notable that when Labour returned in 1964, it
> did not attempt to go back to the 1947 position.
>
> The critical point, in other words, is that the so-called 1947
> planning system ... is really two systems. One was the system as
> imagined in theory, and as given legislative expression in the
> 1947 Act. The other was a very different system, as actually
> operated in the 1950s, and the 1960s. It worked within the
> general framework set up by the 1947 Act (with some amendments,
> particularly on the financial side), but with quite different
> emphases from those intended by the founding fathers of the
> system. In particular, the elementary but important fact about

this actual system is that it depends basically upon an
interaction between the private developer and the public
planners" (Hall et al. 1973 pp.390-1).

3. THE MAIN CHANGES IN THE 1947 ACT CONCEPTION OF LAND POLICY: 1950-80

This section will concentrate on the two most significant changes to policy
measures and institutional arrangements, firstly the removal of the measures
for collecting betterment and subsequent attempts at replacing them; and
secondly, the revisions to the development plan provisions. The first
completely undermined the system as conceived in 1947, leaving government
land policy able to regulate development but with few powers to promote it
and structure the land and property market as a whole, i.e. to engage in
"positive planning" as it is often called. To quote McAuslan,

> "the consideration of the problem of land values in an age of
> comprehensive planning is a consideration of the waxing and
> waning of the emphasis placed on public development and positive
> planning" (McAuslan 1975 p.603).

Having lost the powers to engage in such "positive planning", development
plan changes were motivated by an attempt to re-inject at least some
strategic direction, or policy "consistency and continuity" into a practice
that had become increasingly localized and preoccupied with detail (see
Hebbert 1977 chapter 4). Yet, although government land policy has found it
difficult to maintain a capacity for "positive" planning (development
promotion) or "strategic" planning (determining land allocation within some
kind of regional or national assessment of the scale and location of land
needs for various purposes), the measures for universal land use regulation
(development control) backed by some kind of development plan have
persisted. Nor were they subject to serious questioning until the late
seventies. Why has this been so? Can measures designed within the totally-
different legislative context, let alone social and economic context, of
1947 still be relevant to the 1980s? The changes relating to direct
government intervention in land ownership were largely motivated by
ideological considerations, which were then adapted to the particular
development pressures of the time. The changes in the development plan
arrangements were a direct response to the changing development conditions.
During the 1950s, planning authorities drew up development plans which
identified areas for comprehensive redevelopment (bombed city centres or
areas of slums), segregated uses by zoning, reserved sites for community
facilities of various kinds, and provided quite generous allocations of
land around urban areas within a general guiding principle that settlements
should be compact in shape and that the merging of settlements should be
resisted. The general use of green belts to resist development was
encouraged by central government from 1955 (MHLG Circular 42/55).

Meanwhile, through development control, planning authorities sought to
improve the quality of the built environment, marginally influencing
building design, and the street scene through advertisement control. As the
finance available for public investment was reduced and confined to specific
programme needs (for schools, hospitals etc), so the emphasis in development
control shifted from allowing development only if it was demonstrably in the
general interest, to refusing it only if it demonstrably was not.

During the 1950s as the performance of the economy improved, private
investment, commercial and residential property development substantially
increased. As Oliver Marriott has described (Marriott 1969), city centre

redevelopment for shopping and office purposes became prime investment opportunities, while residential development on greenfield sites around urban areas expanded vigorously as encouragement was given by government to the extension of owner-occupation. For city centre redevelopment property developers were able to work in co-operation with local authorities who sought the revitalization of centres but had little funds to invest in this themselves. The local authorities assisted in land assembly while property developers provided the development (see Marriott 1969, Ambrose and Colenutt 1975, Gough 1979). The problem both faced was that the development plans of the 1950s were insufficiently sensitive to the changing ideas of town centre built form and investment opportunities of the 1960s. For residential developers, the problem was simply that once they had run out of the land allocations of the early plans, local authorities were increasingly unwilling to release further greenfield sites (unallocated or "white" land), because local residents, often occupying new housing developments, resisted further development (Drewett 1973, Saunders 1977).

It was largely these difficulties in property development which led to the change in the development plan provisions of the planning system. The problem of land speculation and the windfall gains created by the operation of the planning system periodically preoccupied central government (see Cullingworth 1980 chapter 7, for example). But devising solutions was caught up in party ideology. It was not until the collapse of a surge in property investment in 1973 that a sufficient consensus was achieved on the need to reduce the opportunity for the making of substantial profits out of property speculation.

3.1 The Land Values and "Positive" Planning

Because the development charges introduced in the 1947 Act impinged immediately and tangibly on the financial interest of private land and property owners and developers, it is perhaps not surprising that this measure was vociferously attacked from many quarters. Some argued, as they still do, that such an infringement of individual rights was fundamentally unacceptable, just as others argued that land is a community asset and should not be in private hands. The middle ground is held by those concerned with efficiency considerations; the efficiency of the land and property market as a market, its efficiency in providing the land and development infrastructure for industry, commerce and housing, the efficiency of public sector provision of physical infrastructure (see Chapter 1, purpose (2)). The first such consideration might lead to only limited intervention, to avoid inhibiting market responsiveness to changing conditions. The other two considerations emphasized the need for cheap and available development land. This requirement for cheap land is of course in conflict with the profit-maximizing interests of land owners and developers.

During the 1950s, Conservative administrations were committed to freeing the land and property market from government controls. It was argued that the 100% development charge in effect inhibited landowners from bringing land forward for development and developers from developing it. Whether or not a lower level of development charge would have had a different effect has often been debated, although had the public sector been prepared to undertake development on a sufficient scale, engaging in compulsory purchase as necessary, the problem would have been a minor one. As it was, those objecting to government restrictions on private land and property interests could ally themselves with those who felt that the development charge led to internal inefficiencies within the land and property market, with the result that land was not available for development. In 1953, the

development charge was abolished. However, local authorities were still
left with the power to acquire land for their development needs at existing
use value. Several authorities had considerable land holdings anyway,
resulting from purchases before the war, and since the war for housing and
comprehensive development purposes. Allowing local authorities to acquire
land cheaply created an anomalous dual market in land, depending on whether
it was purchased by a private or public agency. In 1959, this anomaly was
removed, with local authorities being required to purchase at market value.
In the 1961 Land Compensation Act, land owners were also given powers to
serve "purchase" notices on local authorities if a planning decision (e.g.
zoning a site for a park or a school) meant they could not put their
property to a "reasonably beneficial use". These provisions were extended
in 1968 and 1973 to include compensation for owners whose selling price was
substantially lower than it would have been without the planning proposal
("blight notices")[17]. As McAuslan points out, this further strengthened
the position of private property (see McAuslan 1975 pp.684 et seq.).
According to McKay and Cox, the 1959 Act marked "the lowest point to which
the state's role in controlling land values and development planning had
fallen since ... 1919" (McKay and Cox 1979 p.82). Subsequent attempts to
recoup at least some of the ground lost to property interests have left the
situation little changed in 1980, with effects on the form and content of
local plans which will become evident in Part II.

Labour governments have twice reintroduced legislation designed to regain
control of the location and price of development land from the market and to
secure the collection of at least part of the financial gain from development
to the community. Both were intended to increase the capacity for "positive
planning" and both suffered in this respect from isolation from ongoing land
use planning. The Land Commission, established in 1967, and abolished by
the Conservatives in 1971, had powers to purchase land for development
purposes, to dispose of land to public and private interests, and to raise a
"betterment levy", fixed at 40%, on "development value". It was to be a
national land assembly authority, independent of local authorities though
furthering their planning policies. Local authorities were thought not to
have the entrepreneurial skill for the task required (Cox 1980).

The Commission was expected to play a major role in the market, structuring
land values by its land dealings, as well as through the betterment levy.
More importantly, it was to make land available for private development, but
it found few friends. Not only did it encounter the usual criticism that
the levy inhibited development and the whole exercise was an unwarranted
intervention in property rights, but its scale of operations was so small
that it had little impact on "positive planning" or overall land prices,
while local authorities objected to the existence of an agency which
appeared to interfere with their own efforts in land use planning. The
Commission on the other hand concluded fairly quickly that it was impeded
in its aim of helping to provide the right land for development in the right
places by local authority planning policies "which are directed at the
containment of urban growth and the preservation of open country" (Land
Commission Second Report p.4 quoted by Drewett 1973 p.242). It actually
echoed the residential developers' arguments about over-restrictive policies
pursued by shire county planning authorities, and sought to overturn these
by applying for planning permission on strategic sites and taking refusals
to appeal (Cullingworth 1980 chapter 13). The Commission in total purchased
2800 acres and raised £71 million in betterment levy (see Drewett 1973).

---

[17]The Acts referred to here are the 1968 Town and Country Planning Act and
the 1973 Land Compensation Act.

The 1975 Community Land Act was by contrast administered by local authorities, with the exception of the Land Authority for Wales. Both Conservative and Labour parties were prepared by 1974 to introduce legislation on the land value question because of the widespread concern about the effects on land prices of the speculative investment boom of the early seventies and more fundamentally, as Massey and Catalano argue, the deflection of investment into land and development rather than industrial production (Massey and Catalano 1978 pp.171-2). The Community Land Act gave powers to local authorities (to become a duty at some future date) to acquire "relevant" development land. This would then be used for public development or leased to private developers or users. "Relevant" development was defined to include fairly substantial "exemptions" (e.g. agriculture, forestry and mining) and "exceptions" (e.g. land owned by industrial firms). Regard was to be paid to "the provision of the development plan, so far as material" (Community Land Act 1975 S17 SS2a), and initially local authorities were asked to prepare land policy statements, which were to "provide the policy links with the planning objectives of the area and an orderly framework of operation" (DoE Circular 121/75 paragraph 69). This apparently clear intention to link questions of land value and ownership to land use planning, and hence encourage "positive" rather than regulatory planning, was in fact only inserted into the legislation after active lobbying by the planning profession. The Act was supplemented by the 1976 Development Land Tax on development value realized on disposal of an interest in land. This was fixed at 80%, with the first £10,000 of realized value exempt from tax. This tax had been preceeded by a Development Gains Tax, enacted by the Conservative administration in 1974 consequent upon public and Treasury disquiet about the speculative gains being made from property transactions.

The proceeds of the Development Land Tax went to the Exchequer. Returns from sales of land were divided between central government, the local authorities concerned and a "pool" to be distributed among local authorities. However, the Community Land account was to be discrete, and only used for land purchases. Thus, although given the administration of the Community Land Act, local authority powers to use it were circumscribed. In Wales, a different arrangement was establisned, with a Land Authority for Wales acting as a form of regional Land Commission. Bearing in mind the fate of its predecessor, LAW set out to establish co-operative working with local authorities, and to demonstrate that public land development could be self-financing (Hollingsworth and Cuddy 1979). It had the benefit in this that, like local authorities and other public bodies, it could purchase land net of Development Land Tax.

Once again, this land legislation met considerable hostility on ideological grounds, with many Conservative local authorities refusing to have anything to do with it. However, it was more substantially undermined by central government's failure to devote adequate resources to it, and by its emphasis on the need to purchase land which could be resold leasehold to realize profits on the land trading account. As in the late 1940s, short-term economic priorities undermined land policy measures. Not only did this mean that land purchase was focussed on immediately profitable greenfield sites, but that development-oriented local authorities were unable to use the Community Land Act for opportunity purchases for long-term perhaps unprofitable development needs (see Barrett, Boddy and Stewart 1978). Given also the definition of "relevant" development, Massey and Catalano are no doubt correct in concluding that only what they refer to as "former landed property", and property companies, were constrained in their activities by the provisions of the Act. Financial institutions, on the other hand, could well have been strengthened. The industrial sector was largely unaffected (Massey and Catalano 1978 chapter 8).

The Community Land Act was abolished by the Conservatives' Local Government and Planning Act 1980 with the *exception* of the Land Authority for Wales which succeeded in its aim of demonstrating its profitability[18]. Significantly, also, the Development Land Tax has been retained, though set at a lower level (60%), evidence that the spectre of the land speculator has still not been entirely dispelled[19].

Throughout this legislative and institutional ebb and flow in respect of land values, the land use provisions of the 1947 Act have remained intact. No detailed examination of the reason for this has been undertaken as far as I am aware, but several possible reasons suggest themselves - the strong lobby behind countryside preservation and the protection of agricultural land (the "county" interests of Hall's analysis); the inertia built up within local authorities by the existence of a planning bureaucracy[20]. The desire of local politicians to be in a position to exercise control over development (a sort of local fiefdom, or patronage). Another reason, reflecting the discussion in Chapter 1, may be that while land value and ownership measures impinge clearly on specific property interests, the system of land use regulation backed by development plans is open to manipulation by many interests. It also has the appearance of being in the public interest. There are now signs that this long standing support for land use regulation is being challenged. I return to this point later in the present chapter.

3.2 Development Plans

While the question of land values has been an issue of intense political controversy, legislation about development plans appears to have been largely the product of professional and administrative ideas, legislative ratification and administrative interpretation. There was little parliamentary discussion about the development plan provisions of the 1947 Act, and hardly more in the 1968 Act. This lack of political interest, except from planners and local authorities, has been repeated over the changes to development plan arrangements in the 1972 Local Government Act and the 1980 Local Government and Planning Act. It is not until 1977 that we find an all party House of Commons Select Committee calling for a "review of the development plan system" (House of Commons Expenditure Committee 1977 paragraph 86). Debate has occurred largely among the professional institutes (particularly the Royal Town Planning Institute and the Royal Institute of Chartered Surveyors) and the local authority associations (currently the Association of Metropolitan Authorities, the Association of County Councils and the Association of District Councils), each of which has its associated organization of planning officers. Active lobbying by these organizations has led to changes both in legislation and its subsequent interpretation. However, recently, and reflected in the comments of the Expenditure Committee noted above, criticism of development plans is being mounted from other quarters, notably by the House Builders' Federation who argue that too little land has been allocated in plans, and the CPRE who complain that too much land has been released.

---

[18]It now has to purchase land at market value rather than net of Development Land Tax.

[19]For good accounts of the Community Land legislation in theory and practice, see Massey and Catalano 1978 chapter 8, Barrett, Boddy and Stewart 1978, McAuslan 1980 chapter 5, Grant 1978 and Barrett 1981.

[20]The Land Commission was easy to abolish; the Community Land Act was supposed to generate no extra staff needs.

The main change to the 1947 Act provisions in respect of development plans
came in the 1968 Town and Country Planning Act which introduced two types of
development plan, structure and local plans. This enacted proposals which
had been put forward by the influential report of the Planning Advisory
Group on *The Future of Development Plans* (The PAG Report, MHLG 1965). The
specific form and arrangements for structure and local plans will be
discussed in more detail in Chapters 3 and 4. Here the general intentions of
this so-called "radical revision" (MHLG 1965 paragraph 1.25) and the factors
behind it will be summarized. In essence, the PAG report sought to:

1) reintroduce a strategic planning framework into local authority
    land use decisions;

2) find a way of making the form of plans more relevant to the task
    of "physical reshaping", "modernization", "redevelopment" and
    "wholesale renewal" of large towns and cities (MHLG 1965
    paragraph 2.1); and

3) reduce the administrative burden placed on central government
    by the inquiries into local authority plans ("to simplify
    planning administration" - MNLG 1965 paragraph 1.1).

A subsidiary aim was to encourage more public support for planning. The
Report did not consider either development control or the land values issue,
and in retrospect its recommendations suffered from the failure to consider
development plans within the context of government land policy as a whole.

Given the discussions about outline plans and detailed development plans
prior to the 1947 Act, one may well ask, as several contemporary
commentators did (e.g. TPI 1966, SCLSERP 1971, 1973), why legislative change
was needed. The PAG Report itself argued for the reintroduction of the
thinking about outline plans which preceded the 1947 Act (MHLG 1965
paragraph 1.22). In retrospect, it seems fairly clear that the problems the
PAG report sought to overcome lay not so much with the legislation but with
the way it was used by central and local government. To start with, central
government lost interest in regional planning during the 1950s, so that there
was no strategic framework to guide local authorities in preparing their
plans. In other words, central government did little to promote central
policy consistency and continuity. Plans were therefore "filled" with local
policy concerns, moderated by the representations of government departments
and agencies consulted during plan preparation. Most local authority
politicians and their planning staffs meanwhile were inexperienced in the
preparation of plans which related broader social and economic policy
considerations to detailed land use and development proposals. They also had
inadequate access to information or understanding of how to use it.
Consequently they fell back either on the models of pre war town planning
schemes, or produced plans which were little more than maps of existing uses.
Development plans, therefore, typically became comprehensive land allocation
maps, though rarely did the specified land allocations relate to the development pressures for urban expansion and renewal which local authorities in
many areas began to encounter during the 1950s as the economy picked up. For
town centres and comprehensive development areas, plans had a format similar
to New Town Master Plans, with detailed specification of uses, building bulk
and density.

Consequently, the plans were criticized as "rigid", or inappropriate
"blueprint" documents. Decisions based on them, or increasingly in breach
of them, often appeared arbitrary rather than rational. Because the
public sector was slow to implement proposals, plans were accused of

causing "blight". Meanwhile, property interests adversely affected by the plans generated a large number of detailed objections to plans, which resulted in lengthy inquiries which had to be conducted by central government. The net result was that development plan preparation was a slow and cumbersome process, the results of which were not necessarily helpful to the local authority or central government in its tasks of land management in the 1960s (see Hebbert 1977 chapter 4). One consequence of this was that authorities produced their own interim plans and guidance documents. This proliferation of non-statutory plans accelerated in the 1960s, when central government delayed approving development plan revisions whilst regional strategy was evolved in the light of projections of substantial growth. In the South East and the West Midlands, this production of an agreed regional strategy took ten years, during which substantial development decisions were made outside the context of development plans (e.g. further New Towns; the motorway programme; substantial land releases for housing purposes). A worrying feature of the proliferation of informal plans and proposals was that many, at both central and local government level, were not the subject of public discussion. Local planning authorities often had "bottom drawer" plans which were never even the subject of political scrutiny. (McLoughlin 1973b).

Hebbert (1977) argues that in the 1950s land use policy became predominantly localized and incremental, backing away from the centralized and planning form of the 1947 Act conception. However, some "policy consistency and continuity" was produced through development plans, not because of centralization of policy control but through a common policy direction pursued at the local level. In this light we can perhaps see one factor behind the 1960s review of development plans as the struggle by development interests (linked to the then politically-acceptable aims of economic growth and technological modernization) to break the hold on land release of farmers and the environmental conservation movement. But it is worth noting one further contributor to policy consistency and continuity, namely the definition of those matters appropriate for a local authority to consider in making a planning decision. Although a development plan was and is one such consideration, other "material" considerations can also be used as the basis for decision. In the 1947 Act, local authorities appeared to be given the discretion to include a wide range of matters in both plans and other "material" considerations. In practice, this range was severely limited to so-called "amenity" aspects. This happened in part because of the attitude of the courts to what constituted the legitimate territory of the public interest in land use matters. But it also reflects both the attitude of government, *and* many local authority planners at this time (see Harrison 1972, 1979, McAuslan 1980 chapter 6).

The 1968 Act firstly distinguished two types of plan, the broad strategic *structure* plan, and the detailed development or *local* plans. The structure plan is based on a *survey* of the plan area. Publicity for the survey material and consideration of representations arising from that survey is required. The plan, a written document or *statement*, has to be publicized and objections to it received. It is then submitted to central government (from 1971, the Secretary of State for the Environment) for modification and approval, along with a statement as to how publicity has been carried out. The Secretary of State can receive further representations and exercise his discretion about whether to hold some form of local inquiry or hearing. In practice, the procedure has been to hold an "Examination in Public" in which the Secretary of State hears the local authority's case and that of other bodies, with the issues to be discussed and parties whose views are to be represented decided upon by central government (DoE 1973a).

Local planning authorities may then "if they think it desirable" prepare a
local plan for any part of their area (1971 Act S11 SS(1)). The only
compulsion on them is to prepare an "action area" local plan if such an
area is designated in a structure plan[21]. A local plan consists of a map and
a written statement, the term "map" implying that boundaries on the map can
be specifically linked to boundaries on the ground and hence sites
specifically identified. Publicity and an opportunity to receive
representations and objections are required during and after preparation of
the plan. The plan and a statement about publicity are sent to the
Secretary of State who checks that correct procedures have been followed.
The local planning authority "may, and shall in the case of objections so
made in accordance with regulations ... cause a local inquiry" to be heard.
The organization of a local inquiry into objections to the plan, and
adoption of the plan, are, however, matters for the local planning
authority. It is the authority who adopts the plan and makes modifications
subsequent to an inquiry, not the inquiry inspector or central government.
It thus judges its own plan. The local plan must conform generally to the
approved structure plan, although it was assumed in the 1968 Act that both
plans would be prepared by the same authority.

Despite the professional and administrative concern to promote a strategic
framework to guide land use change which was sufficiently flexible to cope
with rapidly-evolving development situations, administratively the revised
development plan system reflects a hierarchical system of policy control.
Central government approves broad strategic policy, while devolving concern
with detailed matters, to local authorities, including the inquiry into the
specific proposals which would be likely to generate many objections. In
the terms of central-local relations, it reflects an "agency" view of local
government (Jones 1979), with centralization of policy and decentralization
of administration. The central issue here of course is whether such
separation of broad policy from its detailed realization is possible. The
discretion available to the public sector was if anything extended, since
there was no requirement for all objections to a plan to be heard. In local
plan inquiries, some objections could be ignored on the grounds that they
related to already approved structure plan policies (DoE 1977)[22]. Central
government, not the citizen, determines what is to be discussed in the
Examination in Public. Thus while the citizen appears to gain from the
requirements for publicity and the opportunity to make representations in
plan preparation, he may lose under the changes to inquiry procedure.

In exercising this apparently wider discretion introduced in the 1968 Act,
planning authorities are required to have regard:

> "(a) to current policies with respect to the economic planning
> and development of the region as a whole; (b) to the resources
> likely to be available for the carrying out of the proposals of
> the structure plan; and (c) to such matters as the Secretary of
> State may direct them to take into account" (1971 Act S7 4).

This may be contrasted with the 1947 Act which refers merely to the
specification of sites for various purposes. In other words, as McAuslan
has argued (McAuslan 1980 Chapter 6), the legislation itself specifies

---

[21]This requirement was removed in the 1980 Local Government, Planning and
Land Act.

[22]The key issue here is the definition of a "relevant objection" - see DoE
1977 paragraphs 3-5 and chapter 6.

aspects of the breadth of policy concerns that can enter into land use policy matters, rather than leaving it open for interpretation and, as happened in the 1950s, potential limitation. The breadth of concern is further elaborated in regulations which add social policy considerations to economic and financial ones (1974 Regulations No. 1486 Reg. 17 (Schedule 2 part II (iii))).

Finally, the 1968 Act formalized a move away from the universality of the 1947 Act arrangements. While all authorities must produce structure plans, there is no obligation to produce local plans except in the case of structure plan action areas. Further, central government advice soon invented three types of local plan - action area, district and subject plans. An authority therefore could choose whether or not to prepare a plan and if so, of what type. Such variety was quite possible in the 1947 Act. The 1968 Act and the advice and regulations which followed it encouraged greater specificity.

During the 1970s, the 1968 Act has been put into practice, if very slowly. Ten years later, by the end of 1978, only 24 structure plans had been approved in England and Wales, out of a total of 81 required; the first local plan was not adopted until 1976, and only 13 had been adopted by the end of 1978. Meanwhile, legislative changes have encouraged once again a drift away from strategic policy control. This has primarily been due to the impact of local government reorganization in 1974 which created a two-tier local authority structure, metropolitan and shire counties, and metropolitan and shire districts, each with their own political and administrative organization. Planning functions are divided between the two, with counties preparing structure plans and able to prepare local plans. Districts are responsible for most development control matters and can prepare local plans.

The Royal Town Planning Institute was deeply concerned at the consequences of separating "policy" from "implementation" in this way, and pressed for measures to protect the ability of structure plans to guide local plan preparation by districts (RTPI 1972). This led to the requirement in the 1972 Local Government Act for the production of development plan schemes, prepared by counties in consultation with districts. These were supposed to indicate priorities for local plan preparation. The Act also required counties to grant a certificate of conformity in respect of a local plan, to ensure that district-prepared local plans conformed to the structure plan. Despite exhortations from central government to engage in harmonious relations over land use policy (DoE Circular 74/73), the problems of county-district relations have bedevilled land use planning since reorganization came into effect. The power of the districts has been further strengthened by first, the 1978 Inner Urban Areas Act, which allowed local plan adoption prior to structure plan approval in designated inner city areas, and the 1980 Local Government and Planning Act, which extends this provision to all areas. This latter act also introduces several minor adjustments to development plan arrangements.

One consequence of local government reorganization is that districts now have more de facto control over the content of planning policy, whether as expressed in plans or in development control decisions. This in turn has consequences for central government in so far as it has strategic interests in the way land is used and developed. That it has had such concerns during the 1970s is evident in the pressure it has exercised on local authorities in relation to land availability for housing, the treatment of green belts, and the provision of land for industry (Healey 1982b). Meanwhile, local authority planners are arguing that a negotiative and promotional style is

more appropriate to the problems of their areas than a plan-based style
(Collins 1980, Davies 1980, Hill 1980, also Jowell 1977). This in turn has
been met with central government advice limiting the scope of matters
appropriate to consider in development plans (Burns 1980). Whereas in the
1950s it was local authority practices which encouraged the reduction of
development plans to land use maps, it is now local authorities who accuse
central government of reducing local plans to old-style development plans.

4. THE SITUATION IN 1980

To the local authority land use planner of 1980, development control is at
the heart of the system in which he is involved, justifying his existence in
considerable numbers both to administer the control machinery and to provide
policy guidance for its operation. Not much remains of the work on slum
clearance and urban renewal which occupied him in the 1960s and his role in
managing the land market, so vital to the 1947 Act, is largely ignored. In
communities suffering economic contraction, many planners are actively
involved in economic initiatives of various kinds, but their skills and
legitimacy in engaging in such activities are open to question. It could
be argued that the renewed interest in development control in the late
1970s was a reflection of the appreciation that it is all that planners
have left (see RTPI 1979).

Yet overseas commentators, particularly Americans, find the wide discretion
with which development control powers are exercised hard to understand (see
McBride 1979). The explanation of course is that it derives from the 1947
conception when the public sector was expected to dominate development
activity. Many, however, argue that the exercise of this discretion leads
to uncertainty about development intentions, inconsistent decisions, and
general arbitrariness. There are signs that this uncertainty, or lack of a
clear development framework, increased during the seventies, although
whether this was because of the delay in producing structure and local plans
or was inherent in the evolving relationship between planning authorities
and development interests is unclear. McAuslan has also claimed that the
discretion involved in the definition of "material" considerations has
allowed the courts and central government to limit the breadth of issues
that the 1968 Act encouraged. He argues that there should be less
discretion in development control and more weight given to plans (McAuslan
1980 p.151), as does the District Planning Officers' Society (DPOS 1978).
Whatever the cause, criticism of development control has increased recently.
In addition to the accusations of arbitrariness, the machinery is said to
grind too slowly, causing costly delays to developers already operating
with tight profit margins (see, for example, the Dobry report on development
control, DoE 1975). The present and previous governments have sought to
reduce delays by increasing the amount of development which falls through
the net of public control. In this they find themselves opposed by
environmentalists concerned with detailed design control, property owners
wishing to preserve the good neighbour protection service offered by
development control at present, and planners who argue that strategic
developments are not necessarily distinguished by their size.

Meanwhile, the development plans which may at least reduce some of the
apparent arbitrariness in development control are heavily criticized.
Thanks to the energies of the 1979 Conservative administration, nearly all
of England and Wales had an approved structure plan by the end of 1981.
Only 98 local plans had been adopted, however[23]. Not surprisingly,

----
[23] DoE records.

development plans are said to be slow and expensive to produce, and when available are outdated, difficult to change, and/or irrelevant. Local authorities argue for more local control; more emphasis on producing specific policy guidance or promotional activities relevant to the problem in hand; more discretion to engage in a wider range of small-scale interventions; and more powers to co-ordinate *public* sector development. Developers and sections of the public on the other hand claim to seek more certainty, less arbitrariness and hence less local authority discretion. Developers are inclined to argue for more central control to ensure policy consistency, and also seek help with infrastructure co-ordination. There are thus pressures both to dismantle the hierarchical policy control model underlying the present development plan system and to reinforce it, as well as a lack of confidence in statutory plans as a way of expressing policy.

Underlying this discussion over who should define policy and in what form is a further discussion noted by Roberts:

"If the heart of planning is really in the creation of 'policy' documents, then the focus of central government energy should be on systematizing, co-ordinating and integrating the future plans of the local authorities. If, however, it is in reality with the day-to-day decisions, then central government should be concerned not so much with the broad sweep of the brush but the particular appeals on particular applications" (Roberts 1976 p.85).

In effect, we have here three models for the way government land use regulation should occur. In the first, government provides a development framework within which the market can operate, removing the uncertainties of the unfettered market. This involves the production of publicly available development plans which express this framework clearly and precisely. It also involves consideration of the various ways in which the content of such plans could be determined. In the second, government is an arbiter between competing interests in land. No plan is needed here, the emphasis being on inquiries at which all affected parties present their views. Although the final decision lies with the government, there is no longer an assumption that government by itself can determine where the public interest lies. In the third, government makes its own assessment of the issues involved and the public interest in respect of the way land is used and developed. It retains regulatory powers over land use but demands wide discretion in the way they are exercised, and seeks to link land use regulation to a variety of other initiatives to promote development. Formal development plans may be less helpful to government here than a variety of private and semi-public policy statements.

Many local authorities are currently pressing for this third model, but this is not just a case of public officials seeking more power. Planners and local authority politicians are being pushed into this sort of approach partly by the shortage of resources and unpredictability of development initiatives, and partly by pressure from industrial and other private business interests seeking government assistance in times of extreme economic difficulty. Thus we now find local authority planners encouraged to explore a "partnership" approach with the private sector (see Davies 1980; see also DoE Circulars 71/77, 44/78, 9/80, and 22/80), an approach advocated some time ago by Denman (1974), and the Sheaf Report (DoE 1972).

However, McAuslan has recently argued strongly that this retreat into administrative determination of the public interest in land use planning should be resisted. He sees such determination as likely to maximize administrative efficiency rather than a balanced assessment of all interests.

An alternative interpretation is that it encourages a "corporatist" way of operating (see Chapter 1). Currently he sees the courts as the only serious challenge to what he refers to as the dominance of government's "public interest" ideology in the planning field, but he finds the courts to be concerned primarily with the protection of property interests. By contrast, as noted in Chapter 1, he believes that there should be much more emphasis on citizen involvement in determining and sustaining planning policy (McAuslan 1980). I will return to this argument in Chapter 9.

These debates of the late seventies suggest that land use regulation in Britain is at last being seriously questioned. Are we about to see the remaining parts of the 1947 Act dismantled? The rhetoric of the 1979 Conservative government sometimes seems to suggest that all regulation will be swept away with a return to something like a free market in the use and development of land. Many of its critics certainly believe this is what is intended. Yet on closer investigation, most of the discussion is not about the removal of regulation but its replacement by one or the other of the above models. It is, then, the form and purpose of intervention, rather than the amount of it, which is currently being debated, a debate which is long overdue. The outcome of the debate will affect the role of structure and local plans, both in the way current legislation is interpreted and in the proposals for legislative change. Clearly, however, this debate, with its potential outcome in a complete replacement of the 1947 legislative inheritance, is taking place in a very different economic climate to that of the 1960s. Then a development boom was under way which could be presented as encouraging general affluence. Now most interests fear the opposite; hence the hostility to "regulation" and the hope of "promotion".

5. THE EFFECTS OF LAND USE POLICY

The British land use planning system thus gives central government a considerable role in determining strategic policy. In practice power to determine the content of policy is widely diffused and likely to vary from locality to locality. The system was designed to guide urban redevelopment, town expansion and new town construction, while preserving the countryside. It is currently adapting to various forms of economic decline mixed with growth pressures outside the main urban centres. It was intended to provide a framework for public sector investment and now operates through a process of negotiation with private development interests. As Lyn Davies has commented, the main characteristic of British planning practice in the 1980s is that it has none (Davies 1982). What then have been the outcome of thirty years of land use regulation?

We might conclude that given the potential variation in the way the planning system could be used from place to place, no general assessment is possible. As I note in Chapter 8, it is not easy to generalize about the outcomes produced by the use of local plans. Nevertheless, the few evaluative studies that exist, notably that of Hall *et al.* 1973, do come to some important conclusions.

Hall's study argues that the effect of containing urban growth, complemented by the construction of new towns, has been to benefit those in rural areas (through rising property values and attractive environments), young mobile skilled workers and firms seeking large well-serviced sites (new towns), at the expense of the poor urban dweller who has suffered from the consequences of very high urban land prices caused by limiting the amount of urban

development (Hall et al. 1973 Chapter 12). We might conclude that the
planning system has organized the process of suburbanization in Britain,
but has not resisted it.

Drewett (1973) claims that restricting the land available for urban
development without price control has made land more costly and increased
development costs, particularly of housing. First time buyers are therefore
disadvantaged. However, studies in other countries show that urban land
costs have been rising dramatically in most capitalist countries (e.g.
Darin-Drabkin 1977), so it is not clear what the specific contribution of
land use planning has been. Drewett (1973) and a study by JURUE give some
support to the case made by developers that planning control not only
affects development costs through land prices, but through delay in handling
applications (JURUE 1977). However, the costs of delay and the causes of
it are hotly disputed.

Much is made today of the argument that land use policy inhibits development
as well as making it more costly. This is said to happen because development
initiatives are stifled by the existence of complex and costly planning
procedures and the restrictive attitudes of local authorities. This may
well be the case in some areas, particularly those operating green belt or
agricultural protection policies. Yet other studies indicate that
development interests have gained. Elkin (1974), Ambrose and Colenutt
(1975), Gough (1976) and Saunders (1980) illustrate how local authorities
have assisted developers in urban renewal for commercial purposes through
land assembly, provision of infrastructure (especially road realignment),
and the waiving of specific planning restraints (in return for small-scale
"planning gains"). The first two of these studies argue cogently that the
developers gained much more out of these activities than the local
community, low-income families in residential property in such areas
characteristically being displaced. Even Drewett, who stresses the costs
of land use policy, notes the way developers use planning information in
site search (both in scanning development plans and in consulting planning
officers (Drewett 1973)). On the other hand, many small firms have
suffered, through urban renewal schemes which have displaced them and land
allocations in development plans which have declared them to be non-
conforming.

What about the countryside? Hall's study claims that urban expansion has
been effectively limited. Coleman, on the other hand, is highly critical
of this conclusion, arguing that there has been extensive deterioration of
land around urban fringes (Coleman 1976). She attributes this to the
inability of land use policy to ensure the positive use of land. Other
studies illustrate that while green belts have on the whole been
protected from urban development (Mandelker 1962, Gregory 1970), there are
major problems in preserving them in productive agriculture (SCLSERP 1976,
Munton 1983). Studies of other environmental policies also cast doubts on
their effectiveness. Blacksell and Gilg (1977) conclude that in an area
designated as an Area of Outstanding Natural Beauty (AONB) in Devon, there
was actually a higher rate of approval of applications within the AONB than
outside, although more conditions were attached to permissions. A similar
picture was found by Preece (1979) in the Cotswolds AONB, although he
concludes that though development has not been more restricted than
elsewhere, design standards have been raised. Perhaps this is all that
might be expected. Meanwhile Newby (1979) argues forcibly that the
environmental and agricultural conservation policies pursued in structure
plans in rural areas have benefitted the farming industry and the new ex-
urban middle class who have moved into such areas, at the expense of rural
workers.

To conclude, I quote Lyn Davies' assessment of the achievements and failures of the planning system:

> "There has been some effective co-ordination of development, creating a good, local environment: some of the new and expanded towns; some town centre schemes; much of the growth in villages, small towns and suburbs. Planning in all these cases has worked largely by creating a climate of certainty about public sector intentions, enabling a comparatively risk-free private sector investment combined with effective and co-ordinated public developments. There has been, too, a measure of protection and preservation, seen in the containment of towns and the maintenance of green belts; in the conservation of historic urban environments; in the creation of national parks and areas of outstanding natural beauty; in the control of advertisements. And there has been the contribution of planning, with other legislation, towards the control of pollution, ranging from clean air and rivers, to the restoration of mineral workings".

But,

> "notwithstanding the vision and the hopes, the problems have not been solved or the reality has failed to live up to expectations: urban renewal, especially where it has had to rely solely on the public sector; urban transportation; the quality of much of the new development, whether through positive planning or development control, ... Economic regeneration, whether at regional, or local urban, or rural, scales has proved intractable during periods of decline, as have the closely related problems of spatial inequality". (Davies 1982 pp.12-13).

What is not clear is what has produced this particular mixture of achievements and failures. I have stressed the importance of policy measures and institutional arrangements. Others have blamed planners themselves (Dennis 1970, Gower Davies 1972, Regan 1978). Blowers by contrast argues that planners have limited power (Blowers 1980), a conclusion supported by Ambrose and Colenutt's study of city centre redevelopment in Southwark and Brighton (Ambrose and Colenutt 1975) and my own work with Jacky Underwood on London Borough planners (Healey and Underwood 1979; Underwood 1980). Central government's role in limiting the effectiveness of the planning system has also been stressed (Cullingworth 1975, McKay and Cox 1979), while Hebbert emphasizes the influence of the environmental and farming lobbies (Hebbert 1977).

One general conclusion is that central government, the courts, local authorities, business interests and planners have exerted considerable influence, while the public, apart from environmental pressure groups, have had little impact on the outcome of planning policy. Those disadvantaged in society as a whole have benefitted least and have had their problems increased rather than decreased by the system in operation, despite a real intention to do otherwise in 1947. The claim that British land use planning contributes to improving the welfare of the disadvantaged is therefore not easy to substantiate, unless it can be demonstrated that central and local government have the interests of ordinary people at heart in matters of land policy.

In Part II of this book I will be examining the interpretation and use of a
particular tool in the British planning system.   In doing so, I will examine
both how far the form of the tool has limited the uses to which it can be
put, and how different interests have managed to manipulate the way the
tool has been used to suit their own ends.   In Chapter 8, I then consider
what local plans have been used for, returning to the question of the
outcomes of the British planning system and the interests it has served in
Chapter 9.

CHAPTER 3

Structure Plans

1. BRITISH DEVELOPMENT PLANS

In this chapter, I propose to outline the concept of "structure plans" as developed in the PAG Report (MHLG 1965), translated into legislation, and interpreted by central government and local authorities. I then consider the procedures which have evolved for producing structure plans, concluding with an assessment of the content of plans.

As has been indicated in Chapter 2, British development plans have distinctive characteristics. They are *guidance* frameworks, intended to *co-ordinate* and *regulate* the activities of a range of development agents in the public and private sectors. They are not zoning ordinances of the kind found in the U.S. Although land may be zoned in plans for specified uses, landowners have no *right* to develop land in the manner zoned. They are more like what was understood in the U.S. as a "general plan" (Haar 1951), but they are not master plans, in the sense of the development programming maps of a development agency which controls its own land and finance, such as a New Town Corporation. A development plan may be prepared in a master plan form either because, as in some slum clearance schemes, the local authority is the major land owner and developer, or because the plan preparers made the erroneous assumption that as much control could be exercised over a variety of development agents as a New Town Corporation can exercise over itself.

British development plans are not general social and economic development plans either, although the legislation gives some latitude to interpret them in this way, nor are they agency corporate management plans intended for use in co-ordinating and directing local authority investment, although some commentators were critical of the PAG proposals because structure plans did not concern themselves with local authority corporate management (McLoughlin 1966; Eddison 1968).

Within the 1947 Act conception of the planning system, in which the public sector was to undertake most development, this development was to serve the ends of national and economic policy as relevant at the local scale. Development plans were thus to provide principles for translating such policy into spatial allocations and detailed development, co-ordinate the public sector development effort, and indicate the basis on which small-scale private development would be regulated. In effect, the plan was both to provide a *rationale*, demonstrating that public sector decisions were not arbitrary, and a *tool* for efficient management.

In practice, this ideal was rarely realized in the 1950s, as I have shown in Chapter 2. The revised development plan system of 1968 was an attempt to recover the capacity to link detailed development to social and economic policy as evolved at regional and sub-regional level. The two-tier hierarchy of plans, reviving the idea which had influenced discussion about development plans prior to 1947, was aimed at achieving both more central direction over policy and more local discretion in the detailed realization of these policies. Plans were to demonstrate clearly the rationale (or "reasoned justification") for policies which it was expected would be implemented substantially by private sector development agents. With developers prepared to challenge plans prior to adoption and subsequently, and with the growing interest among certain groups in their local environment, it was important that policies were defensible. The 1968 Act therefore attempted to recover the role of development plans in the efficient management of development and in providing a rationale for public intervention which had come to look increasingly arbitrary.

During the 1970s, however, this aim has been challenged, firstly by doubts as to how far development guidance frameworks, especially those pitched at a longer timespan, can increase the "rationality" of the planning system. This challenge derived from debates in planning theory, as well as practice. Those who supported the notion of comprehensive guidance frameworks criticized development plans as emphasizing the *product* (the plan) rather than the *process* of policy guidance, with the result that the production of a one-off plan (although subject to amendment) became more important than on-going policy review. Others challenged the rationality of such comprehensiveness in the first place, accepting the incrementalist argument that it was more relevant to focus on the short term, on marginal adjustments and on evident problems[24].

The second challenge questioned the capacity of plans to present rational principles which would gain widespread support, given an increasing awareness that interests conflict in respect of land and development. Consequently, it is commonly recognized now that plans embody *political choices* about the way land is used and developed, choices which may encounter sustained opposition both during discussion about the plan and subsequently. Thirdly, it has become increasingly apparent that what central government may want out of the planning system is not necessarily the same as what local authorities seek. Consequently, local authorities have sought to increase the discretion available to them in defining the form and content of plans, while central government has set out to decrease it.

It is probably true to say that criticism of development plans is at least as great today as it was in the early 1960s. Once again the attempt to provide a defensible rationale for public sector decisions and to provide a co-ordinative framework to increase the efficiency of public and private sector development investment is struggling against the pluralism of the public sector and the conflicting demands on it, as will become evident in this and later chapters. The dilemma facing development plan production was

---

[24]See Drake 1975 for the debate among structure planners, and Banfield 1959 and Etzioni 1973 for the general issues.

well put some time ago by SCLSERP, which doubted the capacity of the new
development plan system to make any improvements on the old:

"54. The essence of our findings was that whatever may be the purposes
to which the planning system is put, it has always been inherent in
the system that decisions within it upon central and local government
intervention in the use and development of land should not be made
ad hoc but in accordance with pre-determined policies. The vehicle
in which those policies are formulated and expressed in accordance
with the statutes is the development plan. The basic presumption
of the development plan concept is that it is possible to describe,
for a time many years ahead, what will be a desirable physical
environment, and to specify policies and proposals by which that
desirable state might be achieved.

55. It is a presumption that raises difficult questions. In the
first place, the demographic, social, economic and technological
changes which will influence the development of the physical
environment are to a large extent themselves unpredictable. The
development pressures they will exert, and the future response
of society to those pressures, must largely be conjectural for,
while elective and consultative processes can provide some
indication of society's present attitudes, there is no way of
ascertaining what those attitudes will be in the future. Moreover
democratic governments, both central and local, change through
time; their priorities also change, and present governments
cannot by their plans bind their successors.

56. Secondly, while plans are drawn up primarily in terms of the
physical environment, and while the powers to which they relate
are exercisable in connection with the development of land and
buildings, the underlying issues with which the plans are
concerned and their objectives are frequently social and economic.
Thus the area of debate extends to include not only physical
development questions, but also much more difficult ones
concerning the desirability or otherwise of particular social
and economic changes. There are, furthermore, major
uncertainties about the causal relationships between such
changes and physical development which, to say the least, give
rise to doubts about the likelihood of plans for land and
buildings being effective instruments for achieving social and
economic ends.

57. Thirdly, the power which eventually determines what development
will occur is very widely distributed. The multiplicity of
authorities, bodies and individuals in whom power resides all
pursue their own objectives. Most of them are not subordinate to
the local planning authority and that authority is in no position
to foresee and take account in its plans of all the criteria
upon which developers of all kinds will eventually make their
specific proposals. Nor can it be assumed that, at the time the
development plan is being prepared, consultation with these bodies
will reveal what their future actions and reactions will be.
Moreover, landowners die and companies go into liquidation. What
is acceptable this year may be rejected next year.

58. Finally, society is not homogeneous in composition or outlook.
What might be seen by some of its members as a desirable
environment - convenient, efficient and visually satisfying, may

not be thought so by others. One man's benefits may be another's
costs; interests may be in direct conflict and irreconcilable.
In the present state of the law, development plan proposals
virtually determine land values and very considerable sums of
money can be at stake. It would be unrealistic not to expect the
interests involved to do everything possible to influence plans
in their favour before they are finalized" (SCLSERP 1973).

This chapter outlines the way structure plan scope and content has evolved.
Essentially this definition has been the product of central government
guidance, local interpretation and central government reaction to that
interpretation. To a large extent, it is a debate between levels of
government, and between officials (mainly planners, central government,
administrators). Thus it could be described as an example of technocrats
limiting, in managerial style, the opportunities for the exercise of local
discretion by politicians and other local interests in determining how land
is used and developed in their area. Yet it is important to assess how far
these officials, the "technocrats", have been influenced by their political
masters and other interests.

This discussion is limited to the situation in England and Wales. The
development plan arrangements in Scotland are significantly different. The
Scottish regions, much larger than counties, were asked to prepare regional
reports. These were produced quickly and provided both information and
assessments of resource priorities to the Scottish Development Department,
which co-ordinates public sector development investment in a much more
integrated way than in England and Wales. Structure plans are only produced
if necessary, while local plans have to be prepared for all parts of the
country (see McDonald 1977, Diamond 1979 and Wannop 1980 for aspects of the
Scottish system). The Scottish Development Department also produces
National Planning Guidelines on various issues, to assist local authorities.
Several commentators argue that these arrangements are preferable to those
in the south. Regrettably there is as yet no definitive account for
Scotland or England and Wales of either structure plans in either theory or
practice. Most of the published material is scattered among professional
journals and conference reports. The best general account of structure
plans so far remains Drake *et al.* (1975). Other contributions tend to
concentrate on particular aspects of structure planning such as methodology
(Batey and Breheny (ed.) 1978, Barras and Broadbent 1979); public
participation (particularly the Linked Research Project into Public
Participation in Structure Planning[25]); the Examination-in-Public (Bridges
and Vielba 1976); and, most recently, on the content of plans (Rawson and
Rogers 1976; Jowell and Noble 1980; Gault 1981; White 1981).

2. STRUCTURE PLANS - THE CONCEPT

The term "structure plan" originated in the PAG Report and reflects the
essentially physical view of urban areas held by the writers of that report.
Two types of strategic plan were identified: urban and county structure
plans. Urban structure plans were to emphasize:

"the broad structure of the town, and (deal) in policies, objectives
and standards, rather than in detailed and static land use
allocation of the town map". (MHLG 1965 para. 2.5).

_____

[25]Obtainable from Sheffield University

The task of urban planning at this time was seen by the report to be the
remodelling of urban form to make it more relevant to the demands and needs
of the 1960s. Essentially, the PAG Report embodies a notion of the city as
a collection of artefacts, rather than a set of social, economic and
political processes which produce such artefacts. The term "structure
plan" was transferred directly into the 1968 Act. By 1970, when central
government produced a glossy advisory document to aid plan preparers,
Development Plans: A Manual on Form and Content (MHLG 1970), "structure"
had come to mean:

> "the social, economic and physical systems of an area, so far
> as they are subject to planning control or influence. The
> structure is, in effect, the planning framework for an area
> and includes such matters as the distribution of the population,
> the activities and the relationships between them, the patterns
> of land use and the development the activities give rise to,
> together with the network of activities and the systems of
> utility services" (MHLG 1970 para. 3.6).

This represents a slightly more sophisticated notion of social processes and
spatial patterns, but what exactly is subject to "planning control and
influence"? In this phrase lie the seeds of the debate on scope and
content of both structure and local plans. Increasingly, central government
has leant on the legislation which says that a structure plan shall
formulate:

> "the local planning authority's policy and general proposals in
> respect of the development and other use of land in that area
> (including measures for the improvement of the physical
> environment and the management of traffic)" (1971 Act S7 SS(3)(a)).

"Planning control and influence" in this definition is largely limited to
the exercise of development control powers. As to the distinction between
strategy and detail, the Manual advises that:

> "an issue of structural importance is a matter on which the choice
> will affect either the whole, or a substantial part, of the area
> concerned" (DoE Circular 98/74 para. 3(a)).

This seems simple in general terms but in practice raises considerable
problems as has been evident in both structure plan modifications and local
plan inquiries[26]. Structure plans can specify areas and locations but not
precise boundaries and sites. They can specify broad quantities, in the
form of totals of people and jobs to be allowed, but can only allocate
these within a structure plan area in so far as such allocation is of
strategic importance. They can express general criteria to guide
development control decisions but should not contain development control
policies as such. Given the split created by local government
reorganization between the authorities preparing structure plans (the
counties), and those doing most of the development control work, it is not
surprising that a persistent objection by districts to structure plans is
that policies are too detailed.

What is the purpose of structure plans? Appendix I provides extracts from
central government advice on their functions. According to the PAG report,

---

[26]see Solesbury 1974 p.98 *et seq*; Finney and Kenyon 1976.

plans are to "set out" and "clarify" the local authority's "development and
redevelopment objectives", the "physical structure of the town, and
transport policy", and provide a base for detailed planning and development
control. The object of this presentation is to bring policies before the
public and to the Minister for his approval (MHLG 1965 para. 2.6). In other
words, the plan must be available for scrutiny by citizens and central
government. The Manual puts more emphasis on "interpreting national and
regional policies", and "providing a basis for co-ordinating decisions".
Here we see a greater concern with the role of plans in the efficient
management of development. The Manual also clarifies what detailed
planning involves, which now includes "providing a framework for local plans"
and "indicating action areas" (MHLG 1970 para. 3.10).

By 1974, central government advice has become more succinct. Structure
plans have three main functions:

> "(a) to state and justify, to the public and to the Secretary of
> State, the authority's policies and general proposals for the
> development and other use of land in the area concerned
> (including measures for the improvement of the physical
> environment and the management of traffic) ...
>
> (b) to interpret national and regional policies in terms of
> physical and environmental planning for the area concerned ...
> (such) policies tend to be primarily economic and social ...
>
> (c) to provide the framework and statutory basis for local
> plans, which then in turn provide the necessary further
> guidance for development control ..." (DoE Circular 98/74
> para. 3).

This wording has persisted with some simplification into the comprehensive
memorandum on structure and local plans (DoE Circular 55/77, reissued with
minor revisions as DoE Circular 4/79). These functions emphasize the role
of the plan in justifying the way the public sector intervenes in land use
and development; the importance of relating spatial phenomena to social and
economic ones; and the role of the plan in translating strategic policy, *as
approved by central government*, into the detailed operation of development
control. It is worth noting that the only important change introduced by
Circular 4/79 is the omission of "the public" from the first paragraph.
This small alteration reflects the position central government has
increasingly adopted that it is itself the main check on the discretion of
local authorities. This tendency confirms McAuslan's interpretation of the
dominance of the administrative determination of the public interest
(McAuslan 1980), and the drift towards central government's role in this
determination which he believes the 1980 Planning and Local Government Act
further emphasizes (McAuslan 1981).

Schedule 1 of the 1974 Regulations (SI 1974 No.1486) provided a list of
"matters to which policy is required to relate" (see Appendix I). This list
of topics or subjects is similar to that found in the Development Plans
Manual (MHLG 1970 para. 4.23), and is commonly found in planning documents.
I discuss the nature of this "topic" classification in Chapter 6. Despite
the emphasis on comprehensive strategy and "structure", the tendency both in
advice and in practice has been to concentrate analysis and policy production
on these individual topics, rather than on the processes which might
interrelate them (such as the operation of the local economy, or development
processes).

Schedule 1 also provided a list of matters which the structure plan must contain. These require structure plans to include some assessment of "the area" and the changes occurring within it, to relate to New Town and Town Development proposals, to estimate present and future population and employment levels and distribution. The plan preparers must also demonstrate the "regard" they have had to policies "with respect to the economic planning and development of the region", "to social policies and considerations" and "to the resources likely to be available" for carrying out policies and proposals. In addition, the "broad criteria" in relation to the control of development must be specified (but not, of course, *detailed* criteria!), as must the relationships between policies in the plan, and relationships with neighbouring authorities (see Appendix I). Finally, Regulation 9 requires that the plan includes a "reasoned justification" for policies and proposals, though later central government advice indicates that this should "be kept as short as possible consistent with an adequate justification" (DoE Circular 4/79 para. 2.18). The time span of structure plans is not specified in early advice. Later circulars state that they should "look forward about fifteen years" (DoE Circular 4/79 para. 2.2). There can be no doubt that authorities were encouraged in this advice to undertake adequate background research, to face economic, social and resource issues, and interrelate their analyses into an integrated policy document; in other words to provide a well-founded rationale for policies. Following the Local Government, Planning and Land Act 1980, these regulations were revised, and Schedule 1 has been removed. County planning authorities are now required merely to show how they have considered current national and regional policies, social considerations and resources (SI 1982 No 555). More detailed advice relating to topics is likely to appear in a new circular to replace 4/79.

The structure plan itself must consist of a *written statement*, which contains all the above matters, and a *key diagram* which shows as far as practicable the policies and proposals in the written statement, but this must avoid allowing boundaries to be identified (SI 1974 No.1486 12(1)). The argument here is that it must not be possible for property interests to identify precisely how their interests will be affected, as their right to object occurs only in the arena of a local plan. Policies and proposals must be clearly distinguished in the plan (the use of capital letters is common), and any local plan "action areas" must be specified. The 1980 Act introduced a distinction within the written statement between the statements of polcies, and the "explanatory memorandum", or reasoned justification. Thus central government no longer approves the written statement as a whole, merely the policies. The written statement, when submitted to the Secretary of State for the approval of policies, must be accompanied by a statement indicating how the authority has engaged in the publicity and consultation requirements, both before and after definition of the plan policies (1971 Act S8(3)). In this way, the Secretary of State can check that the local authority has engaged in an adequate level of what was initially understood as "public participation".

The 1968 Act made no attempt to define this concept. In 1968, government seems to have felt, as did the PAG report, that allowing public involvement in plan preparation might generate more public support for plans and thus reduce the numbers of objections. Unclear what this would involve, a report was commissioned from the Skeffington Committee. This report (MHLG 1969) made a number of recommendations on how citizens could be encouraged to become involved in plan preparation. It is worth quoting their definition of public participation in full:

"We understand participation to be the act of sharing in the
formulation of policies and proposals. Clearly, the giving of
information by the local planning authority and of an opportunity
to comment on that information is a major part in the process of
participation, but it is not the whole story. Participation
involves doing as well as talking and there will be full
participation only where the public are able to take an active
part throughout the plan-making process. There are limitations
to this concept. One is that responsibility for preparing a
plan is, and must remain, that of the local planning authority.
Another is that the completion of plans - the setting into
statutory form of proposals and decisions - is a task demanding
the highest standards of professional skill, and must be
undertaken by the professional staff of the local planning
authority" (MHLG 1969 para. 5(a)).

It does not seem to have occurred to the group of councillors and planners
who made up the Skeffington Committee that there were other ways in which
public sector decisions about land and development might be made than by
the "highest standards of professional skill". In its recommendations, it
is clear that the public's role was essentially that of providing information.
The Committee did not seem to appreciate that citizens might seek to change
planning policies, and that this might conflict with the established
political processes by which local authority policies are determined. In
fact, the Committee, and many planners who conscientiously attempted to
encourage public involvement in planning, completely failed to appreciate
that the issues raised were political ones and could not be adequately
discussed in isolation from an understanding of the relation of the citizen
to the state[27].

More recently, the term public participation has been replaced, among
central and local government planners, with "consultation", and professional
discussion currently focusses on ways of undertaking this without causing
delay. In retrospect, it is possible to interpret the concern with public
participation in planning as an attempt to negotiate consensus among the
increasingly evident conflicting interests in the way land is used and
developed *in advance* of the formal arenas for debate about the content of
plans, (i.e. the Examination-in-Public and the Public Local Inquiry). As we
will see in Chapter 6, this has sometimes been successfully achieved.
Where conflicts are substantial, however, it becomes impossible to negotiate
them away, and the opportunities for public involvement merely provide
further occasions for battles to be fought out. In the case of structure
plans, these battles increasingly relate to conflicts between central
government and local authorities. However, one significant consequence of
the current disillusion by central government and local authorities with
what at its best was a genuine attempt at open government is that
negotiations about the content of planning policies are being driven back
inside the public sector and the interests it finds it necessary to work
with. This puts more emphasis on the administrative determination of the
public interest and on corporatist ways of working[28].

---

[27] See Damer and Hague 1971 for a critique of the Skeffington report, and Hill
1976 for a valuable discussion of the wider question of the citizen and
the state in the planning field.

[28] There is an enormous body of literature on the public participation issue;
see Barkers's (1979) bibliography. There are many structure plan case
studies, but for a review of experience see Drake and Thornley (1975),
Whitehead (1976) and Boaden *et al.* (1979).

3. STRUCTURE PLAN PRODUCTION

Diagram 3.1 summarizes the main stages in preparing a structure plan, derived from the guide to procedures contained in DoE Circular 4/79 (Appendix A). Production involves the preparation of a draft plan by the county authority and its approval, after consideration and modification, by central government. Most of the procedures originate in the 1968 Act, though the more detailed parts about consultation derive from Regulations. The most important area of administrative elaboration is the Examination-in-Public. The 1968 Act provided for an inquiry into objections to the plan in the same way as for old style development plans and for local plans, although the latter were to be organized by local government. It was anticipated that there would be fewer objections to structure plans because of their broad strategic nature. The prolonged inquiry into the Greater London Development Plan, a prototype structure plan, disabused central government of this expectation[29]. The Department of the Environment therefore invented the "Examination-in-Public" (the EIP). This enables:

> "the Secretary of State to concentrate public proceedings on those matters arising in a structure plan (including issues which may not have been the subject of objection) which in his view need to be examined in discussion" (DoE 1973a para. 2.13).

It was argued that to deal with all objections in an inquiry would involve too much consideration of detail, duplication of local plan objections and, the spectre hanging over the new development plan system from the old, "delay". Administrative efficiency has thus taken precedence over the citizens' right to object where property interests are affected. This raises the interesting question of why it is necessary to have a public examination of any kind. It could be argued that the examination is a move towards the principle of open government. It can also be seen as a mechanism for demonstrating that the approved plan, and any modifications central government chooses to make to it, has some rationale behind it and is supported by some interests. The question of course is which interests central government favours in organizing the EIP and modifying plans. The issues to be discussed and the parties represented at the EIP are selected by Department of the Environment officials, who also brief the Examination Panel, two of whom will be central government officers anyway[30].

Within the overall procedure for preparing structure plans, there are two main areas in which officials exercise substantial powers of discretionary interpretation. The first is in the area of policy formulation, undertaking background investigations for the plan, engaging in the required consultations and proposing policies. How these are conducted, and how the political questions involved are discussed with councillors, rests in most cases with the county planners[31]. However, it would be incorrect to assume that the policies in structure plans submitted to the DoE are determined by planners. In many cases, the concerns of politicians are reflected by a

---

[29] It lasted for over two years and over 28 000 objections were made.

[30] EIP Panels consist of an independent Chairman, often a QC, and normally two other members, from the Planning Inspectorate, and one from a government departemnt.

[31] McLoughlin found that three-quarters of professional staff preparing structure plans were planners, as opposed to officials from other departments (McLoughlin 1973a).

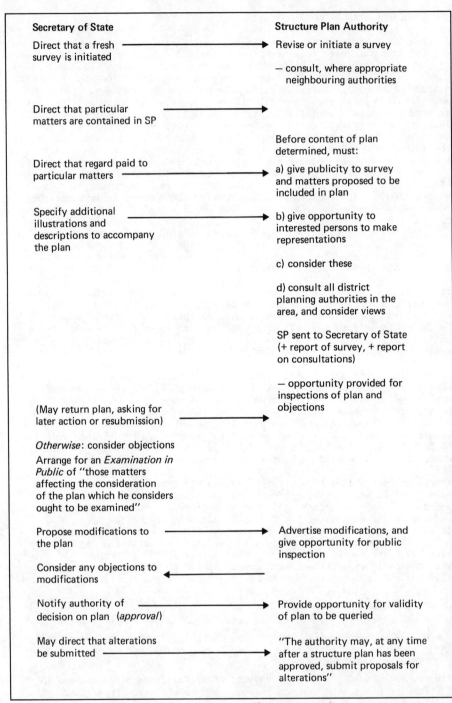

Secretary of State

Direct that a fresh ──────────→ Revise or initiate a survey
survey is initiated

                                                   − consult, where appropriate
                                                    neighbouring authorities

Direct that particular ──────────→
matters are contained in SP

                                                  Before content of plan
                                                  determined, must:

Direct that regard paid to
particular matters ──────────→ a) give publicity to survey
                                                  and matters proposed to be
                                                  included in plan

Specify additional
illustrations and ──────────→ b) give opportunity to
descriptions to accompany   interested persons to make
the plan   representations

                                                    c) consider these

                                                  d) consult all district
                                                  planning authorities in the
                                                  area, and consider views

                                                  SP sent to Secretary of State
                                                  (+ report of survey, + report
                                                  on consultations)

                                                  − opportunity provided for
                                                  inspections of plan and
(May return plan, asking for   objections
later action or resubmission) ──────────→

Otherwise: consider objections

Arrange for an *Examination in
Public* of "those matters
affecting the consideration
of the plan which he considers
ought to be examined"

Propose modifications to ──────────→ Advertise modifications, and
the plan   give opportunity for public
                                                  inspection

Consider any objections to ←──────────
modifications

Notify authority of ──────────→ Provide opportunity for validity
decision on plan (*approval*)   of plan to be queried

May direct that alterations   "The authority may, at any time
be submitted ──────────→ after a structure plan has been
                                                  approved, submit proposals for
                                                  alterations"

Diagram 3.1.   Structure Plan preparation.

process of osmosis in the way planners approach policy formulation,
particularly where there has been some stability at the political level
(Healey *et al*. 1982a). Darke describes a situation where politicians in
effect took over the definition of policies from officers (Darke 1982),
while Blowers discusses the way planners first limited what politicians
wanted to do. Subsequently, both planners and politicians found themselves
mediating between other conflicting interests (Blowers 1980 Chapter 7).
Thus, as we will see in relation to local plans (Chapter 6), planners may
have less control over the content of plans than appears at first glance.

Once the plan is submitted, DoE officials (in the regional offices) have
the opportunity to exercise considerable discretion in arranging the
Examination-in-Public and determining its general content, considering the
Panel's report, and producing modifications. It is only at this last stage
that Ministers are likely to be involved. Political control over, and the
public accountability of, the production of structure plans is therefore
likely to be limited despite the complex procedures for consultation and
approval. In making modifications, it is evident that officials pay
considerable attention to Ministers' views, (e.g. in relation to housing
land availability or the *extent* of green belts). Other matters, however,
such as the DoE's attitude to the green way green belts are used, appear to be
matters of administrative interpretation.

Diagram 3.2 illustrates the progress made in structure plan production. By

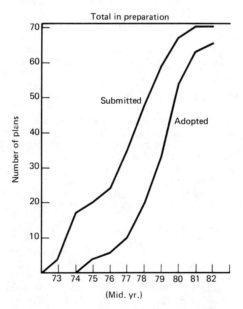

This table excludes the GLDP, the regulation
8 plans, and plan alterations.

Avon is the outstanding plan, withdrawn from
submission when political control of county
changed in 1981.

Source: DoE

Diagram 3.2. Progress in Structure Plan preparation.

the end of 1980, the only structure plans not submitted were for Central/
North Lancashire, Dorset (excluding South East Dorset) and the Isles of
Scilly. Because the Isles of Scilly had no resources to prepare a structure
plan, DoE officials did this for them, thus putting themselves into the
curious position of examining their own plan. By this time, however,
several counties were coming forward with structure plan alterations, 30
being submitted by June 1982. This slow passage from the old development
plan system to the new was partly the result of local government
reorganization, with many authorities not starting structure plan work
until the new counties were established and staffed. Another reason was
the complex assimilation of information and discussion of policy options
which was seen to be necessary to produce a plan. Most took at least three
years to reach submission stage, in contrast to the Scottish regional reports
which were produced in a year. A third reason is that the DoE itself moved
slowly in examining and modifying plans, although during Michael Heseltine's
period as Secretary of State, the approval of plans was speeded up (as
Diagram 3.2 shows). Several of the shire county structure plans in the
South East were held up at the regional offices, however, while regional
strategic policy was discussed at the political level, particularly in
relation to the width of the Metropolitan Green Belt (DoE 1978b).

Despite this apparent slow progress, those areas where structure plans were
first prepared and approved were areas with a perceived priority need for
strategic guidance (see Diagram 3.3). In the West Midlands, local
authorities, encouraged by the DoE, aimed to produce draft structure plans
before reorganization. By 1980, the West Midlands County Council had
already submitted the second structure plan for the area. Nor did
authorities wait until approval before implementing policies. Local plans
were often started prior to submission, while submitted (draft) structure
plans have been used (and upheld) in development control appeal cases.

4. INFLUENCES ON THE SCOPE AND CONTENT OF STRUCTURE PLANS

The PAG report and the Development Plans Manual assume that structure plans
will reflect local problems and issues. To some extent this is the case.
South East county structure plans do not contain the same policies as those
for the Northern conurbations. Plans for predominantly rural areas have
different emphases to those from urban areas. Yet the preparation of each
plan involves choices about scope (what problems and issues to examine)
and about content (how problems and issues are explored and what policies
derived). What determines how these choices are made?

Certainly in the earlier years of plan preparation, planners found the
amount of discretion apparently available to them difficult to cope with.
Central government advice was ambiguous and the role of structure plans
within local authority decision-making was unclear (Thornley 1975). At this
time, however, planners were strongly influenced by the rational planning
methodologies of procedural planning theory. These offered standard
approaches in the form of decision sequences from goal identification
through analysis and policy generation to evaluation, or a "mixed scanning"
variant of this, and emphasized the use of quantitative techniques (Drake
1975; Barras and Broadbent 1979). Plans were directed at accommodating
growth, as derived from earlier regional strategies, despite increasing
evidence that such forecasts were going badly wrong (Davies 1975). But, as
Barras and Broadbent have noted, data analysis went little further than an
elementary level, there was little analysis of development processes,
resources were treated in a limited way, objectives were broad and vague and
little attention was given to social and distributional effects. In general,

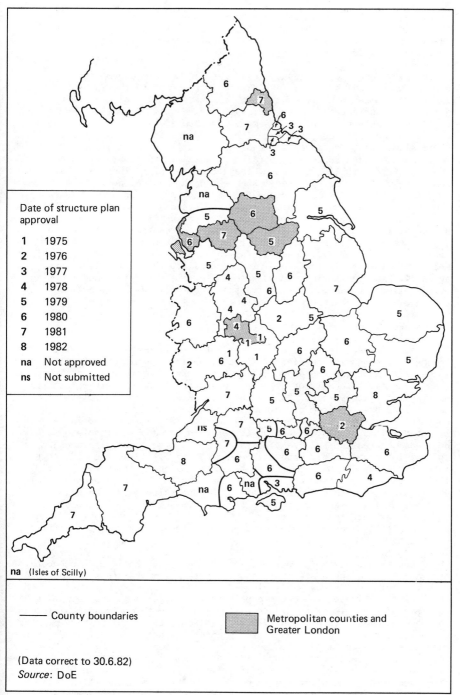

Date of structure plan
approval

1	1975
2	1976
3	1977
4	1978
5	1979
6	1980
7	1981
8	1982
na	Not approved
ns	Not submitted

na (Isles of Scilly)

——— County boundaries

Metropolitan counties and
Greater London

(Data correct to 30.6.82)
Source: DoE

Diagram 3.3.   The location of approved Structure Plans

plans appeared fragmented in their approach with inadequate justification for the policies chosen. Other commentators have noted the lack of clarity on resources (Eke 1977) and inadequate attention in early plans to implementation and monitoring (McLoughlin 1973a).

Later plans focus more on specific issues rather than attempting comprehensive reviews. This was partly in response to the famous "key issues" circular (DoE Circular 98/74) produced by the DoE to encourage quicker plan preparation, and partly to the changing economy. Langley notes that "recent structure plans are more preoccupied with the social problems of stagnation and decay than were their predecessors" (Langley 1979 p.15). Where significant development pressures are still expected, as in the South East, implementing regional restraint policies is the dominant concern (Healey et al. 1980). Several of the northern conurbation plans have adopted a deliberately political stance towards central government, using the structure plan as an advocacy document, to press for more favourable treatment in resource allocation (e.g. Merseyside, (Struthers and Williamson 1978), and West Yorkshire (Briscoe 1978). A few plans have taken a deliberately redistributive stance, attempting to direct resources to disadvantaged groups and to alleviate urban unemployment (e.g. South Yorkshire (Darke 1979)). Cambridgeshire adopted a set of social policies related to the problems of rural inaccessibility (Bruce 1980). These advocative and redistributive policies have rarely survived modification by central government, which claims that such policies stray outside the sphere of "planning control and influence". A fair comment on structure plans as submitted is that they are wide-ranging in scope but most are vague and unspecific in the treatment of issues.

This lack of specificity is often attributed to planners' incapacities (inadequate economic training; failure to understand distributional issues; inadequate understanding of development processes; preoccupation with method over content). Probably of greater importance has been their concern to make policies acceptable. Policy choices spelt out too explicitly might generate opposition from councillors, from the districts, and from other powerful interests. The use of an "allowance for local needs" in several structure plans otherwise seeking to restrain the amount of development provides a revealing example of a compromise phrase adopted as acceptable to many interests. Only when this has to be specified do the different interpretations which can be given to it become apparent (Healey et al. 1980). Bainbridge describes how distributional issues were progressively whittled down in the preparation of the Bedfordshire structure plan (Bainbridge 1978), an account supported by the chairman of the planning committee at the time (Blowers 1980 Chapter 7), who argues that structure plan preparation was dominated by the search for consensus among different interests.

This lack of explicitness could be interpreted as a tactic by "technocrats" or "managers" to insinuate their own interpretation of issues and policies into the political arena. How else did a discussion of the importance of the redistribution of resources appear in the Surrey structure plan, or the problems of economic stagnation take equal place with environmental issues in the Kent plan? (See Flynn 1979 for a discussion of the role of planners in the latter.) Yet although these "planners' ideologies", of which there were several by the mid-1970s (see Healey and Underwood 1979), may have been allowed considerable free rein, there can be little doubt that planners have been sensitive to the political priorities of their own counties, to pressures from the districts with whom consultation was usually extensive, and to advice from central government. Public participation exercises have

also sometimes affected planners' thinking. It could be argued that to
retain their authority, county planners have worked to translate their own
view of politician's priorities into planning policies, making their own
assessments of the nature and relative weight of different interests. Only
where their capacity to do this has been challenged (as in South Yorkshire
and Bedfordshire), have politicians been called on to construct the consensus
which a structure plan must appear to express if it is to be a long term
guidance document. There have been no cases so far where a structure plan
has become so politically contentious that an incoming council withdraws the
plan for alteration. Only in Avon County did something like this happen in
1981 when a newly-elected Labour council withdrew a submitted structure plan
prior to the Examination-in-Public in order to review the policies.

In arriving at a policy content for structure plans, counties have also had
to consider the views of districts, of local pressure groups, of private
sector interests and major public agencies and other government departments.
In many ways, there is little difference in the processes of consultation
on structure plans and those for local plans which I shall discuss in detail
in Chapter 6. Apart from the work of Darke and Blowers mentioned earlier,
there has been little systematic study of the way different interests have
influenced policy content of structure plans. A possible generalization
from the limited evidence available is that district councils and local
pressure groups have been most vociferous in their attempts to influence
policy (notably in public participation exercises); while public agencies
and government departments have exerted considerable influence wherever
their interests are affected. The private sector's influence on plan
content is less obvious, but can be identified in the amount of land noted
in structure plans of the 1970s as already committed for development. This
happened because substantial amounts of land were released in around 1970,
much more than was required by effective demand, in response to central
government exhortations to make more housing land available[31].

County planners have also been faced with a major co-ordination problem in
drawing up structure plans. Their authorities control few of the major
public sector capital programmes. Since 1974, water, drainage and sewage
provision is provided by Regional Water Authorities. Power supplies are
provided by national agencies. Districts control housing investment, and
in metropolitan areas, social services and education as well. The
metropolitan counties are left with only transport as their major investment
field and even here, despite the requirement that transport investment
programmes are based on structure plans, such links are often difficult to
sustain because engineers' departments are accustomed to operate
independently. Even where the will to co-ordinate is present, the financing
of transport projects follows a different timetable to the preparation of
structure plans (see DoE Circular 104/73, and Bayliss 1975). A few counties
are able to report successful co-ordination within their authorities (see
Unsworth 1977, Parker 1978), or with the housing work of districts (e.g.
Hertfordshire's Countywide Housing Study, Hertfordshire CC 1979), or with
infrastructure agencies (Patterson 1978). The central problem here is that
public sector investment is dispersed among a plurality of
development agencies, each operating different forms of capital programming
(all on much shorter time-spans than structure plans) and each relating in
a different way to central government (Stewart 1977).

Without central government co-ordination and commitment to long-term

---

[31]See Drewett 1973, DoE 1975b, Healey 1982b.

investment programming, public sector proposals can only be expressed in generalities, if at all, in structure plans. Fundamentally, the problem of co-ordination in structure plan preparation is a reflection of the political and economic uncertainty facing central government ministries and the entrenched sectoral organization of government. It is no wonder that structure planners, and regional strategic planning in general, have been preoccupied with the problems of co-ordination and inter-organizational relations (McLoughlin and Thompson 1975, Thompson 1975, Friend, Norris and Carter 1978).

There can be no doubt that *central government* has had a considerable influence on the scope and content of structure plans. The mechanisms available to it to exert an influence on plan production have been advice, both formally in circulars and informally; the way the Examination-in-Public is conducted; and in modifications, since it is central government which *approves* the plan. The DoE's views on structure plans have themselves evolved during the 1970s. In the Development Plans Manual in 1970 (MHLG 1970), counties were advised to cover issues comprehensively. By 1974, they were to concentrate on "key issues" (DoE Circular 98/74). By 1976, it was stressed that the focus on policies should be on land use and development issues (see Mabey 1976, and the various structure plan modifications).

The DoE has repeatedly stated that structure plans must be seen as separate from local authority corporate plans, though there may be some interrelationship (Hack and Pailing 1972, DoE Circular 4/79 para. 2.79). Turner, commenting on the experience of metropolitan county structure plans, claims:

> "The DoE has now completed a retreat into the shell of 'fuzzy' land-use planning, insisting and advising at every opportunity that this is all that structure plan policies are to be about. A peripheral concern with environmental quality ... is also permitted to obtrude .... It would appear that the Civil Service is imposing its own administratively tidy or convenient interpretation on events in a way that seeks to distance structure planning from strategic issues of current concern and preserve departmental responsibilities" (Turner 1977 pp.176-77).

County planners in many areas resent this apparent limitation on the part of central government. Meanwhile, central government planners claim that structure plans have given inadequate treatment to social policies and the distributional effects of policies, despite advice (see DoE 1973b and Langley 1979). DoE planners argue that they are not limiting the scope of structure plans. All that county planners seek to do can be accommodated within the legislation. It is merely a matter of making careful distinctions between reasoned justification and actual policies (Mabey 1976, Langley 1979). Perhaps the heart of the dispute lies in an explanatory comment in Circular 98/74:

> "Structure plans represent the stage in planning at which such policies are integrated with the economic, social and environmental policies of the county and expressed in terms of their effect on land use, environmental development and the associated transportation system. (The material on economic and social policies in the written statement should therefore be limited to those policies which have implications for land use, environmental development or transportation)." (DoE Circular 98/74 para. 3(b)).

In other words, the DoE are stressing once again that structure plans should confine themselves to those matters which are under planning influence and control. This largely means those matters which can legitimately be considered in relation to a development control application. However desirable it might be to affect district public housing policies or impose conditions on the occupancy of private housing, the planning system has only limited powers to exercise such influence.

This dispute on content will be found in a more acute form in relation to local plans. In the case of structure plans, counties find themselves criticized for having both too much regard for social and economic policies (beyond the land use remit) and too little regard for social effects. A possible interpretation here is that central government wishes to be seen to be concerned with the translation of social policies into spatial terms and with the social effects of policies. But it does not carry the political burden of having to demonstrate the often uncomfortable results of such an exercise. Nor does it always approve of the policies which result (as in South Yorkshire and Cambridgeshire). The provision in the Local Government, Planning and Land Act 1980 whereby the DoE's approval of structure plans is limited to the policies only, *not* the reasoned justification, may be interpreted as a recognition of the increasing political differences between central government and county councils. It is not yet clear in practice whether this is anything more than a symbolic gesture.

At the Examination-in-Public and modification stages, the policy interests of central government become more evident. As yet there have been few general reviews of Examination-in-Public discussions or modifications (but see Jowell and Noble 1980 and Gault 1981). The interests most commonly invited have been the major public developers, districts, private developers and industrialists, with the public represented by amenity groups or organized national lobbies such as Shelter. In the Staffordshire Examination-in-Public, Bridges and Vielba (1976) noted that industrial interests were recruited specifically to participate in the discussion on employment and were given wide scope to express their views, although apparently they had not objected or made representations in respect of the plan. Darke (1979) also notes the importance of industrial interests in Examination-in-Public proceedings.

As to modifications, many are directed at removing over-detailed policies and clarifying wording. This may seem a matter of mere procedure, but the former gives more flexibility to districts and the latter reduces charges of incompetence against the planning system[32]. More fundamentally, over-restrictive or over-directive policies have been relaxed or removed. Green belt extensions have been cut out, as have South Yorkshire's job priority areas. Limitations on industry have been relaxed in most structure plans seeking to restrain development. Around the conurbations, major additional housing land allocations have been included. Meanwhile policies which go beyond "planning control and influence" have been amended or removed. As noted above, this particularly affects social policies. Jowell and Noble conclude that:

---

[32] Gwilliam 1978 quotes a minor wording change to a policy, suggesting that it reflects an unnecessary preoccupation with detail. But the policy (in the Leicestershire structure plan) is changed from conserving the *value* of abandoned rural railways in providing access to the countryside to actually conserving the *routes* themselves.

"attempts to include 'social' policies within the 'policies and
proposals' part of the structure plan have met with the disapproval
of the Secretary of State. Policies providing for the promotion
of facilities or changes in policy, the designation of priorty
areas, or the advancement of local needs, have not generally
survived central government scrutiny. Many have been removed
from the plan. Others have been allowed to remain, but have
been relegated to ... reasoned justification ..." (Jowell and
Noble 1980 p.308).

It is worth noting that this treatment of social policies *predated* the 1979
Conservative administration.

Such modifications could be interpreted as central government taking up the
interests of cities versus rural counties (using the terminology of Hall's
study discussed in Chapter 2) or development interests versus the defenders
of "the environment". Encouraging development can now be presented as
having broadly-based public support from firms seeking to make profits and
people interested in obtaining and retaining jobs. However, it is
significant that in the South East, development restraint in the counties
is no longer a rural interest, but an urban one as well, since if firms
locate in the outer South East there are fewer to contribute to inner
London's regeneration. In other words, in the 1970s it became evident that
encouraging development outside the conurbations was assisting the process
of deconcentration or "suburbanization". Thus central government is
continuing to allow "organized" suburbanization through the planning system,
though this sytem has had little power to ameliorate the social costs of the
suburbanization process borne by those left behind in inner cities. A more
convincing interpretation is that through structure plan modifications,
central government, sensitive to economic problems, is supporting industrial
and commercial interests against over-restrictive "environmentalist"
counties. The 1979 Conservative government has in addition been particularly
receptive to the land availability arguments of the house-builders' lobby.
Many social welfare concerns, such as conserving land for public housing
projects, are conveniently presented as beyond the influence and control of
planning. It is worth noting as a final comment that these policy changes to
structure plans made on behalf of and sometimes by the Secretary of State for
the Environment are not subject to any further scrutiny other than political
challenge by local authorities and pressure groups. If the House of
Commons Expenditure Committee was concerned about the lack of parliamentary
scrutiny of regional strategy, so too should it be concerned about structure
plan modifications (House of Commons Expenditure Committee 1977 para. 81).

Central government thus appears to be giving considerable weight to
industrial and property development interests in its decisions on plans.
Many local authorities, especially in the last few years, have also used
structure plan preparation, or implementation, to develop a closer working
relationship with business interests. It is this sort of partnership which
was given encouragement by DoE Circular 44/78, and more recently in
exhortations to local authorities to work closely with builders and
developers in assessing land availability (DoE Circular 9/80). Counties
have been encouraged to make their assessments of housing land availability
in conjunction with builders, producing five year programmes which in
effect review and roll forward the structure plan.

Business interests have persistantly put pressure on central and local
government to reduce planning restrictions on their operations, particularly
since 1979. The House Builders' Federation has been most evident in its

lobbying (with representations to the House of Commons Expenditure Committee and the Property Advisory Group (DoE 1980)). Meanwhile, they have expanded their specialist staff in order to make more effective representations at structure plan Examinations-in-Public and in local plan preparation and inquiries. The activities of other interests are less visible, though regional Confederation of British Industry representatives have contested policies at Examination-in-Publics, put pressure on local authorities to assist local firms in their expansion plans and in their labour problems (in particular, providing cheap housing for key skilled workers). These two groups, however, are in as much disagreement with each other as with local authority structure plans (Healey et al. 1980). Industrial and commercial interests compete with residential developers over land allocations; while larger national firms compete with smaller local ones (Healey et al. 1982a; McNamara 1982a).

To conclude, structure plan production is predominantly a technical and administrative process, in which the large area of discretion available to planners to draw up policies and justify them is in practice limited by:

1. the strong sectoral patterns of government organizations overlying the apparent "pluralism" of the public sector development effort;

2. the political priorities of county authorities and their relations with districts;

3. the policy interests of central government ministers and the interpretation of these by central government officials; and

4. the way in which the views of national industrial and development interests and local business and environmental lobbies filter into the thinking of ministers and local councillors on the one hand, and central and local government planners on the other.

Whatever the effects of structure plan policies are or will be, the plans are clearly more limited in scope than might be expected in strategic plans intended to link economic and social policy to spatial strategy, and less specific in focus than one might expect of plans intended to give guidance to the preparation of detailed (local) development plans and development control. The plans may appear more rational than their predecessors under the 1947 Act, but their lack of specificity may make them less usable. Consequently the decisions they are supposed to guide may continue to be uninformed by strategic considerations and appear arbitrary to those affected by them.

By 1980, there was a substantial body of professional criticism of plans[33]. The politicians on the House of Commons Expenditure Committee have been calling for a review of development plans since their report in 1977, although Ministers of the present and previous government maintain that plan production merely needs speeding up (e.g. Heseltine 1979). Many critics support the idea of something like the Scottish system of regional reports. This proposal was first mooted by Drake et al. (1975), who advocated the preparation of County Reports, which would cover all county

[33]For example, see Drake et al. 1975, Smart 1977, Turner 1977, Bruton 1980a, Fisher 1980.

policies and investment, and be submitted to central government for approval.
Local authorities could then at their discretion prepare land and transport
plans and local plans. This solves the problem of integrating county
spending at central government level but gives central government less
control over policy[34]. The distinctive nature of Scottish planning is
sometimes forgotten in this enthusiasm for regional reports, notably the
"comprehensive scale of direct or agency participation by Government in
initiating change in urban and rural conditions" (Wannop 1980), and the
greater co-ordination of government investment through the Scottish
Development Department.

Some alterations to the Examination-in-Public procedure have also been
suggested by Bridges and Vielba. These have since been picked up by the
House of Commons Expenditure Committee and others, notably that the DoE
should be "cross-examined" at Examination-in-Publics in the same way as
other participants (House of Commons Expenditure Committee 1977 para. 82,
Dunlop 1976, Bridges and Vielba 1976 para. 84-86). Bridges and Vielba also
suggest that the Examination-in-Public should occur before policies are
finalized in the plan, rather than after final submission. In other words,
they consider the Examination-in-Public to be an important vehicle for the
public exploration of policy issues, in addition to its role in assisting
central government to evaluate local authority policies. Both these
proposals for the Examination-in-Public in effect encourage a move to a
"participatory democracy" approach by government into land and development
issues. A recent report on public participation from the RTPI, however,
puts more emphasis on bringing the public into the negotiative process
prior to formal inquiries (RTPI 1982).

These proposed changes, however, do not face up to the central dilemmas which
compromise any attempt at providing a strategic guidance framework to
co-ordinate and regulate the activities of many development agents. These
are; firstly, that there is no guiding agency with sufficient powers over
other development agents to ensure reasonable compliance with any strategy;
secondly, there is political disagreement about the way land should be used
and developed (development versus conservation; commercial development
versus houses and factories; speculative value-increasing development versus
low-cost serviced land for industry and community needs); and thirdly, all
development agents are operating in an uncertain economic and political
climate. Thus while interests cannot agree on the content of plans, they
may nevertheless seek their production to help reduce their investment risks.
Inevitably, local plans are faced with the same dilemmas. But it is
sometimes suggested that, because these are more specific, have shorter
time horizons, are prepared and implemented by districts, while interests
may be locally more homogeneous, the dilemmas are more easily resolved.

As will be evident in Part II, this has not proved the case. Before
embarking on the detailed investigation of local plan production and use,
Chapter 4 summarizes the evolution of the concept of a local plan and the
procedures surrounding its production.

---

[34]For support for the regional report idea, see Smart 1977, Briscoe 1978 and
    the House of Commons Expenditure Committee 1977.

Local Plans

1. LOCAL PLANS AND LOCAL PLANNING

Local plans received much less attention than structure plans in the PAG
report, the 1968 Act and subsequent discussion, though there had been some
pioneer work on detailed development plans for town centre redevelopment in
the early 1960s (MHLG 1962). This neglect arose for two reasons. Firstly,
it was assumed by many that planners had by tradition and training the skills
and understanding necessary for the work involved. The priority was to
encourage strategic thinking about the way land was used and developed.
Secondly, PAG's idea was that the preparation of local plans was to be a
matter for local discretion. Having prepared structure plans, it was up to
planning authorities to decide whether local plans were needed and in what
form these should be.

During the early 1970s, local plans continued to receive little attention, as
most planning authorities were preoccupied with the preparation of structure
plans and coping with the immediate consequences of local government
reorganization. However, this latter event had fundamental effects on the
way local plans have been approached. In the first place, the authorities
preparing structure plans were no longer in a position to determine what
local plans should be prepared. This had to be negotiated with the new
district authorities, often both politically and professionally determined
to assert their status and power vis-á-vis the counties. This separation of
strategic from detailed plans in turn created problems for central
government. While overtly maintaining the principle that local plans were a
matter for local discretion, officials became increasingly concerned at the
way local authorities were using local plans since this threatened to affect
central government's strategic interests - in respect of particular policies
and in relation to the planning system as a whole.

Meanwhile, the ideas which planners brought to the local planning task in
the mid-1970s, and the political priorities which have helped to shape
these, have been rather different from those which influenced the writers of
the PAG report. As the social and economic problems of inner urban areas
became increasingly evident, many planners in these authorities sought to
redefine local planning as providing a local framework of social and economic,
as well as environmental and physical, policies. Outside the conurbations,

such a social emphasis led to concerns with the social problems of rural inaccessibility and the protection of "local" activities from the pressures created by the continuing decentralization of firms and people from the main urban areas. By the late 1970s, anxieties about the state of local economies were widespread.

In other words, in many shire and metropolitan districts and London Boroughs, "local planning" was seen as something much wider than the production of local plans as allowed for in legislation. Depending on the nature of local political and economic priorities, and on the way districts organized themselves, "local planning" could encompass the general policy framework for the authority as a whole. It could provide the integrating device for local authority renewal programmes. In some areas, it became the arena within which articulate citizens debated with authorities future strategies for the location of development. And of course in many authorities, it was looked to by development control staff to provide guidance for their own activities.

Inevitably, these varying expectations of "local planning" created a tension between the priorities of counties in respect of the implementation of structure plan policies, and the way districts interpreted "local planning". This tension was often further complicated by the confusion which existed widely in the mid-1970s between local planning, local plans in general and *statutory* local plans. Many planners by this time had taken on board the notion that planning was a process of policy review, implementation and monitoring. As a result, the production of *plans* was of much less consequence than the *process* of producing them (e.g. Turton 1979). Nevertheless, the legislation enabling district planning authorities to prepare local plans gave a locus and legitimacy for this process. Thus the preparation of a statutory local plan was used as the vehicle for a process of policy review.

However, while transferring from the old style county development plans to structure plans, planning authorities had become accustomed to prepare and use a wide range of policy guidance documents; small area site-specific plans discussed at length with the public; "bottom-drawer" plans which never left the planning office but could guide development control decisions; council-approved policies relating to particular types of development; strategic policies for the whole of a planning authority area; design guides, development briefs and detailed standards and criteria used commonly in development control. One task of policy review in many of the new districts became the identification and review of these documents. Yet because of this tradition of producing "informal" planning guidance, many authorities initially gave little thought to the particular characteristics of *statutory* local plans. The use of informal plans had in any case been encouraged by central government in the early 1970s as part of the policy to persuade local authorities to release more housing land (see DoE Circular 122/73). Many planning authorities proposed simply to convert these informal plans and policy statements into statutory local plans. Others, particularly those who emphasized the importance of a policy review process, saw the preparation of statutory local plans as the opportunity to systematize the plethora of policy documents.

As will become evident in Part II, many factors in practice influence the way authorities consider and prepare local plans, one of which has undoubtedly been the mixture of idealism and naivity which characterized many of the planners involved in local planning work in the mid-1970s. Due to the very rapid expansion of planning authorities consequent upon local government reorganization, many local planning teams were young and inexperienced, and their planning education, reflecting the preoccupations of the late 1960s, gave them little preparation for the world of local planning and development control at district level (see Fudge *et al.* 1982; Healey 1982a). Very few local plans have in fact been prepared by those involved in the town centre plans, slum clearance projects and village plans typical of the 1960s. In any case, that experience would have been of only limited relevance in the very different economic circumstances of the late 1970s.

Central government, in its turn, has been uncertain how to approach local plans. Alarmed at the tendencies among districts to widen the scope and content of plans beyond land use matters, it has increasingly sought to influence the way statutory plans have been prepared. As a consequence it has forced many authorities to become aware that a *statutory* local plan is a particular type of planning guidance document not just a general framework to be adapted to the purpose in hand. Not surprisingly, this discovery has been unwelcome in many cases. Further, central government has attempted to force authorities to convert their various informal plans into statutory plans. Authorities, meanwhile, argue that how they approach the provision of a policy framework for their planning functions is *in the legislation* a matter for local discretion. The Local Government Planning and Land Act 1980 has complicated the situation still further by giving districts more power in relation to counties. This means that central government has *less* capacity to influence their planning activities through its approval of structure plans. Thus we have here an interesting example of central government attempting to assert control over local authorities while at the same time appearing to encourage local discretion, but in a policy field where central government has no financial control (see McAuslan 1981).

This chapter provides an introduction to the detailed account of local plan production and use which follows in Part II. It concentrates on describing the way the concept and procedures relating to statutory local plans as interpreted by central government have developed since the PAG report. It concludes firstly, with a review of the scale of statutory local plan preparation; and secondly with a summary of the source material which provides the basis for Part II.

2. THE EVOLUTION OF LOCAL PLANS IN LEGISLATION AND ADMINISTRATIVE INTERPRETATION[35]

The PAG report (MHLG 1965) presented detailed local plans as "a vital component of the planning process" (para. 5.7), but they were only to be prepared if relevant to "local planning problems and policies" and if adequate technical resources to prepare them were available (para. 5.6). They were to provide the detail to urban and county plan policies but, since these policies would have been approved by central government, local plans would not need central government approval themselves (paras. 5.2-5.4).

This devolution of responsibility was one of the items that led to considerable debate at the time. It was argued that local authorities might not be capable of the task:

"Can local government as at present constituted - be equal to the enlightened and dispassionate discharge of these very grave

[35]This section is based on Healey 1979a.

responsibilities and *will the public in general regard local government as being so equal?"* (Heap 1965 p.610).

There was also concern about the potential compromise to citizens' rights (Heap 1965, TPI 1966, McAuslan 1975, Purdue 1977). This could occur firstly where strategic plans pre-empted detailed decisions and secondly because the local planning authority would become judge and jury in its own case. This latter point is a matter which still leads to considerable concern (see Chapter 6.4).

The emphasis in local plans was to be on the guidance, co-ordination and promotion of development, as the following quotations from the PAG report make clear.

> "It is at this stage that general policy and broad proposals are rendered into detailed local terms, enabling the residents of the area concerned to appreciate and comment on the specific proposals for their area. Equally important, it is only when planning policies are carried forward to the point of detailed local interpretation that they can serve as a useful guide to developers and as a basis for co-ordinating public and private action in development and redevelopment. We would again stress the function of plans not primarily as a control mechanism but as a positive brief for developers, public and private, setting the standards and objectives for future development" (para. 5.3).

The purpose of local plans, in PAG's view, was therefore:

> "(1) to implement the intentions and fill in the detail of the policies and proposals in the submitted plans;
>
> (2) to provide planning authorities with a recognized means of planning at the local level - whether for a new development, improvement or any other purpose;
>
> (3) to encourage authorities to undertake comprehensive environmental planning at the local level;
>
> (4) to provide the basis for development control, for detailing land use requirements and sites for public buildings, to help to answer questions on land searches and to provide developers with positive guidance on development standards;
>
> (5) to help the public understand and take part in the detailed planning of their town" (para. 5.8).

These purposes have persisted in slightly modified form in all subsequent central government advice. They reflect PAG's view of local planning authorities as engaged in the efficient management of a collective development effort.

Three types of local plan were suggested:

> (1) Action area plans - "areas on which attention is to be concentrated over the next ten years or so. In effect, they constitute the initial programme for implementing the submitted plan. These are the areas where large scale development, redevelopment or improvement will be undertaken and which therefore need to be planned as a whole" (para. 4.1).

(2) District plans - for those areas with urban plans, to
    supplement action area plans. "Eventually a mosaic of local
    plans can be built up for the town as a whole, setting the
    action areas in a wider context and relating one action area
    to another. Local plans of this character will provide a
    more detailed basis for development control than the urban
    plan itself, and a means of developing the environmental
    area concept, applying the techniques of traffic management
    in a co-ordinated way" (para. 5.16). (The "environmental
    area" concept is a reference to Buchanan's work on the
    organization of traffic in towns (Buchanan 1963.)

(3) Town maps (for smaller towns) and village plans to "give
    clear guidance on the scale, pace and location of development
    in accordance with the policy set out in the county plan ...
    to make specific land allocations, reserve sites for
    important public uses and show the framework for traffic
    movement" (para. 5.23).

As with the proposals for urban and county structure plans, these types of
plans reflect the pre-1974 organization of local government, with
Metropolitan and County Boroughs likely to be involved in action area and
district plans, while counties would prepare town maps and village plans.
Of the three types, however, action area plans were seen as the most
important, reflecting the contemporary preoccupation with large-scale urban
renewal.

The 1968 Act did little further than specify the form of the plan and
outline procedures. Local plans were to be prepared at the discretion of
the local planning authority, but were to follow procedures laid down in
some detail, reflecting the suspicion in which central government held
local authority competence. In effect, the discretionary nature of local
plans was a significant shift away from the "universal" arrangements for
the planning system embodied in the 1947 Act. The purpose of the
procedures was partly to ensure conformity with the structure plan, although
this was not a major issue at the time since it was assumed that most local
plans would be prepared by the structure plan authority. More importantly,
the procedures required public involvement at various stages, provided for
the citizen's right of objection to proposals and indicated where central
government retained the right to step in. Publicity was required on the
matters to be included in the plan and on a draft of the plan. A statement
on how publicity and public involvement has been undertaken must accompany
the plan. An inquiry must be held if an objection is received. It is
these procedures relating to public involvement and the obligation to hold
an inquiry which have been substantially amended by the 1980 Local
Government, Planning and Land Act.

A local plan was to consist of:

"a map and a written statement and shall:

(a) formulate in such detail as the authority thinks appropriate
    the authority's proposals for the development and other use
    of land in that part of their area, and for any description
    of development or other use of land (including in either
    case such measures as the authority thinks fit for the
    improvement of the physical environment and the management
    of traffic), and

(b) contain such matters as may be prescribed or as the Secretary
of State may in any particular case direct" (1971 Act 11 (3)).

The map must be on an ordnance survey base (SI 1974 No. 1486 para. 18(b)).
Action area plans were specified as a particular type of local plan,
designated in a structure plan. Local planning authorities were to derive
the advantages of the 1961 Land Compensation Act in such areas, which
allowed land to be purchased for planning purposes at the time the plan
was adopted. (This power was removed by the Community Land Act 1975.)

It could be said that the lack of further detail about the form and content
of local plans reflected inadequate consideration given to the subject.
It is perhaps fairer to point out that the legislators, as opposed to
administrators, intended to provide local planning authorities with much
more discretion than in the old-style development plan so that they could
develop relevant and flexible responses to the very varied situations they
actually encountered. During discussion on the Bill, the Minister of State
for Housing and Local Government at the time argued:

> "I wish to make a plea for flexibility.... Local plans, as we
> envisage them, will vary considerably in their type and scope, and
> we would be losing some of the benefits of the change that we are
> making if we tried to prescribe too rigidly the requirements
> that would apply to all local plans...."(Cullingworth 1980).

The Minister then went on to discuss the various types of local plans,
drawing no doubt on ideas then being developed in the Ministry and later to
emerge in the Development Plans Manual (MHLG 1970). In addition to action
area plans, he suggested there may be "*district plans* covering a larger
part of the area of a planning authority", possibly with smaller local
plans developed at a later stage for part of this area. A village
expansion scheme is provided as an example. In addition, "one might have
a different kind of local plan" which might "deal with opportunities for
access to the countryside or facilities for recreation", or the "phased
working of minerals within an area"[36]. This seems to be the first mention
of what by 1970 had become *subject plans*.

To supplement the limited guidance on local plan preparation in the Act,
the DoE provided further instructions and advice in regulations[37], the
Development Plans Manual (MHLG 1970), a few advice notes, and a circular
(DoE Circular 55/77, revised as 4/79). The Development Plans Manual
provides the first formalization of the three types of statutory local
plan - district, action area and subject. This was included the following
year in the regulations. The concept of a local plan as presented in the
Manual follows the PAG report fairly closely, which itself built on the
earlier work at the MHLG (see MHLG 1962). The emphasis in both action
area and district plan prototypes was on the restructuring of urban areas,
related to the major urban renewal programme that was given so much
attention at the end of the sixties. The origins of subject plans are
more obscure. They are hinted at in the PAG report (para. 5.21) and in the
parliamentary discussions on local plans quoted above. The PAG report's
reference to village plans is not developed in the Manual. In practice,
subject plans have come to be used for a considerable variety of open land

---

[36]Quoted in Purdue 1977 pp.62-63.

[37]First produced in 1971 and revised after local government reorganization
in 1974, SI No. 1486 1974.

and countryside situations.

Local authority planners were thus presented with an apparently general tool
for the detailed guidance of development and development control which they
could use according to local circumstances. Yet they were also given
fairly precise instructions as to the types of variation in local plan form
and content which could be contemplated. The "closely related" functions
of local plans in general were as follows, according to the Manual:

"1. Applying strategy of structure plan.
   Local plans must conform generally to the approved structure
   plan (3, 10 3); they will develop the policies and proposals
   in it, showing as precisely as possible the changes proposed
   in the development and other uses of land.

2. Providing detailed basis for development control.
   The broad guidance on development control in the structure
   plan will be refined where local plans have been prepared.
   These will give more precise information to developers by
   allocating sites for particular purposes, by defining the
   areas to which particular development control policies will
   apply, and by explaining those policies in terms of
   standards and other criteria.

3. Providing basis for co-ordinating development.
   The planning policies and proposals in local plans will be
   used as a basis for co-ordinating public and private
   development and expenditure over the areas covered by them.

4. Bringing local and detailed planning issues before the public.
   While the structure plan is intended to bring before the
   public matters which affect the structure plan area as a
   whole, a local plan will be concerned to draw their attention
   to more detailed planning issues in parts of that area; it
   will do so in terms that will inform property owners and
   developers how their interests will be affected and where the
   opportunities lie" (para. 7.4).

There is no mention here of PAG's concern to "encourage authorities to
undertake comprehensive planning", or to "help the public understand and
take part in the detailed planning" of their area (see above). Once again
central government advice emphasizes the role of the local plan in the
effective management of development in line with the structure plan. The
public are to be informed rather than involved in this exercise.

The three types of local plan may overlap. *Action area plans* are "for
smaller areas of intensive, relatively short term change" (para. 7.5).
District plans should cover the full range of issues in relatively
extensive parts of the area for which a structure plan has been approved;
these may be towns, villages or tracts of countryside in a county, or parts
of large towns (para. 7.5). They have the following particular
functions:

"1. In general, to set out the planning policies for each area,
   to re-state and amplify the long term planning intentions of
   the structure plan, to describe specific proposals and to lay
   down development control criteria;

2. In urban areas, to apply the structure plan policies for

environmental planning and management;

3. In rural areas, to apply the structure plan policies for
managing the rural environment" (para. 8.6).

This appears to be a broader conception of district plans than that of the
PAG report, where it was confined to urban aras. It also subsumes PAG's
town and village plans[38].

Subject plans were designed "to cater for special planning issues" (para.
7.5). Reclamation in a river valley, restoration of derelict land,
co-ordination of landscaping on a motorway are put forward as examples
(para. 10.6). Subject plans could also be prepared on a particular issue
to provide guidance in advance of the preparation of a more comprehensive
district plan, or where a comprehensive district plan is not needed (para.
10.3). It was suggested by some that the kind of "topic" papers typical
of structure plan preparation and also being prepared by several London
Boroughs could become subject plans (MacMurray 1974). The DoE have since
advised against this interpretation of subject plans (Mabey and Craig 1976).
The DoE's argument here is that a subject plan must be a discrete,
isolatable subject. Housing or employment cannot therefore be appropriate
for subject plan treatment, nor, apparently, is green belt. This view has
been strongly contested by the District Planning Officers' Society (DPOS
1978), although it is the counties which have probably made most use of
subject plans.

As discussed in Chapters 2 and 3, local government reorganization
complicated the development plan system by dividing development plan
functions between two types of authority. Central government's regulations
and advice at this time reflect the concern expressed by professional
planners (RTPI 1972) that this organizational separation might undermine
the new system. Ironically, the machinery introduced as a result of this
concern, the development plan scheme and certification procedure, added
further procedural complications.

DoE Circulars 74/73 and 58/74 outline the development plan scheme and
certification procedure introduced in 1972 as amendments to the revised
Town and Country Planning Act 1971. The exhortatory tone of the circular
is no doubt a reflection of central government's anxiety to maintain the
development plan system as introduced in 1968. Counties are urged to
prepare such schemes quickly, in consultation with districts, but the
presumption is in favour of districts preparing local plans. However, a
county might prepare a subject plan for a policy applicable over a wide
area, or where a county proposes to initiate much of the development
itself or where a major county road scheme is involved. It is suggested
that structure plan authorities should prepare a "planning brief",
indicating how the policies of the structure plan relate to local plans
within their area.

Local planning authorities are advised, however, that should disputes
arise between counties and districts over development plan schemes or
certification, the Secretary of State will only expect to use his formal

---

[38]With local government reorganization, some potential for confusion has
been introduced between district plans and district planning authorities.
Because of this, the Scottish Development Department has advised against
the term (SDD 28/76 para. 4.4).

powers of arbitration as a last resort (para. 8 and para. 11). The first
such formal dispute over a development plan scheme (Manchester and Salford
District Councils' objection to the preparation by Greater Manchester
Council of a Green Belt and Open Land Subject Plan) occurred in 1978. The
DoE ruled that the County should prepare a green belt subject plan only.
Manchester city also objected to the adoption by the county of two river
valley subject plans. Here the DoE ruled that each district should adopt
the plan for its part of the river valley, having previously ruled that
joint adoption was not possible.

Few other areas have engaged in such protracted procedural disputes.
However, informal disputes have been common, particularly where counties
have proposed to prepare plans. As a result of these disputes, in many
cases development plan schemes have not been regularly updated. Nor are
they necessarily an accurate reflection of the local plan programme
actually being pursued by districts. Initially, districts tended to
include all the policy statements and small area plans that happened to be
in hand or contemplated at the time of reorganization. More recent schemes
may still contain optimistic estimates of the progress of work. Yet the
development plan schemes have been one of the few sources of information
available to central government on the way the local plan tool is being
used. In the consultation draft for the most recent circular on
development plans following the 1980 Act (DoE Circular 23/81), central
government actually attempted to use the development plan scheme as a
vehicle for cutting down on the number of local plans being prepared (see
later).

Schedule 2 of the regulations (SI 1486 1974) specified the content of
local plans. The list of matters to which proposals must relate is the
same as that for a structure plan. The schedule also specified what should
be included in the Written Statement. Again, this is the same as for
structure plans, with the omission of estimates of present and future
population levels, and "the economic planning and development of the region
as a whole" (Schedule 1 Part II). This seems to imply that, in local plan
preparation, there will be no need to engage in an independent attempt to
relate to economic and regional policy or predict population and employment.
Many local plans are nevertheless based on just such work, either because
these matters were not adequately covered in structure plans, or where
structure plan predictions now appear in error, or where there are
differences of opinion between counties and districts (see Chapter 6).

Until 1976, central government advice on local plans focused on
procedures, on methods of presentation and on the need for harmonious
relations between the two tiers of local government. Otherwise, local
plans were seen as a local authority concern, to be used as local
authorities saw fit in relation to their problems and resources. Between
1976 and 1978, three major advisory documents were produced which among
other things gave advice on content. These were DoE Circular 55/77 and
the two DoE Advice Notes (LP 1/76 *Development Plan Schemes and Local Plans*
(DoE 1976) and LP 1/78 *Form and Content of Local Plans* (DoE 1978a))[39].

Local Plans Advice Note 1/76 was able to reflect emerging practice.
Claiming that too many plans were being proposed, often of an inappropriate
type, it offered advice on when plans should be prepared:

---
[39] There were in addition a few other advice notes on local plans, but many
fewer than for structure plans.

"Local plan coverage for areas of planning need should be aimed
for, to enable development to be controlled effectively and
economically and to provide an up-to-date planning context for
the Community Land Scheme" (para. 2) (introduced under the 1975
Community Land Act).

Informal local plans (i.e. non-statutory plans) should be replaced as soon
as possible:

"Plans which have progressed through all the statutory procedures
have certain strong advantages. In particular, if development
control is to operate effectively and economically without
recourse to *ad hoc* decisions, an up-to-date statutory framework
is required" (Para. 10).

Material not appropriate to a statutory plan could have the status of
"supplementary planning guidance" (para. 4), such as design guides or
detailed schemes (Appendix I). As to content:

"Local plans are land use plans. Although other policies may be
included as part of the reasoned justification to support and
explain the land use proposals and policies, local plans will
be the executive instrument in respect of the land use element"
(para. 15).

Here central government is firmly limiting the scope and content of plans to
the narrow interpretation of "planning control and influence" they had
arrived at in relation to structure plans. Local plans, even more so than
structure plans, were to be guidance documents for the exercise of
development control. DoE officials argued vigorously at this time that
local plans could not contain proposals which would not be allowable as
"material considerations" in a planning decision. However, the position in
planning law is currently fluid on the definition of material considerations.
In any case, development plan considerations are in addition to, not part of,
material considerations. As Purdue (1977), Hamilton (1977) and Loughlin
(1980) argue, development plans by including social and economic
considerations as encouraged by the 1968 Act could *widen* the scope and
content of development control decisions. Jowell and Noble (1980) argue that
central government has effectively prevented this from happening in structure
plans (see Chapter 3). I will assess in Part II how far it has been
successful in relation to local plans.

DoE Circular 55/77 provides the first comprehensive statement of central
government advice on structure and local plans. Among other things, it
pulls together the comments made over the years on the types of local plan.
District plans are for situations which need comprehensive review and
proposals; they should normally be for larger areas, though not necessarily
for administrative districts. Smaller area district plans may be needed to
deal with urgent issues (para. 3.7). On action area plans, the advice
virtually repeats that of the Development Plans Manual. It is subject plans
which have led to most controversy (see Hebbert and Gault 1978, DPOS 1978).
The circular states clearly that subject plans are appropriate only where
the subject can be treated in isolation and:

"either (1) there is a need to develop local policies and
proposals in advance of comprehensive plans

or (2) other matters in that area are of insufficient
importance to justify planning comprehensively" (para. 3.9).

Green belts, recreation and amenity and leisure were the subjects of the first three subject plans to be deposited. However, despite earlier advice to the contrary, DoE officials now argue that green belt is not a sufficiently discrete subject for a subject plan since it requires consideration of the developed/open land boundary. Many counties are proceeding with such plans nevertheless, to safeguard green belt boundaries until district plans are prepared (see Chapter 5, Hebbert and Gault 1978, and Elson 1979).

Three further points are worth emphasizing from the Circular, which highlight particular problems identified by the DoE in the light of current practice. The first is the nature of proposals (paras. 3.28-3.32). These should either define a specific site for development or define the specific area in which particular policies will apply (para. 3.29), and should be limited to those proposals which will be started within ten years (para. 3.30). The reasoning behind this is to avoid unnecessary blighting, to prevent public confusion over proposals which cannot in practice be implemented via a local plan and to avoid delay in plan adoption which might occur if a plan was encumbered by contentious but non-land use proposals. Some authorities may nevertheless argue that a local plan is a useful vehicle for *informing* the public about its general intentions and policies as they affect an area.

The second point concerns the content of local plans. Following Advice Note 1/76, the circular reiterates that proposals should be confined to those "for the development and other use of land or for any description of development or other use of land" (para. 3.28). Subsequent to this circular, the London Borough of Camden was threatened with High Court action by a local group over a proposal in their draft Borough plan which was claimed to be *ultra vires* as it distinguished between users. Camden amended their proposal.

Thirdly, the circular returns to the issue of the need to replace non-statutory plans and policies (paras. 4.3-4.6). Local authorities awaiting an approved structure plan are advised to "progress" urgent local plans as far as possible through the required procedures. As long as such plans are formally supported by the planning authority (by a council resolution) and conform generally with "matters proposed to be included in the structure plan", the Secretary of State will view such a local plan as a "material consideration" in relation to development control appeals. Informal local plans which are not to be converted into draft local plans "must be treated as having lapsed and cannot be taken into account in the exercise of development control" (para. 4.5). This would appear to be a clear warning to local authorities on the future attitude of the planning inspectorate at an appeal. The only exception is "supplementary planning guidance" such as notes on development control or housing layouts. If such guidance has been approved by the Council and been subject to public consultation, the Secretary of State will accept it as a material consideration (para. 4.6).

It should be noted that central government is assuming that its power over local authority planning policy and its detailed operation lies in its capacity to overturn refusals or conditional permissions at appeal. It should be noted that it does not have the same power over local authority permissions. It thus exercises power through appeal decisions only where the policies involve *resisting* certain types of development. The DoE's advice also assumes that it can control the way the Inspectorate decides on appeal cases. Although the Inspectorate does heed DoE Circulars, and is

given confidential briefings on contentious applications[40], there is
circumstantial evidence to suggest that the Inspectorate acts as
independently of central government as it can.

Local Plans Advice Note 1/78 concentrates in particular on the nature of
proposals and their presentation in the Proposals Map and Written Statement.
Proposals should be precisely defined and represent a firm decision to
develop a site or apply a policy in an area (para. 12). The emphasis is on
clarity, which should, the advice note hopes, help the public understand
what is proposed and consequently formulate their objections (para. 12).
The relation of local plans to resources and implementing agencies is
discussed (paras. 28-29, 37, 88). The DoE's position on the validity of
distinguishing between users as opposed to uses is stated explicitly:

> "Proposals for housing development will arise in respect of the
> public and private sectors and other authorities and bodies,
> but the proposals should not distinguish between them. Land
> can only be allocated for residential use generally" (para. 16).

The general tone of the circular and both advice notes is directive, with
central government setting down firm guidelines for local authorities. This
apparent firmness is somewhat undermined by two factors. Firstly, according
to Advice Note 1/78 and most earlier advice, the legislation is supposed to
allow a "flexible approach to cater for differing local needs, circumstances
and resources" (para. 3). If a local authority argues that its response is
reflecting this flexibility, is it not justified? Secondly, if a local
authority does go against central government advice, how far will central
government step in to correct this? In theory, central government's formal
powers of intervention are to be treated as a last resort (Circular 55/77
para. 3.23). In practice, central government intervention in local plans
has been increasing.

1978 brought a minor legislative change in the arrangements for local plans,
allowing local authorities in special areas designated under the 1978
Inner Urban Areas Act to deposit local plans prior to the approval of
structure plans so long as they conformed to a structure plan in preparation.
This provision was made as it was feared that the delays in structure plan
preparation were holding up the provision of site specific guidance
frameworks for inner city regeneration programmes. Some authorities made use
of this provision, but by this time there were doubts about the relevance of
statutory local plans to inner city situations (see Chapter 5). The
revisions introduced in the 1978 Act were incorporated in a revised general
circular on structure and local plans (DoE Circular 4/79).

By mid-1979 when the new Conservative administration took office, the
complexities of local plan inquiries and the procedural problems of local
plan amendments were added to the longstanding DoE concern with the slow
preparation of plans and the tendency of authorities to use plans for other
purposes than the guidance of physical development. Almost immediately, the
new Secretary of State for the Environment initiated work on what became
the Local Government, Planning and Land Act 1980. Initially, officials were
asked to produce items of legislation relating to central government control
over local authorities which could be cancelled, apparently to give
authorities more "local discretion and autonomy" and "better value for money"

---

[40] As was revealed in the case of the controversial Coin Street Inquiry,
concluded in 1982.

(DoE 1979 para. 11). DoE officials used this opportunity to revise areas
of the legislation which were causing administrative difficulties, as well
as removing apparently unnecessary controls. The proposals for repeal of
legislation in relation to local plans included:

"power to require preparation or amendment of development plan
schemes and to prescribe their contents and procedures;

specification of content of local plans by direction;

prescription of availability for inspectors of local plans
other than at a local office;

prescription of content of public participation statement;

the requirement that the adoption of a local plan must be
delayed until the structure plan is approved" (DoE 1979 p.8-9).

The first two appear to be a retreat from the earlier increase in DoE
concern with content. Both these and the second two could be purveyed as
reducing interference in local authority discretion, although the longstop
role of central government in relation to public participation had probably
helped to ensure that authorities did attempt a reasonable degree of
consultation with affected citizens. The fifth power extended to all areas
the special provisions for local plan adoption in advance of the structure
plan introduced for inner areas by the 1978 Act.

However, as McAuslan (1981) has convincingly shown, these legislative
amendments taken in total (and the "bonfire of controls"[41] constituted quite
the opposite of an increase in local discretion and autonomy. In the
planning field, Ministers were preoccupied with "speeding up" the planning
system, and making land available for development. Pressure was therefore
put on local planning authorities to make planning decisions more quickly,
to prepare local plans quickly and only when necessary, and to prepare
five-year housing land availability statements. It seems likely that
Ministers would have dispensed altogether with structure and local plans,
but were advised to retain these by officials. This in turn led to DoE
pressure on local planning authorities to prepare local plans efficiently.
The arguments used to support retaining structure and local plans probably
related to the need to demonstrate some "consistency and continuity" in
planning policy (see Chapter 2), and to avoid the situation which developed
ten years previously when land was released outside the framework of
statutory plans in response to central government pressure on the housing-
land availability issue. At both stages, central government was responding
to an effective lobby of house building interests.

The proposals for legislative change went through various adjustments
before the 1980 Act was finally enacted. In addition to some tidying up
relating to amendment procedures and to those for revoking existing old-
style development plans, the Act contains the following significant
provisions:

1. Local plans can be adopted in advance of structure plans, but
only if the Secretary of State approves. (This in part safeguards
the County's strategic interests, but it also ensures that Counties

---

[41] A repeat of a similar exercise in the early 1950s, embodied in the 1979
White Paper included all areas of the DoE/DoT remit.

and Districts together do not use these "expedited procedures" to
over-ride structure plan modifications.)

2. Publicity and "public participation" is only *required* when a
draft plan has been prepared, replacing the earlier requirement
for public consultation on matters to be included in the plan.

3. A Public Local Inquiry into a local plan is not necessary if
objectors are prepared to agree to have their objections dealt
with in writing.

The Act also weakens the position of counties in safeguarding their strategic
interests in development control decisions, since counties have lost their
power to direct districts to refuse applications on structure plan grounds.
This has been replaced with encouragement to consultation. Taking the
amendments to the planning legislation as a whole, the position of counties
and the structure plan as a strategic guidance framework have both been
weakened, as has the role of the citizen, both as participator in local
plan preparation and as objector.

However, the weakening of the counties' role has in turn created problems
for central government in safeguarding its own strategic interests. It can
no longer rely on negotiations about structure plan content, given the
potential weakness of the link between county structure plans and district
local plans and development control. As a consequence, DoE regional offices
have recently been giving much more attention to local plan progress, which
often involves them in closer contact with the district planning authorities
than they have been accustomed to. The evidence that local plan preparation
was not after all a matter for local discretion is provided in a
controversial phrase in a draft of what became DoE Circular 23/81:

> "County planning authorities in consultation with district planning
> authorities are invited to *agree* by 30 September (1981) the need
> for local plans in a review of their development plan scheme *with
> the appropriate DoE Regional office*.... The Regional office will
> wish to be satisfied that the work proposed on the preparation of
> a local plan is realistic, justified and can be carried out
> within a year..." DoE 1981 para. 12 (my italics).

As planning authorities were quick to point out, the 1980 Act had abolished
the DoE's interest in the content of development plan schemes. The wording
of the final version of the Circular[42] thus refers to "consultation" with
Regional offices rather than "agreement". Two other amendments to the
above extract from the draft circular are also worth noting:

> Firstly, "local plans are not needed where the structure plan
>   provides an adequate planning framework or where little
>   or no pressure for development is expected".

> Secondly, "The absence of a local plan, or the fact that one is in
>   the offing, is not in itself sufficient reason for
>   refusing an application" (DoE Circular 23/81 paras 10
>   and 11).

---

[42] A new circular is due in late 1982 which provides considerable advice on
the form and content of local plans, developing the direction of advice
of the late 1970s.

We may thus conclude that the current view in central government is that the only value of local plans is in areas under private sector development pressure where such plans can expedite local planning decisions and assist the development industry. However, the areas of the country affected by such development pressure are much less than they were in the 1960s. Economic recession has meant that for the conurbations, for Wales, Scotland, the Midlands and Northern England, the key land policy questions are not how to regulate and channel development pressure but how to promote it. Thus, if the DoE view is correct, local plans are of most relevance in the areas around the conurbations, particularly in the South, which are still experiencing development pressure, fuelled by the continuing process of suburbanization. This is of course the reverse of the priorities the writers of the PAG report had in mind when they put forward the idea of local plans. It can also be argued that they would barely recognize the concept of a local plan now embodied in DoE advice.

Many local authority planners have been very critical of the DoE's view of local plans, as I indicated in the introduction to this chapter. Local authorities argue that such a limited view makes local plans inappropriate for local problems and needs. Perry noted in 1976:

> "the sad irrelevance to practical planning of much of the legislative paraphernalia and government advice emanating from the 1971 Act" (Perry 1976 p.139),

and Hambleton, around the same time, maintained that:

> "the influence of the statutory requirements runs very deep, and seems to be stunting the development of creative, problem-solving approaches to local planning" (Hambleton 1976 p.176).

In part, this debate results from the different perceptions of central and local government planners. The former take a vertical "top-down" view of local plans, as a further mechanism for ensuring policy consistency within a sectoral concern with land use matters and a hierarchical model of policy control. It is because of the inadequacies of the hierarchical model consequent upon the weakening of the Counties' role in strategic policy as a result of local government reorganization and the 1980 Act, that central government has become increasingly concerned about the preparation of local plans. Local authorities are more aware of the inter-relatedness of local problems and the many ways in which the public sector impinges on them.

But central government is also warning local government planners of the limitations of planning powers and of the prospects for inter-sectoral co-ordination at any level of government. These warnings are officially presented as guidance on procedures, but mask two important policy concerns. The first is to restrict the interventionist enthusiasm of some local authorities, who stray into restrictions on private development initiatives which go beyond those justified by physical and environmental reasons. As with structure plans, this restriction tends to exclude many policies and proposals directed at social welfare ends (for detailed evidence on this point see Chapter 6). Legal precedent is used to argue that economic and social considerations are not legitimate in detailed land use planning matters, yet as I have noted the position in law is less definite than the DoE supposes. The DoE's limitation to land use matters is thus a matter of *policy*, not of law. Central government also claims that many of the informal local plans used by local authorities are not subject to public or even political scrutiny. Here central government appears to be upholding the principle of open government, and the rights of the citizen. It is

also, of course, upholding the rights of the property owner to object to
proposals (while at the same time seeking to reduce the time spent on
inquiries). Thus there is a strong suggestion that central government is
seeking to limit the extent of intervention in private property rights which
some local authorities may seek.

Central government's other concern is with the credibility of the planning
system as a whole. The fear here is that local plans will be incompetently
produced, a fear persisting from the 1960s when local authority capacity to
take the discretion offered to them was doubted. If policies are unclear,
or incapable of implementation, if developers cannot easily "read" plans,
then the whole exercise of attempting to make public sector land use
decisions appear rational will be undermined. What central government -
politicians and planners - think they want out of land use planning is not
at all clear. The present government's increased support for development
interests is complemented by rhetoric maintaining support for environmental
conservation (e.g. Heseltine 1979, Baron 1980). The image is created that
the two interests can be readily "balanced". The reasons for the delays in
preparing structure and local plans are presented not as the result of
difficulties in finding a politically-acceptable balance, but because
planners are dilatory.

Central government, at both political and administrative level, thus
commonly portrays local authorities in the planning field as "inefficient".
No doubt they sometimes are. However, this position ignores the possibility
that local authorities may have different political priorities from those of
central government when using the tool of a local plan. In addition, the
preparation of such plans may involve difficult local political problems
where significant interests are in conflict over the way land is used and
developed. I explore how local authorities have interpreted and used the
tool of a local plan, and how far they have been affected by central
government advice in Part II.

3. HOW MANY LOCAL PLANS HAVE BEEN PREPARED?

DoE planners Mabey and Craig (1976) estimated that 3543 statutory local plans
were proposed for adoption by 1980, according to development plan schemes.
Bluntly, they considered that this was far too many. More recently, a
figure of 200 adopted by the mid-1980s has been suggested by central
government, with Ministers maintaining this may still be too many. However,
a recent survey of over 50 authorities suggested that many more than this
are contemplated by authorities (Fudge et al. 1982b).

By the end of March 1983, 372 statutory local plans had been placed on
deposit for receipt of objections. 171 had been adopted[43]. The majority
have required an inquiry into objections. Diagram 4.1 shows that the
deposit of local plans rapidly accelerated in 1980 and 1981, with the rate
of adoption lagging behind this. The acceleration in deposited plans partly
reflects the 1980 Act provision to deposit plans in advance of structure
plans. In the main, however, it is the result of the approval of most
structure plans by the end of 1980 (see Chapter 3).

Table 4.1 shows that three quarters of deposited and adopted plans have been
district plans. Table 4.2 shows that 60% of local plans deposited have been

---

[43]The source of this data is the DoE.

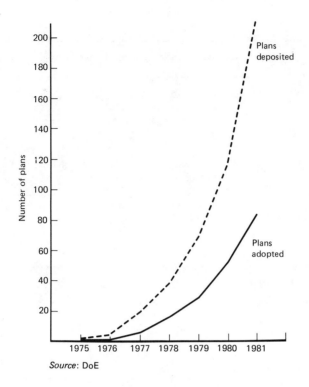

Source: DoE

Diagram 4.1.   Local Plans Deposited and Adopted (31.12.81)

prepared by the County Districts, with only 13% prepared by upper-tier
authorities (the GLC, Metropolitan Counties and shire counties), though
counties have prepared most subject plans. This suggests that local plans
are by no means concentrated in urban areas. Diagram 4.2 tends to confirm
this, showing a considerable scatter of plans outside the main conurbation
areas. This diagram does not discriminate between large and small area plans
and thus gives a misleading picture of plan coverage. It is worth noting
that in areas where structure plans have been approved, only some districts
have prepared statutory local plans so far. Other districts have either
been working more slowly or do not see statutory local plans as necessary.
However, this data gives no indication of the scale of local plan
preparation in total as it leaves out those which authorities do not intend
to become statutory. The discussion in this chapter has suggested several
reasons why the statutory format might be avoided. Part II (Chapters 5-8)
attempts a comprehensive account of the variety of ways in which the tool of
a local plan is being employed, based on experience between 1974-80. I
explore how far such a tool is adaptable to specific circumstances,
essentially neutral, to be used to serve whatever purposes individual local
authorities wish to pursue, and how far the tool itself constrains its
content, the way it is produced and used. My aim is to illustrate the
interplay between enabling legislation and its discretionary use. This
involves attention not only to the formal use of the tool, statutory local
plans as deposited and adopted, but to the whole range of similar sorts of
local plan or local planning policy exercises undertaken by local

TABLE 4.1

Deposited Plans	1975	1976	1977	1978	1979	1980	1981	Total	%
District plans	-	2	7	15	25	38	79	166	77.6
Action area plans	2	1	6	2	5	6	4	26	12.1
Subject plans	-	-	1	2	2	3	14	22	10.3
Total	2	3	14	19	32	47	97	214	100.0

Adopted Plans	1975	1976	1977	1978	1979	1980	1981	Total	%
District plans	-	-	2	6	10	18	25	61	72.6
Action area plans	1	-	2	4	3	3	5	18	21.4
Subject plans	-	-	1	-	-	2	2	5	6.0
Total	1	-	5	10	13	23	32	84	100.0

(Source: DoE)

authorities. These chapters are based on as broad a review of such exercises as I have been able to construct.

However, a comprehensive review of local plans prepared between 1974-80 proved to be an impossible task. Even by confining myself to England, there are 411 local planning authorities which might be preparing plans. The Department of the Environment has records of all the Development Plan Schemes produced by the authorities, which purport to provide a programme for local plan preparation. But as already noted, many of these were never updated after the mid-1970s and are not considered accurate estimations of plans actually in preparation. The only other record held by the Department is that of statutory local plans deposited, with details of inquiries and adoption. This is maintained by scouring the official publicity notices[44]. To supplement this list, I have scanned the

---

[44] My information on statutory local plans was kindly supplied by the DoE.

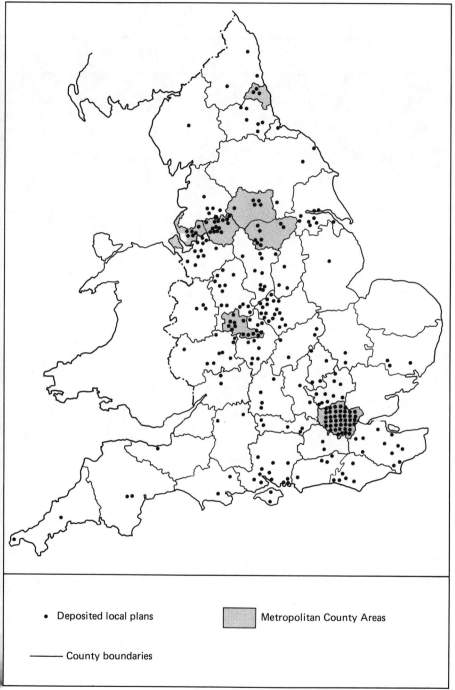

- **•** Deposited local plans

▨ Metropolitan County Areas

——— County boundaries

Diagram 4.2. The location of Local Plans deposited.

TABLE 4.2

	District	Action area	Subject	Total	%
GLC	-	1	-	1	0.5
Metropolitan counties	-	-	5	5	2.3
Shire counties	5	1	13	19	8.9
London boroughs	24	9	-	33	15.4
Metropolitan districts	22	6	-	28	13.1
Shire districts	115	9	4	128	59.8
Total	166	26	22	214	100.0

(Source: DoE)

professional journals and newsletters from the mid-1960s to the end of
1978 (Healey 1979a); more recent material in these journals including lists
of "plans received" in The Planner and Planning Bulletin; local plans and
related papers held at the School of Advanced Urban Studies, Bristol; the
collection of plans and related material in the Department of Town Planning,
Oxford Polytechnic; and my own collection of nearly 100 local plans.

The material held at SAUS provides an indication of the enormous amount of
what might be called "local planning advisory documents" which local
authorities actually produce. On the one hand there are documents
associated with local planning exercises - position statements, community
reviews etc., on the other, there are development briefs, design guides and
environmental codes (statements of detailed development control standards).
In between are a range of policy guides on particular issues, proposals for
specific sites or areas, and the "bottom-drawer" plans inherited from the
1960s which were often not subject to any form of political or public
scrutiny, as well as plans for General Improvement Areas, Housing Action
Areas and Conservation Areas. Many authorities had a large number of small
area projects and plans. Coventry Council had 24 Action Area proposals at
one time (Trafford and Hanna 1977). In Hampshire, 190 separate plans and
policies existed for South Hampshire at the time of reorganization (Brown
1974).

In this study I have limited myself only to those documents which are
studies for, drafts or final versions of a local plan or other local policy
statement (omitting those reports which are primarily concerned with
corporate planning). I have also confined myself to the period 1974-80.
My scan covers 274 plans, 117 of which had been deposited as statutory plans
during the period (43%). These plans were produced by 180 local authorities
or 44% of the total in England. My impression is that this probably
represents about 50% at least of the plans prepared in the period. There is
no way of telling how representative these authorities are of all
authorities. However, I am confident that they represent a wide spead of
different political and economic situations. The only notable area of poor
coverage is from the Yorkshire area and the North East. Williams (1978)

gives a useful account of a survey of local plan preparation in the North East which confirms many of my own findings. I have read about half of the plans and for many of them I have found published comments by those preparing the plans. Tables 4.3, 4.4 and 4.5 summarize the plans included in this review.

There are several ways in which the discussion of the production and use of local plans could be organized. Case studies provide the most revealing insights into how local plans are produced and used, but it is then difficult to draw generalizations. There are also very few examples where existing material allows coverage of all the aspects of production and use. An alternative was to arrange the chapters according to the different groups involved in and affected by local plans. Again, existing work only touches on this aspect tangentially. Such an arrangement would also make it difficult to identify the interplay of interests in plan production and use, and to focus precisely on the nature of local plans as a tool. I have opted therefore to organize the chapters according to stages in production and use, concentrating in turn on purposes, method, content and outcomes. Chapter 5 explores the reasons why local plans have been prepared, allowing discussion of the purposes of plans. Chapter 6 summarizes what is involved in preparing local plans, including, for statutory plans, the stages of inquiry and formal adoption. Chapter 7 takes stock of the plans as produced, examining their form and content. Chapter 8 then considers what information there is on the way plans are used. While the first three chapters are concerned primarily with the production of policy statements within government agencies, Chapter 8 shifts the emphasis to the interplay of government agencies and those involved in the development process.

Each chapter has a different organization, depending on the nature of the material to be discussed. However, throughout the discussion I emphasize the following themes:

(1) Given that the formal purpose of government intervention in land use and development is to further some definition of the "public interest", how is this "public interest" established in the production of local plans?

(2) Who and what influences the way the public interest is defined, and the role of the plan in producing specific development outcomes? How visible and accountable are these influences?

(3) How far are these influences local, how far are they organized around the hierarchical model of policy control embodied in the current form of the legislation, and what is the relationship between the form in which plans are produced and presented and their content?

(4) What role does local plan production and use have in influencing land use and development change.

(5) What are the consequences of the way local plans are produced and used; what costs are incurred, what benefits accrue and to whom?

Finally, in view of the lack of any previous systematic discussion of local plan preparation, with many contributions scattered among professional journals and working papers, I have attempted to reference my account to this diffuse literature as fully as possible.

TABLE 4.3 Type of local authority by status of plan

	Statutory: deposited				Probably statutory			Non-statutory	Unclear	Total plans
	D	AA	S	Total	D	AA	S			
Met county/GLC	-	1	-	1	-	-	3	-	2	6
County	4	1	5	10	-	-	7	-	3	20
Met district	8	5	1	14	3	3	-	6	10	36
London borough	18	7	-	25	6	1	-	4	-	36
County district	56	8	3	67	24	-	1	21	63	176
TOTAL	86	22	9	117[45]	33	4	11	31	78	274

D : District

AA : Action area

S : Subject

[45]Due to error, one plan is not included in this figure.

TABLE 4.4 Type of local authority by size of plan area and status of plan

	Statutory: deposited			Probably statutory			Other			No information	Total
	Small	Large	All district	Small	Large	All district	Small	Large	All district		
Met county/GLC:	1	-	-	-	3	-	2	-	-	5	6
County:	3	7	-	-	6	-	1	1	-	2	20
Met district	11	2	-	5	1	-	4	6	-	7	36
London borough	14	2	9	1	3	3	3	-	1	-	36
County district	39	13	5	15	8	2	61	4	1	28	176
Total	68	24	14	21	21	5	71	11	2	37	274

Small: Less than 20% district area

Large: 20% + district area

All district: Whole area of district

TABLE 4.5   Status of plan by size of plan area

	Small	Large	All district	No information	Total	%
Statutory: deposited: District	45	17	14	10	86	31.2
Action area	21	1	-	-	22	8.0
Subject	2	6	-	1	9	3.3
Probably statutory: District	15	13	5	1	34	12.3
Action area	4	-	-	-	4	1.5
Subject	2	8	-	1	11	4.0
Non-statutory	27	2	2	-	31	11.2
Unclear	44	6	-	24	77	27.9
Total	160	56	21	37	276	99.4
%	58.0	20.3	7.6	13.4	99.3	

(For definitions of small, large, all district, see Table 4.4).

PART II

CHAPTER 5

Why Prepare a Local Plan?

1. INTRODUCTION

A local plan is a tool, a means to achieving some purpose or policy. A statutory local plan is a distinctive version of a local plan tool, which local planning authorities may prepare at their discretion. How have local authorities exercised this discretion and to what ends? Who and what has determined the way this discretion has been deployed? In answering these questions we are led centrally into the debate between local authorities and central government about the nature of a local plan, and the distinctive characteristics of a statutory local plan. This chapter explores this debate, and then examines what can be discovered from the local plans actually prepared during the 1970s about why they were undertaken.

So far as the legislation is concerned, a statutory local plan is a *site-specific development guidance framework*. An important strand in the debate about the nature and value of statutory local plans has been the claim by many local planners that a local plan should be much more than this, as I have noted in Chapter 4. Some consider its central role as a method for clarifying and reviewing policy and programmes. Others view it as a vehicle for expressing local authority policies on a wide front, related to local problems and local needs.

In making such claims, local planners are presenting their role and that of the plan they are preparing as one which involves managing resource allocation within their authority's area, particularly that of the public sector. For some, the purpose of this was to ensure that local authority resources were used as efficiently and effectively as possible in the general interest. Other local planners were informed by a concern to assist disadvantaged groups threatened by market pressures. In neither case were market processes given much attention in discussion, or in the plans themselves. However, many local plan teams did make attempts to involve local communities actively in plan preparation, with a few examples where the latter actually took over. In effect the production of local plans in the mid-1970s was caught up in the shifting ground of contemporary planning ideologies, in which notions of "corporate planning" rubbed shoulders with "social planning" and participatory democracy, and mixed uneasily with an emphasis on defining the quality of the design of the built environment (see Perry (ed.) 1974; see also Healey, McDougall and Thomas 1982). To quote Robin Thompson, who was responsible for the preparation of the Borough Plan for the London Borough of Camden:

> "At present, local planning inhabits a no-man's-land between the small-scale, physical inheritance of architecture and surveying and the broader policy perspectives derived from the social sciences" (Thompson 1977a).

This situation was reinforced by the fact that most local plan teams in the new metropolitan and shire districts contained young staff recently exposed to the new planning ideas of the 1970s. A survey in 1980 found that 60% of the staff in the districts were under 35, and a third of the staff in the metropolitan districts were between 25 and 29[46] (a quarter in the shire districts). It is probable that many of these young local planners not only lacked experience in the preparation of site-specific guidance frameworks but were unclear about exactly what the role of a local planning authority was and could be. Meanwhile central government advice provided little assistance on how to relate the planning tools available in the legislation to the specific political and economic characteristics of local authorities (see Chapter 4). This partly reflected central government's official stance that local plans were a matter for local authorities to develop. It is also likely that central government was unsure about the problems which preparing local plans might actually involve.

The difficulties of preparing local plans were in any case increased by the effects of deepening recession which eroded the economic base of many areas and altered the nature of development pressures in other areas. Associated with these economic changes, local politics in many areas have become more volatile. This has created problems both of interpretation - what are the land and development demands and needs of an area; and policy continuity - will the policies advocated by the local authority change during the preparation and life of the plan. In other words, it has become difficult to produce site-specific policy guidance where the strategic context is uncertain or liable to change over short periods.

Finally, it should be noted, that despite the emphasis in professional debate on plan-making and "policy work" during the 1970s, local plan production was not necessarily accorded high priority by local authorities. Counties were absorbed in structure plan preparation and review. Districts had a constant stream of development control issues to deal with. Urban districts, particularly the Metropolitan districts, usually had a range of development, conservation and, more recently, economic regeneration programmes and projects which occupied their attention. Consequently, there were many reasons why local authorities might not take up the discretion available to them to prepare plans, and many more possibilities of deflection from the task when plan preparation was underway.

In this chapter, I will explore firstly the discussion among central and local government planners on the purposes of local plans; why they should be prepared and for what sorts of situations. I conclude by summarizing what this debate suggests about the various purposes which the tool of a local plan might be used to pursue. I then examine, from my review of plans, what plans have actually been used for, concentrating at this stage on why they

---

[46]These figures are based on a study commissioned by the SSRC *Manpower Requirements for Physical Planning* (Amos 1982).

have been initiated and for what sorts of areas.

2. THE PURPOSES OF LOCAL PLANS

2.1 *Central Government Advice*

So far as central government is concerned, the purposes of a local plan remain those stated in the Development Plans Manual, to be found inscribed in most local plan written statements produced since. These are:

1. to apply the strategy of the structure plan;

2. to provide a detailed basis for development control;

3. to provide a basis for co-ordinating development;

4. to bring local and detailed issues before the public (see Chapter 4).

Although the last two purposes derive from the hierarchical policy control model embodied in the statutory land use planning system, the second two at face value provide considerable leeway for discretionary interpretation. Co-ordinating development could take policies and proposals into a very wide arena of public and private sector development investment, whereas local and detailed issues, especially as *perceived* by the public, are likely to include matters well outside a "land use" remit. The "particular functions" of district plans quoted in Chapter 4 from the Development Plans Manual also encourage a wide interpretation of the role of local plans, with their emphasis on setting out planning policies and long-term "planning intentions" for an area, and on managing the rural and urban environment. "Planning" and "environment" here are open to liberal definition.

Even in the late 1970s, when DoE advice was firmly stating that local plan proposals should be confined to land use matters, considerable scope was suggested for local plans. In Advice Note 1/78, local authorities were exhorted to use the Development Plan Scheme to determine priorities in the preparation of local plans, and the following are suggested as considerations to bear in mind when establishing such priorities:

"action areas as defined in the structure plan ...;

areas where the use of powers under the Community Land Act is envisaged to initiate development;

areas with a large industrial content;

areas with inner city problems;

major growth areas indicated in the structure plan;

areas under pressure for development;

areas with land availability problems;

areas where particular planning issues need to be resolved" (DoE 1978a para. 6).

This list reflects central government's preoccupations at the time, but leaves wide scope for interpreting "planning issues", stressing only that proposals in respect of these should relate to "the development and other use of land" (para. 10). The Advice Note gives no indication of how such proposals might assist areas with a "large industrial content" or "inner city proposals". DoE Circular 44/78 added the issue of private sector land availability to the list, noting that local plans should reflect strategies which "look forward to the best balance of amount, size, locations and hope of industrial development", which should in turn help areas with "serious inner city problems" (para. 23). But no advice is given on how land use strategies will actually do this.

The new Conservative administration from 1979, firmly prejudiced in the view that much local authority planning was at best a waste of time and at worst inhibiting economic regeneration, encouraged the increasingly jaundiced view held by officials in the DoE of local plan production. DoE Circular 9/80 demanded that local authorities maintain a five year supply of housing land whatever the state of play on local plans. Circular 22/80 emphasized that "prematurity" agreements, i.e. that permission was not to be given for a planning application because a local plan to sort out competing demands for land had not yet been prepared, would no longer be supported on appeal so local authorities should progress their local plans with all speed. However, Circular 23/81 advised authorities that they were preparing too many "low priority local plans".

> "Local plans are not needed where the structure plan provides
> an adequate planning framework or where little or no new
> development is expected". They are needed "to provide locations
> for future supply of land for housing and industry; to define
> the precise boundaries of areas of restraint, or to co-ordinate
> programmes of land management, e.g. by indicating preferred areas
> for mineral working. They will seldom be needed for a village
> or a small town that is not expected to change very much"
> (DoE Circular 23/81 para. 12).

Running through this advice is a contradiction typical of central government statements about land use planning. On the other hand, plans and proposals must confine themselves to the "legitimate" sectoral territory of land use and development matters. At the same time, they must be demonstrably relevant to the issues of political salience for Ministers. During the 1970s these have shifted from social issues and the environment, via the inner city and industrial promotion, to land availability for private sector development. It is left to the local authorities to find a path through these contradictions. In doing so, the local authorities reflect the different and often equally contradictory political and economic pressures to which they in turn are subject.

2.2 Local Planners: Early Ambitions

As I have already noted, local plan teams in the newly-created metropolitan and shire districts were not in the best position to address the task of developing relevant planning guidance. Many were new to the work involved and to their authorities. Several authorities were newly created, leading to uncertainty as to the political and organizational constraints which might confront local planning work. Often there was no data which related to new district areas. Consequently, there was in many cases little knowledge to build on which could have provided them with an awareness of political priorities and the nature of land use of development issues in their areas. In such cases, early exercises in local plan production were by accident or design necessarily "learning processes" for all involved. Yet even where there was a substantial inheritance from previous authorities, as in many of the former county boroughs, or where counties continued with local plan work, as in Hampshire, Berkshire, and Cheshire for example and in London, where reorganization occurred a decade before, the direction of policy was uncertain. This arose not just because structure plan policy disputes were often unsettled until the late 1970s. Policies in approved structure plans were also overtaken by the collapse of the growth predictions of the late 1960s, and the shift in policy in the late 1970s towards economic regeneration.

Yet the public statements of planners around 1974 barely discussed such difficulties. Instead, they conveyed both an ambitious collective programme for local plan preparation (see Section 4.3), and ambitious and idealistic notions about the functions of local plans. The flavour of local planning thinking at this time is conveyed in a collection of papers published in the planners' professional journal (Perry (ed.) 1974). These reflect planners' contemporary preoccupations with corporate planning; with a "total approach" to co-ordinated local authority investment programmes (deriving from the Sunderland Guidelines study by McKinsey and Co. of a planning approach for the new metropolitan districts (DoE 1973c)); with positive discrimination in favour of the needs of disadvantaged groups (following the ideas made familiar to planners in the United States by Gans (1968)); and with the quality of the urban environment. Perry stresses three points:

> "The first is that local plans can be one of the main vehicles for securing corporate planning of local authority activities. District plans, in particular, relate to conveniently-broad parts of local authority areas, have timescales relevant to planning activities in other local authority services, and need not be myopically concerned with physical development alone ... Secondly, local plans must form the main agent for public involvement in planning, and as much effort must be expended in adapting to this purpose as in securing their implementation as satisfactory physical development. Local plans could be the bridgehead for the public into the local government stronghold, and could be used to make authorities aim to provide services that really respond to peoples' needs, rather than aiming to be narrowly business efficient. The third contention is that local plans have failed hitherto even to secure consistently high environmental quality and that, in order to achieve this, local planners must intervene more positively in the design process" (Perry 1974 p.492).

MacMurray (who worked on the Sunderland study) stressed the importance of client group analysis, and of developing an understanding of the causes rather than symptoms of problems. Local planners should aim to contribute to policy production in local authorities through research which identifies local issues, and through advising on the work of other departments. But the "core of the local planners' work is to plan, design and control the implementation of public and private sector development" (MacMurray 1974 p.493). Edwards, writing from Coventry which was then an exemplar of the link between land use planning and corporate planning, elaborated on how this approach should be developed. Local plans could be used to emphasize "area-oriented" problems and co-ordinate the City Corporation's activities within areas (Edwards 1974). Whitney, from Liverpool, was more cautious.

He supported the importance of co-ordination with other local government activities if "locally experienced and interrelated needs are to be met", but was uncertain of how this co-ordination and relevance could be achieved (Whitney 1974). His authority had after all been demolishing large areas of the city under slum clearance programmes without more than a very generalized conception of "people's needs".

It was left to two planning assistants from Nottingham (which had also been energetically demolishing its inner areas) to inject a note of caution:

> "Local planning could become the poor relation within the corporate planning set-up also. Local planning as a means of understanding the total needs and priorities within small areas, or among specific social groups, remains a largely uncharted area and both within the profession and without, an unpopular notion. Local planning departments and sections remain a relatively insignificant part of the total complex of day-to-day decisions relating to the destiny of our urban environment. It is arrogant to suppose that solutions lie within the profession, or even within local government as a whole".

> As to MacMurray's arguments, these "would appear to add up to a plea for 'more power to the people' and 'more power to planners as self-appointed guardians of the people'." To implement such an approach, they comment, "will require a fundamental rethinking within local authorities, legislative changes in parliament embracing a widening of the scope of local authorities' planning powers, and more statutory opportunities for grass-roots views to be voiced" (Bowen and Yates 1974 p.502).

Meanwhile, as far as DoE officials could tell from reviewing development plan schemes, the main factors determining the priorities for the local plans being proposed in development plan schemes in 1975 seemed to be:

> "the local situation - existence of obsolete plans and/or strong pressures for development;

> - the financial implications of the plans;

> - the availability - both in numbers and in terms of time - of suitably skilled staff;

> - the strategic importance of the plan to the county and/or region as well as the district;

> - the existence of development investment proposals which cannot be implemented without a local plan" (Mabey and Craig 1976 p.71).

To this list, other commentators added criteria which reflected local political considerations, notably the demand for equal attention to all parts of a district (Yates 1975, Whitney et al. 1976). Thus, preparing a plan for a part of a district which had a particular land use and development problem could be seen as unduly favouring that area.

The view of local planning as providing effective policies to meet community needs through efficient co-ordinative mechanisms had widespread support among practitioners at this time, and, as Cockburn (1977) suggests, linked social planning and community development initiatives with the technical rationality of structure planning exercises. Yet it was already an anachronism in the circumstances which were accelerated by local government reorganization. Political life in the new districts was increasingly organized on party political lines, with councillors less likely to accept guidance from officers, and community groups of one kind or another increasingly critical of both their councillors and officers. Consequently conflicts over ends, priorities and needs have become more evident. Meanwhile in central government financial cutbacks to what had until then been an expanding local government enterprise made the setting of priorities within local authorities a much more difficult and contentious issue. Innovative reviews initiated by planners of policies and programmes in relation to the needs of particular groups and areas are liable in such circumstances to get lost as the definition of policies and programmes becomes increasingly a matter for politicians.

Partly in response to this, many planning departments have been forced back onto their statutorily-defined territory of regulating the use and development of land. Others have moved away from policy review to initiating and progressing development projects of various kinds. Many planners have also become skeptical of the role of documents in providing policy guidance, putting much more weight on the process of policy review and relating policy to action, rather than the formal production of plans. As a consequence of this learning process about local planning, the debate about local plans has more recently focussed on the following three questions. Firstly, what is the role of area and site-based policy guidance where conflict over priorities and lack of resources creates substantial political and economic uncertainty; secondly, if this first question is answered positively, what is the value of a local plan in providing such a framework; thirdly, if a local plan is considered desirable, what is the value of preparing it in a statutory format?

2.3 The Debate About Statutory Local Plans

Some authorities, in both metropolitan and shire districts, have concluded that, while some form of policy framework for guiding development is required, possibly in the form of a site-specific framework, there is no need to become embroiled in the procedures involved in statutory plan making. These authorities are avoiding the various constraints on form and content which the statutory format appears to impose, thus operating with unfettered discretion. So what do statutory local plans offer which makes many authorities choose nevertheless to prepare them?

Statutory local plans differ only in degree from any other local authority policy statement. They are an administrative not legal device. They are advisory not mandatory in that authorities are not required to make a decision as specified in a local plan. The proposals within them, as in any other policy statement, are not legally binding on anyone. They merely carry more weight to certain parties who make significant resource decisions. But who are these parties? In some authorities, housing, education and transport departments in the districts and counties may give more credence to a statutory than to an informal policy statement. However, they are not legally impelled to take account of the provisions of any local plan, and may ignore them whether statutory or not. It is only in the context of the making and upholding of decisions on planning applications that the provisions of statutory local plans are of any importance, since in making a decision, local planning authorities are required to consider the relevant development plan. Even here, development plan policies are assessed in the light of other "material considerations" (see Chapter 2) when decisions on planning applications are made. So however much local

planners would prefer statutory local plans to "bind" the investment
decisions of other public sector agencies (see, for example, DPOS 1978) or
determine more directly the outcome of planning applications (McAuslan
1980), their main role lies in the way local planning authorities conduct
their regulative powers in relation to private sector development
initiatives. How important this role is in turn depends, firstly, on
whether any private sector development initiatives are likely to come
forward which would not be acceptable to the authority and secondly, on the
extent to which central government, through its decisions on appeal,
supports local plan policies. Thus the role of statutory local plans
depends crucially on the degree of central government support for them.

Central government, however, has not only presented ambiguous advice to
local authorities on the content of plans. It has also fluctuated in the
degree of support to be given to statutory plans. In the early 1970s,
when under pressure from development interests, the famous land
availability circulars were produced calling for the allocation of more
housing land (DoE Circulars 102/72 and 122/73). These advised authorities
to prepare informal local plans to override restrictive and allegedly
outdated old-style development plans. By the mid-1970s, the criticisms of
local authority "bottom-drawer" plans, which in many cases received no
public scrutiny, as well as the continued existence of development plans
often prepared ten to twenty years previously, led the DoE to stress the
early completion of replacement statutory local plans. Consequently they
advised local authorities that informal plans would no longer be supported
on appeal (DoE Circular 55/77; see Chapter 4). While DoE advice has
continued to stress the importance of statutory local plans for use in
appeals, it has at the same time been pressing local authorities to give
attention to other "material considerations", notably speedy and helpful
treatment of industrial applications (DoE Circular 71/77), ensuring adequate
residential land availability (DoE Circulars 44/78 and 9/80), and generally
less restrictive attitudes to development (DoE Circular 22/80). These have
cast some suspicion in the minds of authorities and developers as to how
far central government will uphold the policies and proposals in statutory
local plans.

Central government, then, appears to argue that local authority planning
policies for the use and development of land should be expressed in a
statutory local plan to provide a clear, openly-discussed and challengeable
statement of the principles by which a local authority will exercise its
planning regulation powers. Yet it is ambiguous in how far it will itself
support such principles in a plan. Several local planners also accept this
limited land use role for statutory local plans. Some argue that they will
provide a firm basis for judging planning applications and constructing
appeal cases (Wilson 1977a, Thompson 1977b); others that they will replace
outdated plans[47], or remove blight (Thompson 1977b). As Thompson states:

> "Some (local authorities) are succumbing to the allure of the
> non-statutory plan. Tempting though the freedom from statutory
> entanglements may be, this approach will not solve critical
> problems such as blight, and its champions find the going hard
> on appeals. Camden played the game and opted for a statutory
> plan" (Thompson 1977b p.148).

---

[47]Drew Stevenson of Westminster City Council, in a discussion on local
plans in London, 26 June 1977).

The District Planning Officers' Society, in their report of 1978 which reviewed the experience of local plan production in the West Midlands in relation to the arguments for and against statutory local plans, concluded that such plans had the following advantages:

"it provides a means of public scrutiny of local authorities' policies";

"it provides formal safeguards for those whose interests are affected";

"it provides a basis for corporate decisions and an aid to co-ordination";

"statutory status provides a firm basis for investment and other decisions by public authorities";

it helps on appeals (DPOS 1978 para.3.42).

It noted two other arguments sometimes put forward for statutory plans, that they "create the planning service" (i.e. provide a justification for the existence of planners other than those in development control), and that they provide a methodological discipline. Rightly they conclude that a local plan is merely a tool, to be used as part of a package of instruments to solve specified problems and achieve specified objectives. Such a tool can hardly be used to justify having a planning service. The role of planning departments is an issue of a much more general nature than the question of the selection of appropriate tools for a particular task. Nevertheless, this does not invalidate the point that the process of preparing a development guidance framework and implementing the proposals within it may itself produce more outcomes than the formal existence of the plan as a document, as will become clear in Chapter 6.

We may thus conclude that the distinctive characteristic of a statutory local plan is its role within the relationship between central government and local government over planning matters. So long as its content is more or less in line with the strategic policy of approved structure plans and is not overridden by central government policies as expressed in current circulars, statutory local plans provide a legitimacy to local planning decisions. Frequently, such legitimacy gives strength to the local planning authority in its dealings with private sector development initiatives. However, local planners and their authorities may seek to use this tool for other purposes, to provide a methodological discipline, or to legitimate an exercise in policy review or even to change a prevailing policy. In so doing, they are deflecting the statutory tool for their own particular purposes. In Chapter 8 I will consider how valuable local plans, statutory or otherwise, have been for any of these purposes. It is a sad comment on the way local planners thought about the nature of the task they were engaged in that they gave so little attention to the nature of a statutory local plan and what the tool of a local plan could be used for until experience forced them to.

To conclude, the following chart summarizes the potential uses of local plans as suggested in central government advice and in the discussion among practitioners. Since how a plan is used relates to who is using it and for what ends, I have organized the chart around different interests. Given the conclusions of the preceeding discussion, I have indicated which plans would appear to require statutory preparation in order to fulfill the purpose indicated. One may conclude from this chart firstly that many

Potential Uses of a Local Plan

Interests in whose decisions the plan to play a central role	Way plan to be used	Value of statutory format	Source
1 Internal to Local Planning Authorities	Assists in making decisions about development applications (see also 9)	(✓)	Formal local plan function DPOS 1978. Wilson 1977a, Thompson 1977b
	Replaces obsolete plans; or where confusion over plans; removes blight; clarifies policy (see also 6 and 7)	(✓)	Mabey and Craig 1976 Thompson 1977b
	Provides a methodology for local public policy review		Turton 1979 DPOS 1978
2 Other local authority departments, government depts, public agencies	Co-ordinates and provides a programme for public development investment (see also 6)	(✓)	DPOS 1978
	Forces government bodies to discuss their future intentions		Thompson 1977b
	Injecting an area and spatial dimension into sectorial programmes		Edwards 1974 Trafford 1975 Luithlen 1977
3 Providers of funds or authorization to use funds to the local authority	Enables use of related powers (e.g. CL Act)	(✓)	Local plan advice note 1/78 Mabey & Craig 1976
	Provides programme with which to bid for resources under related legislation (e.g. Inner Urban Areas Act; Housing Investment Programme)		Local plan advice note 1/78
4 County Planning Authorities	Realizes the strategy of the structure plan	(✓)	Formal local plan function
	Assists county to prepare structure plan		

Potential Uses of a Local Plan (contd)

Interests in whose decisions the plan to play a central role	Way plan to be used	Value of statutory format	Source
5 Local Authority Councillors	Demonstrates the council's interest in an area, issue, or group		Yates 1975 Whitney *et al.* 1976
	Forces attention to position of local authorities; *vis-à-vis* structure plan policies, or central government policies		
6 Land and property developers	Provides information which may make investment decisions more efficient		Thompson 1977b Drewett 1973
	Provides beneficial externalities via co-ordination of related development to mutual advantage (see also 2)	(✓)	Formal local plan function DPOS 1978
7 Public at Large	Demonstrates the rationale of government decision-making, opens local authority policy to public scrutiny	(✓)	DPOS 1978
	Provides opportunity for local people to determine/ influence future of their community		Marsh 1980
	Informs the public of local authority policy	(✓)	Formal local plan function Thompson 1977b
	Provides for 'natural justice' right of those with a property interest to object where local authority policy or proposals directly affect their interests	(✓)	Formal local plan function DPOS 1978
8 Farmers and other defenders of the countryside	Provides security of protection from development	(✓)	CC
9 Secretary of State	Assists in handling appeal decisions	(✓)	Circulars
	Assists implementation of structure plan policies as approved by SOS		

interests may perceive a benefit in the preparation of a local plan, even
of a statutory local plan; secondly, there is considerable scope for
conflict over what the purpose of the plan actually is.

3. WHY HAVE LOCAL PLANS ACTUALLY BEEN PREPARED?

The main source I have used for making an assessment of why plans have been
prepared is the plans themselves. Yet the reasons for preparing a plan
are rarely articulated clearly in plan documents. This reflects both an
assumption that preparing a local plan is necessary for itself, despite
the discretion in the legislation, and a lack of clarity as to precise
purposes. Sometimes of course, such vagueness is deliberate for political
reasons. I do not think this is always the case, however.[48] Some
indication of the implicit purpose of a plan can be obtained from careful
reading. Didcot's first interim local plan was prepared in an attempt to
force certain policies into structure plan modifications (Didcot Interim
Local Plan, South Oxfordshire DC). A key reason for preparing the Waterloo
District Plan (LB Lambeth) was to obtain Borough control over a former GLC
Comprehensive Development Area. In Eagle Street, (Coventry MB), the local
authority's policies changed from slum clearance to rehabilitation, and the
Lapworth Plan (Warwick DC) expresses the local authority and the public's
concern to resist powerful development pressures.

The problem of interpretation is further complicated by the changing way in
which issues are treated. Plan production exercises may have started off
in the 1960s for town centre redevelopment schemes, slum clearance areas
or villages, or for substantial greenfield developments in line with
regional growth proposals. Many of these exercises petered out during the
1970s as the development climate changed, but others continued, perhaps
because the local authority could not escape its commitment to preparing a
plan. One of the most remarkable conclusions to emerge from detailed
study of the history of the development of policy guidance within an area
is the long period of time over which policies have developed and the
persistance of issues to which planning departments find themselves giving
attention (Healey et al.1982a).

Because of the difficulties of determining the intentions of plans, beyond
the formal statement of purposes which very often is merely a restatement
of standard local plan functions, the following review of plan purposes
merely provides examples of the potential uses of plans listed at the end
of Section 2. Section 3.2 then explores more systematically the sorts of
areas for which local plans have been prepared.

3.1 *Origins of Local Plan Production*

(1) Factors Internal to the Local Planning Authority

Confirming DoE advice, and the land use interpretation of the role of local
plans, a large number of plans, both statutory and non-statutory were being
produced to clarify policies for development control purposes. Sometimes

---

[48]I am still at a loss to determine the purpose of Darlaston District Plan
   (Walsall MB), and while Brunswick Town District Plan (Hove DC) is
   concerned with conservation issues, I cannot discover why a statutory
   plan was considered necessary.

they were needed to replace outdated plans - where too little land has been allocated in the past (e.g. Mundford Village Plan and Dereham Policy Review (Breckland DC); Horsham Area DP (Horsham DC)); or too much (e.g. Newton-le-Willows Local Plan (St. Helens MB)); where public investment proposals had been abandoned or changed, and where areas could be released from blight, notably in a number of town centre plans; or to eliminate so called "white land" (Warwickshire CC's Green Belt Subject Plan; High Wycombe Area DP, Wycombe DC); or where an area is subject to new development pressures and a framework for determining the location of new development is needed for the first time (as in several Cornish small towns and villages). In many of these examples, a plan is used to resolve the question of which among a number of possible sites should be released for development. These are clearly all areas under some private development pressure, although several plans were attempting to reduce the amount of growth allowed for in plans of the 1960s and/or permissions of the early 1970s. In other words, they reflect local authority adjustments to reduced growth expectations.

Two other sorts of clarification are worth noting here. One is found in areas where structure plans have allocated substantial growth, and the local authority seeks to demonstrate to often critical ratepayers and constituents that the development programmed will be adequately co-ordinated and phased. Examples here are the South Hampshire growth area plans (notably Fareham Western Wards, Hampshire CC); Sutton Coldfield District Plan (Birmingham MB) and Abbey District Plan (Leicester DC). The other occurs in cases where local authority policy has changed with respect to its own developments, notably in the housing field. Several action area plans reflect the shift from clearance to rehabilitation, although in these cases the role of development control in implementing the plans is likely to be minimal. Examples here are the Eagle and Eden Street Action Area Plans (Coventry MB). More recently, authorities may be marketing former housing sites to the private sector.

Few plans appear to be justified on methodological grounds alone. Perhaps the London Borough plans could be considered as an example. Here, the strategic Greater London development plan (GLC 1976) was so general and so little addressed to the problems of the Boroughs in the 1970s, that most Boroughs believed they should undertake their own general policy review in order to derive specific policies for land use and development. This is one reason why so many are aiming to produce Borough-wide plans (see Table 4.4). Another reason is that the Boroughs until 1972 were required in legislation to prepare their own development plans, and have been reluctant to give up this task. Two other methodological reasons appear among the plans. Hoyle District Plan (Penwith DC) is justified on the grounds that since the area is newly under development pressure, it has never had the local plan "treatment" which it is assumed to be needed. Hoyle is one of the Cornish settlements referred to above. Liverpool MB undertook the Walton-Fazakerly District Plan for an area on their northern fringe as an experiment to test the value of statutory plans. They concluded that they had no value in the Liverpool area, and have not prepared any such plans since.

(2) Origins in the Demands of Other Local Authority Departments and Public Agencies

There is much less evidence of this factor leading to local plan production. The major exceptions are firstly the activities of housing departments, and secondly, where the local authority is a major landowner.

The two of course are often related as the local authority becomes an owner
of development land through purchasing for housing schemes. I have already
referred to urban renewal plans where the strategy has shifted to
rehabilitation. Several planning departments have also been closely involved
in preparing the annual Housing Investment Programme bids, which may then
feed into local plans. Where the local authority is the main landowner/
developer, as in some areas of council housing, or where local authorities
have build-for-sale programmes, or where the intention is to sell off to a
private developer, a local plan may be needed to determine the exact amount
of land to be developed, and the alignment and programming of infrastructure
(e.g. Skippindale Action Area Plan (Scunthorpe DC), Abbey District Plan
(Leicester DC), Chineham District Plan (Hampshire CC), Basford and Forest
Fields DP (Nottingham DC), Buckingham Town Plan (Aylesbury Vale DC),
Tranmere and Rock Ferry District Plan (Wirral MB)). Several plans include
areas for industrial development linked to local authority promotional
policies, (e.g. Farnworth District Plan (Bolton MB) and Rochdale Town Centre
District Plan (Rochdale MB)), but it is not clear whether any of these
originated in the need to allocate industrial land.

Several plans for small towns and villages have been initiated as a
consequence of local authority investment action in the building of bypasses
(e.g. Hadleigh District Plan (Babergh DC); Kimberley and Eastwood District
Plans (Broxtowe DC); Melbourne Village Plan (South Cambridgeshire DC)).
Finally, a number of plans are closely linked to exercises in corporate
local authority policy review. Some of these reflect the range of local
authority policies and do not confine themselves to land use matters (notably
Wandsworth Borough Plan 1st draft (LB Wandsworth); Watford Borough Plan
(Watford DC), and to some extent Gloucester City Local Plan (Gloucester DC).
These tend to be prepared for the whole authority, as might be expected.
In other instances, although informed by a corporate planning exercise, the
plan itself is confined to land use matters (e.g. Waltham Forest Borough
Plan (Waltham Forest LB) or to small areas (e.g. Eagle Street and Eden
Street (Coventry MB)).

(3) Origins in Bids for Resources

Increasingly during the 1970s, as central government has sought greater
control and direction over local authority spending, plans or policy
statements have been demanded of local authorities to justify resource bids
(Hambleton 1981). Repeatedly, planners have argued that such policy
statements should be based on development plans, since the latter provide
the only evident mechanism for co-ordinating development investment arising
from different spending programmes. Community Land Act transactions were
supposed to be based on development plans, and Transport Policies and
Programmes on structure plans. However, I have found very few examples
where such resource bids have initiated local plan production. In a few
cases, reference is made to the use of Community Land Act powers (e.g.
Rochdale Town Centre District Plan (Rochdale MB); Beckermet, Egremont and
St. Bees Village Plans (Copeland DC)), and the relationship with HIPs has
already been mentioned. In the Wirral, four non-statutory local plans were
produced as the basis for bids for Inner City programme funds. Four plans
were deposited under the Inner Urban Areas Act which, prior to 1980, allowed
statutory local plans to precede in designated areas before structure plan
approval (Farnworth DP (Bolton MB), Rochdale (Rochdale MB), Brunswick DP
(Salford MB), and Basford, Forest Fields (Nottingham DC), but all these were
probably initiated well in advance of the legislation, and were not directly
linked to resource bids. Finally, the few Countryside Management Plans may
have been prepared with Countryside Commission grants in mind. The Loose

Valley Draft District Plan (Maidstone DC) arose itself out of a Countryside Management Project, and plans for derelict land may have provided extra support in bidding for derelict land grants. Several other river valley local plans have been attempts to co-ordinate the investments of several local authorities and their departments rather than a direct bid for resources (e.g. the Mersey and Medlock River Valley Subject Plans (Greater Manchester CC)).

In very few cases can it be said that the demand for a policy framework for projects when bidding for resources actually initiated the preparation of a local plan. If a local plan already existed, it probably provided useful data, policy background and proposals, when bidding for resources. If one was not available, the timescale of most finance bids would have precluded the preparation of a plan specifically for a bid. Exceptions here are the Wirral plans already referred to, and the East Moors District Plan (Cardiff DC), which was produced in response to the unexpected closure in 1978 of a major steelworks. In this case, the production of the plan was closely linked to obtaining resource commitments from the Welsh Development Agency and the Land Authority for Wales. However, as we will see in Chapter 6, the activity of plan preparation has often been important in *obtaining* resource commitments from other departments and agencies for particular projects.

(4)   The Structure Plan as Initiator of Local Plans

A first glance at many plans suggests that the policies of the structure plan are a major factor leading to local plan preparation. All statutory action area plans originated in structure plans, until the legislation was altered in the 1980 Local Government, Planning and Land Act. Local plans are often referred to in structure plans to determine the specific amounts and locations of structure plan proposals, to define boundaries to protective zonings (such as green belts), to co-ordinate substantial growth (as in Abbey District Plan (Leicester DC), Fareham Western Wards, (Hampshire CC), or to work out various forms of key settlement policy in rural areas (e.g. Markfield District Plan (Hinkley and Bosworth DC); Coleorton and Ashley Woulds District Plans (North West Leicestershire DC)). This appears to suggest that the hierarchical sequence of plan production does operate in practice. Perhaps the best example can be found in South Hampshire, where growth areas as part of the South East regional strategy were defined in 1972 in a general way in the structure plan. Further land within these areas was not to be released until local plans had been adopted. The first was not in fact adopted until 1979. Yet this sequential relation between structure plan policies and local plan development seems to have been unusual. Many of the growth areas and green belts were defined before structure plans were prepared and were merely translated into structure plan terms. Far from determining priorities for local plan preparation, some structure plans merely contained what districts already perceived as their priorities.

A few plans started life in order to contribute to the formation of structure plan policies as the experience of Oxfordshire illustrates. Oxfordshire opted for directing growth to selected small towns to relieve the pressure for housing and industrial development in Oxford and the rural areas. The Vale of White Horse District Council actively sought growth for Wantage and Abingdon, with plans for expansion in both towns proceeding in parallel with the structure plan. Meanwhile neighbouring South Oxfordshire was less happy about receiving further growth particularly at Didcot where there was an insatiable demand for cheap commuter housing when the town was

brought within 45 minutes of central London via the High Speed Train. South
Oxfordshire produced a plan for Didcot premised on limited growth. Both the
Vale and South Oxfordshire Districts aimed via their plans to determine the
content of the structure plan. The County, and subsequently the Secretary
of State, preferred growth at Didcot rather than Wantage, which meant that
plan-making had in effect to start all over again (Caddy 1981). Further
confusion has arisen in some areas over the modifications to structure
plans. In Wycombe District where development pressures and policy
uncertainty were sufficient during structure plan preparation to warrant
the preparation of a "Residential" Subject Plan to define which of a number
of white land sites would be released, and where progress was well under
way towards a district plan for a substantial part of the district, the
preparation of the district plan was halted for two years while the County
determined the distribution among the districts of the additional housing
totals inserted into the structure plan by the Secretary of State's
modifications. The county was given a maximum of two years to make this
determination, and for political reasons took this amount of time.

Finally, some counties with approved structure plans seem to have prepared
very few local plans (compare Diagram 3.3 with Diagram 4.1). Why have so
few plans been deposited in the West Midlands or Cleveland, compared to
Greater London? Why have so many plans been deposited in Leicestershire,
Hampshire and Staffordshire and so few in East Sussex? The answer is
complex, relating to the nature of each authority's problems and its
attitude and approach to local plans, but it is worth noting that the
initiation in a structure plan of a policy change requiring spatial
definition does not of itself mean that a local plan providing that
definition will be quickly produced. It is for this reason that many
counties have attempted to produce local plans as holding devices, as with
green belt subject plans. However, as we shall see in Chapter 6, this
produces its own problems.

(5) Local Political Demands for a Local Plan

Although councillors have been actively involved in the preparation of
some local plans, and have expressed other views on occasion as to the
content of such plans, I have no evidence of councillors actually
initiating a local plan. Local councillors and interest groups which
exert political pressure have frequently influenced the agenda of problems
or areas for attention. Planners have then put forward a local plan as a
tool for acting on the problem. As a result, councillors and citizens may
then be drawn into the preparation process. Councillors in some areas have
certainly had views on the areas for priority local plan attention (Yates
1975; Whitney et al. 1976), and at Wandsworth demanded a complete revision
of the local plan to reflect Conservative views after a local election. A
similar demand has been made by recently-elected left wing Labour
councillors in relation to the North Southwark district plan. However,
there is more evidence of councillor disinterest in and active hostility to
local plan preparation than of active initiation of plans (Healey 1977).
Chapter 6 explores further the role of councillors in plan preparation.

(6) Origins in the Demands of Developers

The extent to which development interests have been responsible for
initiating local plan preparation is difficult to assess. I deliberately
excluded development briefs from my review of plans, though some local

plans contain development briefs within them. For a few, the distinction
is difficult to make (e.g. Elmdon Heath/Lugtrout Lane/Wheretts Well Lane
Action Area Plan (Solihull MB); Holme Action Area Plan (Scunthorpe DC)).
Such development briefs assist the local authority in managing its relations
with private sector or other public sector interests on a major development
site. In several cases it is likely that the site concerned was identified
initially by development interests. I came across a number of cases where
developers brought forward large development sites, using private
consultants often acting on behalf of a consortium of developers, to
prepare a small area plan and development brief (e.g. Central Berkshire;
Thornhill District Plan (Cardiff DC)). There were of course a large
number of cases where the intentions in preparing a plan were to strengthen
the local planning authority's hand in resisting development pressures.
As I will suggest later, development interests have been a pervasive but not
necessarily visible influence on local plan preparation. Plans often
contain general policies which express community interests, but the sites
which are allocated for specific uses and projects may have arrived in the
plan by a quite different route from that suggested by the plan.

(7)   Farmers, Defenders of the Countryside and the Public

These three groupings, though often with conflicting interests in how land
should be used and developed, have been grouped together since a common
mutual concern is to resist further development. There is much evidence,
to be discussed in Chapter 6, that the public have played a considerable
role in plan preparation. In a few cases, they have been substantially
responsible for plan policies (e.g. Covent Garden Action Area Plan (GLC),
Lapworth District Plan (Warwick DC), and in two cases in Warrington DC
(Rixton Brickworks and Walton Park)) appeared to have demanded the plans.
In the former case, the council were fighting a High Court case against
the construction company, Christian Salvesen, concerning the use of the
derelict brickworks for tipping purposes. Even if there are few cases
where members of the public singly or collectively have actually initiated
a plan, there is evidence that many people, perhaps those who live in more
affluent and environmentally attractive areas, consider a local plan a
desirable product for their areas. It is also likely that local planning
authorities may feel the need of a plan where land for development is to be
allocated for one reason or another, and local hostility to this is
expected. A local plan can thus, as suggested earlier, legitimate the
authority's position. Farmers' interests are usually well-protected by the
Ministry of Agriculture, although the National Farmers' Union has supported
the preparation of local plans.

(8)   The Secretary of State

Although central government retains the power to direct the production of a
local plan, this power has not yet been employed. Since central government
ministers are currently skeptical of plans, a formal direction is currently
an unlikely occurrence. However, there is circumstantial evidence to
suggest that DoE Regional officers have advised certain local authorities
quite firmly that they should prepare plans, if they want their policies
upheld on appeal.

To conclude, it can be suggested that despite the wide range of factors
which could initiate the preparation of a local plan, the most important
factors have been those which relate to the way a planning department sees
its role and function. It is planning officers who suggest that the

preparation of a local plan could further the purposes of an authority,
rarely other interests which impose such preparation on the authority.
This might be seen as giving considerable discretion to local planners
to determine the content of plans. However, most of the examples already
quoted suggest that local plan preparation is quite closely tied to land
and development issues, despite planners' grander ambitions. This
suggestion is confirmed in the next section.

3.2 *The Types of Problems to which Plans are Directed*

The previous section considered the reasons why plan preparation was
undertaken in relation to the agencies and groups likely to perceive some
value to their interests in preparing a plan. If most plans relate to
land and development issues, then one factor influencing plan preparation
is clearly the nature of the land use and development issues which an
authority faces in its area. However, there is not necessarily a direct
correlation between a particular type of issue and the preparation of a
plan. As the previous section illustrates, plans may be prepared because
the public demands them, because councillors wish to see all parts of their
authority receive the same "planning treatment", or because officers wish
to demonstrate the role of a local plan. Nevertheless, identifying the
issue(s) with which local plans are concerned provides an important
objective assessment of what local plan preparation is about, to set against
the previous discussion of apparent intentions. To make such an assessment
I have produced a simple typology of "land use and development issues",
developed from the suggestions given in formal advice and from what emerged
from an initial review of all the plans I have seen. In constructing it, I
have attempted to interrelate the types of locations involved with the nature
of the development processes active in the area, and with local authority
policy. Of the 274 plans in my collection, I have been able to allocate
228 (83%) to a specific issue within the typology. In what follows I
discuss the typology first, and then provide an assessment of which issues
appear to be associated with most plans (Tables 5.1 and 5.2).

3.3 *Land Use and Development Issues for Which Local Plans might be Prepared*

1. Areas under Heavy Development Pressures, where the Local Authority
    Seeks to Contain and Restrict Market Operations

These are the areas for which development plans have traditionally been of
major significance, from the Town Planning Schemes of the 1932 Act to the
planning studies reviewing old-style development plans of so many areas on
the outer margin of metropolitan areas in the 1960s. I have divided this
category into 3 subgroups:

(a) The city centre/inner city boundary

Here high value central city uses might be expected encroaching on areas of
low income housing and older industrial firms. I have only come across 3
plans of this nature, all in London (see Table 5.1). Some of the inner
London Borough-wide plans also contain policies for this kind of area
(notably Camden Borough, and Hammersmith and Fulham Borough Plans). Within
London, these plans cover some of the most contentious development sites,
notably Coin Street and Hay's Wharf, in the area of Waterloo and North

TABLE 5.1

Types of area/issue	Met. counties/ GLC	Counties	Met. districts	London boroughs	County districts	Total	%
Areas under heavy development pressure							
a. City centre/inner city boundary	-	-	-	3	-	3	1.3
b. Immediate urban fringe	3	4	3	-	6	16	7.0
c. Outer urban fringe/small farms/villages under commuter pressures	-	2	1	-	29	32	14.0
a. Major growth areas	-	2	-	-	3	5	2.2
b. Minor growth areas	-	1	1	-	23	25	11.0
Opportunity sites	2	-	6	4	6	18	7.9
Town centre plans	-	1	8	9	24	42	18.3
Areas of open land	1	6	1	-	7	15	6.6
Inner city areas	-	-	9	1	6	16	7.0
Areas with a large industrial content	-	-	-	1	2	3	1.3
Small towns	-	1	1	-	14	16	7.0
Villages	-	-	-	-	13	13	5.7
Plans for substantial urbanized areas	-	-	1	13	3	17	7.5
Other	-	2	1	-	4	7	3.1
Total	6	19	32	31	140	228	99.9

Note: The plans on which this anlaysis is based are all those within my review of plans for which an issue of concern could be identified

TABLE 5.2

Types of area/issue	Met. counties/ GLC	Counties	Met. districts	London boroughs	County districts	Total	%
Areas under heavy development pressure							
a. City centre/inner city boundary	-	-	-	1	-	1	1.0
b. Immediate urban fringe	-	-	2	-	2	4	4.1
c. Outer urban fringe/small farms/villages under commuter pressure	-	1	1	-	8	10	10.2
a. Major growth areas	-	2	-	-	1	3	3.1
b. Minor growth areas	-	1	1	-	11	13	13.3
Opportunity sites	1	-	3	3	2	9	9.2
Town centre plans	-	-	2	8	12	22	22.5
Areas of open land	-	3	-	-	3	6	6.1
Inner city areas	-	-	4	-	1	5	5.1
Areas with large industrial content	-	-	-	-	2	2	2.0
Small towns	-	1	-	-	3	4	4.1
Villages	-	-	-	-	4	4	4.1
Plans for substantial urbanized areas	-	-	-	10	1	11	11.2
Other	-	2	1	-	1	4	4.1
Total	1	10	14	22	51	98	100.1

Note: The plans analysed here are all those deposited as statutory plans by the end of 1980 for which an issue of concern could be identified.

Southwark District Plans. In Chapter 8, I will discuss the role of these
plans in relation to conflicts on specific sites. At this point, it is
worth noting that I have found no example of such plans outside London, nor
of similar situations within plans for larger parts of cities. This is no
doubt because only London now has substantial pressures for central city
expansion.

(b)   The immediate urban fringe

This is similarly an area in which substantial development gains can be
realized by converting open land into developed land. Due to the long
history of containment policy (see Chapter 2), nearly all larger towns and
cities in England have long-standing policies and plans regulating the
details of this conversion process, often by the use of green belts.
Sixteen plans were identified for this sort of area, 7 of them in
preparation by shire or metropolitan counties. Several of these are aimed
at making necessary adjustments to green belt boundaries consequent upon
structure plan policies. In many cases the adjustments to the inner edge
of green belts are likely to be very small indeed since anything other
than major inroads on green belts are likely to have already been made.

(c)   The outer urban fringe, and small towns and villages under commuter,
      tourist and retirement pressures

It is these areas which are experiencing the effects of the continuing
decentralization of people and firms, from conurbation cores. This has
been particularly marked in the south, as the 1981 Census shows. However,
the collection of plans includes examples from the Midlands and Cheshire.
Twenty-nine or 14% of all the plans were in this category, and there were
possibly more which for lack of evidence have been classified as small
towns (8) or villages (9). It seems reasonable to conclude from this that
these decentralizing processes and the development pressures they create
have been responsible for generating considerable work on local plans.
The proliferation of village plans in the 1960s was of course in part a
response to these same processes, if not always realized as such.

2. Major and Minor Growth Areas

In these areas planning policy has sought to concentrate the growth which
would otherwise be scattered among small towns and villages as above.
Several of the larger "growth areas" which persist from the 1960s were
managed through New Town Development Corporations and so do not appear as
local plans. Elsewhere, such growth is being managed using local authority
planning powers. In Central Berkshire, substantial growth is being managed
by a series of development briefs and small local plans. In South Hampshire,
by contrast, it is felt that local plans were needed to determine which
sites to allocate before development briefs are drawn up. The reason for
the difference in treatment appears to be that in Central Berkshire the
development sites had already been identified and could be listed in the
structure plan. In South Hampshire, the sites had to be selected. Yet,
very few local plans have been found which can reasonably be said to relate
to major growth areas. Apart from those in Central Berkshire and South
Hampshire, the only others were the Abbey District Plan (Leicester DC) and
Ashford District Plan (Ashford DC). These plans really only differ in
degree from the much larger group where a small amount of growth is proposed
in structure plans. Local plans are then produced to allocate this. Many
of these are for small towns and villages in areas under development
pressure, which differ only from category 1c in that some growth is to be

allowed (e.g. Groby, Markfield and Ratby District Plans in Leicestershire,
Southam District Plan in Warwickshire and Chineham District Plan
(Basingstoke DC)). A few are towns which formerly had a Town Development
Act expansion agreement (e.g. Banbury, (Cherwell DC) and Tamworth (Tamworth
DC)). Thirty plans or 23% of plans were in this category, 5 (group A) for
major growth areas, 25 (group B) in minor growth areas.

3. Opportunity Sites

I have used this category to cover three sorts of situations.

(a) "Prime development sites", notably around motorway junctions, where
there are substantial development pressures. The three examples found here
were Bickenhill/Marston Green DP (West Midlands CC), Oldbury with Langley
DP (Sandwell MB) and Enderby/Narborough DP (Blaby DC). The first two are
within conurbation areas. The third is at the junction of the M1 and M69
and involves allocating housing and industrial land while protecting areas
of high agricultural value. Clearly, several more such sites were included
within larger plans. Many authorities would be more likely to use a
development brief than a local plan for this kind of site.

(b) The second group consists of sites where a major development opportunity
had been created by the removal of a particular land-using activity from an
area, such as the removal of docks downstream (Bristol Docks Local Plan)
or the transfer of markets to larger sites (Covent Garden Action Area Plan
is the most famous example here). Seven plans in this group were identified.

(c) Thirdly, several plans have been produced for sites which have the
potential for development, particularly for commercial or industrial
purposes, but where there is no evidence of current development interest in
them. Eight plans in this category were identified, including Beckton
District Plan (LB Newham) and the Local Plan for Wapping (LB Tower Hamlets)
for part of the Docklands area; rundown inner city areas with land which
could possibly be used to attract industry (Clough Street Action Area
(Burnley DC), Darlaston District Plan (Walsall MB)); and urban fringe areas
in the north west which might attract housing and industrial investment
(Walton - Fazarkly District Plan (Liverpool MB); Newton-le-Willows District
Plan (St. Helens MB)). This group of plans merely expresses the hope that
economic investment might take place if available land were presented to
potential investors more positively through the medium of a plan.

4. Town Centre Plans

Forty-one (22.5%) town centre plans were identified, but the town centres
presented different sorts of problems. Several involved urban renewal where
substantial private investment had been underway for some time. In these
cases, the plan was a continuation of earlier informal plans or Town Maps of
the 1960s. Elsewhere, the problems were mainly concerned with traffic
management. In 9 plans, conservation of a historic core was the primary
concern. (Two Conservation Area plans are included here, Brunswick Town
(Hove DC), and Widcombe Priority Area (Bath DC)). In 6, the primary concern
was with revitalizing run-down centres. All these were in metropolitan
districts, and could also be included as inner city plans.

5. Areas of Open Land

This category excludes plans concerned with defining the green belt, but includes those concerned with: (1) areas of dereliction following mineral working (e.g. Ryton/Greenside Quarries Subject Plan (Tyne and Wear MC); Rixton Brickworks Subject Plan (Warrington DC)); (2) programming of mineral excavations and afteruse (3 plans, 2 being Minerals Subject Plans); (3) dealing with potentially-conflicting open land uses (e.g. Dungeness Countryside Subject Plan for Agriculture and Conservation, Sand and Gravel (Kent CC); Development on the Lincolnshire Coast Subject Plans (Lincolnshire CC)); and (4) Countryside Management Plans (5 plans - 4 were for river valleys. The fifth, Walton Park Subject Plan (Warrington DC) is for a large area of parkland, mostly owned by the local authority). Counties had a major involvement here, producing 7 out of the total of 15 plans.

6. Inner City Areas

I have already suggested that category 1a and 6 of the plans in category 4 might properly be considered as concerned with inner city areas. Similarly, several of the large area plans (category 10) also cover inner city areas, especially in London. In addition, 16 plans for specifically inner city problems were discovered. Six of these were not in London or the metropolitan districts, but in large towns in the shire counties. Three had made use of the special provisions in the Inner Urban Areas Act. (The fourth Inner Urban Areas Act plan, Rochdale, is a rundown Town Centre.)

7. Areas with a Large Industrial Content

This category has been included because it is referred to in Advice Note 1/78. However, although several plans in other categories included land allocations for industry (e.g. the growth areas (category 2), inner city plans (category 6) and the large area plans (category 10), very few were solely confined to industrial matters. One was an Employment Subject Plan (LB Lewisham), an attempt at converting a "topic" paper into a plan. Another was a small industrial action area (Bardon, North West Leicestershire)).

8. and 9. Small towns and Villages

Twenty-nine plans fell into these two categories, 13% of the total. Most were concerned with small scale land allocations and traffic problems. A few village plans were for groups of villages, some where growth was to be encouraged and others where it was to be restricted (e.g. Ashby Woulds and Coleorton District Plans (North West Leicestershire DC)). One village had grown substantially since the 1960s but had no adequate centre (Broughton Astley Central Area Action Area (Harborough DC)). Another plan was concerned with the deteriorating environment of a declining village (Swinefleet District Plan, (Boothberry DC)). The number of these small area/small settlement plans raises questions about the appropriate size of plan areas. The DoE has been particularly concerned about the numbers of small area plans being produced. I return to this issue in Chapter 6.

10. Plans for Substantial Urban Areas

By way of contrast with the previous category, 17 plans (7.5%), were
produced for the whole of an urban local authority's area or a substantial
part of it. Thirteen of these plans were in London, following the example
set by the London Borough of Camden. Outside London, I have come across
few equivalent examples, and those I did find were for areas where
considerable development interest is to be expected in any sites the
authorities concerned allocate in the plans (Greater Chester (DC),
Gloucester City (DC), and Watford (DC)). It is worth noting that the
metropolitan districts have not followed the London example, typically
producing small area local plans.

11. Other

Finally 6 plans could not be allocated to any category and are listed below
out of interest:

Intensive Livestock Units Subject Plan (Humberside CC),
for a distinctive category of "development" (Deposited).

Severn Gorge District Plan (Shropshire CC),
for a collection of industrial archaelogy sites (Deposited).

Longford Action Area (Coventry MB); clarifying the allocation
of housing land in a rundown industrial village, given
the fixing of a roadline (Deposited)

Askam and Ireleth District Plan (Barrow-in-Furness DC).
Industrial dereliction in an area of high landscape value
(status unclear).

Grimsby/Cleethorpes Population and Housing Subject Plan (Grimsby DC).
Reallocation of housing land (status unclear).

Local Plan for South Oxford (Oxford City DC). Mixture of inner
city and urban fringe issues (status unclear. To be
incorporated in Oxford City District Plan).

Rossendale District Plan (Rossendale DC). Declining industrial
settlement, suffering poor housing, high unemployment,
and environmental dereliction (Deposited).

I make no claim to comprehensiveness in the collection of plans I have
reviewed. Nor are the 228 plans examined necessarily a representative
sample of all local plans prepared during the 1970s. Nevertheless, there is
never likely to be comprehensive information available. If we make the
albeit shaky assumption that these plans do bear some relation to the total
effort in local plan preparation at this time, then Table 5.1 gives us some
indication of the issues with which local plans were most likely to be
concerned. Perhaps two fifths were for small towns and villages in areas
beyond the conurbations, mostly under development pressure (categories 1c,
2, 8 and 9). Another fifth were for town centres, and around 15% were for
inner city areas and large urban complexes. When we examine plans deposited
as statutory plans we are on firmer ground in drawing conclusions, since the
universe of deposited plans is known. Of the 83% which could be allocated
to a category, a very similar pattern was found as with all plans (Table 5.2)

This strongly suggests that local plans are being prepared, as the PAG Report and DoE advice has consistently advised, where land use and development change is taking place. Two qualifications must be made to this conclusion. Firstly, outside London, local plans for inner city areas are not common and are typically for very small areas. This suggests that local plans are seen as less relevant to areas where change is occurring as a result of economic decline and disinvestment, although often produced as part of a long tradition of small area plans in those areas often associated with housing renewal programmes. Secondly, it is difficult to assess how many areas in total are experiencing the same problems as identified plans are addressing, but yet plans are not perceived as necessary.

4. CONCLUSIONS

From this albeit patchy account of why local plans are being prepared, we may conclude that a substantial number, whether statutory or not, are directed at the traditional task associated with land use planning, that of marginally adjusting market pressures for development, containing them within compact settlements and keeping them limited in their local impact. In other words, local plans are managing the local adjustments necessary to the continuing implicit national settlement strategy of contained urban dispersal we have had since 1947 (Hall et al. 1973). Despite changes in regional policy in the mid-1970s aimed at reversing policies and market strategies which accelerated dispersal from the conurbations, despite attempts to retain economic activity within inner city areas, and despite the apparently restrictive policies of many of the plans for small towns and villages, there is no sign that the way land is being allocated in local plans is more than marginally affecting these dispersal trends. As we will see, most restrictive plans contain let-out policies for local needs which would allow further development. Successive Secretaries of State have in any case relaxed plans which were seen to be restrictive. In this, of course, local plans were usually continuing the direction of planning policy set by structure plans.

Meanwhile, within the conurbation areas, local authorities were either still concerned with the problems of restructuring or conserving town centres, with the problems of industrial disinvestment, or with coping with the consequences of their own clearance programmes of the 1960s, especially where these were overtaken by public expenditure cutbacks in housing finance. Apart from the few town centres where private sector development interest in shopping and offices continued, and these were mostly in the south, local authority policies within these conurbations have been to attract investment, whether in infrastructure, housing and environmental improvement, or, more fundamentally in economic activity. While it is known that local plans can perform a function in allocating land among competing users, it is not at all clear whether there is any value in plans where no interested users are in sight, except perhaps to legitimize a change in policy from that embodied in development plans of twenty years ago.

It looks then as if local plans are in fact being used to clarify land allocation policies. Perhaps this is all one might expect a site-specific guidance framework to do. But it is hardly what was envisaged in the ambitions of local planners in the mid-1970s. This leaves a question as to whether this apparent conformity with central government advice has occurred because local authorities have deferred to it or given in to central government pressure. To the extent that a statutory local plan is

useful to a local authority because it is likely that the policies within it
will be supported by Inspectors and the Secretary of State on appeal, this
may be the case. But a more significant though ill-recognized influence has
been the underlying economic and social processes which have led to what is
in effect dispersed suburbanization and conurbation disinvestment. It is
these processes which have created the problems to which local authorities
have had to address themselves. They have also produced the pressures,
from industrial and house building lobbies for example, on central
government which have affected the formulation of its advice on the content
of local planning policies. In other words, the *appearance* of the operation
of hierarchical policy control in the planning system is produced by
underlying processes affecting all levels of that system.

What is striking about the plans themselves, and local planners' discussions
of their task during the 1970s, is how little attention has been given by
planners to these underlying processes. Local planning authorities,
particularly the districts, tend to see their situations as unique, rather
than part of processes affecting a region or the nation as a whole. They
also, as noted earlier, tend to present policies and proposals as the
outcome of considering community demands and needs, rather than as the
responses to the pressures from development interests which they often are.
I will explore the way various influences are brought to bear on the
content of local plans in detail in Chapters 6 and 7. I return to the
possible reasons for this demeanour of innocence about social and economic
process and spatial change in Chapter 9. At this point, I merely note that
such innocence is rapidly disappearing from planning departments in areas
most severely affected by recession, largely in response to political
demands from central and local government to find innovative alternatives
to conventional planning policies.

Local Plan Production

1. THE FORMAL PROCEDURES

In this Chapter I will be concerned with the processes through which local plans are produced. In effect, I am exploring a particular example of the formulation of policy guidance and the definition of projects and proposals within local government. It might be expected that the way authorities formulated their policy guidance in relation to land and development matters might vary very considerably, reflecting the social and economic differences between areas and the political and organizational differences among local authorities. However, if such guidance is to be prepared in the form of a statutory local plan, and the previous chapter has suggested situations where this may be the case, authorities have to follow sets of procedures laid down by central government in legislation and accompanying regulations. The following notes summarize what is involved:

Formal Requirements	Comment
Having decided to prepare a local plan, (or been directed to by the Secretary of State),	No such direction has occurred. The LGPL Act 1980 removes the Secretary of State's power to direct the content of plans. A draft circular on Development Plans of March 1981 made the contentious proposal that DoE regional offices should agree the need for (and hence content) of local plans with local authorities. The final version requires local authorities to discuss the need for plans with regional offices (Circular 23/81).
the planning authority "may, if necessary, carry out further survey work in addition to that carried out by the county planning authority during preparation of the plan".	

The authority must also "take such steps as will, in their opinion, secure:

(a) that adequate publicity is given in the area in question to relevant matters from a report of any survey carried out ... and to matters they propose to include in the plan;

(b) that persons who may be expected to want to make representations about the matters proposed to be included in the plan are aware that they may do so; and

(c) that such persons are given the opportunity for making representations".

These representations must be considered by the planning authority; which must also consult the county planning authority (or the district for county prepared plans) "with respect to the content of the plan" and "afford that authority a reasonable opportunity to express their views, and take these views into consideration".

The completed plan (consisting of a written statement and a map on an ordnance survey base), accompanied by a certificate of conformity with the structure plan where the plan is district-prepared, has to be put on deposit for public inspection with this fact advertized.

Copies of the plan, the certificate of conformity and a statement on how the authority has carried out the requirements for publicity must be sent to the Secretary of State,

who may direct the local authority not to proceed to adoption if he is

The LGPL Act 1980 removes the requirement to publicize matters arising out of a survey. This removes the suggestion that two stages of consultation, on survey and on issues and proposals may be required.

The LGPL Act 1980 extends the provision of the Inner Urban Areas Act 1978 for deposit and adoption of local plans prior to structure plan approval. This can only be done with the Secretary of State's approval, and the plan must conform with county policies. If structure plans subsequently alter these policies this will be stated in the structure plan. An adopted local plan will then be declared as not in conformity.

The LGPL Act 1980 removes the Secretary of State's power to direct where the plan is to be publicized and the form of the publicity statement.

This has so far happened in one case the Waterloo District Plan which, anomalously, was based on extensive not satisfied with the publicity procedures.

'public participation.

The planning authority "may, and shall where relevant objections are made in accordance with the regulations, hold a public local inquiry or other hearing". The inquiry must then be held by "a person appointed by the Secretary of State".

The LGPL Act 1980 allows objections to be dealt with by written representations if all parties are agreed.

Currently all have been from the Planning Inspectorate.

The authority must consider this person's report of the inquiry, "decide whether or not to take action in the light of the report and on each of its recommendations" and make a statement of these discussions, which must be available for public inspection. If modifications to the plan are proposed, these in turn must be advertized, objections received and a possible further inquiry held. When all this has been done, the planning authority is then in a position to adopt the plan.

Three such second inquiries had been held or proposed by the end of 1981: Sutton Coldfield DP (Birmingham MBC), Westminster BP (Westminster LB), Wigston DP (Oadby and Wigston DC).

See DoE 1979 (Circular 4/79) Annex B paras. 9-27; Local Government Planning and Land Act 1980.

There are two important general points to stress about these procedures. Firstly, they derive from a view which sees the definition of planning policy as part of a linear process, starting with the formulation of national and regional policy, followed by the articulation of such policy with local authority strategic concerns into a spatial strategy, the structure plan. This is then worked up in detail in local plans to provide guidance for development control. Yet as much of recent public policy literature stresses, such linear processes of policy formulation are not commonly found in local authorities. The formulation of policy is an ongoing and evolving affair, not necessarily marked by formal statements of changes of direction. Evolving policies are brought to bear on and in turn are affected by day-to-day decisions on both routine matters and occasional projects and enterprises which authorities may be involved in. Thus the reality of policy formulation in contemporary British local government is more of an interactive than a linear process (Barrett and Fudge 1981, Healey 1982b section 2).

This interactive process takes on an interorganizational dimension in the planning field, since the procedures, following the linear model, allow for the influence of one public sector organization on the content of the policy of another. Central government influences the content of structure plans; counties influence the content of district local plans. If the linear process worked well, central government would have little concern over the

content of local plans. Where it does not, then central government may
have to cast a closer eye on the content of local plans than in theory is
necessary. One issue to be explained in this chapter is, therefore, how
effectively the hierarchical control model has worked in imposing central
government and county interests on the form and content of local plans.

The second point to note about the procedures is that they embody
instructions to the authority as to the way policy guidance should be
formulated. Policies and proposals should be based on adequate information
(survey), have evidence of the consideration of a wide range of interests
and have wide support (consultation), and should afford interests affected
by particular proposals, the opportunity to object. Compared with the
requirements for the production of other policy statements by local
authorities, such as those accompanying bids for housing and transport
finance (HIPs and TPPs), these procedures are more complex and require much
more consultations, public debate and scrutiny. I will consider in Chapter
9 why local plan preparation is so encumbered in this way. However, these
procedures express three different models of policy formation: a technical
one, based on analysis and issue identification by experts; a consultative
one with a range of possible forms of consultation; and a semi-judicial one,
where local authority policies are debated and scrutinized in an apparently
objective arena[49].

The important question to explore in relation to any such procedures is
what their effect is upon the content of policy; in particular, do they
systematically give or deny access to interests differentially or are they
neutral. Further, since exactly how legislative procedures are to operate
is always open to interpretation, who controls that interpretation, with
what possible effects on the content of policy? This chapter thus explores
the interrelation between the processes by which plans are produced, the
content of debate about policies and proposals, and the interests which may
have access to and influence over these debates.

This chapter is divided into two main sections. The first considers the
process of plan preparation, up to the production of an approved plan by the
local authority. The second deals with plan scrutiny and applies to
deposited plans only. However, these processes of plan production take
place over timescales which are often prolonged. The next section provides
an indication of how long it has taken to prepare plans, as a context for
the rest of the chapter.

2. THE TIMESCALE OF PLAN PRODUCTION

What studies there are of plan production seem to indicate that many plans
have taken an inordinately long time in preparation, and that this length
cannot be related in any simple way to cumbersome procedures, delays in
structure plan approval, the type of authority preparing the plan or the
type of issue being considered. Hampshire county planners, when working
on their structure plan hoped to have local plans for the major growth areas
approved by 1975-76 (Brown (1974)) (see Diagram 6.1). In fact the first
was not approved until 1979. The delays here can be attributed to the time

---

[49] Regan (1978) makes a distinction between the professional, technical and
judicial elements of the planning system. This ignores the consultative
elements, which, as I will show, are of considerable importance.

taken by the DoE to approve the structure plan, problems over infrastructure, changed investment intentions among those with development interests, combined with increased public resistance to the scale of growth proposed and the way the county proposed to service it (Healey 1982c).

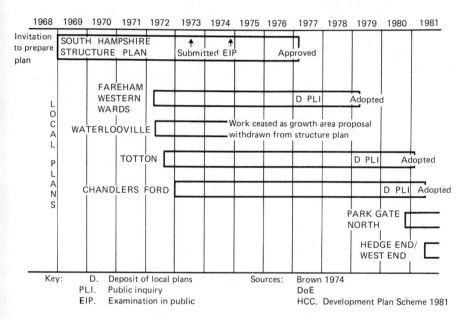

Diagram 6.1. South Hampshire: Progress on the Growth Area Local Plan

The situation in London during the 1970s has been little better. Fifteen of the 33 London Boroughs claimed to be preparing Boroughwide District Plans around 1975 (Healey 1977). The Greater London Development Plan was approved in 1976, yet only one Borough Plan had been deposited by 1977, 5 more by the end of 1979 and 3 more by the end of 1980. The plan deposited first, Camden's Boroughwide Plan, was produced in the remarkably short time of two years, although this was only possible because of the amount of background work on studies, plans and policies already existing (Fudge 1982). Others have taken 6 (Hammersmith) or 7 (Westminster) years to prepare. Several Boroughs have been working on plan production since the late 1960s in one way or another, and still no statutory plan has been forthcoming (e.g. Enfield, and Redbridge), although the circumstances of London have been rather different from that of the rest of the country. Nine Boroughs proposing Boroughwide plans or large-area borough plans were still in the preparation stages by the end of 1980.

Vine's study of four small towns in the Midlands, which one might imagine presented less complex problems, demonstrates that these too have taken around four years in each case from initiation to deposit or equivalent (see Diagram 6.2). In only one case (Towcester, South Northamptonshire DC) can the delay be related to belated structure plan approval, and here the authority was advised two years before approval that their plan did not meet the statutory requirements (Vine 1980). In my review of plans, however, I identified a considerable number of plans which were either halted awaiting structure plan approval (e.g. Church DP (Hyndburn DC) and Rossendale DP

(Rossendale DC in Lancashire)), or where a policy dispute between the
county and district invalidated work on a local plan (see Caddy 1981).

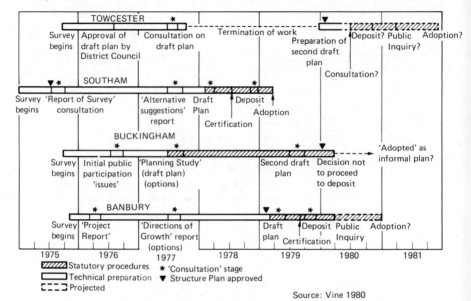

Diagram 6.2.   Progress on Selected Country Towns Local Plans
in the Midlands

My own data on the timescale of plan preparation is too sketchy to allow
quantification, but indicates that no simple generalizations can be made.
The recent survey of 10 local planning authorities by Fudge et al. (1982a)
reaches a similar conclusion.   A survey of the local plan preparation in
the West Midlands suggested an overall preparation time of 21 months (DPOS
1978), and another by Couch gives 2 years, 7 months (Couch 1978).   Perhaps
the most reliable estimate is provided by recent work by Bruton et al.
(1982) on a number of statutory local plans which have reached adoption
stage.   This gives a "typical" production time of over four years, with
three years up to deposit, and a year and a quarter from deposit to
adoption (Table 6.1).   Such an average, however, masks the very
considerable difference between plans that required an inquiry and ones
that did not (Table 6.2).

Fifty-five plans had been adopted by the end of 1980.   The average time
taken from deposit to adoption was 15 months, though some took less than 6
months and others 2 years or more.   Only one third of plans were adopted
without an inquiry, and most of those without an inquiry have so far been
small area plans.   Those adopted most quickly so far have been Bishops
Itchington DP and Southam DP, both of Stratford-upon-Avon DC.   Those taking
longest from inquiry to adoption have been Sutton Coldfield DP (Birmingham
MD) where a second inquiry was necessary, with Fareham Western Wards
(Hampshire DC), Belbroughton DP (Bromsgrove DC), River Tees Subject Plan
(Cleveland CC), and several of the London Borough Plans, all taking over 2
years.

If there is one consistent factor affecting the time scale of local plan
production in the 1970s, it has been the disorganization produced by local

TABLE 6.1

Stages in Typical Plan Preparation	Timing in months	Running total
1. Preparation and publicizing of local plan brief	1.5	1.5
2. Preparation of Report of Survey and associated public participation	18.0	19.5
3. Preparation of draft local plan and associated public participation	12.0	31.5
4. Production of 'final' version of local plan	2.0	33.5
5. Certification	1.0	34.5
6. Deposit	1.5	36.0
7. PLI	7.0	43.0
8. Inspector's report received	2.5	45.5
9. Modification on deposit	4.0	49.5
10. Adoption of local plan	2.5	52.0
Total	52.0	52.0

(Source: Bruton et al. 1982b)

TABLE 6.2

Time from deposit	Average	Range	Number of plans
No inquiry	6.7	2-13	17
Inquiry	18.5	7-29	38
Total	14.9	2-29	55

(Source: DoE)

government reorganization. The detailed case studies of local plan preparation undertaken recently by Fudge et al. (1982a) illustrate the problems involved in providing local planning guidance for new authorities and new areas, often with little information base, where both councillors and officers had to feel their way to discover what policies might be, coupled in many cases by substantial staff changes. There are signs that plans are now being prepared more quickly. The DoE currently officially expects local plans to be prepared in a year (DoE Circular 23/81), though unofficially appreciates the difficulties of this. As Wilson argues, if there is any point in preparing a local plan, it is likely to be the need to resolve a significant issue around which there are considerable conflicts of interest (Wilson 1977b). Resolving these is unlikely to be a quick matter.

3. PLAN PREPARATION

This section examines the way plans are prepared up to the point at which
they are either "approved" as prevailing policy by a local authority, or
placed on deposit as a statutory local plan. Essentially, this section is
about the methodology of local plan-making. However, this discussion of
methodology will be quite unlike early textbooks on town planning, which
gave instructions on how to draw up plans for towns (e.g. Keeble 1969).
Nor will it be in any way similar to the discussion of systematic methods
for preparing strategic policies, as for example presented in relation to
subregional plan preparation by Cowling and Steeley (1973). Both of these
approaches reflect an assumption that plan preparation is essentially a
technical process. In the introduction to this chapter, I indicated that
the procedures for *statutory* local plan preparation involve two other
models of policy formation, consultative and semi-judicial. I also noted
that the relation between policy formulation and action was more likely to
be an interactive phenomena than a sequential one. Consequently, the
technical elements of plan preparation have to be discussed and assessed
alongside those which involve such interaction. As a way of organizing an
account of these interrelationships, I consider first the problem of
determining what sort of plan to prepare (if any!). I then examine who is
likely to be involved in plan preparation. This is followed by a
consideration of the more "technical" problems involved in identifying
issues and developing proposals where this is the task of "experts", i.e.
planning officials, followed by a parallel examination of consultation
processes. I conclude by considering who and what determines the content
of plans.

3.1 *What Sort of Plan to Prepare?*

Having decided to prepare a local plan, a local authority has to consider
what issues will be addressed in the plan and what area will be covered by
the plan's policies and proposals. The selection of a plan's focus and
attention presents both political and intellectual problems. Politically,
certain issues and areas will be given priority attention in council
affairs from time to time, but it may not always be politic to declare this
selectivity (see Chapter 4). Intellectually, it is a difficult task to
disaggregate the causal factors which underlie what are seen as "issues",
determine the scale at which they should be examined, and specify the
activities and areas to which policies and proposals should be directed.

One obvious way out of the dilemma of selection is to attempt a
comprehensive ("all-issues") plan for the whole of a local authority area.
Such an approach avoids the need for further spatial specification except
in relation to the area over which a particular policy may apply, or the
location of a particular project. Yet 58% of the plans in my scan were for
small areas. Clearly, many local authorities prefer to concentrate plan-
making effort on particular locations. The resolution to the area problem
does not necessarily solve the problem of the range of issues to address,
however. Planners commonly talk of the need for comprehensive or "total"
approaches to plan-making (see Chapter 5), yet assumptions are made, often
implicitly, about the boundaries of the concern of such exercises, and about
the focus to be taken in formulating proposals.

The scope for discretionary interpretation by local authorities in
determining both what areas and what issues to cover is potentially vast.
The legislation for statutory plans formally provides for this discretionary
interpretation. The 1972 Local Government Act in effect encouraged district

councils to take such discretion. Central government has ever since been seeking ways of drawing back some control over interpretation, as previous chapters have indicated. The key focussing device, as offered in DoE advice since 1976, has been that proposals should be confined to those relating to land use and development. DoE advice has also stressed the different functions of the three types of statutory local plan: the comprehensive district plan; the small action area plan for areas of intensive change; and the subject plan, for issues about which proposals can be made in isolation from other issues. Advice also stresses that small area plans are unlikely to be able to address issues adequately and also take more time to prepare than larger area plans. Large area district plans are consequently advocated.

Local authorities may not choose to prepare statutory plans, and if they do, can bend the above definitions to suit their circumstances. I have already discussed in Chapter 5 the debate about the advantages and disadvantages of statutory versus non-statutory plans. Here my emphasis is on whether plans should be for single issues or all issues, large areas or small areas. DoE advice and the regulations provide a vocabulary which has structured local planners' debates, although it has been largely confusing. In Section 3.3 I return to the issue of the scope of the plan.

As Table 4.5 showed, 58% of plans in my review were for small areas. Excluding the plans for which no information on size was available the proportion is 67%. 88% of the non-statutory plans or those with unclear status were for small areas. There seems no doubt that despite DoE advice, local plans in the 1970s were seen as small area plans, although there are signs that this is changing. One reason for this relates to the types of areas for which plans have been prepared (see Table 6.3). As was noted in Chapter 5, most plans have been prepared for areas beyond the conurbations (small towns and countryside under severe development pressure, minor growth areas, small towns and villages), for town centres, inner city sites and special landscape areas or opportunity sites. 75% of the plans for these sort of areas are small ones and the proportion rises even higher if we subtract the areas under severe development pressure (80%). Are local authorities then merely preparing plans for those few special areas which need something more than the general guidance of the structure plan, a general code of standards for detailed development, or a development brief?

The DoE clearly thinks that many of these small area plans are either unnecessary or would be dealt with more effectively within a larger plan, and there is some evidence to support their case. One reason why so many small area plans were being proposed and prepared during the 1970s was the continuation of such activities from the 1960s. At this time, private and public sector development was on a substantial scale, as is only too clear from the PAG report. Town centres were being renewed; villages and towns beyond the conurbations were being expanded by appeal or by design; inner city areas were being rebuilt particularly through slum clearance and public sector housing programmes. In contrast, parts of the urban fabric were being specifically conserved. Because the preparation of overall development plans was discouraged, firstly by the changeover to the new style plans, and secondly by the speed with which proposals for development or for managing conservation and change in specific areas came forward, local authorities at reorganization often had a considerable collection of small-area proposals on hand. I have already quoted Hampshire's 190 operative plans and policies (Brown 1974). In Coventry's structure plan, 24 Action Areas were proposed (Trafford 1975), and Sheffield had 33 local plan areas (Adamson (1975). It could be argued that these small area projects are a necessary response to the demands of the land and development

TABLE 6.3

Types of area/issue	Size of plan area			Total
	Small	Large	All area	
Areas under heavy development pressure				
a. City centre/inner city boundary	2	1	-	3
b. Immediate urban fringe	6	9	-	15
c. Outer urban fringe/small farms/villages under commuter pressure	16	10	5	31
a. Major growth areas	1	4	-	5
b. Minor growth areas	19	5	1	25
Opportunity sites	15	2	-	17
Town centre plans	39	3	-	42
Areas of open land	9	5	-	14
Inner city areas	15	1	-	16
Areas with large industrial content	2	-	1	3
Small towns	15	1	-	16
Villages	12	1	-	13
Plans for substantial urbanized areas	-	1	14	15
Other	4	2	1	7
Total	155	39	22	222

situations local authorities were facing at that time. However, our work in London in the mid-1970s suggests that such "responsiveness" was hardly directed by any clear sense of purpose and direction. Rather, in many areas it probably reflected *ad hoc* reactions to the latest demand on the planning authority (Healey and Underwood 1977).

Inspection of several small-area plans raises questions about whether a local plan was the most appropriate vehicle for conveying the information contained within it. Several action area plans might have been more appropriately treated as development briefs, i.e. statements of the layout, design and phasing considerations to guide a particular development project which has already been agreed in principle. Solihull MBs Elmdon Heath/ Lugtrout Lane/Wherretts Well Lane Action Area Plan is an example. It covers a very small area (24.5 ha) intended largely for industry, adjacent to a large site allocated to British Leyland (Rovers) for a new assembly plant. Several action area proposals that have never been progressed also turned up in the review, no doubt because either the development did not materialize or because a development brief or similar was considered adequate (Moorfield Action Area Plan (Liverpool MD); Holme Action Area Plan (Scunthorpe DC)).

Meanwhile there has been a shift away from the action area format since it no longer brings any particular benefits. According to original advice, action area plans were to be for areas where substantial land use and development change could be expected within ten years. Land acquisition for the purposes of comprehensive planning was likely to be easier to justify on the basis of such a plan. During the 1970s it has become evident that substantial development change is not forthcoming on the scale envisaged in the PAG Report. In addition, the Community Land Act absorbed the special land acquisition powers which Action Area designation offered. There is thus no real advantage in them unless an authority wishes to have a hierarchy of statutory local plans, in which case an action area plan can be lodged inside a larger district plan. Several London Borough Plans have done this, (e.g. Camden), although another alternative is to "inset" plans for special small areas.

In theory, the special *subject plans* should remain of value to local authorities, allowing them to deal with single issues rather than a range. The nine subject plans formally deposited by 1980 covered a diverse range of topics (green belt, minerals, river valley recreation management, caravans and camping, intensive livestock, derelict land, a park, conflicting countryside activities), and in many cases cover more than one topic. Stratford-upon-Avon's Leisure-in-the-Valley subject plan covers hotels as well as waterways; Warrington's Rixton Brickworks subject plan covers minerals, waste disposal, scientific sites and open land; Kent's Dungeness Countryside structure plan for Agriculture, Conservation, and Sand and Gravel obviously covers all these. In practice, subject plans are being used not so much for *isolatable subjects* but for open land and countryside issues, and in particular where the county are in charge of preparation (see Table 4.3).

This reflects firstly the tradition of planning thought which puts housing, employment and transport as the central issues for any properly comprehensive study. In Dungeness, these clearly are *not* the central issues affecting landscape and development. Here they are conservation of a delicate landscape and wildlife environment, accommodating tourist pressures and the constraints on both of the presence of a nuclear power station. In effect, the Dungeness subject plan deals with an isolatable *area* rather than an isolatable subject. Secondly, the subject plan format allows the preparation by counties of plans for issues affecting the county as a whole, without prejudicing the preparation by districts of their own district plans. This arises because subject plans can overlay district plans, but the latter may not overlay each other. Nevertheless, there have been frequent protests about county-prepared subject plans, particularly for green belts. Districts in Manchester formally objected to the Development Plan Scheme which allocated to Greater Manchester Metropolitan County the task of preparing a Green Belt Subject and Open Land Plan, and there have been several other informal disputes (e.g. Essex, Oxfordshire and Avon).

It is probable that the DoE would happily dispense with subject plans, although an invention of their own. While countenancing green belt reluctantly and accepting minerals subject plans, they have effectively dissuaded authorities from proceeding with subject plans for the traditional topics of planning study - housing, employment, transport, community facilities, etc. Three such examples - Wycombe's Housing Subject Plan, Hove's Residential Subject Plan and Lewisham's Employment Subject Plan were all discouraged by DoE regional offices. The DoE argument here, as with green belts, is that the subject is not sufficiently isolatable to be dealt with on its own. Their case is supported by the controversy at the River Tees Subject Plan Public Local Inquiry. The plan dealt with

recreation and amenity, and objectors argued that the conflicts between
recreation and port-related industrial uses were so great that a
comprehensive review should have been undertaken to ensure full consultation
with all river users and riparian owners[50]. Yet if structure plans can
provide a reasonable context for area plans (as in action area plans), why
can they not for subjects and issues?

The DoE seem to be encouraging local authorities into using the district
plan format if possible. In 1980, 80% of the plans deposited were district
plans, so why not use the district plan format for all plans? The problem
here, for both local authorities and the DoE, is that, according to the
regulations, district plans are for areas "where detailed planning matters
need to be studied and set out in a comprehensive way" (DoE Circular 4/79
para. 3.12). In particular, the Circular goes on to say, "a district plan
will enable a review to be carried out of the interrelationships between
planning issues at a detailed local level" (para. 3.12). Local
authorities claim that this takes time, and that sometimes a "holding" plan
is needed, to define boundaries indicated in structure plans (e.g. green
belts), or deal with urgent issues (as in the Rixton Brickworks case). The
DoE claims that plans where these interrelationships are not adequately
worked out, either because a subject plan format has been used, or because
a district plan involved inadequate "study", could be challenged at appeal
or in the courts as inadequate. The River Tees case just quoted is an
illustration of the possibility. No such appeal has however yet been
contemplated so far as I am aware, and the DoE's concern here could just
be put down to neurotic wariness over the effect of local authority
discretion on the overall credibility of the planning system. The ingenuity
of developers such as the West Midlands firm of Bryants should not of
course be underestimated. They have already taken Solihull and the DoE to
court for not holding an inquiry into their objections to the Solihull Green
Belt Subject Plan.

In any case, the DoE's interest in these distinctions has been overtaken by
their concern with speedy local plan production. I will consider in
Chapter 9 how far central government has any real interest in whether and
how local authorities produce plans. Present advice would suggest firstly,
that if plans can be produced and modified quickly there will no longer
be a problem over "layering" of plans; "holding plans" can be replaced as
necessary by more definitive plans. Secondly, confining the focus of the
plan, to land use issues where a plan is "really needed", is emerging as
much more important than a comprehensive review of interrelationships. As
with structure plans, the emphasis is shifting towards "key issues", rather
than "all issues". Having implanted the plan typology, central government
may now be seeking simplification. However, past experience suggests that
local authority behaviour is not necessarily amenable to central government
exhortation. Local authorities will still have to resolve the problems of
selection - of issues and areas - when contemplating producing a local plan.
Section 3.3 returns to this question.

Do all these fine distinctions between types of plan matter to anyone other
than the central and local government officials charged with the detailed
operation of the planning system? The answer is probably very little, but
with the following qualifications. Firstly, central government's concern
over the type of plan to prepare is part of its wider concern to limit the
content of plans, and hence the policies which are subject to the

---

[50]Pers. comm. E. A. Hill.

consultation and inquiry requirements associated with statutory plans. In effect, they are reducing the agenda available for public debate and scrutiny, unless local authorities choose to reveal policies for such debate and scrutiny in other ways. Secondly, the existence of different types of plan creates confusion to almost everyone else concerned in any way with local planning guidance.

3.2 Who Prepares the Plan?

Many people at one time or another will find themselves involved in the preparation of a local plan, even if it is only by receiving a leaflet asking for comments through the letterbox. Some of these people are required to be involved by regulations; others are drawn in as a result of local authority consultation programmes or their own demands. I discuss most of such involvement in Section 3.4 as consultation. Here I concentrate on those who largely control plan preparation, taking the managing role in determining the approach and method, progressing the task through the stages that are decided upon, filtering material and comments received and determining the final form and content of whatever constitutes the output of the process.

There is no systematic evidence on who manages plan preparation.* Plans do not always provide such information, though articles about plan preparation often refer to it. But I think it would be a reasonable conclusion that most plans, especially in shire districts, have been prepared by small local plans teams in planning departments, reporting intermittently to their members. In metropolitan districts and other large urban authorities, more complex arrangements may be found, but most local plan exercises are still likely to be the responsibility of special teams of a few officers. The form and content of plans is therefore predominantly determined by the interpretation these local planners make of the major issues of concern, the policy priorities in respect of them and the way in which these should be expressed. This does not of course mean that local planners act independently. They are subject to formal political control, and to a wide range of other influences which may affect the way a planning department considers issues and priorities, in addition to any particular influences which may develop during local plan preparation. Yet they play an important role in filtering pressures of various kinds and in converting them into formal policies and proposals. It is in this task that the 'expertise' of planners is particularly important, professional ideologies and traditions mixing with local circumstances and formal procedures to produce the way issues are discussed and policies expressed in plan documents. Underwood (1980) in her study of local planners in Haringey gives a good account of this process at work.

Although most plans are district-prepared (see Table 4.3), counties have some involvement in plan preparation. Under the 1968 Act, it was of course assumed that counties would prepare local plans as detailed expressions of their own structure plans. Few counties after 1974 were in the fortunate position of Coventry which, as a county borough, had already prepared their own structure plan, closely linked to a corporate plan. Several shire counties, however, with similar post-reorganization boundaries, effectively directed the early local plan work of districts while the latter built up their staffing. Hampshire prepared the local plans for the first three growth areas specified in the structure plan itself (Fareham Western Wards AA Plan, Chandlers Ford and Totton District Plans), and commenced work on some town centre plans. Leicestershire, which similarly had a structure plan approved in the mid-1970s which contained policies for considerable

*Fudge et al 1982 provides useful evidence to fill this gap.

growth at a number of locations, gave substantial guidance to its districts,
which prepared small area village growth plans in a similar format (Hollox
1978). (Glenfield DP (Blaby DC); Ratby, Markfield and Groby DPs in Hinkley
and Bosworth DC; Coleorton and Ashby Wolds DPs in North West Leicestershire
DC). Hertfordshire persuaded its districts not only to agree to the
preparation of district-wide plans, but to a common format for specifying
land allocation policies. This was associated with their concern to ensure
an effective restraint policy (Griffiths 1979). Berkshire, though
preferring to use development briefs to manage the substantial growth in
parts of central Berkshire, handed over the Newbury and Thatcham DP to the
district prior to deposit. Another example of a local plan prepared largely
by the county but handed over to the district for deposit is Tamworth DP in
Staffordshire[51].

Several local plans, including many of the county-prepared ones, are
prepared by joint county-district teams. The Norwich Central Area Local
Plan was jointly prepared by the City Council, and County Highways and
Planning Departments. Rochdale's Town Centre District Plan was prepared by
a county-borough working party, linked to making resource bids related to
the Urban Aid Programme. Where no formal joint working arrangements exist,
good working relations at officer level between the counties and districts
may assist plan preparation.

However, how far counties have been involved in local plan preparation has
depended considerably on the history of relations between counties and
districts. In metropolitan areas, the districts were more likely to have
both staff, information and organizational continuity from before
reorganization, while the metropolitan counties faced problems of developing
strategies for quite new administrative areas. In some cases, metropolitan
districts have largely ignored their counties: Manchester district, which
lost nearly half its staff to the county, has been aggressively independent
of the county in its work in general. Nevertheless, reasonable co-ordination
took place over the district's City Centre Local Plan, and the district has
been content to let the county prepare plans for the river valleys since
these involve several districts, and the city can gain by the resources the
county is prepared to invest in river valley landscape and recreation
management (Healey 1982d).

By contrast, in Oxfordshire the staff of the old county moved out to the
districts. These then proceeded to work on local plans, especially in
South Oxfordshire and Vale of White Horse, while the county built up a new
staff and store of knowledge about the area through structure plan
preparation. This perhaps accounts for the more complex policy disputes
between county and districts here, and for the abortive work on local plans
noted by Caddy (1981). And in the cases where counties initially played a
considerable role in plan preparation, this role has been increasingly
challenged as districts have become more organized. For its most recent
growth area local plan, Hampshire County Council has had to agree to hand
over preparation to Eastleigh district. However, the district has very
limited resources to devote to the task, so the county is providing the
district with a "local plan brief", which in effect contains a substantial
amount of the processed information base and policy ideas on which the
district can work (Healey 1982c).

County-district disputes over who should prepare plans have already been

---

[51]Pers. comm. E. A. Hill.

noted. To some extent these relate to jockeying for position between the
two tiers in the new local government structure: district councillors
resent interference by their county colleagues in their territory; district
officers often feel likewise. To some extent, such disputes are solely
about the appearance of responsibility and relate in no way to the content
of policies. Thus Manchester City has formally objected, not to the
preparation of river valley subject plans by the county since it
acknowledges that only the county has the resources to do this, but to the
formal *adoption* by the county of a local plan for part of Manchester City's
area. The argument here is that this gives the county more control over
land and development matters than it otherwise would have, though in fact
such county adoption makes no difference to how development control is
handled. However, Manchester City is particularly concerned at the
precedent this could provide should there be a real policy dispute between
the county and the district. Manchester City remains an objector to the
county-prepared Green Belt Subject Plan because this allocates sites into
the green belt which the City, with few greenfield sites, would prefer to
see as available for development. The City first objected to county-
preparation of the plan. The DoE determined that the county should prepare
and adopt the plan but for green belt matters only. The district has since
objected to the deposited plan. Meanwhile, the DoE has determined that the
first river valley plan which is likely to reach deposit stage should be
deposited in bits, district by district! (Healey 1982d).

A similar sort of dispute has occurred in Oxford. Once again the issue
concerns green belt, and in particular the revision of the inner boundary of
the Oxford Green Belt. The structure plan requires some land take for
housing and industrial purposes, and Oxford City is demanding more since it
is land hungry. The surrounding districts view the potential loss of open
land with some concern and have wished to maintain both close influence over
the determination of where development should go and control over the
detailed formulation of policies. Consequently, districts combined to
prevent the county preparing a green belt subject plan. Currently, districts
and the county in combination have prepared district plans for each
district's part of the Oxford fringe. But the County refused to certify two
of the resultant local plans, and again the DoE was drawn in to arbitrate.

Apart from these situations, counties have been involved in particular sorts
of areas and problems, as already noted. In some cases, the plan deals with
an area which straddles two districts. Examples here are the GLC's Covent
Garden Action Area Plan, for an opportunity site created by the removal of
London's major vegetable market south of the river. The plan area is in the
boroughs of Westminster and Camden. In a few cases, districts have attempted
joint preparation for a cross-boundary problem (e.g. Islington and the City
of London in relation to Smithfield). However, such joint working seems
both rare and difficult. Shropshire's Severn Gorge District Plan is for an
archaeological heritage area in Wrekin and Bridgnorth districts
Cleveland's River Tees Subject Plan includes parts of all the Teesside
districts. Other plans are prepared for county-wide issues, such as
Humberside's Intensive Livestock, and Coastal, Caravan and Camping Subject
Plans. The most common group of county-prepared plans are those which seek
to implement key strategic policies which involve drawing boundaries in
areas with strong development pressure, notably green belt and minerals
subject plans. These account for one third of all county local plans
identified in my review.

Despite this local plan activity by counties, most local plans are prepared
and adopted by districts. The DoE has encouraged this and districts prefer
it. Most appear to have been prepared within planning departments, though
there are a few examples of preparation by an interdepartmental team, often

linked to some form of corporate arrangement. Coventry's Action Area Plans
and the Foleshill Policy Guide were derived from the framework set by the
Programme Area Teams of the Corporate Plan, with interdepartmental teams for
plan preparation, although these found counteracting the strong departmental
emphasis within the corporate planning exercise difficult (Trafford 1975).
Islington's Borough Plan and Watford's District Plan had close links to
corporate arrangements in their preparation.

In Haringey, an attempt was made to use local plans to provide a land
resource base to annual capital programming (Frith 1976, Underwood 1980).
Waltham Forest's Borough Plan is the land and development dimension of its
corporate plan, although, given this link, it is remarkably narrow in its
focus on land use. In Wirral MD, four small area local plans (Birkenhead
Central Area, Seacombe, Tranmere and Rock Ferry, North Birkenhead) were
quickly prepared with the co-operation of the housing department and the
community development section of the social services department. The
impetus here was the opportunity for Urban Aid Programme funds (Adcock 1979).
The contrast with Liverpool City, where departmental traditions have
inhibited experiments in area management, let alone co-ordinated resource-
based local plans, is striking.

How far the statements in plans about working arrangements for plan
preparation reflect actual working relationships is difficult to determine
in the absence of detailed case studies. Other departments may feel that
their perception of issues and their priorities have been distorted by
planners, while planners may feel that their colleagues in other departments
lacked real interest and commitment (see Underwood 1980, Healey and Underwood
1979). This reservation possibly applies even more to the involvement of
the infrastructure agencies - County Highways, the Water Authorities, the
Gas Board and CEGB; and other major public sector interests, notably the
Ministry of Agriculture (MAFF) and the National Coal Board. It is rare for
these agencies to be involved in joint working arrangements. A notable
exception is Cardiff City's East Moors Local Plan, produced in 6 months in
close co-operation with the Welsh Development Agency and the Land Authority
for Wales. The impetus behind this so far non-statutory local plan, as
noted in Chapter 5, was the unexpectedly sudden decision to close the East
Moors Steel Works, and the concern of the City and other interests (notably
BP Pension Trust, a major landowner) to see the site attract industrial
development.

Humberside had a less harmonious working group for the preparation of the
Intensive Livestock Subject Plan. This included, in addition to
representatives of the county and districts, the Yorkshire Water Authority,
the CPRE, MAFF and the NFU. Given that the plan aims to moderate the
"amenity deterioration" caused by intensive pig farming (3.7% of all the
U.K.'s pigs were apparently to be found in this area in 1977), it is perhaps
not surprising that "there was not unanimous agreement between all the
groups of the Working Party" on the plan's proposals. In Stafford's Stone
DP, however, MAFF did not notice the structure plan's allocation of good
quality farmland for development: their objection only came forward when
the plan was placed on deposit. Normally, however, MAFF and the other main
public sector interests appear satisfied with procedures for consultation
and rarely get involved in formal preparation arrangements. As we will see,
they have been able to exercise considerable influence on the content of
plans through consultation.

So far, plan preparation has been discussed as if it were an entirely
administrative process, involving co-ordination in various forms between
public sector officials. It is a reasonable conclusion that this

substantially reflects the reality of local plan preparation. However, this activity is subject to at least the formal decision-making power of councillors, while the requirements for publicity and public consultation about plan content have drawn in local interest groups in various ways. It is also true that many local planners have considered it important to involve politicians and the public in plan preparation, as a way of generating proposals and obtaining political commitment to them.

In some cases, councillors have been active members of plan preparation working parties, or special committees have been established to review ongoing preparation work (e.g. Coventry's Eagle Street Action Area Plan, Lapworth District Plan (Warwick DC) (Wilson 1977a, Bruton and Lightbody 1979)). For the Hampshire growth area plans, the team of planning officers was complemented by a special members' panel which kept in close touch with plan preparation throughout. These were linked to joint committees of councillors of both the county and relevant districts. How these political arrangements work out depends on the general way in which officers and members relate to each other in a particular council. Hampshire county happens to have a tradition of delegation to small groups of members; in other councils, all decisions are in effect referred to majority group meetings, or to a caucus of key members.

Similarly, the political style of councils affects how far the public is drawn into plan preparation. In both the Eagle Street and Lapworth plans, local residents demanded considerable attention from the council in plan preparation, the former as a result of the "consciousness-raising" work of the local Community Development Project (Trafford and Hanna 1977). The latter case, as the chief planning officer wryly comments, is "a rural area characterized by a well-to-do commuter population who jealously guard it from the conurbation development pressures of which they are a part" (Wilson 1977b p.779). In a few cases, local plans have actually been prepared from start to finish by working parties including residents. In Coventry's Eden Street Action Area Plan, residents were brought in from the beginning by a council clearly anxious to avoid the confrontations experienced over its previous Eagle Street Plan. Perhaps local residents were satisfied with the result, as there were no objections and this plan became the first local plan to be adopted in Britain (in December 1975). In Westminster Borough Plan and Lambeth's Waterloo DP, residents were closely involved in discussing plan proposals (see on, Section 3.4), though not formally in plan preparation. The same can be said of the Covent Garden Action Area Plan (GLC). Two other cases with very close public involvement throughout are Warrington's idiosyncratic subject plans for Rixton Brickworks and Walton Park. Both seem to have been initiated in response to public concern (Chapter 5).

Finally, it is worth noting a number of other arrangements or possibilities identified in my review, though none of the plans involved, perhaps significantly, have so far emerged into deposited plans. Maidstone's Loose Valley District Plan has grown out of a countryside management project, involving a variety of recreation, landscape and farming interests. Several other such exercises are known to exist. Cheltenham's Central Area Interim District Plan was initiated when the council rejected a consultants' plan (by Hugh Wilson and Womersley). A consultants' plan was also rejected for Covent Garden, though this time by the public. Consultants have also undertaken special studies for plans in a few cases, although I know of no plan proceeding to deposit which has been substantially consultant-prepared, although consultants were involved in plans for several growth area development proposals in the late 1960s/early 1970s, some of which eventually emerged as local plans in the scan (see

Foster 1975). Two examples illustrate the sort of relationships involved.
The Thornhill District Plan (Cardiff CB) is a draft-written statement,
building on an earlier master plan for an urban fringe green field site near
the M4. This was prepared by agents acting on behalf of a consortium of
local landowners and including the city council. In Lower Earley (Central
Berkshire), Shankland Cox first produced a plan for substantial development
for the council. This was rejected by the various landowners involved. A
revised plan was then prepared on behalf of the consortium of landowners
and developers, which became the basis of the development brief which has
subsequently guided development there (Davis 1982). However, except for these
few examples, landowners and developers are rarely involved formally in plan
preparation, as will become clearer in Sections 3.4 and 4. The exception is
where the local authority itself is a major landowner (e.g. Abbey District Plan
(Leicester City Council), Skippingdale Action Plan (Scunthorpe DC), Chineham
District Plan and Fareham Western Wards Action Area Plan (Hants CC), Newburn
District Plan (Newcastle City MD)). The Estates Department of the council is
then likely to be involved. It is also possible that with the present
government's emphasis on working with the housebuilders on land availability,
more private sector involvement in plan preparation may be on the way (as a
forerunner, see Newton-le-Willows District Plan, St. Helens MD). The joint
local authority/HBF land availability studies have certainly had some effect on
the information base upon which discussions about housing land allocation are
likely to take place.

3.3 *The Method of Plan Preparation: Identifying Issues and Developing
     Proposals*

If local plan preparation is largely a task managed by local planners
working in districts, how then have they gone about it? From the material
I have looked at, a comprehensive review of the methodological approaches
used in local plan preparation is not possible. Published documents are the
product of a preparation process and do not necessarily reveal its form of
operation. A few plans appear to have adopted the methodological sequence
of the rational planning model (goals - analysis - alternatives -
evaluation) following the early structure plan experience (e.g. Darlaston
District Plan (Walsall MB)). A more common approach is to proceed from
survey, to issue identification (which may involve consultation and
discussion with councillors), to the formulation of options for action (or
alternative policies) which become the basis of a consultation exercise.
Policies and proposals are then drawn up, with a further stage of
consultation before the policies and proposals are finalized. Diagram 6.3
provides a recent illustration of such an approach. This is of course a
variant of the survey-analysis-plan sequence. There are few examples where
technical methods have been used to develop alternative proposals, although
the Hampshire growth area plans were developed by considering different
alternative transport and land use arrangements, and evaluating these.
However, the proposals which were contained in the three adopted plans were
in each case substantially different from any of those initially arrived at.
In retrospect, such technical derivation of alternatives did not prove
particularly helpful (Healey 1982c).

Several more recent plans have collapsed the background work,
concentrating on identifying "issues and options". This recognizes that
there may be no need or time for formal survey, and that the central
question is to identify the issues about which the plan is to make

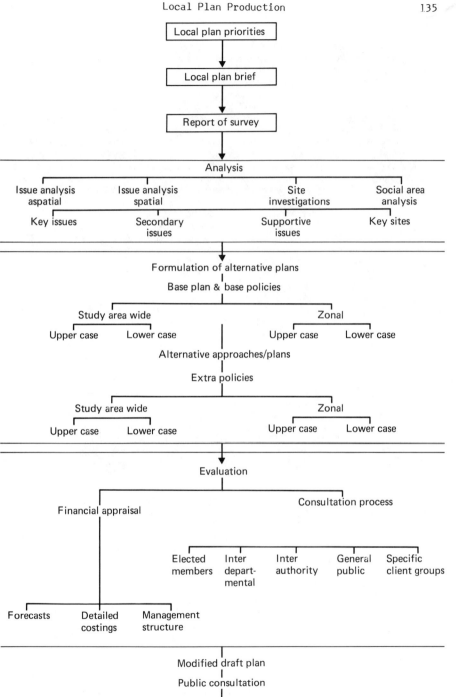

Source: Booth and Edwards 1981

Diagram 6.3.   The Local Plan Preparation Process in
Barnsley MD

proposals[52]. As one local planner commented, in relation to a metropolitan district, the danger was that local plan preparation could be swamped by information; whereas the plan, in terms of its policies, was probably already extant, contained in the minds of councillors, senior planning officers and development control staff[53].

To some extent "issues and options" papers are a variant of the "position statement" advocated as part of general local authority policy review exercises (see DoE 1973c). Such a policy review was the starting point of Camden's borough plan[54]. In such a large and complex area, this identified an enormous range of issues and existing policies. To organize their approach to this range in a manageable form, the local plan team adopted a "mixed scanning strategy" which allowed broad review of all issues, with concentrated effort on the priority problems (Thompson 1977b). This approach was also found helpful in structure planning (Drake 1975)[55]. There is little other evidence of methodological sophistication in local plan preparation. A few teams have contemplated using AIDA, a decision-making technique for devising policy options from related variables; others have tried to assess the financial implications of proposals. This too is a transfer from structure planning (see Bather, Sutton and Williams 1975). Following the methodological shift in structure planning, many local planners advocated a "needs-based" approach (Duerden 1979), reflected in Islington's Borough Plan (Islington LB), Camden Borough Plan (Camden LB), Liverpool City's approach, and Bolton MD's Farnworth District Plan. A few plans also demonstrate that their preparers have concentrated on what is the main issue in hand, without concerning themselves with any specific methodology. Apart from the subject plans, examples here are Elmdon Heath, Lugtrout Lane and Wherrett's Well Action Area Plan (Solihull MD); Rural Areas District Plan (Uttlesford DC).

It might be expected that the method of local plan preparation would depend on the nature of the issues to be considered, the characteristics of the area involved and the nature of political priorities in the area. Thus Hampshire's growth area plans require much more consideration of the costs and benefits of alternative arrangements of land uses, than those for inner city areas, which may be dominated by a concern with how to regenerate local economies; or for green belt areas where the main consideration is to restrict development. To some extent plans do vary in this way.

Yet when one looks at large numbers of plans it becomes evident that certain common methodological principles are very widely used. The most notable of these is the "topic principle". This involves dividing the material to be considered into "topics", such as housing, employment, industry, commerce, retailing, education, community facilities, transport, conservation. Such an organizing principle can be found in reports of survey, consultation documents and in the organization of plans themselves. Curiously, while

---

[52]Many examples can be cited here, e.g. Westminster City Plan (Westminster LB Atherstone District Plan (North Warwickshire DC); Enderby/Narborough (Blaby DP); Askam and Ireleth District Plan (Barrow-in-Furness DC).

[53]Pers. comm. J. Bird.

[54]Pers. comm. C. Fudge.

[55]Robin Thompson had been researching into structure plan preparation before leading Camden's local plan teams. The notion of "mixed scanning" derives from Etzioni 1973.

there has been extensive discussion of the sequence by which plans and
policies should be arrived at in the planning literature, there has been
very little comment on the "topic" method for organizing issues. It appears
to be a taken-for-granted method, or a fall-back position in default of
anything else. The Development Plans Manual encourages it in its advice[56].
My own interpretation is that planners have found it convenient to retain
this way of dividing the material they deal with because it relates to the
land use classifications, embodied in the *Use Classes Order*, which are used
when dealing with planning applications. Policies and proposals can then
be grouped to allow ready translation for development control officials
and applicants. With the shift away from detailed specification of
particular uses and their form of development towards more concern with
activities, this translation is less straightforward than it was.
Policies now sometimes discriminate on other grounds than use (such as local
users). However, local planners have had some difficulty in thinking
through what this might mean for the way local plans are developed and
organized.

However, local planners cannot be taken to task too severely for their lack
of methodological awareness, since there has been very little discussion in
professional debates about the methodological problems which have to be
faced on local plan preparation. This is partly because the focus of
methodological development has so heavily concentrated on the development
of strategic policies, using systematic methods. Yet the reality of local
plan preparation is that of producing detailed and largely site-specific
policy guidance as a collective operation involving a large number of people.
In my view, this is an area which requires much more development in the
planning field. I provide the following notes as an introduction to such a
reconsideration.

In preparing a plan, plan preparers are faced with the problem of determining
the focus of the plan, and the range of issues it will consider. In many
instances these have been decided in the decision to prepare the plan, and
the determination of the area to which the plan is to apply. The focus and
issues may derive from the structure plan, the major development changes
going on in an area, political priorities, areas of major public concern.
Where the focus and range of issues are not evident, however, it is necessary
to find some way of discovering them. The rational model stresses ends as the
way into this task. The Geddesian survey-analysis-plan formula sends plan-
preparers off into information collection. The topic approach encourages them
to undertake sectoral studies. None of these provides much guidance on the
questions of focus and range, still less on how the various issues might be
related together. The mistake that many local planners have made is to assume
that if they follow the correct sequence of activities, a plan will emerge.
As a result, they have paid much less attention to the context in which a plan
is being prepared, the precise reasons why a plan is appropriate at a
particular time and the main difficulties that are likely to be encountered in
producing it. Planners have perhaps wanted policy ideas to emerge creatively,
unencumbered by institutional constraints and past history.

The first task that a local plan team should face up to is understanding the
political context within which a plan is to be prepared. This would include

---

[56]When the systems approach to plan-making was advocated, these topics were
sometimes presented as the "components" of the urban system.

not only the policies in structure plans and the advice of central government as to procedures, form and content of local plans, but also local political pressures and priorities, other central government policies and the modes of operation of the local authority itself and other public agencies with an interest in the plan. As Thompson stressed in relation to Camden's plan: "to be effective a local plan must be firmly formulated within the confines of its operational context" (Thompson 1977b p.145).

Secondly, some way of understanding the social and economic processes affecting the various activities found within an area of study is needed. At the level of a local authority's concern these activities may have little connection with each other apart from spatial contiguity. Local residents in Eagle Street living in council properties and dependent on several sources for their low incomes, including a large slice of state income support, have few direct links with adjacent car and engineering plants whose employees are mostly to be found in owner-occupied housing on the outer margins of Coventry. In the 1960s, planners were attracted to the notion of an "urban activity system" as a way of defining interrelationships, focussed on the notion of a local "employment base". However, the relation between the location of employment and of other activities is much more complex than this suggests, and its spatial expression is by no means contained within small areas. A more recent development is the focus on "local economies" as a subset of the national economy (Broadbent 1977 Chapter 3). This may have some value for substantial freestanding urban areas. However, few local plans are produced for such situations, as we have seen. For most local plans, the analytical problem is to relate the changing behaviour of the activities occurring within the plan area to each other and to the forces which are structuring each activity. These may be operating at a national or international scale. As Wandsworth planners and councillors concluded in their study of employment change in their Borough, the local authority had very limited powers to control the employment policies of large firms which contributed most to labour shedding. They therefore proposed to concentrate their effort on assisting small and often local firms (LB Wandsworth 1976).

Thirdly, where local plans are to focus on land use and development issues as the DoE demands, social and economic processes and policies have to be translated into land uses and development projects. Here again, little guidance is available. Much of the geographical literature discusses correlations between patterns of land use and possible factors producing these. Yet local planners need to know about the processes by which demands and needs for land and property are generated, their specificity and predictability. Neo-classical economists offer models of land market operations, yet acknowledge that land and property transactions do not operate successfully as "markets". Sociologists, who tend to give more attention to processes, infrequently address questions about the land and development expressions of the activities they discuss. One result of this is that while many plans attempt to assess the need for dwellings within the plan area, using demographic calculations, and convert this into requirements for additional dwellings and land, few plans contain any analysis of the processes by which land for housing, or for any other activity, becomes available. In this context, the present government's exhortations to local authorities to consider housing land availability could have one salutary effect, among its other less desirable consequences. Yet it would be unfair to accuse planners of paying little attention to these development processes. Local planners and those working in development control often have a good working perception of them. The problem they face is in conceptualizing this and relating it to the other bits of knowledge they possess.

As a technical or intellectual process of relating knowledge about the social and economic processes affecting the way land is used and developed in an area to the specific concerns of a local planning authority, then, local plan preparation has not so far been particularly impressive. This conclusion has to be set against evidence that planners do sometimes perform a challenging function in their authorities, widening the range of issues addressed by politicians, other departments and the public (e.g. Underwood 1980), partly because of their concern with the interrelationships between the activities of other departments and public agencies. The main difficulty which local plan teams have found, though rarely articulated as such, was that they had no adequate way of conceptualizing the task they were engaged in and their role in relation to it. However, the intellectual difficulties planners have in developing such an understanding, which are by no means small, have perhaps been less significant than they might have been because of the role of consultation and "public participation" in determining the agenda of issues and proposals addressed in local plan preparation.

3.4 *The Method of Plan Preparation: Consultation*

Whereas there is no formal requirement in statutory procedures to carry out surveys or any other technical investigations in preparing a local plan, central government assuming that much of this is provided in structure plans, the legislation and regulations give considerable attention to consultation and publicity. This element of preparation should therefore not be underrated. Local authorities are required to make "persons" with an interest in the "matters proposed to be included in the plan" aware that they have an opportunity to make representations on these matters (DoE Circular 4/79 Annex B para.10). Until recently it was understood that this should be done *before* the plan was finalized, i.e. before deposit in the case of statutory plans. Two sorts of consultation are involved here. The first, with public agencies, has a long history; the second, with the public at large, was an introduction of the late 1960s, as discussed in Chapter 3. Why are they both given such attention in legislation?

A possible answer is that central government was interested in participatory democracy. There is, however, little evidence to support this interpretation, although some local government planners have had this in mind. A more plausible explanation is that central government was responding to the increasingly vociferous environmental lobbies of the late 1960s, active at both local and national level. (As noted in Chapter 3, some people hoped that involving the public in plan preparation would allow a consensus to be negotiated prior to the deposit of plans, to reduce the scale of objections.) A third possibility is that public consultation was seen as providing a sort of preliminary vetting of local authority policies, a check on their competence, in which central government had limited confidence. For both central government and local planning authorities, the most significant role for public consultation in plan preparation is to give support to the planning authority's policies where significant conflicts over land use and development exist. The fact of engaging in an apparently public debate on policy alternatives helps to legitimate the policies arrived at. The process may also co-opt some sections of the public into giving support to policies. In a very few cases, as noted in Section 4.2, citizens may have a very significant role in plan preparation, but these are rare, and have been associated more with the political demands of certain groups of citizens than any ideological concern by planning officers to participate with citizens in meeting community needs.

Public consultation is, then, about accountability and political support. Consultation with the government departments and the main public agencies may be related to the latter's concern to protect their own interests. Circular 4/79 lists those "likely to be interested in local plan proposals":

Ministry of Agriculture, Fisheries and Food
Ministry of Defence
Department of Education and Science
Department of Employment
Department of Energy
Department of the Environment (including the Property Services Agency)
Home Office
Department of Industry
Department of Trade
Department of Transport

Countryside Commission
Crown Estates Commissioners
Forestry Commission

Nature Conservancy Council
Post Office (Postal Regional Headquarters)
Post Office (Telecommunications Regional Headquarters)
Regional Council for Sport and Recreation
Regional Health Authority
Regional Water Authority

DoE Circular 4/79 para. 3.57. (England only).

This list excludes the energy authorities (Gas Board, CEGB, NCB, BNF) as well as British Rail or British Steel, but those are normally consulted, and are subsumed in the above list under the relevant departments.

The traditional way that planning authorities engaged in consultation, and which is still followed for most development control applications is by correspondence. For organizations and individuals accustomed to scan papers to identify points which affect their interests, this is an efficient procedure. However, planners may also seek to obtain agency commitment to a specific scheme or agreement to use a site. Delays and conflicts here can become among the most time-consuming elements of plan preparation. LB Newham found that negotiating with the Gas Board over a major site of the latter's so-called "operational land" was a near impossible task, and it was only at the inquiry stage that the Board were forced to discuss the issue (Beckton DP). In Featherstone DP (Wakefield MD), the NCB owned significant areas of housing and land which the local authority would have liked to have seen developed, but was difficult to negotiate with. Local authorities have usually been careful to obtain MAFF's views and many land allocation proposals reflect these. Nevertheless, MAFF failed to respond to the opportunity for consultation in the Stone DP already referred to, which led to a major objection, with the Secretary of State calling in the plan.

These apparently routine consultations are often crucial to the content of plans. Firstly, public agencies may be the source of proposals. School and health sites, and roadlines, are typical examples. On the one hand, as Thompson (1977b) argues, plan preparation has the beneficial effect of forcing secretive departments and agencies to "display their hand" so far as their future programmes are concerned. Manchester City planners argue that local plan preparation was responsible for bringing to light important

British Rail proposals for linking main stations across the city centre,
proposals which were obviously crucial to the city centre local plan. On
the other hand, because of the blighting effects of proposals (and resultant
purchase notices), public agencies may be reluctant to reveal any proposals
that are not already in agreed expenditure programmes. Thus in the case of
the Beckton District Plan (Newham LB), the local plan preparers achieved
some success in getting various agencies and departments to take on projects
into agreed expenditure programmes, but the completed plan merely reflected
this successful negotiation, rather than determining it. In another case,
the eduction authority actually changed its school site proposals as the
plan was deposited, no doubt alarmed at the implications of having its
proposals included in an adopted local plan (Basford, Forest Fields and
Radford DP, Nottingham DC).

Secondly, local plan preparers may seek to obtain commitments by public
agencies and departments to particular projects, as in the Beckton case.
Typically, these are infrastructure projects; road construction, traffic
management schemes; reservoir construction or sewage works. Once again, the
problem is to persuade a Highways Department or a Water Authority that a
project which falls in a particular local plan area should have priority.
Vine's study of local plans for four small towns provides several examples
(Vine 1980). Where it is impossible to obtain agreement to a road proposal,
local plans have adopted a variety of solutions. In Buckingham, although
part of a bypass has been started using developer contributions under Section
52 agreements, the county council has still not agreed a line for all of
the road. In Didcot (South Oxfordshire DC), the draft local plan was only
able to indicate half the length of a road, which only made sense if
completed. Bakewell DP (Peak Park Joint Planning Board) reserves a swathe
of land for a road, as does East Hertfordshire's District Plan. A
solution increasingly adopted to this dilemma of uncertainty as to when a
necessary piece of infrastructure is to be built is to require contributions
from developers. This has long been the practice in growth areas such as
Hampshire but with public expenditure cuts the practice is increasing (see
Enderby and Narborough DP (Blaby DC); Horsham Area District Plan (Horsham
DC), the South Hampshire growth area plans). However, this may create
further problems. In Chandlers Ford District Plan (Hants CC). a road which
was intended ultimately as a district distributor road was only shown for
part of its length, so that developers could not argue that they were
contributing to a district rather than an access road.

Finally, public agencies may contribute to the plan through their assessment
of the allocation of sites for development. The most important agencies
here are MAFF, as already suggested, and the Regional Water Authorities. The
Chandlers Ford Plan provides an interesting illustration of the role of both
agencies. Following the structure plan, a large amount of development was
proposed on a greenfield site in the ownership of a single estate. Most of
the land was in a few tenanted farms. However, the county was advised by
the Water Authority that due to sewage difficulties, development could not
proceed for about a decade. The landowning firm who was interested in
seeing the land developed, hired its own firm of water engineers, which
concluded that the alleged constraints could be removed with much less
investment than the Water Authority had anticipated. The Water Authority
and the county accepted this case, and the county went on to prepare a
draft plan, a process based largely on a technical assessment of sites,
traffic flows, conserving farm units, etc. However, by the time the draft
plan was published, the landowner had encouraged MAFF to invest in one of the
tenanted farms and did not wish to see this land developed. Consultation
around the draft plan then largely involved the landowner and MAFF
negotiating over the location of development (Healey 1982c).

For most of the government departments and public agencies, local plan considerations are at best peripheral to their primary concerns and at worst an irritating infringement of their own autonomy to determine the principles and priorities for allocating resources. Yet their investments or attitudes may be fundamental to the future development of an area. Consequently, planners have been encouraged to go beyond routine consultation and break into the bastions of these agencies through developing informal contacts. An interesting phenomenon has been the employment of planners by some public agencies to help manage their relationships with planning authorities, formalizing the informal contact networks which frequently develop.

How successful local planners are in "bending" the programming and location of investment projects depends to a large extent on the past history of relationships with these agencies, and on the bargaining counters local planners may command. Now that the Regional Water Authorities have settled down after reorganization, relationships with planning departments seem to be operating smoothly (see Hickling, Friend and Luckman 1979, Bishop 1980, Healey *et al*. 1982a). This is partly because Water Authorities are required by law to service new development. Consequently they have a close interest in the land released to development by planning authorities on greenfield sites since this could affect their own investment programmes. However, highway authorities are under no such direct pressure, unless a land allocation proposal is likely to cut across a potential road line. Except in respect of incurring blight notices, local planners have little bargaining weight with agencies responsible for social infrastructure, since these react to demand. During the 1970s, with falling populations in many areas and public expenditure reductions, providing social infrastructure in co-ordination with other local plan considerations has proved particuarly difficult.

There can be little doubt that public agencies have been influential in determining local plan content. And it is evident that consultation with them occurs in a different way to public consultation, using bureaucratic procedures and modes of operation. If officials refer to the greater role these days of informal contact networks among public agencies, they are merely noting that the mode of operation of bureaucracy is changing in Britain - from the use of formal procedures in hierarchical structures of responsibility to open structures with more individual responsibility to negotiate. It is possible that this change makes the local planners' job of co-ordinating with several agencies more effective, as commitments may be achieved by clever manipulation. However, these influential negotiative processes are not readily visible or available for public scrutiny, and are comparable to the kind of bargaining among major interests which has been given the name of "corporatist" (see Chapters 1 and 9).

By contrast, consultation with the public at large rarely takes this form. In a few cases, the public and the public agencies are lumped together and "consulted" via a letter or publicity statement and a copy of the plan. The citizen usually has to read the plan in a library or at the planning office in such cases. However, the requirement to produce a report on "public participation" undertaken (the public participation statement) which has to accompany a deposited plan has probably forced a number of authorities to do more than the above. In several authorities, public consultation in any case has developed as part of the normal activity of the planning department, or the council as a whole.

Public consultation can be undertaken in many forms. I have already referred in Section 3.2 to public involvement on working parties to work out

and test policy options. More usually comment and discussion on the
planning authority's ideas is sought through public meetings, exhibitions
(often mobile), questionnaires to individuals, questionnaires to organizations,
meetings with selected organizations, news releases and use of radio and the
local press. In some areas, despite planners' attempts to arouse interest,
there has been limited response. Cherwell DC circulated 12 000 questionnaires
in Banbury. Only 2% were returned (Vine 1980). Epping Forest's experience
with their Queens Road Area District Plan was little better (13%). By
contrast, there is the example of the Lapworth District Plan (Warwick DC).
As already noted, this plan concerns a wealthy urban fringe area. The
purpose of the plan was to determine the boundaries of the green belt and
thus clarify the status of an area of "white land". The planners were
concerned to allocate some land for local needs, taking a wider area than
the immediate vicinity into their calculations (Wilson 1977b). Local
residents, who had previously organized themselves into a preservation
society to oppose the M 40, swung into action again in defence of the green
belt. The local authority circulated a questionnaire to one in five
residents and had a 74% response rate (Bruton and Lightbody 1979, Bruton
1980b). The result of this involvement, which continued on into the public
inquiry, was that the plan became progressively more restrictive. It is
worth noting that this plan took two and a half years from publication of
draft policies to deposit. Yet it was for a very small area, and the final
document is very slight. Fareham Western Wards (Hampshire CC) is another
example where the public demanded increasing involvement in local plan
preparation. Here, however, local people disputed the county's strategy for
servicing new development, as well as the scale of growth proposed. It
took the Inspector's judgement to change the content of the plan.

In some areas, amenity groups, specialist interest groups or residents'
groups manage to achieve the status of a regular consultee. In other words,
they transfer from being part of the "public at large" to the status of a
"major agency". This difference in status is likely to be marked not just
by the frequency of formal contact over planning matters, but by the
accessibility of the planning authority to representatives of such groups,
and by the influence such groups have over the content of policies and
proposals. It is also probable that in some areas, certain development
interests achieve the same status, building on their close contact through
negotiations over particular planning applications (Healey et al. 1982a).

The three questions which need to be addressed about public consultation are,
firstly, how far it has changed both the content of plans and the relations
between the local planning authority and citizens; secondly, which members
of the public have become involved; and thirdly, whose interests have the
changes served. The answers to all three questions in the Lapworth example
are fairly clear, but this is typical only of affluent urban fringe areas.
The likelihood is that there is significant variation between the nature
and impact of public consultation from one area to another, and that
generalizations can only be made at the level of the nature of land and
property interests in an area, the form of the local authority's
relationship to its constituents and the changing patterns of economic
investment in a locality. The only useful generalization that can be made
without better research into these questions than we currently have is that
those who get involved in local plan consultation tend to be middle class
owner-occupiers. There is also some evidence to suggest that those with
development interests tend to by-pass consultation, waiting until a plan is
finally produced to decide whether it suits them or not (Bruton et al. 1981).

3.5 Who and What Determines the Content of Local Plans?

Those engaged in plan preparation, after doing whatever research and
consultation is seen to be necessary, are faced with a mass of information -
facts, opinions, ideas, objections - which somehow have to be processed into
justified proposals, to form a local plan. The conventional critical
interpretation is that this is all done in the planners' terms, i.e. it is a
technocratic process (Kirk 1980). Were this the case, then planners' values
would be reflected in proposals (notably concerns for "rationally"-derived
policies, for encouraging and protecting good design, and in many areas in
the 1970s, helping the disadvantaged), constrained by structure plan
policies and by DoE advice. Yet there is evidence that this technocratic
process has from time to time been substantially swayed. The most noisy
of these deflections to the planners' path have occurred where local groups
have demanded entry into preparation and have been successful in changing
policies. Even on a lesser scale, public involvement provides planners
with a great deal of information - about sites, issues and priorities. This
itself may change the way planners think about plan content. Less visible
but arguably much more significant has been the role of public agencies
and other government departments. Even less visible, but yet emerging from
detailed case studies (Healey et al. 1982a), is the effect on plan content of
those with private development interests. It is probably therefore
inappropriate to describe the planner as a technocrat in local plan
preparation. S/he is more a mediator, a filterer of an array of changing
interests. This may in part account for h/her lack of attention to the
methodological issues raised in Section 3.3. It also makes it more
difficult to identify h/her contribution. This is of course a problem for
planners. More importantly, it is a problem for the rest of us. To whom
are local planners, and the others who make a significant contribution to the
content of plans, accountable? Here we have to ask how far have
councillors been aware of local plan preparation and able to interpret the
meaning of policies and proposals?

In some cases, there can be no doubt about the active involvement of
councillors, as in the examples quoted in Section 3.2. There are other
examples where a subgroup of planning committee councillors keeps a
watching eye on plan preparation. Examples are reported where councillors
have changed policies, and planners in both Sheffield and Manchester report
that councillors in practice set the climate within which plans and other
work are undertaken. It is for this reason that the London Borough Plans
for Islington, Westminster and Kensington and Chelsea have different
emphases and priorities. More disturbing are reports that councillors
do not understand the plans they have approved, or approve them in
principle but do not feel bound by them. The first throws doubt on the
ability of councillors to act as an adequate check on administrative
discretion. The second questions the relevance of the plan preparation
exercise itself.

Finally, it is worth considering the other side of the coin. Did the
process of plan preparation produce any outcomes in itself? Did it change
the activities of any of those who became involved in its preparation?
Three sorts of effects of the process of preparation are commonly noted by
planners. The first is that public and hence political consciousness is
raised about certain issues during discussion about the plan. These may or
may not be areas to which the final plan actually addresses itself. (A good
example here is local needs policies in areas where development is in
general to be restrained.) Similarly, they may or may not be issues
injected into discussion by the planners. Secondly, the process of
preparation may produce resource commitments, as in the Beckton case.

Thirdly, the activity of preparing a plan may develop working relationships within the planning department, and between it, other departments, public agencies, local groups and development interests which may persist after plan preparation has been finished. It is for all these reasons that it may be claimed that the process of plan preparation is more important than the product.

In other words, local plan preparation may improve the efficiency and effectiveness of some aspects of local authority work and may make this more visible and accountable. But these two gains are not necessarily compatible, as has often been pointed out (e.g. Fudge 1976). The desire for efficiency and effectiveness is likely to stress the role of interorganizational consultation and manipulation, co-ordinating the large interests. The search for accountability leads to public debate, letting all interests have a say. It is perhaps a significant tendency of the late 1970s that planners became more interested in the first and less in the second, a tendency which McAuslan has highlighted in the changes in the 1980 Local Government, Planning and Land Act (McAuslan 1981).

4. PLAN SCRUTINY

In a number of cases, local authorities prepare local plans with no intention of making them statutory local plans. In this case, none of the formal procedures for consultation described in the previous section apply, though these are often undertaken. More frequently, authorities are undecided about whether or not to convert their plans into formal statutory plans by going through the often lengthy certification, deposit and adoption procedures.

As Marsh (1980 Chapter 7) notes, many local planners view these procedures as a tiresome and costly addition to an already lengthy process of plan preparation which brings few extra benefits. As he suggests, local authorities may at this stage feel defensive about their plans, often so elaborately prepared. They may thus accede to the temptation not to deposit the plan. A recent report from the District Planning Officers' Society in fact recommends the removal of inquiries as statutory requirement (DPOS 1982). It is difficult to tell how many plans are in a position to be formally deposited but yet this has not been done. South Oxfordshire has been using its small town local plans for some time and so far has deposited none of them. Two of the plans studied by Vine (1980) are in a similar situation. The DoE's attitude is ambiguous. Local authorities are urged to prepare statutory plans. Yet to overcome the problem created by the delayed approval of structure plans, the Inspectorate were asked to support plans which had been through the appropriate procedures up to deposit (DoE Circulars 55/77 and 4/79).

To local authorities, the reasons for going through the plan scrutiny stages relate to whether full statutory support is likely to help them in dealing with planning applications, whether statutory status gives the plan additional status in other arenas, such as negotiations within their authority, and whether the public is likely to demand statutory status. Yet there are other reasons why plans should be subjected to semi-judicial review. One is of course the formal protection of property interests, although these also have the opportunity to appeal at the level of planning applications or purchase proposals. The process may also involve some parties who ignore consultation opportunities in plan preparation. More importantly, it allows scrutiny of the plan proposals from a point of view external to the local authority. Consequently, many interested parties

recognize it as a final check on local authority discretion. This is also
one of the reasons why local planners are nervous of this stage of plan
production. However, many people even when involved in an inquiry, do not
appreciate that although an inquiry is held by someone outside the local
authority, this person makes recommendations only to the authority. It is
up to the authority whether these are taken on board[57].

In this section, I will concentrate on who gets involved in plan scrutiny
and the extent to which plan proposals are changed through this process.
Unlike plan preparation, there have been two systematic studies of
inquiries and I have drawn substantially on both. The first is a study by
Marsh of 8 inquiries (Marsh 1980). The second is a study by Bruton,
Crispin, Fidler and Hill at Birmingham Polytechnic of a much larger number
of inquiries (Bruton et al. 1981, 1982a, b).

4.1 Depositing the Plan

Once a local plan has been approved by the local authority, it has to be
certified as in conformity with the structure plan. It is then put on
deposit with an opportunity for objections to be made. A copy is also sent
to the DoE whose function is to check that procedures have been correctly
followed. At this stage, then, there are three checks made on the form and
content of the plan-certification, DoE procedural review, and the
opportunity to object.

The certification of conformity with the structure plan is an explicit
policy control. Local authorities have been concerned about potential
problems at this stage, but most plans in the end progress through this
stage quickly. This is mainly because problems have been ironed out in
advance, or because where conflict is likely, plans have not been deposited.
If a county formally refuses to certificate a local plan, the district may
appeal to the DoE to arbitrate. The DoE has been reluctant to intervene,
and until recently there were few cases which reached the stage of a
request for intervention.

However, there was a run of cases in the early 1980s where counties have
opposed district plan proposals which involve more peripheral conurbation
development than structure plan policies imply. The most contentious case
has been in Bromsgrove, where Hereford and Worcestershire County claim that
the district plan has allocated an industrial site in the green belt and
not restricted residential development to that for local needs only[58].
This is a major strategic issue so far as the county's structure plan is
concerned, as well as being an interesting expression of the way the
continuing pressure to allocate greenfield sites is pushing against shire
county restraint policies. This dispute has gone to the DoE for
arbitration. In another case in Leeds, the DoE directed Leeds City to
revise the Marley Local Plan to exclude a proposal for industrial and
warehousing development on green belt land adjacent to the M 62, to bring
it into conformity with West Yorkshire structure plan. The DoE then called
in an application by Tarmac Ltd, for development on the site concerned
(Planning 471, 4 June 1982 and 473, 18 June 1982). In Newcastle, however,

---

[57]Bruton et al. 1982a highlight the extent of the confusion in the minds of
those participating in inquiries.

[58]Planning 463, 9 April 1982, p.12, see also Planning 480, 6 August 1982,
p.12.

the DoE ruled that a local plan which Tyne and Wear county refused to certify was in conformity, arguing that the dispute between the district and the county - over shopping policies for Newcastle city centre - should be resolved at the local plan inquiry (*Planning* 480, 6 August 1982).

Other conformity problems have arisen either at this stage or during inquiry, but these are usually seen as technicalities. The Buckinghamshire Minerals Subject Plan had a longer time period than the structure plan. Fareham Western Wards (Hampshire CC) was claimed to be out of conformity because it accepted lower population totals than the structure plan, but this did not prejudice conformity as the structure plan allocations were for a longer time period. Abbey District Plan (Leicester DC) shifted a major development site because of pollution problems. It is probable that a fairly liberal view of conformity is taken. It is worth citing one interesting case at this point: Hertfordshire's Structure Plan was modified by central government to reduce the extent of green belt, removing a green belt around Bishop's Stortford. The county and East Hertfordshire District have colluded in bringing it back. It appears in the latter's local plan, which conforms with the former's structure plan *amendments*, as is now possible under the 1980 Act. Not surprisingly, the DoE formally objected to the plan, and are of course unlikely to approve the amendments.

Because in relation to local plans, the DoE's role is formally procedural, it cannot officially require a local authority to alter the content of a plan where it disagrees with a policy. In such a case, it has to make a formal objection, just like any other aggrieved party. As I have argued elsewhere (Healey 1979b), this distinction between content and procedures is not as clear as it appears. DoE regional officers will often have advised plan preparers on the content of plans as well as format during preparation. Authorities may also send draft plans to them for comment and advice, and there is considerable evidence of substantial modifications made as a result of DoE advice on draft plans sent to them. They may advise that the scope of the plan is inappropriate, covering matters over which the planning authority has no formal control (such as social policy or management issues); they may indicate infelicities in wording, or inadequacies in the local plan map, or that the format of the plan as a whole is inappropriate (e.g. with the residential and employment subject plans referred to earlier). In a few cases, they have evidently considered the local plan to be incompetently prepared and have suggested a rethink. The only formal case of a plan being returned after deposit was the Waterloo District Plan (Lambeth) where it was claimed that despite extensive public involvement in plan preparation, the statutory procedures had been incorrectly followed.

It is thus clear that the DoE is not content to leave policy control over local plans to the structure plan. This is evident not only in the pre-deposit discussions just referred to, which appear to be occurring on a larger scale than was originally envisaged, but in the increasing number of formal objections to plans. A few of these objections have been procedural, over the way policies are expressed (e.g. Abbey District Plan, Leicester DC). Most frequently, however, they have related to green belt matters and local needs policies. In the first case, the DoE has attempted to ensure that green belt is treated consistently. It thus objected to Sutton Coldfield District Plan's use of the term "interim" green belt, as creating two categories of green belt (Birmingham DC). It has also objected to attempts to write green belt extensions back into local plans after they have been cut out through structure plan modifications (e.g. in East Hertfordshire DP). In the local Leeds case, the DoE has been concerned about whether it is legitimate for planning policies to distinguish between housing land allocations for local

and non-local people. Although such policies are to be found in a large
number of areas under development pressure, the DoE has objected only to
policies to exclude second home purchasers, in attractive rural areas. This
is an extension of similar modifications to structure plans.

4.2 Objections

Exactly how those with a potential interest in a local plan find out that
it has been deposited and that they can object is not at all clear. Earlier
public consultation may build up awareness of the plan. Development
interests may be on the look out for plan deposit. The local authority may
publicize deposit extensively (Bruton et al. 1981). In some cases,
objections are clearly orchestrated, as with the 357 objections to the
Eagle Street Action Area Plan (Coventry MD) (Marsh 1980), and the 1401
objections to the Wandsworth Borough Plan. The former was organized by
local community development officers, the latter by the fierce political
opposition to the then Tory council. The Birmingham Polytechnic work shows
interestingly that while public consultation processes may increase the
interest in the plan and hence in some cases the numbers of objections, many
objectors had no involvement in public consultation and vice versa (Bruton
et al. 1981).

Despite all the DoE's attempts to confine the scope of local plans to land
use and development matters and to non-strategic issues, those who do find
out about the plan and object, do not necessarily accept such limits.
Objections may relate to matters which should be in the plan but are not,
to matters discussed in the plan but not reflected in proposals, and to
the general case on which the plan is based. The assumptions of the London
Borough plans in particular have been challenged by articulate groups often
consisting of or advised by other planners (e.g. Camden, Westminster,
Hammersmith). Some objections may support the plan, or be a counter-
objection to someone else's objection. How then is the local authority to
decide whether an objection is relevant, and consequently whether an inquiry
should be held?

DoE advice on inquiries (DoE 1977a) states that an objection is not
relevant if:

(1) it is made outside the time limit;

(2) it is not properly made to a proposal in the plan (although
    the distinction between policies, proposals and other
    considerations in a plan is not always too clear - see
    Chapter 7);

(3) it challenges the strategic policies already approved in
    the structure plan;

(4) it challenges proposals which are not properly part of
    a local plan, or which raises issues which are wider than
    the land use remit.

This is a clear statement of the boundaries of the content of a local plan,
as the DoE sees it. Marsh (1980 p.28) claims that the DoE sought a narrow
definition of objections to avoid the consideration in inquiries of
alternative proposals for development or general challenges to a plan.
Interestingly, the Sand and Gravel Association has challenged the
Buckinghamshire Minerals Subject Plan in the high court because the inquiry
did not allow the consideration of alternatives sites. Although allowed by

DoE advice, the Association claims that such a procedure is contrary to natural justice. (*Planning* 480, 6 August 1982.) However, in practice, local authorities, often on the advice of the Inspector appointed to hold an inquiry, have taken a liberal view on all these points, with around two thirds of local plans so far adopted subject to an inquiry.

The dilemma for the DoE and local authorities in respect of local plan inquiries is that while, for the DoE, the adoption procedures are the opportunity to allow property interests to object to proposals which affect specific sites, they also provide an opportunity for continuing public debate about the desirability of particular policies and proposals. The DoE, in defining relevant objections and in attempting to limit the content of plans, has been trying to keep the role of local plan inquiries to the first purpose. However, with the increasing demands for public scrutiny of the validity of a wide range of public development proposals, their efforts have been in vain. Local authorities and Inspectors recognize that inquiries are *de facto* a significant arena for public and often overtly political debate.

Evidence of this can be found both in the wide definition of relevant objections, and in the acceptance of late objections. These are usually heard if an inquiry is already arranged. Objections lodged during an inquiry may even be heard. The local authority may assist objectors to frame their objection in an appropriate form (e.g. Atherstone District Plan (North Warwicks)). Challenges to strategic policy may be accepted (notably at Fareham Western Wards (Hants CC) and Sutton Coldfield (Birmingham MD)). This practice may increase where local plans are deposited prior to structure plan approval, as is now possible in the 1980 Act. Challenges which raise non-land use issues are normally accepted, for example, the objection to Camden's proposal to discriminate between private and public nursery education, and in the demand at Lewes (Town of Lewes DP) that housing proposals should discriminate positively towards local people in housing need.

In general, Marsh concludes that local authorities err on the cautious side, holding an inquiry and accepting objections if there is any doubt about relevance (Marsh 1980). Inspectors also seem to take this receptive position. This partly reflects the uncertainty about the scope and content of local plans. It may also reflect local authority concern to continue a consultative style built up during public consultation in plan preparation, or a more explicit political concern to ensure that no pressure groups can claim that their views have been suppressed.

Underlying the question of the definition of relevant objections, however, is the issue of accountability. The DoE wishes to confine local plan inquiries to ensuring that planning authorities account for their policies to property interests, assuming that normal political processes by which councils approve local plans provide an adequate accountability check on the general desirability of policies and proposals. Yet it must be asked why property interests need this double check. They can in any case object again if a planning application is refused. If, however, property interests are allowed this opportunity, it is reasonable to argue that so too should everyone else. If this is accepted, questions then have to be asked about who decides whether objections are relevant and whether an inquiry should take place. Officers must report to their members on the objections heard and make recommendations abut the need for an inquiry. It would not be difficult for officers and members to define away an objection. Bryant's objection to the Solihull Green Belt Subject Plan was defined as not relevant because it questioned the structure plan. No inquiry was held.

Yet other such objections have been heard. Bryant have taken the council
to the high court for a ruling here, bringing the DoE into the action on the
grounds that the latter should have ensured that the council hold an inquiry.
The result of this action is not yet known.

Many other objectors, whose objections are potentially relevant, would find
it difficult to seek such remedies if their objection was ignored. Their
only consolation is that so far objections tend to be heard, but there is no
guarantee that this will continue. It is worth noting that Hampshire County
Council nearly decided against holding an inquiry into their Fareham
Western Wards Action Area Plan which generated 478 objections and a
contentious inquiry on strategic grounds (Marsh 1980). Local authorities
now face severe financial constraints. The 1980 Act allows objections to
be dealt with by written representations if all parties agree. This appears
a sensible provision in several cases where objections are few and minor
(e.g. Groby District Plan (Hinkley and Bosworth DC), Longford Action Area
Plan (Coventry MD), Brunswick District Plan (Salford MD)). In Oldbury
District Plan (Sandwell MB), all parties had agreed to modifications, but
prior to the 1980 Act, an inquiry still had to be held. However, the
legislative change creates an opportunity to avoid an inquiry by persuading
objectors, to have their objection dealt with by written representations.
This clearly goes against the demands for open presentation of objections
to an impartial assessor. Given such demands, it is likely in practice that
it will not be politically possible to avoid many inquiries as a result of
the 1980 Act.

4.3 Who Objects and About What?

There is an enormous range in the numbers of objections received to a plan.
Sometimes there are none (as in the case of Eden Street Action Area Plan
(Coventry)). Only two, both from developers, were made to Solihull Green
Belt subject plan (Solihull MD), and in many other cases, only a handful
of objections are received. Several plans have produced hundreds of
objections. LB Wandsworth's Borough Plan held the record by the end of 1981
with 1401, overtaken in 1982 when over 8000 objections were made to Greater
Manchester County Council's Green Belt Subject Plan. Table 6.4, from Marsh's
study, gives some idea of who objectors are. Most are either amenity groups
or individuals. However, the presence of commercial firms at inquiries is
not infrequent, and most are legally or professionally represented (Marsh
1980 p.87a).

The number of inquiries by individuals and amenity groups raises questions
about the role of public consultation in plan preparation. As already noted
the PAG report and the DoE hoped that public consultation programmes would
reduce the numbers of objections. This seems to have been the case in Eden
Street Action Area Plan (Coventry MD). Bruton *et al.* cite Brunswick
District Plan (Salford MD) as a similar case. On the other hand, in other
cases public involvement in plan preparation actually increased the numbers
of objections, by identifying points of conflict which could not be resolved
into consensus agreement (as in Lapworth District Plan (Warwick CD)),
(Bruton *et al.* 1981), or merely raising awareness of the issues involved
(e.g. through the residents' working groups at Westminster, and Kensington
and Chelsea (Marsh 1980 p.135)). Marsh concludes:

> "The great majority of objections arise out of informal channels
> of communication already established between the local planning
> authority and potential objectors during public participation;
> and from routine contact between the local planning authority

TABLE 6.4

Local plan inquiry	Total No. of recorded objections	No. of objectors heard[59]	Type of objector heard			
			Central/ local govnt.	Commercial organizations	Amenity groups[60]	Individuals
1	2	3	4	5	6	7
Beckton	110	23	1	1	12	9
Covent Garden	28	12	1	6	2	3
Eagle Street	357	8	-	4	3	1
Fareham	478	112	2	6	13	93
Galley Common	9	4	-	1	-	3
Groby	9	5	-	2	2	1
Lewes	97	13	1	1	6	6
Sutton Coldfield	122	22	1	2	10	9

Footnotes: [59] i.e. appeared in person or had their written evidence read out.

[60] including all residents' associations, interest groups, etc., and any 'umbrella organization' formed for the purpose of the PLI.

(Source: Marsh 1980 p.87a).

and developers, land owners, commercial undertakings and so forth"
(Marsh 1980 p.61).

Both Marsh and Bruton *et al.* note the limited involvement of developers,
landowners and commercial undertakings in consultation programmes. Bruton
et al. from their interviews with objectors, found some evidence to suggest
that property interests are sometimes professionally advised not to get
involved until a plan has been deposited. This may partly be a recognition
that the implications of the plan would not be evident until proposals were
finalized. It probably also reflects their greater faith in the formal
objection and inquiry procedure and their greater familiarity with it.
Development interests are accustomed to dealing with local planning
authorities at the development control level, often having ongoing and close
contacts (Healey *et al.* 1982a). They may prefer to negotiate over policies
and proposals in an ongoing way, now and again objecting and having an
inquiry, rather than engaging in the more unfocussed general discussions
involved in local consultation exercises. However, although individual
developers and landowners and their advocates appear at inquiries, it is
rare for organizations representing their interests to enter an objection.
An interesting exception here was Dacorum, where the House Builders'
Federation objected to the principle of the mechanism used for phasing
development. Dacorum District Plan contained control totals for specified
time periods. Control totals for later periods were to be reduced if
exceeded in an earlier period. The HBF's concern was about the precedent
that might be set by this "recoupment" policy.

What objections are about is obviously related to the policies in the plan.
However, Marsh found it possible to classify objections into two broad
groups - those related to property, and those related to policy questions.
I reproduce his classifications below (Marsh 1980, p.88 *et seq.*).

1. Property Objections:

(1) Small scale:

> (the loss of part of a front garden or back garden to a road or school
> proposal, for example. One "objector" to Brunswick District Plan
> (Salford MD) merely wanted to propose that a maypole be erected in the
> area).

(2) Substantial sites:

> (as where a major part of a substantial landholding may be affected.
> Marsh quotes the case of a tenant farmer in Sutton Coldfield who stood
> to lose nearly half of his holding of over 200 acres for development).

(3) By a dominant property owner:

> (Marsh quotes here the British Gas Corporation at Beckton, who owned a
> large part of the 2000 acres proposed for docklands re-development).

2. Policy Objections:

(4) "Sins of Omission":

> (where an objector seeks to insert a policy or proposal, or correct its
> emphasis, or ensure back-up resources or proposals are available. This
> last objection is often made where large-scale development is involved

and local residents fear that social facilities will not be provided in
phase, e.g. Sutton Coldfield, Fareham Western Wards).

(5) Technical validity of policies and proposals:

(where it is argued that a policy or proposal will not achieve its
objective. This appears to be particularly common in relation to traffic
management schemes. Bruton et al. (1981) note Tamworth District Plan
(Tamworth) and Banbury District Plan (Cherwell) as examples).

(6) Objections of principle to the plan's major policies and proposals:

(these, of course, will usually challenge the structure plan also.
Marsh notes, in addition to the Sutton Coldfield and Fareham Western
Wards cases, Grosvenor Estates' challenge to Westminster's restriction
of office development. To this may be added the challenge made by
developers and the New Town Development Commission to Dacorum District
Plan, which, like East Hertfordshire's, was in conformity with an amended
version of an approved structure plan. It was claimed that the Inquiry
should not be held. The DoE clearly sympathized with the developers
here, since, as in East Hertfordshire, the amended structure plan and
the district plan attempted to replace policies struck out by the DoE in
approving the structure plan).

Bruton et al. (1981) suggest a further category: the level of detail of the
plan, where a district objects to proposals in county local plans, as in
district objections to Humberside's Intensive Livestock Units Subject Plan.

However, as is evident from Table 6.4, not all objections are heard. This is
partly because some are grouped, as in the Eagle Street Action Area Plan
Inquiry (Coventry MD). Only a very few are defined as irrelevant, as
already discussed. However, a number of objections are in effect negotiated
away. It is common practice for planning authorities to meet objectors
informally prior to an inquiry, or even prior to deciding whether to hold an
inquiry (Marsh 1980 p.64). Such discussions are no doubt used for many
purposes - to explain non-relevance, to help objectors frame their proposals
in a more satisfactory way, to help persuade them to withdraw objections,
and to discuss possible modifications to the plan. There is little
information about the detail of such discussions and the way different sorts
of objections and types of objectors are treated, though it would be of
interest to study those objections which are withdrawn. In many cases, the
local authority proposes a modification to the plan before the inquiry. In
effect, pre-inquiry discussions may produce significant changes to plan
policies. The 1980 Act encourages this still further, with the possibility
of not holding an inquiry as an advantage to be achieved by the local
authority.

Most such modifications are minor, but in the Eagle Street case, a proposal
to demolish 259 dwellings was changed to rehabilitation (Marsh 1980 p.66).
Westminster planners introduced a substantial package of modifications at
the inquiry. Although such negotiations may often lead to desirable results
for the objectors and the local authority, there are worrying aspects of
this process, the most important being that those with an interest in a
proposal as modified might not have an opportunity to object. In some
instances a plan has been withdrawn from deposit, redeposited and amended.
The problem with this negotiation procedure is that it produces a series
of bargaining and counter-bargaining moves between, in effect, a very few
objectors and the local authority. In a few cases, a panel of councillors
closely monitors these negotiations, but this is probably rare. Once again

one has to ask whether there are adequate safeguards against modifying plans in ways which favour certain interests in a way not intended in a plan as deposited. On the other hand, such negotiations can significantly reduce the degree of misunderstanding between the local authority and objectors. Inquiry Inspectors on the whole favour such negotiation. In one famous case, Wandsworth, the inquiry was adjourned after the first day because such discussion had not taken place. It is always possible where the local authority's proposals and approach to objections are highly contentious, as in the Wandsworth case, for the DoE to call in the plan and handle objections itself. This has so far happened only once, and related to the MAFF objection to the Stone District Plan. This was a late objection on strategic grounds apparently due to an oversight by MAFF, and the DoE was in this case assisting the authority.

4.4 The Inquiry and Modifications

The local authority prepares its plan. It has the discretion to determine what objections it has to accept, and may engage in discussions in an attempt to modify these objections. It arranges the inquiry, although the inquiry is held by a person appointed by the DoE, so far always from the Planning Inquiry Inspectorate. The local authority arranges the inquiry and decides whether or not to accept the recommendations which result. It is thus judge of its own case. Its decisions are formally made throughout by locally-elected councillors, but I have already raised doubts about the extent to which these review administrative process. The local plan inquiry is thus distinct from a public inquiry into a planning application, where a decision is made on or on behalf of the Secretary of State. As already noted, most objectors are not aware of this distinction, and are disturbed by its implications when it is made clear to them (Bruton et al. 1981). Inspectors so far have been at pains to clarify their position as advisers, not deciders, to all parties at the inquiry and to create the illusion of independence and hence external review of the plan. Nevertheless they are by no means independent and come to inquiries armed with DoE Circulars, advice notes, and, probably, though it is never admitted, briefing from DoE officials concerned with local plans and policy[61].

Are Inspectors then, a tool of DoE policy in reviewing local plans? To some extent this is true. Inspectors have upheld objections relating to inappropriate content where these are in line with DoE advice. The Camden Inspector recommended modification to the policy discriminating against private nursery schools. The Westminster Inspector (there were actually two) rather wearily dismissed an objector's proposal to restrict private medical facilities to the Harley Street area. These "are a part of normal every day activities in the United Kingdom and it is not a matter for a local plan to express a view or advance a policy on the effect of these on the provision of public medical facilities" (Inspectors' Report p.39). Marsh, however, notes that Inspectors have taken different attitudes to the "land use remit", and that Local Plan Advice Note 1/78 has not been taken literally (Marsh 1980 p.53).

The format and agenda for an inquiry is usually agreed between a "programme officer" appointed by the local authority (usually an administrator but occasionally a planner (Marsh 1980 p.62)), and the Inspector. Objections

---

[61]The existence of this briefing in relation to development control inquirie was finally admitted at the contentious Coin Street Inquiry in 1981.

are likely to be grouped into related sets to construct the agenda for the
inquiry. The actual proceedings are usually approached by the Inspector in
a flexible way, although tending to follow the format of an appeal inquiry
(the objector, followed by the local authority), with major objectors and
the local authority represented by a legal advisor. Individuals and amenity
societies normally find themselves given considerate attention to compensate
for their lack of experience in such situations. Marsh concludes that
Inspectors seem to have adapted the format of the inquiry to local
circumstances, which vary from the major confrontation between developers and
local authority at Westminster and Dacorum, or citizens and local
authority as at Fareham Western Wards, Eagle Street and Sutton Coldfield,
to a few owner-occupiers anxious about their properties (Marsh 1980 p.109).
However, Lewes DC had cause to complain that the Inspector at the Town of
Lewes District Plan Inquiry refused to accept a local inquiry format which
excluded legal representation, although the authority and the objectors had
agreed to it. However, the Birmingham Polytechnic study concluded that the
presence of legal representatives played a very significant part in
determining the tenor of the inquiry[62].

Whatever the uncertainties, eventually, after an inquiry lasting from one
day (Belbroughton District Plan (Bromsgrove)) to nearly five months
(Westminster District Plan), the Inspector produces a report. Two or three
months seems a normal interval. This report usually presents the case put
by the authority and the objector for each objection, concluding with a
recommendation to modify the plan or not, with necessary supporting argument.
The local authority has then to produce a short report for its committee
and for the public on whether it accepts modifications proposed. Marsh has
attempted a qualitative assessment of the "outcomes" of the local plan
inquiries he examined (see Table 6.5). This gives the impression that, of
the recommendations made, a substantial number were modifications. Of
these, nearly all were accepted. Many recommendations relate to
modifications proposed by the local authority itself. But, as Marsh notes,
such a table gives no indication of the significance of objections. Many
are small-scale property objections. Marsh claims that Inspectors tended
to lean towards such objectors on the grounds of fairness unless the
planning authority's case was overriding (Marsh 1980 p.120). Substantial
property objectors were not necessarily successful, (Laing's objections at
Fareham Western Wards, Bryant's at Sutton Coldfield, the Gas Board's at
Beckton and most of Grosvenor Estate's at Westminster all failed), though no
Inspector's modification to meet such an objection was overturned by the
local authority (pp.121-2). However, the tenacity of developers who
believe that a particular site has development potential does not appear to
be much affected by a local plan inquiry. At the Rossendale District Plan
Inquiry (Rossendale DC), a developer who felt he was losing support left
with the comment: "See you at the appeal"[63].

Objections to the general policy of the local authority fared less well,
according to Marsh, although Inspectors did propose modifications to a
traffic management scheme in Lewes District Plan and to the scale, location
and phasing of development at Fareham Western Wards. More recent cases
appear to support Marsh's conclusion. Grosvenor Estate's challenge to
Westminster City Plan's office policy was not upheld, nor was most of the
case made by "People before Profit" in relation to Hammersmith's Plan.

---

[2] Pers. comm. E. A. Hill.

[3] Meeting at Birmingham Polytechnic 31.5.1981.

TABLE 6.5

Local plan	Inspectors' recommendations		LPA's response to Inspector's recommendation that a modification be made			Total number of modifications made to written statement
	That no modification be made (a)	That a modification be made (b)	Accept in full (c)	Partial acceptance (d)	Reject (e)	(f)
Beckton	5	27(8)	27	-	-	20
Covent Garden	12	6(3)	6	-	-	10
Eagle Street	11	15(12)	11	3	1	42
Fareham Western Wards	Not given	27 -	25	1	1	229
Galley Common	2	3 -	0	0	3	0
Groby	2	5 -	4	0	1	3
Lewes	4	10(2)	2	3	2	24
Sutton Coldfield	18	10 -	7	2	1	42

Notes: Columns (a) and (c) The number of recommendations for or against modifications is not a reliable indicator of the overall impact of the inspectors' recommendations e.g. In Beckton, one recommendation against a modification (re Gas Corporation objection) far outweighs in significance the 27 recommendations for modifications in terms of the final 'shape' of the plan.

Column (b) Figures in brackets are recommendations in support of LPA's suggested 'pre-inquiry modifications'.

Column (d) Usually means that LPA accepts the principle implicit in the inspector's recommendations, but cannot accept in full because of practical difficulties.

Column (e) Galley Common and Groby are all 'technical' rejections - see appendix 4 (Resolution of Adoption, Galley Common DP).

Column (f) A modification may vary in magnitude from correcting a spelling mistake to a fundamental policy shift.

Objections to non-land use policies have received differential treatment. At Beckton, housing allocation and tenure policies, which the Inspector claimed would normally be regarded as "beyond the purposes of a local plan" were admitted because of the special circumstances of the area (Beckton District Plan Inspector's report para. 1.38). This modification was accepted by the local authority. In the Town of Lewes District Plan, the Inspector recommended that a proposal be amended to read: "In the allocation of the council's own housing or nomination for Housing Association accommodation, full account will be taken of the needs of people including single persons and childless couples under 40 years of age, who work locally and have local family ties or are in poor accommodation in the town" (Town of Lewes District Plan Inspector's report, p.47). In general, however, non-land use objections have not been successful, as with the objection concerning private medical facilities in the Westminster Plan.

There have, however, been few cases where the Inspectors' recommendations so substantially modified a plan as in Fareham Western Wards (Hants CC). Here, the amount of development intended in the plan period was reduced to two thirds of its original total (from 6000 to 4000 dwellings). The location of development was also altered, as were the phasing provisions including a requirement to complete specified facilities before further development took place. In this case, it is fair to conclude that the Inspector and the public in effect re-wrote the plan. The only other case where the Inspector's recommendations have seriously criticized the whole basis of a plan's policies and proposals is the Wandsworth case. The basis of this criticism was firstly, that the plan went beyond land use issues to make a broad political statement about council policies. Secondly, the policies were not adequately justified by an assessment of the problems of the area. The criticism centred on housing policies which advocated the development of local authority-owned land by private developers and the sale of council houses. Unfortunately, having argued that these policies were not within the land use remit, since they distinguished between the public and private sector as land developers, he then claimed that the policy for the sale of council houses was not adequately supported by an assessment of the borough's housing needs. His report has since been challenged on this count by central government ministers who have informed local councillors in Wandsworth that the Inspector's comment on national housing policies (for the sale of council houses) was inappropriate.

It is worth noting here a significant comment by the Inspector in his report, since it suggests that one concern of central government and the Inspectorate in maintaining the limited definition of the content of local plans is to keep "planning" policies out of the political arena:

> "I take the view that the Wandsworth Borough Plan must be properly designed to serve the interests of the borough under any administration, and that to this end, special care should be taken to ensure that the written statement is couched in neutral terms, whereby it may serve its true purpose without becoming a party political football to be kicked between opposing political goals, rather than a plan to be followed, monitored, and thoughtfully revised as need and opportunity may render change both desirable and practicable."

From what I have already said, however, it is evident that in many cases, the development of local plan policies and proposals is already within the political arena, if by this we understand public debate about the nature and validity of local authority policies[64].

In general, local authorities have accepted the modifications proposed by
Inspectors, although in a few cases, modifications have not been accepted
for technical reasons. However, the standing of the Inspector's
recommendations where these are not accepted has been called into question
by a number of recent cases, and the Inspectorate are known to be seeking
some clarification of their position. The case which has most worried the
Inspectorate related to allotments in the Waltham Forest Borough Plan.
Objectors argued against proposals that these should be allocated for
housing land. The Inspector supported their case, but the local
authority rejected the modification. At Hammersmith, the Inspector
supported an objection to plan proposals for a development by the London
Transport Executive in Hammersmith Centre. The local authority rejected
this recommendation, having given planning permission for the development
between the publication of the Inspector's report and discussion of the
recommendations. The Inspector's recommendations about how the local
authority should allocate its housing tenancies at Lewes was also rejected.

4.5 The Role of Plan Scrutiny

The process of receiving objections to a plan and holding an inquiry
firstly provides an opportunity for the identification and final resolution
of issues which still remain problematic after plan preparation. Secondly,
it leads to a continuation of the negotiative process between the local
authority and those interested in its proposals, which is typically a
major element in plan preparation. Thirdly, it provides an arena for
continuing public debate about a local authority's proposals, notably
where the local authority is in conflict with particular groups over
specific plan proposals or where there is ongoing political conflict between
a local authority and certain of its citizens (as at Wandsworth). Fourthly,
it allows property owners to have the specific adverse consequences of a
local authority's proposal considered as it affects their interests.
Fifthly, it provides an opportunity to check the competence of the local
authority's plan as formulated, a form of "quality control" as Marsh
suggests (1980, p.159). Finally, it allows the DoE to inject its oar
once again, on policy matters as an objector.

There are several reasons why local authorities may feel uncomfortable with
plan scrutiny. One already mentioned is that it exposes their competence
to public scrutiny. Another is that it merely continues conflicts which
can never be resolved to the satisfaction of all parties. A third reason
is that the style of the semi-judicial review, with objectors opposing
local authorities, conflicts with the consultative and negotiative style
which authorities often develop during plan preparation and sometimes in
development control and other work. Is there then a case for eliminating
it, as the DPOS report (1982) argues, especially as in the end, it is the
local authority's decision which prevails? An alternative argument is
that since many conflicts cannot be negotiated away, and that in an inquiry
someone other than the local authority suggests what significance comment
and criticism of policies may have, the inquiry is in fact the most
important part of plan production. How one approaches this debate depends
upon one's view of the competence of local authorities, the rights of

---

[64]Details of the Inspector's report on the Wandsworth Borough Plan are to
be found in *Planning* 456, 19 February 1982 p.5.

property interests, the role and status of local plans and the way in which public authorities should arrive at their policies and proposals.

5. CONCLUSIONS

Statutory local plan production, as this chapter has shown, is a long and often difficult business. Its consumption of resources of manpower and paper may be less than in structure plan production, but it must be considerably more than the preparation of the other policy vehicles (or planning systems) that have developed in and for local authorities in the 1970s (Stewart 1977). It can also be contrasted with these other planning systems in the way a technical or applied research mode of policy formation is combined with consultative-negotiative modes, with public debate, and, in the case of many statutory plans, with a semi-judicial mode. This mixture of modes and its methodological implications is certainly not fully appreciated by most of the planners involved in local plan work. Local plan production also differs in that the consultative-negotiative mode not only spans public sector relationships, but community and private sector interests as well. We may therefore wonder why such an elaborate form of policy production has evolved for detailed site-specific development guidance in land use planning.

One common explanation is that since the planning authority's decisions about land use affect private property interests, it is important that the latter are given every opportunity to state their case. I would restate this argument somewhat differently. If the state is to play a role in determining what land uses and developments are to be permitted, it must, in a society which places importance on the concept of private property, make publicly evident the basis for its decisions. In addition, other government departments ever since 1947 have sought to ensure that their autonomy is not limited by planning policies. The procedures for formal consultation with them helps to protect their interests and ensure that their actions do not at some later stage invalidate plans. Until the 1960s, then, plan production was acceptably a process of applied research and design, with technical experts (planners) to do the job combined with consultation and negotiation with major public development interests. Since then, the recognition of the scale and depth of conflict over not only the way land is used and developed, but the way resources are allocated and distributed in a general way, has encouraged the use of these procedures as an opportunity for public and increasingly overt political debate about the validity of the local authority's policies. Articulate sections of the public and organized pressure groups have been demanding the opportunity to check the plan's validity. Local authorities, in turn, have tended to seek to develop co-operative and negotiative styles of working with the most demanding of such groups reflecting the negotiative style that has become common when working with larger development interests. Consensus agreement is being negotiated to avoid confrontations in arenas such as the public local inquiry. This in turn pushes the development of the plan's policies and proposals back into the administrative arena. Public consultation and the inquiry process had the effect of drawing them into the public and political arena. It is thus no surprise to find that those who argue for more public scrutiny of administrative discretion, in this case to determine "the public interest" in the way land is used and developed, wish to strengthen the semi-judicial aspect of plan production (TCPA 1981, McAuslan 1980).

A further reason for the complexities of local plan production must therefore be that the issues it is concerned with are those around which a substantial degree of conflict exists. This is of course not always the case, as we have seen, nor is it always easy to identify in advance which issues will raise major disputes. The resolution of such conflicts is all the more difficult to contain since the issues typically cut across the conventional divisions of the public sector (departments, levels, elected councils, quagos and quangos) and across major interests within society as a whole. As Foley noted in 1960, the consensus upon which planning was built up after the war masked major internal conflicts of interest. These have become increasingly evident since then. While they can still be more or less contained at the level of generality at which structure plans operate, it is much more difficult to do so as policies are developed into specific proposals.

The form of local plan production is really no different from that for all development plans established in the 1947 Act. For reasons of administrative efficiency - to devolve the work of handling inquiries and to reduce the amount of objections to plans - the form of plan preparation was marginally altered to allow more opportunity for consultation and publicity and to give to local authorities the task of organizing inquiries. In parallel, changing political demands ensured that from time to time the opportunities made available through these procedural changes were vigorously used. In response, both central government and local authorities are retreating into less formalized arrangements. However, these in turn make it even more difficult for the DoE to ensure that local planning policies do not compromise its own policy interests.

In other local government policy fields, central government can fall back on financial control, as in housing, education or transport. In land use planning, it has to depend on advice, on procedural checks, and as we have seen, the occasional formal intervention to establish the boundaries, as it sees them, to local authority activity. As local authorities move further into consultative and negotiative modes of operation, it becomes more difficult for central government to monitor this activity. This perhaps explains the stress in DoE advice of the later 1970s on transferring to statutory plans and, more recently, on producing plans quickly, with the minimum of investigation and consultation. Yet central government in other guises, in a whole variety of ways, is making the issues to which plans are addressed more dynamic and more difficult to resolve. Consequently, however much local authorities may seek to speed up plan preparation, it now often requires more consultation and negotiation and possibly more investigation than it did when public investment resources were expanding. Thus the form of local plan production contained in legislation and regulation raises problems for both central and local government. In order to safeguard their interests, both are likely to develop informal practices to circumvent the limitations produced by the formal practices. As has been suggested, in addition to the local authority and the DoE, these are likely to be other central government or local authority departments and public agencies and, depending on the local situation, often larger development interests, or environmental pressure groups. In other words, how local plans are produced, and whether they are produced, is likely to *reflect* more than it *structures* the ongoing relationship between the planning authority and the various agencies, groups and interests with which it is involved. Nevertheless, the formal procedures for statutory local plan production can be used, with some effort, to force new groups and new issues into this relationship.

Local Plans: Their Form and Content

This chapter examines the plan documents themselves, the products of the processes described in the previous chapter. As with the preparation of plans, their form and content is in theory something to be determined by the planning authority. Compared to old-style development plans, or policy vehicles such as HIPs or TPPs, where a precise format is imposed by central government, local plan documents come in considerable variety. A statutory local plan has to consist of a Written Statement and a Proposals Map on an ordnance survey base. It has also to be accompanied, when deposited, by a statement on "public participation" undertaken in plan preparation. For non-statutory plans, authorities are of course free to choose any format.

Some plans run to well over 100 pages, with photographs, diagrams and maps within the Written Statement. Others are very brief, the shortest being a single fold-out or pamphlet format (e.g. Hemel Hempstead Town Centre Plan (Dacorum DC) or those referred to by McGilp (1981)). The Proposals Map may be within the text, as a foldout bound in with the text, or a map, often very large, in a pocket at the back of the report. Maps may be monochrome or multicolour, with any kind of colouring convention. Some plans explain clearly their purposes and status. In others, this is difficult to discover and in a few it requires considerable effort to determine the date of the plan and the plan area. In some, survey material and a report on public participation is presented together with objectives, policies and proposals. Others state simply the proposals and their justification, with survey material and consultation documents treated as quite separate. And the covers of plans display varying degrees of graphic flamboyance. One might say that the only common element about them is that they are on A4 sized paper.

There are a few common conventions. Following DoE advice, statements of policies and proposals in plans are normally clearly distinguished, in heavy type or capital letters. Some plans use the diagrammatic conventions provided in DoE advice (the Development Plans Manual) and the earlier MHLG ideas on town centre plans (MHLG 1962) (see Diagram 7.1). However, this form of presentation was more appropriate where substantial development was expected and where local authorities could afford the costs of multicolour presentation. Consequently, authorities have increasingly worked out their own presentational forms. Somewhat curiously, given planners' self image as

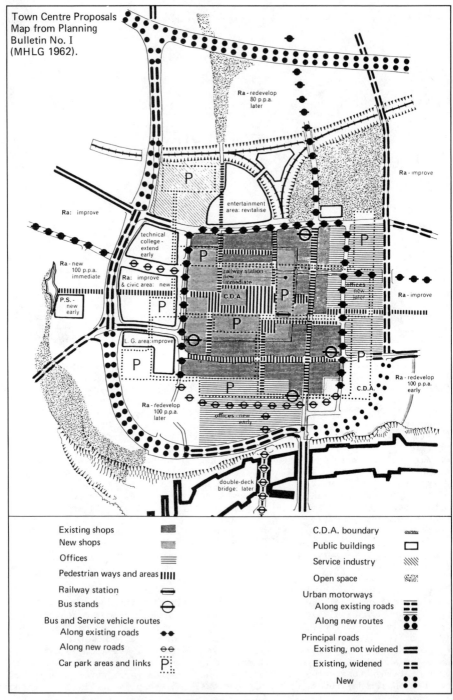

Town Centre Proposals
Map from Planning
Bulletin No. I
(MHLG 1962).

Ra - redevelop
80 p.p.a.
later

Ra - improve

Ra: improve

entertainment
area: revitalise

technical
college -
extend
early

P

railway station
new
immediate

C.D.A.

offices
new
later

Ra - improve

Ra - new
100 p.p.a.
immediate

Ra: improve
& civic area: new

P.S. -
new
early

P

L. G. area:improve

P

P

Ra - redevelop
100 p.p.a.
early

C.D.A.

Ra - redevelop
100 p.p.a.
later

offices new
early

double-deck
bridge: later

Existing shops	▦	C.D.A. boundary
New shops	▦	Public buildings
Offices	☰	Service industry
Pedestrian ways and areas ‖‖‖		Open space
Railway station	⬯	Urban motorways
Bus stands	⊖	Along existing roads
Bus and Service vehicle routes		Along new routes
Along existing roads	◆◆	Principal roads
Along new roads	⊖⊖	Existing, not widened
Car park areas and links	P	Existing, widened
		New

Diagram 7.1(a)

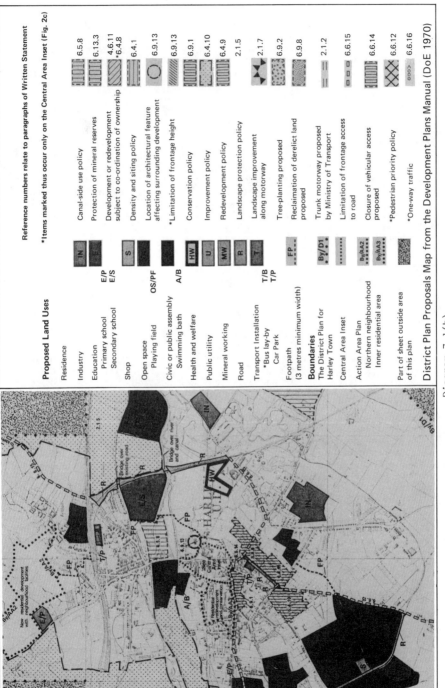

Reference numbers relate to paragraphs of Written Statement

*Items marked thus occur only on the Central Area Inset (Fig. 2c)

Proposed Land Uses		
Residence		
Industry	IN / E	
Education		
Primary school	E/P	
Secondary school	E/S	
Shop	S	
Open space		
Playing field	OS/PF	
Civic or public assembly		
Swimming bath	A/B	
Health and welfare	HW / U	
Public utility		
Mineral working	MW	
Road	R	
Transport Installation	T / T/B	
*Bus lay-by	T/P	
Car Park		
Footpath	FP	
(3 metres minimum width)		
Boundaries		
The District Plan for	By/D1	
Harley Town		
Central Area Inset		
Action Area Plan		
Northern neighbourhood	By/AA2	
Inner residential area	By/AA3	
Part of sheet outside area		
of this plan		

Canal-side use policy	6.5.8
Protection of mineral reserves	6.13.3
Development or redevelopment subject to co-ordination of ownership	4.6.11 / *6.4.8
Density and siting policy	6.4.1
Location of architectural feature affecting surrounding development	6.9.13
*Limitation of frontage height	6.9.13
Conservation policy	6.9.1
Improvement policy	6.4.10
Redevelopment policy	6.4.9
Landscape protection policy	2.1.5
Landscape improvement along motorway	2.1.7
Tree-planting proposed	6.9.2
Reclamation of derelict land proposed	6.9.8
Trunk motorway proposed by Ministry of Transport	2.1.2
Limitation of frontage access to road	6.6.15
Closure of vehicular access proposed	6.6.14
*Pedestrian priority policy	6.6.12
*One-way traffic	6.6.16

District Plan Proposals Map from the Development Plans Manual (DoE 1970)

Diagram 7.1(b)

professionals concerned with their clients' needs and with public discussion
on planning policies, local plans are not easy to read or understand. Their
authors appear to have had an audience of local councillors, local groups
with a specialist interest in planning and sometimes development control
officers in mind when composing their documents. There appears to be little
appreciation that local plans may be of interest to people outside a local
area, such as developers, or that many citizens do not have a sophisticated
grasp of planning ideas and procedures.

Local plans thus appear local in orientation and specific to particular
areas and issues. Nevertheless, despite the superficial variety in form,
there are consistencies in form and in content, just as there are in the way
plans are prepared. I will try to illustrate this consistency-within-
variety first, by brief summaries of seven plans, selected to cover a range
of areas and problems to which local plans are directed. I then consider
the content of the policies contained in plans, in terms of their apparent
aims. I follow this by looking in more detail at the kinds of policies
that plans contain, and the way policies and proposals are intended to be
implemented. In conclusion, I return to the question of the limited
variation to be found in the form and content of local plans, and consider
what has constrained this variation.

1. A SUMMARY OF SEVEN PLANS

So far in this account I have cited brief examples of a large number of
plans. Inevitably this is unsatisfactory, since it is not possible in this
way to illustrate the relationship between local circumstances and the form
and content of plans. To remedy this, I provide here a collection of
accounts of plans, selected from different sorts of areas. Even these
accounts fail to provide the depth necessary to relate the role and nature
of the plan to the economic and political circumstances in which the plan was
prepared. It is only now that such studies are becoming available[65].

I have selected seven plans representing a range of types of area, using the
classification developed in Chapter 5, although all are district plans and
all have been deposited. Three are all-area plans, chosen because these
contain within a single plan a variety of types of area (Gloucester includes
suburbs and town centre, Horsham large settlements and small villages). For
each, I indicate the type of area involved and a brief history of plan
production. I then attempt to summarize the form of the plan and give an
indication of plan content. The plans selected are:

   Farnworth District Plan (Bolton MD): inner city area (Type area: 6).

   Newton-le-Willows District Plan (St. Helens MD): unattractive urban
      fringe land in the north west (Type area: 3).

   Islington Development Plan (Islington LB): all-area inner London
      Borough Plan (Type area: 10).

   Horsham Area District Plan (Horsham DC): all-area town and rural

---

[65] See the ten case studies to be published by Fudge, Lambert and Underwood,
based on the ten case studies undertaken for the DoE in their study of
local plan preparation (Fudge *et al.* 1982); see also E. A. Hill's Ph.D
study of county-district relations in local plan preparation undertaken,
and Farnell 1981).

villages under severe development pressure (Type area: 10 and 1c).

Chandler's Ford District Plan (Hampshire CC): major growth area
(Type area: 2a).

Ashby Wolds Area District Plan (North West Leicestershire DC):
villages in a mining area (Type area: 9).

City of Gloucester District Plan 1981 (Gloucester City Council): all
area plan for town with investment potential (Type area: 10).

Diagram 7.2 shows the location of these plans

Farnworth District Plan: (Bolton MD, Greater Manchester MC) (Diagram 7.3)

Deposited District Plan
Small area
350 hectares
17 000 people

This is an inner city area of social deprivation and physical decay, with
"exhibits chronic social, economic and environmental problems, many of which
represent the last vestiges of the area's former industrial expansion".
Plan preparation was authorized by the District Council in December 1974.
The major problems within the area were identified in the non-statutory
Bolton Metropolitan Borough Plan, which advocated policies for inclusion
in the structure plan and defined corporate policies for the council
itself. A report of survey for the District Plan was published in December
1975, with a report on *Alternative Policies and Proposals* in 1976. A draft
written statement was then published for comment in December 1977. The
plan was in use from this time, though it was not formally deposited until
October 1980, using the Inner Urban Areas Act powers to do so prior to
structure plan approval (in January 1981). No relevant objections were
received, so no inquiry was necessary. The plan was adopted in June 1981.

The stated purposes of the plan, a modified form of the standard local plan
functions, are to implement the strategic policies and targets identified
in the Borough Plan and Structure Plan; "to identify and respond to the
problems and opportunities in the Plan Area and provide a framework for the
guidance of investment on behalf of the local authority, other organizations,
and private individuals; to provide a vehicle for the expression of the
council's corporate policies and programmes; to meet the statutory
requirements of the Town and Country Planning Act 1971 and the Local
Government Act 1972". The first two are the main aims of the plan, which
appears to be directed towards obtaining and directing public and private
investment resources to improve the physical fabric of the area, and
thereby assist in alleviating social and economic deprivation. The plan
is 42 pages long, divided into three parts. Part I introduces the plan,
identifying key issues, priorities for action and resources for
implementation. Part II presents policies and proposals, organized around
topics (housing, industry and employment, transport and movement, shops
and offices, education, community life, recreation, leisure and amenity,
health and community services). Part III presents detailed development
control matters.

In Part I, the plan briefly identifies those aspects of the problems
experienced by those living in the area which the Council has the power to
alleviate (poor condition of the housing stock, high degree of industrial
obsolescence, decline in social and economic well-being of the community,

A   Farnworth District Plan
B   Newton-le-Willows District Plan
C   Islington Development Plan
D   Horsham Area District Plan
E   Chandlers Ford District Plan
F   Ashby Woulds Area District Plan
G   City of Gloucester District Plan

● Local plans discussed in text
▨ Large plan area
── Metropolitan counties

Source: DoE 1970

Diagram 7.2. Location of Local Plans Discussed in the Text

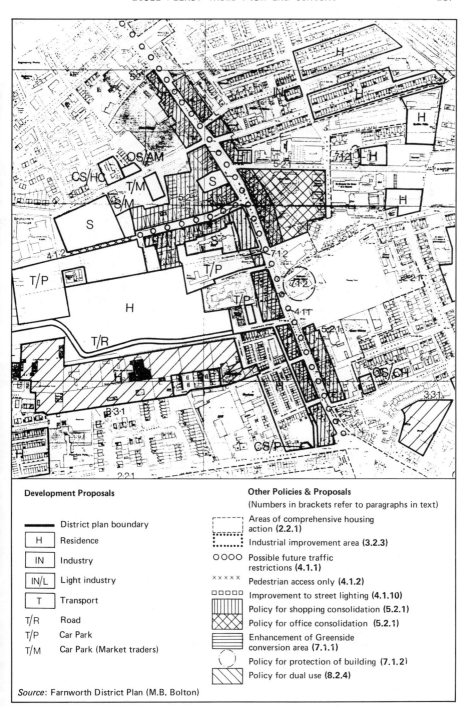

Development Proposals

▬▬▬	District plan boundary
H	Residence
IN	Industry
IN/L	Light industry
T	Transport
T/R	Road
T/P	Car Park
T/M	Car Park (Market traders)

Other Policies & Proposals
(Numbers in brackets refer to paragraphs in text)

Areas of comprehensive housing action **(2.2.1)**

Industrial improvement area **(3.2.3)**

OOOO Possible future traffic restrictions **(4.1.1)**

×××× Pedestrian access only **(4.1.2)**

□□□□□ Improvement to street lighting **(4.1.10)**

Policy for shopping consolidation **(5.2.1)**

Policy for office consolidation **(5.2.1)**

Enhancement of Greenside conversion area **(7.1.1)**

Policy for protection of building **(7.1.2)**

Policy for dual use **(8.2.4)**

Source: Farnworth District Plan (M.B. Bolton)

Diagram 7.3.

depressing nature of the physical environment).   These "key issues" provide
the organizing principle for defining policies.   For housing, land will be
released for private housing, "to widen choice", as well as continuing the
improvement programme; private investment is to be attracted into the area,
with the Council concentrating its own resources in an Industrial
Improvement Area.   To develop a "greater sense of community identity",
cultural facilities will be made available where possible and the Council
will provide publicity, assistance and advice.   Vacant and derelict sites
and buildings, where not used by the above proposals, are to have their
appearance improved if in Council ownership, with private owners being
encouraged to do likewise.   To do all this, however, the Council will need
more resources than it currently controls, and the plan advocates a
"re-direction of investment by other authorities and organizations" as well
as the active involvement of the local community.

Each topic chapter first summarizes objectives, then for each objective,
justifies it and presents proposals (indicated in italics), followed by
supporting Council policies.   For housing, the three objectives are to
"promote a wide range of residential development to promote choice in
housing", to pursue a vigorous improvement policy and to optimize the use
of housing resources.   The first objective will be achieved by allocating
17.04 hectares of land for residential development.   Nearly half of this
is in Council ownership, but some of this will require relocation of firms
before it can be made available.   It is proposed to use Section 250 of the
1971 Town and Country Planning Act to relocate firms on 2.2 hectares of
land so that it can be made available for private housing.   Section 250
allows the Secretary of State to pay a grant to local authorities for the
development or redevelopment of an area.   Evidently, the local authority
can only hope that such grants will be forthcoming.   The plan claims that
the Council will acquire land in private ownership with planning permission
if owners are not proceeding quickly to develop it.   The Council's House
Building Programme is then summarized.   The proposals in respect of
improvement and optimum use of resources involve the Council's housing
powers (for example GIA's, improvement grants, clearance areas, tenant
exchanges) and are nearly all listed as "other supporting council policies".
One of these, of contemporary interest, states: "2.2.6: *The current policy
of bricking up vacant properties as soon as possible, clearing sites and
paying attention to basic properties will be continued.*   This will help to
reduce vandalism and decay and help local residents awaiting rehousing".

In the industry and employment field, 25.65 hectares are to be promoted for
new development.   This land is currently owned largely by British Rail,
with the rest in Council or private ownership.   Two sites were being
compulsorily purchased using slum clearance powers for clearance.   In
addition to making land available for industrial investment, and promoting
the Industrial Improvement Area, the Council will operate development control
policies flexibly and make key worker housing available.   The Department of
Employment will establish a local job centre .   Promoting community life is
interpreted as stemming the decline of "cultural activity".   The area's
"remaining architectural and industrial heritage is to be safeguarded",
with support for an existing conservation area and listing of buildings.
A community centre will be "promoted" within the town centre, although the
Council will not have the resources to provide this.   A range of supporting
Council policies is included, from making Council buildings available
outside normal hours to reducing rents for Council premises to local groups
and making the central bandstand available for children's theatre.   The
Development Control Notes in Part III provide information on such matters
as car-parking standards, the provision of play areas and additional

proposals in relation to shopping and office use. In general, they present
a helpful and flexible attitude. The proposals map, at scale 1:2500
(Diagram 7.3) is monochrome but reasonably readable, if cumbersome. As in
the text, development proposals and other policies and proposals are
clearly distinguished.

The plan is well presented and concise. In addition to land use and
development policies, it includes details of Council housing policies.
Given the centrality of the Council's housing work to realizing plan
policies, this is hardly surprising. It looks as if the plan is directed
at local groups, and potential private investors, i.e. it has a local
political and economic role, though it requires a high degree of literacy.
The key problem for the policies in this plan is of course resources.
Where will the Council obtain the finance to purchase and clear land to
make it available? Will private investment be forthcoming? Certainly this
area is fortunate in receiving some central government grant through the
Urban Aid programme for investment in some of its programmes.

Newton-le-Willows District Plan: (St. Helens MD, Merseyside MC) (Diagram
                                     7.4)

Deposited District Plan
Large area (just)
130 hectares
20 000 people

This is a semi-urban area between Liverpool and Manchester, with
substantial areas of vacant and derelict land which could be brought into
productive use, among large areas of housing and old industry. A report of
survey for the plan was produced in April 1976. Two stages of public
participation were undertaken. The draft plan was certified as in
conformity with the Merseyside Structure Plan in December 1980, the
structure plan being approved the previous month. A Public Inquiry was
held in June 1981, and the plan was adopted in April 1982.

The formal statement on the scope and purpose of the plan merely
reiterates the standard purposes. However, paragraph 1.2 states that a
statutory local plan is needed because the statutory planning framework is
out of date. The Council is now implementing a policy of clearance and
improvement, and the effect of this on the area needs clarification. The
environment of parts of the area is deteriorating in quality; employment
in the area is declining and there is a shortage of "readily available
land for industry". In addition, since the area borders with Greater
Manchester MC and Cheshire CC, it is affected by development proposals in
these counties. To summarize, it is an urban fringe location within the
Merseyside-Manchester conurbation, the land resources of which could be
used to attract new investment in an area of economic decline if problems
of dereliction can be overcome. However, to allocate such land conflicts
with structure plan policies of concentrating development within urban
areas.

The plan is 68 pages long, with 12 chapters, and a Proposals Map (Scale
1:10 000) with 2 insets, both in poor quality monochrome (Diagram 7.4). The
first three chapters outline the background to the plan, the strategic
framework and how the policies and proposals were arrived at (plan options
and alternative solutions). "The most important element in the Plan is
considered to be the availability of land". Three options for the area
were considered: stabilization of population and employment levels; decline

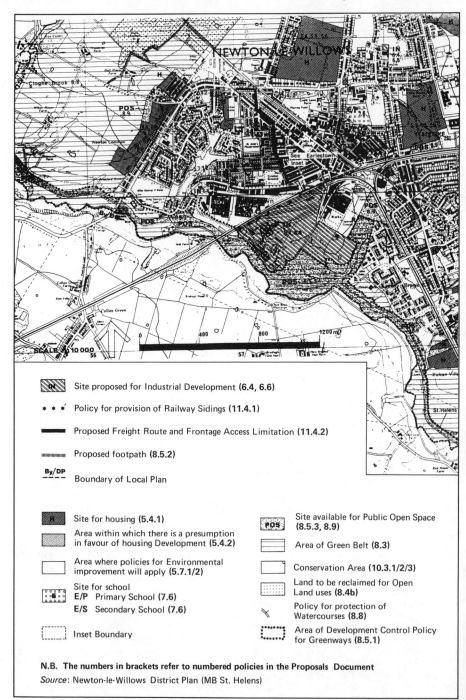

Site proposed for Industrial Development **(6.4, 6.6)**

Policy for provision of Railway Sidings **(11.4.1)**

Proposed Freight Route and Frontage Access Limitation **(11.4.2)**

Proposed footpath **(8.5.2)**

By/DP
Boundary of Local Plan

Site for housing **(5.4.1)**

Area within which there is a presumption in favour of housing Development **(5.4.2)**

Area where policies for Environmental improvement will apply **(5.7.1/2)**

Site for school
E/P Primary School **(7.6)**
E/S Secondary School **(7.6)**

Inset Boundary

Site available for Public Open Space **(8.5.3, 8.9)**

Area of Green Belt **(8.3)**

Conservation Area **(10.3.1/2/3)**

Land to be reclaimed for Open Land uses **(8.4b)**

Policy for protection of Watercourses **(8.8)**

Area of Development Control Policy for Greenways **(8.5.1)**

N.B. The numbers in brackets refer to numbered policies in the Proposals Document

Source: Newton-le-Willows District Plan (MB St. Helens)

Diagram 7.4

in employment but not housing; planned decline of both. The public, when
consulted, not surprisingly, opted for the first. This involved the
allocation of substantial sites for housing and industry. It is made clear
in the plan, though not on the proposals map, that private housing is
envisaged. This reflects the local authority's appreciation of its own
limited resources and dependence on private sector initiatives and grant
aid of various kinds. The plan contains a very brief chapter on "general
development policies". It then has 8 chapters on topics (housing, industry
and employment, social facilities, urban fringe and parkland policies,
Earlestown centre, conservation, transportation and shopping).

Each chapter contains a general discussion of the issues involved, an
assessment of land needs, and specification of sites or equivalent. These
are written in capitals as proposals. An appendix to each chapter provides
"Implementation Notes". Thus, in the housing chapter, the need to provide
enough housing to maintain the area's population is noted, with a comment
on the uncertain contribution of the housing programme to slum clearance
and improvement. Additional housing land needs are identified, with
comments on its current availability (a significant amount is not available
because of development constraints). A total of 22.25 hectares of land is
estimated as required. 18.54 hectares is seen as currently available, with
15.95 hectares available but with constraints. The plan notes: "The excess
of supply over requirements is considered to be more apparent than real
when faced with the practicalities of getting development off the ground".
Local planners have evidently been influenced here by the DoE/House
Builders' Federation land availability studies (DoE/HBF 1979). Open land
sites are then identified, followed by policies for infill sites, housing
and environmental improvement. In the Implementation Notes, the plan
refers to the Council's housing programme including improvement expenditure,
concluding with a statement on the links between these and proposals in
other chapters. The Council, though looking to investment from the private
sector, is clearly prepared to take an interventionist stance and appears
to regret the passing of the Community Land Act: "On the question of the
supply of housing land, it is hoped that the local plan will provide a
basis for obtaining the co-operation of landowners in the release of land
for development, but to be sure that land is made available compulsory
purchase powers may be required under the Town and Country Planning Act in
order to assemble sites at the right time". The authority also anticipates
"purchases of sites, preparation of development briefs and marketing of
sites; provision of information on site availability to builders and
developers". The latter is expected to help local builders most. The
Proposals Map allocates sites for housing and industry; defines the green
belt boundary, defines other areas where there is a presumption in favour
of housing; where environmental improvement policies will apply, and sites
for various other proposals. The Map also lists 11 policies and proposals
which apply to the whole plan area (Diagram 7.4).

Using the argument that local people (in Newton-le-Willows) do not want to
see further decline, the plan in effect facilitates the process of
suburbanization in this region of acute industrial decline and inner city
problems. Although it is not clear where the finance for an interventionist
role will come from, the plan appears to commit the authority to an
important facilitating role in promoting private development. In
presentational terms, the plan is overburdened with explanations of how the
policies were arrived at. It is neither clearly nor confidently presented,
and local people including local builders might have some difficulty
appreciating its contents. It is possible that the function of the plan is
as a political justifications for proposals, rather than as a technical

justification to be used in appeals, or as a basis for bargaining with
developers. Given the type of area and the plan's policies, it seems likely
that any development proposal would be viewed positively by the local
authority, although the county, more concerned with inner city regeneration,
might raise objections.

Islington Development Plan: (Islington LB, GLC) (Diagram 7.5)

Deposited District Plan
All area
1490 hectares
166 4000 people

Islington is an inner London Borough, dominanted by inner city problems,
with few of the pressures of an expanding central area experienced in
neighbouring Camden. The Council undertook a number of preparatory studies
in the mid-1970s and engaged in extensive consultation with local people.
The Council had also prepared a Community Plan which contained policies for
the Borough broader in scope than development planning policies. A first
draft of the Borough Plan was available in mid-1979, with the written
statement deposited in September 1980. An inquiry was held in June 1981,
and the plan was adopted in April 1982. It conforms with the GLDP, approved
in 1976.

The main aims of the plan are "to guide public investment so that the
Council's social objectives are achieved, particularly those relating to the
most deprived residents in the Borough; to promote private investment ...
in order to reverse economic decline, meet the need for new jobs, and to
produce better shopping centres and improved housing; to provide and protect
a full range of modern local community services ... ; to improve and protect
the quality of the physical environment in working, living and shopping
areas". The plan is 229 pages long, with additional diagrams and is divided
into 15 chapters. This length reflects the complexity of the issues
involved in an authority-wide plan for an area of this nature. Its content
and layout are clearly explained in the text. Part I (Chapters 1-3) sets
out "the purpose of the plan, the main trends and issues facing the Council,
and the context provided by the GLDP". Part I in effect summarizes the
area's problems, aimed partly at the concerns of local people, but also
containing data likely to be helpful in supporting the Council's case on
particular applications. Part II is "a review of various topics". (Housing;
offices, industry and commerce; transportation; recreation and leisure;
shopping; education; social, health and community services; design,
townscape and conservation; other development planning policies). "Each
topic is examined as to the issues it raises, the resources and powers
available to the local authority, and the strategy which the Council will
follow. Then follow the development planning policies, beginning with
general objectives, followed by the specific policies which are being
proposed. The policies are shown in capital letters, and a statement of
justification follows each policy". Part III (Chapters 13-15) consists of
the financial and land resources available for implementing the plan". The
plan is supplemented by three non-statutory documents, two for special areas
(the Nag's Head, the Angel) and Planning Standards Guidelines which apply to
all development proposals.

There are 4 objectives for housing development: "to maintain and where
appropriate increase the stock of satisfactory housing; to ensure that
housing provides appropriate and acceptable living standards; to ensure the
provision of a variety of housing to suit the needs of Islington residents;

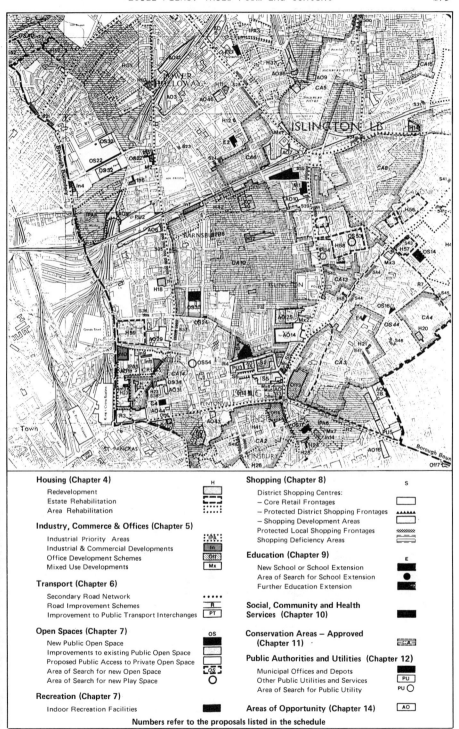

Housing (Chapter 4)   H

Redevelopment
Estate Rehabilitation
Area Rehabilitation

Industry, Commerce & Offices (Chapter 5)

Industrial Priority Areas
Industrial & Commercial Developments   In
Office Development Schemes   Off
Mixed Use Developments   Mx

Transport (Chapter 6)

Secondary Road Network
Road Improvement Schemes   R
Improvement to Public Transport Interchanges   PT

Open Spaces (Chapter 7)   OS

New Public Open Space
Improvements to existing Public Open Space
Proposed Public Access to Private Open Space
Area of Search for new Open Space   OS
Area of Search for new Play Space   O

Recreation (Chapter 7)

Indoor Recreation Facilities

Shopping (Chapter 8)   S

District Shopping Centres:
– Core Retail Frontages
– Protected District Shopping Frontages
– Shopping Development Areas
Protected Local Shopping Frontages
Shopping Deficiency Areas

Education (Chapter 9)   E

New School or School Extension
Area of Search for School Extension   ●
Further Education Extension

**Social, Community and Health
Services (Chapter 10)**

**Conservation Areas – Approved
(Chapter 11)**   C.A.

Public Authorities and Utilities (Chapter 12)

Municipal Offices and Depots
Other Public Utilities and Services   PU
Area of Search for Public Utility   PU ○

Areas of Opportunity (Chapter 14)   AO

Numbers refer to the proposals listed in the schedule

Source: Islington District Plan (L.B. Islington)   Diagram 7.5

to maintain and improve the residential environment of the Borough and to give priority for improvements to those areas which have the greatest environmental problems". In respect of the first objective, it is proposed that:

> "Permission will not normally be given for a change of use from residential to non-residential. Exceptions may include:
>
> i)   where the property cannot provide satisfactory living accommodation
>
> ii)   where the environment is unsuitable for residential use
>
> iii) where the property is subject of a proposal for non-residential use in this plan
>
> iv)   where a loss of housing is necessary to ensure the provision of recreational, educational or community facilities, where these are deficient".

Such a proposal is to be found in many local plans for densely built-up areas with a concern for local housing needs. I have quoted it here because it illustrates the use of performance criteria with which to judge development proposals, as opposed to simple use zoning. It also is a good example of the way policy areas can be interrelated in local plan policies. Someone who wanted to run a small business or open a co-operative shop in their home would, however, still have to search through the other chapters of the plan and the map to see if a modification to this policy could apply. Other housing policies concern density, mix of dwellings, standards or conversion, access for the disabled and hotel development, which in general is welcomed.

In respect of offices, industry and employment, objectives concern the need to ensure appropriate industrial accommodation to meet local employment needs, to improve the environment of business and industrial areas and to ensure that proper consideration is given to the employment implications of all development proposals. Office developments are not restrict (compare other London Boroughs, Lowenberg 1980) as these may bring some employment gain, but "storage, wholesale and distribution uses" (i.e. with low employment densities) are to be located only where they are appropriate and where they contribute to local employment needs". There is also a special objective "to ensure the provision of suitable accommodation for the clothing industry and appropriate controls over outworking". The Council proposes to support the assembly of land for industrial use in appropriate locations, with suitable "areas of opportunity" shown on the proposals map. The general employment policy states:

> "The Council will carefully consider the employment implications of all proposals for development and change of use and will treat these as being material considerations in the determination of planning applications. Subject to the specific land use and environmental policies set out elsewhere in the plan sympathetic treatment will normally be given to developments which bring employment benefits to the borough".

Strictly speaking, part of this policy is redundant, since the policies of a local plan *supplement* material considerations when a planning applications is considered. However, the local authority is here trying to establish that there is no room for doubt about the legitimacy of employment gain and loss

as a factor in development control. It seeks to determine the definition
of material considerations to pre-empt alternative definitions by the
Secretary of State or the Courts. A subsequent chapter on "other development
planning policies", a "catch-all" chapter, includes a statement that the
Council will seek planning gain and Section 52 agreements where appropriate.

In Part III, a review of the financial resources available to the Council
and other public agencies is provided. Despite urban programme aid, it is
concluded that both public and private finance will be lacking to tackle
adequately the Borough's development problems . Availability of land is then
reviewed, with the conclusion that given land shortages, it is important
that all development proposals represent an "efficient use of the site or
building". This is expressed as a proposal though it is not clear how
efficiency would be defined here. This chapter also contains a proposal:
"The Council will continue to press the Government, through the Inner City
Partnership, to ensure that statutory undertakers and public authorities
release surplus land where this is needed to achieve this plan's objectives".
The proposals in the plan are then summarized in two forms: (1) the
Proposals Map (Diagram 7.5), at a scale of 1:10 000, clearly presented using
traditional town planning colours (purple for industry, red for public
buildings, green for open space, blue for offices and shops); (2) *Schedule
of proposals* (Diagram 7.6), which lists each site for which a proposal has
been made, who is to develop it and its existing and future use.

The format of this plan has many similarities with the style pioneered by
the Camden Borough Plan. It emphasizes the physical development dimensions
of Council policies. It reflects careful consideration of the Council's
powers in respect of land use and development. Where the Council has no
direct powers, policies are expressed as intentions or as advocacy statements.
Policies are interrelated systematically, with each set of topic policies
cross-referring to other policy sets. A few specific allocations are made,
and zoning used, particularly where development pressures are to be
resisted. Otherwise extensive use of performance criteria is made. The
plan is firmly oriented to relieving social deprivation, though attempting
to attract private investment in central area uses such as hotels and
offices, as well as housing and industry.

Horsham Area District Plan: (Horsham DC, West Sussex CC) (Diagram 7.7)

Deposited District Plan
All area
5363 hectares
94 860 people

Horsham District lies to the south of the London conurbation, beyond the
metropolitan green belt and adjacent to Crawley/Gatwick. It is under
intense development pressure, which explains the all-area format chosen
(compare East Hertfordshire and Uttlesford District Plans, both adjacent to
Stansted Airport). The plan was initiated soon after reorganization, with
early consultation with parish councils in 1976. Further public consultation
was carried out in 1979, with the first draft of the plan available in July
1979. This was revised by February 1980, followed by further consultation
"with the public affected by the changes". The plan was approved by the
Council in June 1980, at which time the West Sussex Structure Plan was
approved. The plan was put on deposit in October 1980, with an inquiry in
March 1981. The Inspector delivered his report to the local authority in
September 1981, and the plan was adopted in February 1982.

Ref. No.	Scheme (Name of Agency)	Existing Use	Future Use	Site Affected
Industrial and Commercial Developments, 1980 – 85				
IN1	Belgravia Works (Private)	Vacant property	Rehabilitation for industry	157–163 Marlborough Road.
IN2	Tufnell Park Road Yard and Depot (To be determined)	Railway land and Former BRS Depot.	Area should to developed for industry, with improved access.	Land to south of railway between Huddlestone Road and Comus Road.
IN3	Finsbury Park Coal Yard (Private)	Disused coal yards and vacant shop	Industrial	Former Finsbury Park Coal Yard bounded by Clifton Terrace, Wells Terrace, Bus Station, garage adjoining the Bus Station and Lennox Road.
IN4	Camden Dwellings (Private)	Vacant site, formerly residential	Industry	Site of Camden Dwellings, 274/276 York Way
IN5	Balmoral Grove (LBI)	Vacant Site	Industry	St. Matthias Chapel 437–451 Caledonian Road and 5–9 (cons) Balmoral Grove.
IN6	Blundell Street (Private)	Vacant Site	Industry	36–56 Blundell Street.
IN7	Offord Street (Private)	Part vacant site, part storage	Industry	Offord Street (Rear of 31–75 Offord Road)
IN8	69/73 Essex Road (To be determined)	Vacant site and shop	Industry	Nos. 69–73 Essex Road.
IN9	All Saints Street (To be determined)	Cleared site, formerly residential (Slum clearance site)	Industry	Site of 8–36 (even) All Saints Street.
IN10	Westinghouse Site 82–96 York Way	Vacant offices	Redevelopment for industry	82–96 (even) York Way
IN11	All Saints Triangle (To be determined)	Cleared site, formerly residential and church.	Industry or commerce	Street block bounded by All Saints Street, Caledonian Road, Killick Street.

Diagram 7.6

Office Developments, 1980–85 (In these schemes, offices will be the primary use with associated uses as indicated).				
OFF1	Finsbury Park Station (B. Rail and Private)	Vacant land	Redevelopment for offices with new B. Rail booking hall, shops and improvements to bus terminus (See also PT2)	Site between Stroud Green Road, Station Place, Seven Sisters Road and Finsbury Park Station.
OFF2	Holloway Arcade Holloway Road (Private)	Shops and disused ballroom.	Redevelopment for offices and a shop unit.	Site of the ballroom and Nos. 19 to 28 and 2 Holloway Arcade.
OFF3	Duncan Street (LBI and private)	Mainly car park, with some shops and other uses.	Redevelopment mainly for offices with shops, pub, restaurant, sports club, open space, workshops and residential.	Land on the north-east corner of the Angel, reaching up to Duncan Street. It is not known at present whether the factories in Torrens Street will be included in the scheme.
OFF4	Lyons Corner House (Private)	Vacant building.	Rehabilitation for offices with bank at ground level.	1, Islington High Street
OFF5	New River Corner (Private)	Mostly vacant land with some shops	Redevelopment for offices with some shops at ground level.	1–25a Pentonville Road 401–455 St. John Street.

Source: Islington Development Plan (LB Islington)

Diagram 7.6 continued

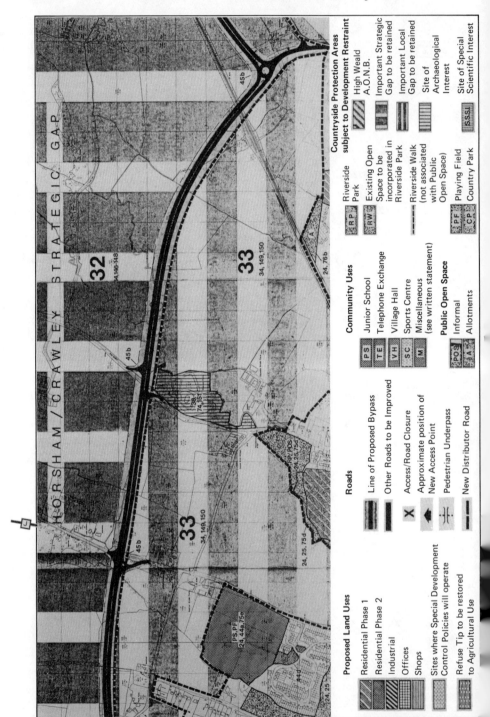

Proposed Land Uses

Residential Phase 1

Residential Phase 2

Industrial

Offices

Shops

Sites where Special Development
Control Policies will operate

Refuse Tip to be restored
to Agricultural Use

Roads

Line of Proposed Bypass

Other Roads to be Improved

X   Access/Road Closure

Approximate position of
New Access Point

Pedestrian Underpass

New Distributor Road

Community Uses

P S   Junior School

T E   Telephone Exchange

V H   Village Hall

S C   Sports Centre

M   Miscellaneous
(see written statement)

Public Open Space

POS   Informal

A   Allotments

**Countryside Protection Areas
subject to Development Restraint**

High Weald
A.O.N.B.

Important Strategic
Gap to be retained

Important Local
Gap to be retained

Site of
Archaeological
Interest

S.S.S.I.   Site of Special
Scientific Interest

R P   Riverside
Park

R W   Existing Open
Space to be
incorporated in
Riverside Park

Riverside Walk
(not associated
with Public
Open Space)

P F   Playing Field

C P   Country Park

The main purpose of the plan, though not clearly articulated as such, is to
clarify the policies of the structure plan. This advocates a policy of firm
restraint, but proposes some additional land release for housing and industry,
to be limited to local needs and local firms. In this policy of selective
restraint, allowing for local needs, it is thus similar to many other local
plans in the areas around the London and West Midlands conurbations (Healey
et al. 1980). The District Plan is less restrictive in its interpretation
of structure plan policies than perhaps the county would like to see, again
in common with many similarly-located districts. The district also
considers a local plan particularly necessary as previous planning documents
are obsolete, since development has exceeded that allowed for. The plan
has 83 pages, an enormous monochrome Proposals Map at scale 1:25 000 with 14
inset maps at 1:5000 (Diagram 7.7). It has 6 chapters. Chapters 1-4
explain how the plan was arrived at (summary of survey and consultation;
discussion of the options for locating new development). Chapter 5
summarizes the main proposals by topic (population and housing; employment
and industry; recreation and open space; agriculture and countryside;
minerals; shopping; community facilities; transport and parking; utility
services; design and conservation; archaelogy). Chapter 6 summarizes the
proposals by policy area. These are a mixture of small settlement policies
and social policies, resulting in a policy statement applicable to every
part of the plan area.

The strategy of the plan is to concentrate land allocation for new
development on the fringe of Horsham and at Broadbridge Heath and Southwater
where a new by-pass has recently been completed. Firm restraint is then
applied to the rest of the area. A key housing policy, developed from the
structure plan, is to reduce the rate of housing development. This is to
be done by phasing the release of land:

> "The release of land for residential development will, when
> monitoring of rates of development reveals a need for such,
> initially take place upon land identified for residential
> development prior to the preparation of (the) plan (Phase I
> Land). When monitoring reveals that these sites are becoming
> exhausted, phased development will be permitted on newly-
> identified sites (Phase 2 Land) when needed".

A note adds that if the "reduction to (a building rate of) 225 units per
annum can be achieved before the end of the plan period", some phase 2
sites may not be released. In other words, the reduction is to be sought
by a continuation of control totals and phased land release. Other housing
policies allow infill and define the boundaries of the built-up areas of
towns and villages (effectively "village envelopes"). No proposals are made
for meeting local housing needs, except through sufficient land allocation,
although development for a range of housing types including small low-cost
units, bungalows for the elderly and larger detached houses are apparently
to be encouraged.

The industrial sites allocated, are to be limited to specified types of
development (light industry, firms that provide opportunities for local
people, unobtrusive factory buildings). Warehousing development is less
welcome. The release of industrial land is to be phased "to meet the needs
of local businesses and employment needs of the local population", but
there is no indication of how this is to be done. Countryside policies
emphasize firm restraint with policies at least as restrictive as those in
green belts. The Council would dearly like to see an extension of the
Metropolitan Green Belt to cover the "gap" between Crawley and Gatwick, but
is unable to propose this as such an extention was removed by the Secretary

of State in modifications. The plan defines its own, very restrictive
proposals for this and similar local 'gaps'. In addition the plan contains
very detailed landscape and design requirements. The following policy is
of particular interest:

> "Although there is no statutory control over farming or forestry
> operations the local planning authorities will seek to ensure that
> such a change as is needed (for example, grubbing up of hedgerows,
> erection of farm buildings, or felling operations) does least damage
> to landscape character or nature conservation interests". (The
> Inspector subsequently recommended that "no" in the first line
> should be changed to "little".)

Ecological and archaeological sites are also to be given considerable
priority against development proposals. Design policies stress the need to
use local materials, particularly red/brown bricks (local stock bricks
where possible), vertical tile hanging, stained weatherboarding and white
painted shiplap, and "The Local Planning Authority will require (the
traditional) predominant vertical emphasis in fenestration to be echoed in
new development".

Actual sites are then specified in each policy area. Where land allocation
for development is involved, proposals specify the site, what its release
is dependent on, if relevant, what infrastructure is to be provided and who
is to pay for it (nearly always the developer), what community facilities
are to be provided and what landscape features are to be protected.
Referring to the allocation of housing land at Southwater, no development
other than that with planning permission will be allowed until the by-pass
is constructed (scheduled to start in 1980/1981); 20 hectares of phase 2
land is allocated, but the developer will have to provide a spine road,
assist with drainage and sewerage works, pay for junction improvements,
allocate a site and (apparently) pay for the construction of a school,
dedicate and lay out public open space. Here we have a plan which contrasts
completely with the previous three plans described. Development is
accepted very reluctantly and must pay for itself. The main objectors at
the inquiry were those whose land had not been allocated for development,
particularly those with sites in the "gap", with the Horsham society making
a number of points on environmental protection and design (including an
objection that "weatherboarding" weathered badly unless well maintained).
The Inspector recommended very few modifications to the plan.

Chandler's Ford District Plan: (Hampshire County Council) (Diagram 7.8)

Deposited District Plan
Large area
22 000 people

This is one of the sites within the South Hampshire Growth Area as defined
in the Strategic Plan for the South East (SEJPT 1970). Substantial
development for housing, industrial and office purposes is proposed (1700
dwellings, 10.2 hectares of industrial land, 13 000 square metres of office
space). It has been prepared by the county. The county intended to
develop all the growth area local plans. In addition, the local plan area
spans two districts (Eastleigh and Test Valley). This plan was initiated
in 1972 (see Chapter 6) and prepared "under the guidance of a Joint
Advisory Committee" of members of the County Council and the two districts.
The county did most of the work on the area for new development, and
Eastleigh district developed proposals for the existing built up area of

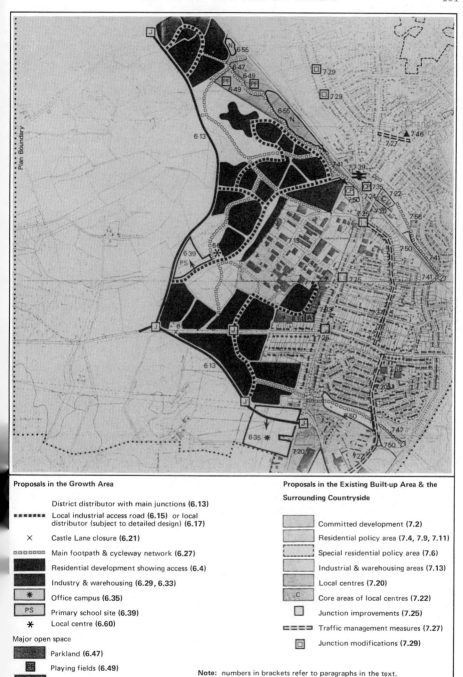

Proposals in the Growth Area

District distributor with main junctions (6.13)

▪▪▪▪▪▪▪ Local industrial access road (6.15) or local
distributor (subject to detailed design) (6.17)

× Castle Lane closure (6.21)

▫▫▫▫▫▫▫ Main footpath & cycleway network (6.27)

Residential development showing access (6.4)

Industry & warehousing (6.29, 6.33)

✳ Office campus (6.35)

PS Primary school site (6.39)

✳ Local centre (6.60)

Major open space

Parkland (6.47)

PF Playing fields (6.49)

N Nature reserve (6.55)

✳ Titlark Farm landscaped area (6.51)

A Allotments (6.51)

**Proposals in the Existing Built-up Area & the
Surrounding Countryside**

Committed development (7.2)

Residential policy area (7.4, 7.9, 7.11)

Special residential policy area (7.6)

Industrial & warehousing areas (7.13)

Local centres (7.20)

C Core areas of local centres (7.22)

▫ Junction improvements (7.25)

▭▭▭▭ Traffic management measures (7.27)

▣ Junction modifications (7.29)

Note: numbers in brackets refer to paragraphs in the text.

Diagram 7.8

Source: Chandlers Ford District Plan
(Hampshire County Council)

Chandler's Ford. There were some initial delays due to uncertainty over the form and timing of major sewerage investment. The County Council took considerable effort over public consultation. "The proposals attracted over 500 column inches in the local press, and this, together with radio and television coverage and household leaflet delivery, made it unlikely that many residents of Chandler's Ford were unaware of the plan or of how they could obtain further information". However, the development land was in the ownership of a single large estate. The landowner and MAFF objected to the county's draft proposals for the location of development since certain farms had been improved in the period between the county's early consultations with them and the publication of draft proposals. The land eventually allocated for development was determined in negotiations between the county, the landowner and MAFF. It was deposited in February 1980, with an inquiry held in September 1980. The plan was adopted in 1981, with only minor modifications made as a consequence of the inquiry.

The main purpose of the plan is to put forward detailed proposals for major growth, provide a framework for co-ordinating public and private investment and establish guidelines for the existing built-up area (Eastleigh) and the growth area. The plan is 39 pages long, with reports on survey and public consultation published separately. The proposals map is multichrome, not unlike the recommendations in the Development Plans Manual, at a scale of 1: 10 000 (Diagram 7.8). It is supplemented by a key diagram, as in Hampshire's other local plans. The plan has 8 chapters. Chapters 1-5 provide the background to proposals. Chapter 6 contains the proposals for new development and Chapter 7 for the existing built-up area. Chapter 8 concerns planning and implementation. This plan thus breaks away from the topic organization, although within Chapters 6 and 7, proposals are organized on topic lines.

The background chapters summarize the issues and objectives of the plan. The allocation of land for development is to be guided by the need to provide additional services, to protect working farms, to conserve landscape features and protect certain areas from traffic noise. Nineteen objectives are identified, developments of the extensive list of broad and general objectives to be found in the South Hampshire Structure Plan. These have been used to help determine the organization of land allocations *within* the area allocated for growth, but in the main express little more than a desire that new development should fit harmoniously with existing built-up areas and landscape. In the end, as noted above, the determination of what land was allocated for development was negotiated with the main interests involved, rather than undertaken as a technical exercise. The proposals for new development indicate general principles, of location, mix and density of housing, position of access and landscaping. However, it is expected that details of development will be defined in development briefs and will probably be tied up in planning agreements. Consequently, proposals in the plans are not precise, nor are the allocations on the proposals map, which remain diagrammatic. The net result is that structure and local plans for this area provide three levels of diagrammatic advice, the structure plan key diagram, the local play key diagram, and the local plan proposals map. This plan does, however, appear to provide local people with a clear idea of the general principles of development to be used in more detailed discussions with developers. Within the existing built-up areas, proposals relate to permitting only that development which is in keeping with the existing character of the area, with proposals for various traffic and environmental improvements. For the countryside areas, standard restrictive policies are reiterated. It is indicated that further land will be develope in the future to meet the growth area targets, but its location is suggested as alternatives rather than a precise specification. The nature of the

Diagram 7.9. Chandlers Ford District Plan Implementation Schedule

infrastructure works and community facilities needed for each stage of
development is indicated. Very little is noted about finance, with no formal
commitment by the County Council to any specific infrastructure works. It is
made clear that developers are expected to provide all on-site infrastructure
and contribute to off-site works. In particular, they are to contribute to
the early stages of an outer peripheral road to give access to the new
development sites. Eventually, when final stages have been constructed this
road is extended to become a local distributor road. The developers are thus
to pay for the first stages of this local road. An Implementation Schedule
indicates what needs to be provided in the new and existing area in each
phase, but with no indication of who will actually undertake the development
(Diagram 7.9). This plan provides an interesting example of a situation for
which local plans in 1968 were envisaged. In Fareham Western Wards, the
county used an action area format for a very similar situation. As with the
Fareham plan, where development was to take place within a dispersed developed
area, the plan depends on private initiative to bring development forward and
pay for much of the necessary infrastructure. In the current development clim
there must be doubts about how far this private investment will be
forthcoming[66].

Ashby Woulds Area District Plan: (North West Leicestershire DC;
                                        Leicestershire CC) (Diagram 7.10)

Deposited District Plan
Small area
2400 hectares
8882 people

This is an area of small villages, within the Leicestershire coalfield, with
problems of dereliction and subsidence, following mining operations. The
villages are subject to the structure plans' settlement policy which allocate
one (Measham) the status of a key settlement. The others are "restraint
settlements". Thus this is a rather special variant of a village area plan.
The structure plan for the area was approved in 1976. This plan was
initiated in 1976 and initial consultations begun. A draft district plan
was published in 1979, including the report of survey. The plan was publiciz
through formal consultations, the press and by public meetings. Considerable
account seems to have been taken of the views expressed. The plan was
finally deposited in August 1980, with an inquiry in June 1981. The plan
was adopted in January 1982.

It is not clear what the main purposes of the plan are, although its central
concerns appear to be allocating small areas of land for housing and industry
improving the environment, conserving agricultural land and mineral resources
The plan is 32 pages long, with a proposal map on a scale of 1:10 000 (6 inch
to the mile) and an inset at 1:2500 (Diagram 7.10). It is organized on a
topic basis (population and housing; employment and industry; minerals and th
restoration of derelict land; landscape and environmental improvements;
education, social and community services; recreation, open space and footpath
shopping, transport, communications and heavy lorry depots, public utility
services). There are 3 final chapters on the main villages. Housing policie
allocate sites and restrict development to within the boundaries of settlemer
as defined on the proposals map, (i.e. "village envelopes"). Similar propos
are made in respect of employment generating development. There are no forma
proposals for minerals, but the plan contains information on existing
minerals permissions and County Council policies. Since the district has
no powers over minerals, its stance here can only be advocative. On landscap

---

[66]See Healey 1982c for a detailed account of this plan.

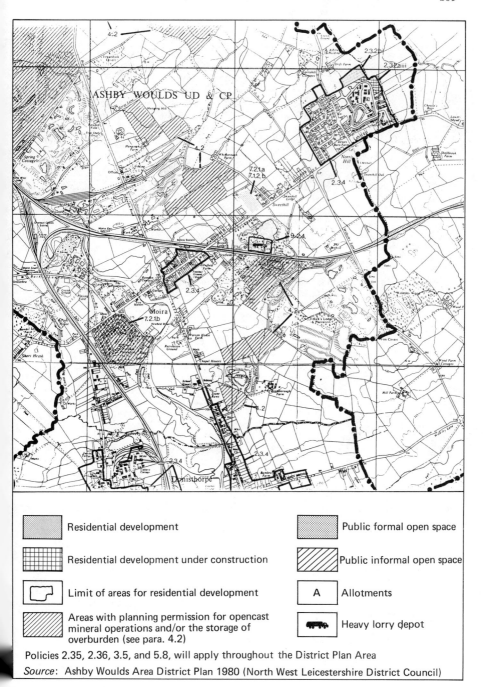

Residential development

Residential development under construction

Limit of areas for residential development

Areas with planning permission for opencast mineral operations and/or the storage of overburden (see para. 4.2)

Public formal open space

Public informal open space

A Allotments

Heavy lorry depot

Policies 2.35, 2.36, 3.5, and 5.8, will apply throughout the District Plan Area

Source: Ashby Woulds Area District Plan 1980 (North West Leicestershire District Council)

Diagram 7.10

"the District Council supports the County Council in its endeavours to
promote amenity tree planting schemes in the area in agreement with
landowners". The District Council will also have regard to sites of Scientifi
Interest when considering planning applications. A site is allocated at
Measham for a high school, but it is not clear whether the County Education
Department supports this. The area policies add very little to the above.

This plan is so limited in content that one wonders why it was prepared.
There is little evidence of major conflict over the use of land, or of
significant demand for industrial and housing land release. Although
environmental improvement is sought, the district council does not appear
to be devoting its own resources to the task.

City of Gloucester District Plan 1981: (Gloucester DC; Gloucestershire CC)
(Diagram 7.11)

Draft, with possibility of deposit
All area
3742 hectares
90 000 people

Gloucester is a regional market town which for many years experienced
relative economic stagnation, but has recently begun to benefit from its
location near the junction of the M4 and M5. In 1978, the city council
embarked on a Central Area Interim District Plan. "It became apparent
during the preparation of (this) plan that many of the issues being
investigated affected the remainder of the City and in some cases to such a
degree that they could not effectively be resolved in the City Centre alone".
A citywide plan was therefore started at the beginning of 1980.
Consultations started on the smaller plan were extended for this plan, with
data provided by the county. The present draft was produced by January 1981,
so this plan can just about claim to be a plan produced in a year. The
structure plan was approved in mid-1981. The local plan was deposited in
May 1982.

The purpose of the plan is to interpret structure plan policies; identify
city problems and issues and policies for resolving them; co-ordinate the
activities of other departments in respect of development; identify what
other agencies should do to achieve plan policies. The plan is 86 pages
long, with a proposal map at a scale of 1:10 000 and a town centre inset,
scale 1:2500 (Diagram 7.11). There are 9 chapters, 3 on background, 5 topic
chapters (employment, housing, environment, transport and shopping), and a
final chapter on co-ordination and programming, concluding with a brief
summary of the main policies. Within each chapter, policies are divided int
core policies, at a general level, and specific *implementation* policies.
The latter emphasize current priorities. A chapter on finance is included
in the first part of the plan.

Significantly, given that this plan was drafted in 1980, the first proposals
discussed are those relating to employment. The aim to promote employment
growth, although this area has few of the problems faced in Farnworth,
Newton-le-Willows or Islington. Core policy E.1 is to "promote, principally
through the identification of land and granting of planning permission, the
release of land for industrial development sufficient to cater for 5 years
requirement". This is calculated around an anticipated employment growth of
7%, with new jobs being created to compensate for job loss in existing firms
as well as employment growth. Implementation Policy E.1.Ca, proposes the
allocation of 40 hectares for industrial development, some of it requiring

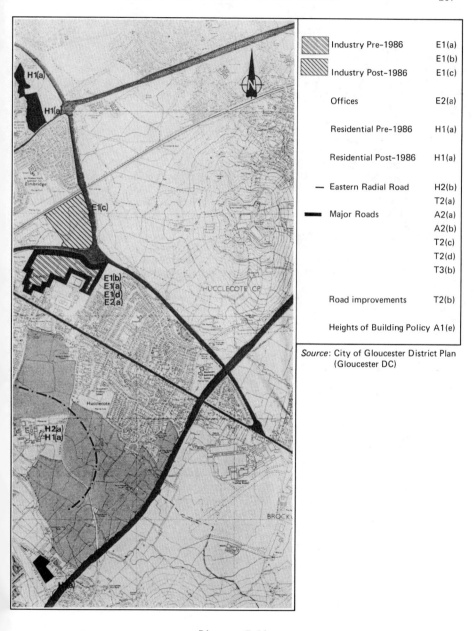

Industry Pre–1986   E1(a)
                          E1(b)
Industry Post–1986   E1(c)

Offices   E2(a)

Residential Pre–1986   H1(a)

Residential Post–1986   H1(a)

— Eastern Radial Road   H2(b)
                           T2(a)
■ Major Roads   A2(a)
                          A2(b)
                          T2(c)
                          T2(d)
                          T3(b)

Road improvements   T2(b)

Heights of Building Policy A1(e)

Source: City of Gloucester District Plan
(Gloucester DC)

Diagram 7.11

on-site infrastructure or access. Where the council is not a site owner, it proposes to act in a promotional capacity. Similarly, land and planning permission for 46 450 square metres of office space is proposed, not to mention land over and above commitments for a further 1500 dwellings. In all cases these figures are for the period 1981-86. It is worth noting that the allocations of housing are equivalent to those for Chandler's Ford, a major growth area, while those for industry and offices are nearly *four times* as much as in Chandler's Ford.

Apart from these land allocations, many policies remain at the level of generalities. "Consideration will be given to the density and quality of housing development, so that a suitable range of house types may be available at all times", but it is not clear what might be considered a suitable range. The Council will "define selected areas where home improvement is considered to be most urgently needed", but has clearly not got round to this yet. When it does so, however, these areas will be awarded high rates of grant. There is also a core policy claiming that "the Council will seek to ensure that there is a satisfactory provision of housing accommodation for those sections of the community whose needs are not adequately met by the private sector". The plan notes that the council will continue building new accommodation and assisting other agencies to make provision for these needs, so far as finances permit, which is of course not very far. A number of traffic improvement measures are proposed, the most important of which being the completion of the inner relief road. This is a major priority for the county, but short-term traffic management measures are proposed in order to make a large area of land available for private housing development prior to the construction of a suburban relief road. Shopping developments are to be concentrated in the central area, although two DIY stores and a superstore are to be allowed on the margins of the centre, adjacent to the inner relief road.

This plan then, sets its cap at obtaining a good slice of the development investment that is currently searching for prime sites and helpful local authorities on the London/Bristol/Cardiff axis. Apart from defining sites, however, the plan is vague about the sort of aspects it will consider when negotiating with developers. Nor does it indicate if and when public agencies will be undertaking apparently programmed investment. According to the implementation schedule, the Inner Relief Road will not start until 1983. This perhaps relates to the speed at which the plan has been produced, uncertainty about whether finance will be forthcoming, and a concern to maintain flexibility for detailed negotiation with developers. It perhaps also reflects an authority whose only prior experience of development promotion has been a 1960s town centre scheme.

These seven examples illustrate the way the content of policies varies with the particular development problems of each area. They also give some indication of the different political and organizational contexts within which each plan has been prepared and how this may affect form and content, although this can only be fully appreciated through detailed case studies rather than an examination of plan documents themselves. The above accounts also show how similar plans are in their presentation and in the way issues are considered. Although each plan uses different presentational techniques and formal organization, an investigation of their contents reflects common assumptions about their scope and content. I will comment later on how this may be explained. However, I now turn to an examination of the policies. Although varying between areas, are there any similarities in the content of policies? To make such an assessment, I have used my overall review of plans.

2. THE POLICY INTENTIONS OF PLANS

Most plans state aims and/or objectives in some form. There are many reasons for not taking such statements at face value. Firstly, statements of aims and what the policies and proposals in the plans actually imply are not necessarily consistent (as some of the examples in the previous section illustrate). Secondly, the policies in the plan are not necessarily those which a local authority intends to follow. For example, the form of their expression in a plan may relate more to local political acceptability than how the authority will actually guide development (as in the Gloucester and Horsham statements on local needs). The alternatives that could have been pursued are not necessarily clear, despite the discussion of options or alternative strategies in some plans. In practice, critical decisions in the plan may have concerned the allocation of specific sites, or the exact quantity of land released in a period. Finally, the policies apparently formulated in plans are not necessarily new. The plan may merely express longstanding policies and attitudes. Nevertheless, there are generalizations that can be made about content of policies in local plans.

The first is that many plans still contain generalized objectives about the quality of life and social well-being (see for example Gloucester and Chandler's Ford), despite these criticisms of such vague statements when used in structure plans. These persist partly because local plans are still seen by some planners and certain sections of the public as guidance documents for the overall development of an area, even though they are in practice usually making limited proposals about land and development. But the policies in local plans concerning land and development matters are not of value in themselves. They are always instrumental to social, economic or environmental policy ends. Consequently, it is legitimate and necessary to attempt to connect land and development proposals to these ends. However, as I noted in Chapter 6, making the connection between such policies and land allocations is not always easy. In addition it may be politically difficult to make clear the nature of the choices that are being made, for example the impact of urban fringe land allocation in Newton-le-Willows on inner city areas, the possible dangers of allocating inner city sites for private housing (Farnworth) or the encouragement of office uses (Islington). It is therefore convenient for several reasons to use general objectives. These also serve to give the impression that a general interest calculus is being used in determining land use and development.

Whatever their stated purposes, most local plans contain proposals primarily about *land allocation*. This partly reflects central government advice that proposals should be limited to those which can be achieved by planning powers. Yet this limitation applies to non-statutory local plans as well. It may be concluded that local planners now also recognize that their field of action is linked to and limited by the nature of planning powers as provided by legislation and/or to the perception within local authorities that local planning authorities are concerned with land and development issues. In both the Islington and Farnworth examples, general policy plans provided the context within which specific land use and development policies and proposals had been derived. However, land allocation is approached in local plans in different ways, with different intentions pursued. In many built-up areas, the plan merely specifies performance criteria, as in most of the London Borough plans. In areas with substantial vacant or derelict land, or greenfield sites, specific land allocations are made. In these plans, the aim is often to limit the amount of land allocated to protect the interests of existing residents and enterprises (e.g. Horsham). The problem here is to determine the amount that will have to be released in order to sustain a defensible restrictive position. Although structure plans may have defined the principles for making this calculation, in terms of numbers of new dwellings within a period (using control totals, as in Hertfordshire), or for whom provision should be made (e.g. local needs qualifications), it is not necessarily a simple matter to workout the amount and location of land to allocate, as the Horsham plan shows. DoE Circulars 44/78 and 9/80 have created further considerable problems for local authorities, since these require that authorities demonstrate that they have five years housing land supply in their areas.

Elsewhere, the primary concern may be to allocate land so that it is co-ordinated with infrastructure provision (e.g. Horsham, Chandler's Ford, Gloucester). In all three instances, the framework of the plan provides the basis for negotiation with developers, highway authorities and water authorities over the timing, scale and detailed design of development. Finally, land may be allocated to enable the planning authority to attract development. This was a concern in the Gloucester plan, but more importantly in Farnworth, Newton-le-Willows, and Islington. In these areas, problems of site clearance are typically involved if land is to be made attractive for private development. The plan expresses a local authority commitment to intervene where possible in land assembly, site clearance and servicing. Only in a few cases is the social concern which often underlies these promotional policies in plans backed by limitations to ensure that the jobs created or the homes built will actually assist local people. Islington was concerned to attract only labour-intensive firms. In Barnsley Town Centre Plan (Barnsley MD), labour-intensive firms are to be encouraged, partly to sustain cheap public transport and so improve the mobility of many low income workers, especially women.

These types of land allocation policies suggest that the policy content of plans may be grouped as follows:

1. those where the main concern is to co-ordinate substantial new development or redevelopment;

2. those where the central emphasis is on promoting development;

3. as a particular form of this, those where a broad programme of social and economic revitalization is sought;

4. those where the object of the plan is to restrict development pressures in order to protect the interests of social groups who would otherwise be displaced by the operation of the market;

5. those where restriction is similarly sought in order to conserve the character of an area and the resources within it.

I have arrived at this grouping from reading the plans, though it echoes closely the general arguments for government intervention in land use and development discussed in Chapter 1[67].

The first concern, the efficient management of substantial new development, was a central task for local plans as envisaged in the PAG report. Given the reduction in development investment, it is not surprising that this is a primary concern in only a few of the plans I have come across. It is likely

----

[67] Obviously I will be accused of bias in ensuring the relationship of the two typologies!

to be the central focus of town centre plans where substantial development is still expected (Bexleyheath Action Area Plan (LB Bexley)); in major growth areas such as Abbey District Plan (Leicester DC) and the Hampshire Plans (Chandler's Ford, Totton, Western Wards of Fareham); in opportunity sites such as Covent Garden Action Area Plan (GLC), Enderby/Narborough District Plan (Blaby DC) for a site at a motorway node; or the increasing number of smaller development sites where infrastructure provision is a problem because of lack of public sector finance. These plans usually contain policies for phasing development, for design and mix of development and for provision of infrastructure and community facilities. In many such plans, a key issue in plan preparation has been negotiating agreement to proposals from residents and environmental groups often strongly opposed to any further development in their areas. As in Chandler's Ford, the bargain struck with local interests is the inclusion of proposals for general environmental protection and enhancement, and design criteria for new development. Yet while a local plan may give *some* assurance to *some* interests about the way the local authority will approach large development proposals, local authorities and developers have increasingly turned to development briefs for the more complex development sites. It is not at all clear how far the local plan framework publicly negotiated in, for example, Chandler's Ford will actually be used to provide the principles of such development briefs.

Although most recent plans acknowledge the need to help small firms and local businesses, there is a major difference between plans which are managing market-generated development investment, and those which seek to promote such investment in their areas. In a few areas, the two policies overlap, as in Gloucester. In London, the promotional interest is primarily selective, to maintain industrial employment and resist up-market office and hotel development which allegedly does not benefit local people (Waterloo DP, LB Lambeth; Camden Borough Plan), although as we have seen, Islington's plan welcomes both these types of development. In northern industrial areas, attracting any sort of private investment is desperately sought. This contrast can be seen between Islington and Farnworth, both areas in receipt of urban programme aid. Islington can contemplate obtaining planning gain from developers. In Farnworth, Bolton MD has to hope for government grants in order to undertake site preparation works in the hope of receiving some private sector investment interest. This raises the question of the role of a local plan in the promotion of development, which I will consider in the next chapter. It is evident that some plan preparers hope that the information provided, on sites and on council policies, may be helpful to potential investors.

Finally, there are plans which adopt a restrictive attitude to market-generated development. In rural areas, new development is commonly to be contained in village envelopes (Horsham, Ashby Woulds; see also Uttlesford Rural Areas District Plan (Uttlesford DC); Wrekin Rural Areas District Plan, (Wrekin DC); the Cambridgeshire village plans). In areas under severe development pressure, typically around London or the West Midlands conurbation, development is to be restricted to that for local needs only. The intention to keep out commuters or large national or regional firms has been undermined by the difficulties of defining what "local" is (Healey *et al.* 1980), and by structure plan modifications which have tended to weaken local needs policies. Yet many local plans seek not only to reduce the rate of development (East Hertfordshire and Dacorum District Plans; Horsham District Plan) but to provide space for the relocation and expansion of existing firms and to encourage local building firms to undertake housing

development[68]. As Larkin (1978) and Shucksmith (1981) have pointed out,
local needs policies appear to be concerned with social welfare, but they
could well have the opposite effect, pushing up land and property prices to
the detriment of those on low incomes, especially where council house
building programmes are small. Much more important in outer urban fringe
areas are conservation, landscape protection and design policies.

The only plans I have come across which express a deliberate intention to
restrict market tendencies to protect low income or otherwise disadvantaged
groups are in London, around the expanding central area (particularly Covent
Garden Action Area Plan (GLC), Waterloo District Plan (LB Lambeth) and
Camden Borough Plan). Otherwise the only social welfare policy concerning
land and development issues found in many plans is that which proposes to
resist the loss of residential accommodation. In Islington and other areas
with declining employment, a similar concern may be applied to industrial
firms, and even to local shops. The aim here is usually to prevent the loss
of properties the use of which benefits disadvantaged groups. It may also
be to encourage intensification within built-up areas, to reduce the amount
of greenfield site development.

From my reading of local plans I find the conclusion unavoidable that, taken
together, they express an intention to facilitate efficient development, as
a combined public/private sector operation out of which private firms gain
profits and local authorities hope to gain jobs, homes, rate incomes,
infrastructure and community facilities, or merely less nibbling away at an
open land environment. In some cases, the thrust of proposals is actually
to create a private sector in an area, as in certain inner city areas. This
conclusion is similar to that reached by Farnell (1981) who found that only
those local plans which were concerned with facilitating development were
progressed through to completion. Others, though proposed, fell by the
wayside due to such factors as lack of commitment by politicians and senior
officers, or difficulties in getting agreement on policies. Local planners
thus appear in practice to be conforming to central government advice in
limiting the scope and content of plans. But has this been produced by the
existence of this advice, or by other factors? I have already suggested
that the nature of planning powers and the perception *within* local authoritie
of the role of local planners may also be a source of the limitation on the
content of policies. Before pursuing this question further, I now look at
the more detailed presentation of policies and proposals.

3. THE EXPRESSION OF POLICIES AND PROPOSALS

How the policies and proposals contained in plans are expressed is
enlightening in what it reveals about the powers which local planners
consider can be influenced by the plan, and about current thinking among
local planners in the UK about the form in which site-specific policy
guidance should be expressed. So I make no apoligies for including a sectio
on what might seem to some the detailed technicalities of plan construction.

Four factors are likely to influence the form of expression of policies. The
first is what powers the authority considers can be influenced by the plan.
This varies from authority to authority. In some places, housing and
planning functions are closely integrated within the local authority (one
suspects this is the case in Farnworth). Elsewhere, the authority is a majo

---

[68]See the work of Elson and McNamara on Hertfordshire; Elson 1982.

landowner, and it may be appropriate to provide detailed development specifications in a plan. In other situations, development will be initiated by the private sector, and the local authority's powers to influence this lie in the development control area.

The second factor is the planners' perception of the difficulties of predicting when and where development investment will take place. During the 1950s, in drawing up plans particularly for parts of the urban fabric, planners tended to assume that the planning authority possessed the powers to determine the form, timing and location of development proposals. Yet even then, except in New Towns and a few clearance areas, their powers were little more than regulatory, with development initiative passing to the private sector. Consequently, while master plans, which specified the form of development both in location and bulk, might be appropriate where the planning authority was the major landowner and developer, elsewhere old-style development plans were claimed to be rigid and inflexible. One of the influences behind the PAG report was the search for ways of expressing policies and proposals which were more flexible, or reflected the reality of a local planning authority's powers. The local plans actually prepared illustrate a variety of responses to this problem.

Thirdly, the form of expression of policies has been influenced by DoE advice (see Chapter 4). I have already noted that proposals are supposed to be distinguished from the plan text in some way. Advice also stresses that local plans should concentrate on proposals only, since policy definition is the task of structure plans. Many plans include policies and proposals, both distinguished in capital letters. The distinction DoE officials now recognize that they were in fact concerned with policies, and that the distinction between policies and proposals has been a confining one[69].

DoE advice also stresses, as already noted, that the content of proposals should relate to land use and development matters, though these may be derived from social and economic considerations. As Section 3 shows, plans tend to keep within this remit, but there are many examples of non-land use proposals, depending on what role local planners are seeking for their plan. The DoE also advises that there should be a careful relationship between the Proposals Map and the Written Statement, so that the implications of proposals for those with property interests are clear. Yet many now contain very few spatially-distinguishable policies. Nevertheless, most authorities use some form of numbering to relate proposals in the text to the map (see examples in Section 2). Advice is also given on the handling of public sector proposals. These should not be included as proposals if a development is already underway, or if land has already been given planning permission for development. On the other hand they should not be included unless there is a firm commitment to construction, as expressed, for example, as a priority in a TPP. The concern here is to avoid facing these public agencies with the cost of compensation for blight. With the current uncertainty over public sector finance, such commitments for necessary infrastructure or facilities are often difficult to arrive at (see Chapter 6).

Finally, the form of expression of policies and proposals may reflect political considerations and the way the local planning authority prefers to manage its relations with those involved in development. Local councillors may not wish to be too specific in policy statements, in order to retain

---

[69]I infer this from discussion at a seminar on local plans at SAUS, Bristol, February 1982.

their discretion to determine the policy which should in fact prevail in
relation to a particular application. Planners and councillors, i.e. the
planning authority, may merely prefer to state the terms in which
negotiations between developer and authorities should be conducted, rather
than specify the outcome in advance. Here authorities are retaining their
interpretive discretion, (although in the Chandler's Ford case, this
discretion was in fact exercised by district councils, not the county who
prepared the plan). Thus under the guise of the need for "flexibility",
the form of expression of policies in plans may not only reflect economic
uncertainty and the limited powers available to planning authorities, but
the balance an authority (often unconsciously) strikes between retaining
its administrative discretion to determine the public interest in a
particular case, and the pressure which plan production creates for prior
and public determination.

It is no wonder that some local planners claim that the wording of policies
may become a major activity in plan preparation. It is often the point at
which professional planners and the local planning authority are most
evidently publicly tested - at local plan inquiries, in development
control appeals, and sometimes in political controversy. Local planners
in different authorities often consult each other for ideas about the
wording of policies and it has even been suggested that there should be a
"bank" of policies to which planners could refer for ideas (Fudge *et al.*
1982). This suggests a considerable shift from the notion of *locally*
developed policies for local circumstances. Nevertheless, this idea is
not as odd as it sounds given the common elements in the content of policies
already referred to.

Reviewing plans, it becomes evident that there are a number of different
ways in which policies are expressed[70]:

    A: Plan-wide policies and proposals.

    B: Site-specific policies and proposals.

    C: Area-specific policies and proposals.

    D: Activity level controls.

    E: User-oriented policies and proposals.

    F: Policies and proposals for phasing and co-ordination.

    G: Management policies.

    H: Intentional and advocacy policies and proposals.

A. *Plan-Wide Policies and Proposals*

1. Defining general principles which will guide a local authority's
consideration of any development proposals; e.g. a presumption against the

---

[70]I have developed these out of some ideas originally put forward in
discussion at Oxford by Martin Elson. The only comparable attempt at a
classification of types of policies of this kind is to be found in Barnard
(1981), based on the former functions of plans.

loss of residential accommodation, or proposals which entail the loss of
employment, or which are not for local needs.

2. Performance criteria to apply to development proposals. These may be
specific to a particular use e.g. "A change to residential use will normally
be permitted if the accommodation can provide acceptable living conditions,
and the environment is suitable for residential use" (Islington DP). This
sort of policy reflects the move away from segregated zonings. Performance
criteria are also used in relation to all forms of development, specifying
the aspects of layout, design, and special provision (e.g. car parking,
play spaces) which the authority will consider. These too reflect a shift
away from the tradition of specified standards. These general criteria may
be found within chapters relating to specific uses, or they may be grouped
as a special set of "development control policies" (e.g. Farnworth).
Camden published its Environmental Code as a special annex to its plan.
Islington's Planning Standards Guidelines are treated as supplementary
planning guidance, referred to in, but not part of, the plan.

B. *Site-Specific Policies and Proposals*

Many plans now only include on proposals maps those sites for which a
specific development is proposed, rather than broad-use zonings. These may
be public sector developments, or land released for the private sector.
Gloucester's local plan shows how little may in the end be mapped. In this
case, the line of a road is mentioned (in an area allocated in the text for
new housing development) though this is not specified on the map. At
Chandler's Ford, the layout of new development is only indicated
diagrammatically. These proposals maps make a striking contrast to the few
which still adhere to the traditional format of detailed layout. Where
this format is used, as in the Wapping Local Plan, it expresses nothing
more than what the authority would like to see on land it does not own and
does not have planning control over (it is within the London Docklands)
(Diagram 7.12). As a supplement to specification of sites in the text and
maps, several plans now include a schedule of proposals. Examples have
already been cited for Islington and Chandler's Ford (Diagrams 7.6 and 7.9).
I illustrate here that from Beckton District Plan (Newham) as it specifies
clearly the commitment of different agencies to site development (Diagram
7.13).

The main problems in expressing policies in terms of specific projects lie
with public sector proposals. Road proposals, often required to make sense
of the other policies and proposals in a plan, can be included if within a
TPP. If not, they may be left out (e.g. Buckingham Town Plan, Aylesbury
Vale DC), or indicated with a broad reservation (Bakewell DP, Peak Park
Joint Planning Board), or an area of search may be indicated (East
Hertfordshire DP). (Diagram 7.14). There have been difficulties in several
plans in extracting commitments to proposals from public agencies, as noted
in Chapter 6. Some, legitimately, cannot give a particular proposal high
priority compared to other demands. Others do not realize the implications
of including a public sector proposal in a plan, as in Basford, Forest
Fields District Plan (Nottingham DC), where the education authority
reviewed and changed its school requirements after the plan was agreed for
deposit. Others are reluctant to reveal their commitments, as in the
dispute between the GLC and Westminster over the publication of road-
widening reservations in the context of the plan.

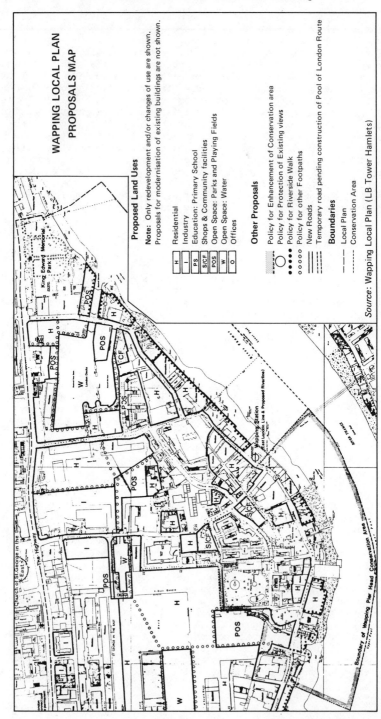

WAPPING LOCAL PLAN
PROPOSALS MAP

Proposed Land Uses

Note: Only redevelopment and/or changes of use are shown.
Proposals for modernisation of existing buildings are not shown.

H	Residential
I	Industry
PS	Education: Primary School
S/CF	Shops & Community facilities
POS	Open Space: Parks and Playing Fields
W	Open Space: Water
O	Offices

Other Proposals

- Policy for Enhancement of Conservation area
- Policy for Protection of Existing views
- Policy for Riverside Walk
- Policy for other Footpaths
- New Roads
- Temporary road pending construction of Pool of London Route

Boundaries

- — · — Local Plan
- ------ Conservation Area

Source: Wapping Local Plan (LB Tower Hamlets)

Diagram 7.12

Area	No.	Project	Proposal No.	Agency	Start required in District Plan	Status/ Comments
West Beckton	1	Prince of Wales I (151 dwellings)	H1	LBN	Under construction	
	2	Prince of Wales II (270 dwellings)	H2	LBN	1979	CPO confirmed
	3	Prince of Wales III (70 new, 120 existing dwellings)	H3 & H4	LBN	1978/9	Existing dwellings being acquired. New dwellings programmed.
	4	14–20 Burley Road	H7	LBN	1978	3 dwellings programmed
	5	Beckton I (235 dwellings)	H5	GLC	Under construction	Allocations to be made
	6	Beckton II (440 dwellings)	H6	GLC	1979	Construction programmed
	7	Private 'A' (170 dwellings)	H8	Private development	1980	Developer to be selected
	8	Private 'B' (210 dwellings)	H9	Private development	1980/81	Developer to be selected
	9	Rehabilitation of other dwellings (initially 100 dwellings)	P1	Housing Association/ LBN	1978	Funds allocated: Inner Cities Construction Programme & Housing Corporation
Cyprus	1	Area 1 (231 dwellings)	H11	LBN	1978	Construction programmed
	2	Area 2 (350 dwellings)	H12	LBN	1980	Agreement to build in principle
	3	Area 3a (300 dwellings)	H13	Housing Association	1979	Funds yet to be allocated. Housing corporation agreement to fund.
	4	Area 3b (210 dwellings)	H14	GLC	1979	Agreement to build in principle.
	5	Area 3c (190 dwellings)	H15	GLC	1980	Agreement to build in principle
	6	Area 4 (350 dwellings)	H16	LBN	1981	Agreement to build in principle.
North Beckton	1	Area 1 (607 dwellings)	H10	GLC	1980	Agreement to build in principle.

Diagram 7.13. Beckton District Plan: Implementation Schedule (part of)

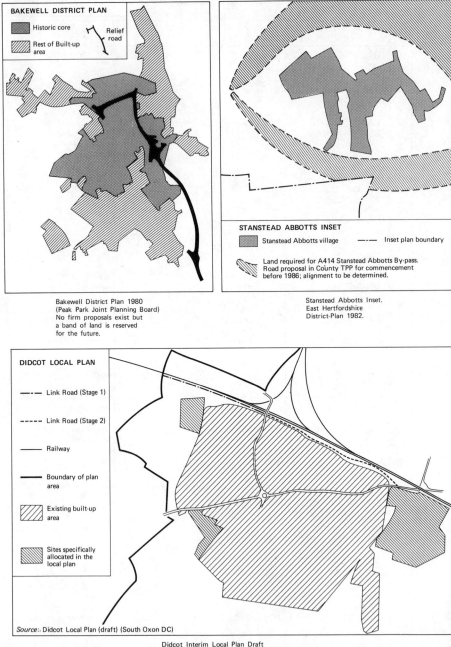

BAKEWELL DISTRICT PLAN

- Historic core
- Rest of Built-up area
- Relief road

Bakewell District Plan 1980
(Peak Park Joint Planning Board)
No firm proposals exist but
a band of land is reserved
for the future.

STANSTEAD ABBOTTS INSET

- Stanstead Abbotts village
- Inset plan boundary
- Land required for A414 Stanstead Abbotts By-pass. Road proposal in County TPP for commencement before 1986; alignment to be determined.

Stanstead Abbotts Inset.
East Hertfordshire
District-Plan 1982.

DIDCOT LOCAL PLAN

- Link Road (Stage 1)
- Link Road (Stage 2)
- Railway
- Boundary of plan area
- Existing built-up area
- Sites specifically allocated in the local plan

Source: Didcot Local Plan (draft) (South Oxon DC)

Didcot Interim Local Plan Draft
(South Oxon District Council) 1978.
Stage 1 was agreed before plan preparation.
Stage 2 was agreed in time for the draft.
But there is no agreement on whether and how
to re-align the difficult underpass below British
Rail main line.

Diagram 7.14

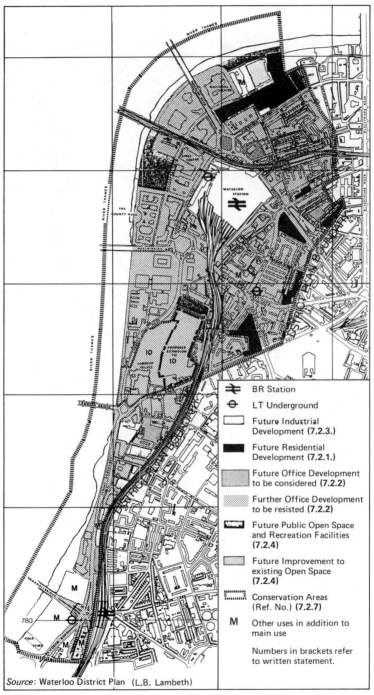

BR Station

LT Underground

Future Industrial
Development **(7.2.3.)**

Future Residential
Development **(7.2.1.)**

Future Office Development
to be considered **(7.2.2)**

Further Office Development
to be resisted **(7.2.2)**

Future Public Open Space
and Recreation Facilities
(7.2.4)

Future Improvement to
existing Open Space
(7.2.4)

Conservation Areas
(Ref. No.) **(7.2.7)**

M   Other uses in addition to
main use

Numbers in brackets refer
to written statement.

Source: Waterloo District Plan (L.B. Lambeth)

Diagram 7.15

C. *Area-Specific Policies and Proposals*

These can be found in two forms; firstly, the sorts of policy areas or
settlement specific policies found in the Horsham and Ashby Woulds plans.
These not surprisingly are common in rural area plans, though many larger
plans have a section on the policies relevant to sub-areas of the plan.
Secondly, zoning may be used to define an area within which or beyond which
an activity is to be excluded or encouraged.

1. Exclusive zoning

Examples here are broad zonings within which special limitations will apply.
The type of example here is the green belt. However, the Secretary of
State's structure plan modifications and objections to local plans have
limited the use of green belts, though local environmental and residents
groups still see them as a powerful tool for restricting development over
wide areas. In areas outside green belts where very restrictive policies
apply, authorities have had to devise alternative forms of firm restriction
on development, for example Horsham's "Countryside Protection Areas
subject to development restraint", and Wrekin Rural Areas District Plan's
"area of special housing control". Other examples of restrictive open land
zonations are AONB's, Sites of Special Scientific Interest, and specific
local inventions such as the "no tipping" zone in Rixton Brickworks Subject
Plan (Warrington). Another form of exclusion is the zoning *for* a specific
use in order to keep out a higher value one. The most famous example here
is the Waterloo District Plan (LB Lambeth) where land is zoned for housing
and industry to exclude offices. This is then overlain, so that the
intention is perfectly clear, with a zonation specifically excluding
offices (Diagram 7.15). Another example is in Newburn Local Plan
(Newcastle-upon-Tyne MD), where land is zoned for industry on the urban
fringe, to exclude housing. Finally, zoning may be used to restrict
development within a specified area. "Village envelopes" are the type of
examples of this, but another is found in the "Diplomatic zone" proposed
in Kensington and Chelsea's Borough Plan.

2. Promotional Zoning

These include longstanding area policies, such as Housing Action and
Improvement Areas, and conservation area; more recent ideas such as
Industrial Improvement Areas; and special zones, such as Islington's "Areas
of Opportunity" for industry. Enterprise Zones are of course an
extension of this principle. While valuable in concentrating local
authority effort and private investment attention, such area zonings may be
criticized because in concentrating benefits in one area they may make
conditions worse in other similar areas. The value of zoning depends on
its capacity to influence investor behaviour into patterns the market would
not by itself have produced. Promotional zonings may give confidence to
existing occupants of houses and factories and attract the new ones in.
Green belt zonation may deter developers from buying land in these areas.
Chapter 8 will consider what evidence there is on whether these effects
actually occur. It should be noted, however, that where no proposals or
zones are indicated for an area, the implication is that existing uses and
the existing character of an area will stay the same. This in itself could
be considered a zonation.

D. *Activity Level Controls*

Here the object is to control the amount of an activity in an area, in
addition to or as an alternative to controlling its location. The
traditional way of doing this has been by density controls (for housing and
industry) and controls on building bulk (or plot ratios) for more intensive
uses such as offices. Density guidance is still provided in many plans,
although simple standards have been replaced by more flexible statements.
Densities may be expressed as a range (as in London, deriving from the GLDP).
In some areas, they are to be in keeping with existing densities. In areas
under development pressure where there is concern to limit the amount of
land released, minimum densities are specified. Such activity controls
have traditionally been used for local design reasons, or to limit
congestion produced by the occupants of developments. More recently, some
authorities have tried to use activity controls for more sophisticated
purposes, such as the regulation of regional growth. In Hertfordshire,
districts are allocated control totals for housing and employment in order
to reduce the rate of growth in each. Districts have then been required to
produce proposals which release land in relation to the control total. East
Hertfordshire and Dacorum District Plans have policies which state that if
totals are exceeded in one period land released in following periods will
be reduced. The DoE and the House Builders Federation are known to be
hostile to this idea, since it appears to run counter to the requirement to
provide a five year supply of residential building land (see Chapter 6
section 4.4).

E. *User-Oriented Policies and Proposals*

DoE advice states firmly that proposals should relate to uses, not users.
Yet several proposals discriminate directly or indirectly towards users.
The DoE argument is that planning powers do not allow such discrimination,
referring to a few key court cases. Yet the legal position here is unclear,
especially if local plans themselves define the scope of material
considerations (see the discussion in Chapter 4). Planning authorities are
on safe ground when discriminating in favour of buildings in the
countryside for farmers and farm-workers only. This has been a longstanding
exception to containment policy. The position is more complex where an
authority is attempting to discriminate in favour of local interests, or
particular groups within the housing market or public sector development.
Policies which discriminate in favour of local firms are common in areas
under development pressure, with the widespread use of conditions limiting
occupancy of office and sometimes industrial developments to local firms or
firms serving the local area. But planning authorities have had difficulty
in devising similar policies to restrict the occupancy of private housing
development to "locals". A common approach is to encourage a particular mix
of development, although surveys tend to confirm the suspicion that cheaper
houses tend to go to non-local people, and more expensive ones to local people
(McNamara and Elson 1981). Horsham District Plan rationalizes this problem
by stating that building larger houses will create capacity in smaller and
possibly cheaper houses (i.e. the 'filtering' theory). In Tamworth and
Rossendale District Plans, policies aimed to attract higher income residents
by encouraging larger houses, but these were successfully challenged by
developers at local plan inquiries[71]. Policies specifically aimed at
reserving areas for public housing development have been discouraged by the

---

[71]Pers. comm. E. A. Hill.

DoE. Nevertheless some have survived into local plans (e.g. Beckton District
Plan, LB Newham). Finally, at Camden, the courts and the DoE combined to
discourage the inclusion of policies which discriminated against private
nurseries.

F. Policies and Proposals for Phasing and Co-ordination

Several examples of these were illustrated in Section 2. They are most
common where substantial land allocations are involved on greenfield sites.
Such policies state investments necessary before the land can be released,
such as water supply or sewerage. These encourage potential developers to
consider making contributions to these works, and the requirement for this
may be specified (as in Chandler's Ford). This of course implies the use of
agreements between the planning authority and the developer if planning
permission is given. Where developers' contributions are not specified,
the requirement provides a baseline for negotiations with developers. In
sites affected by dereliction of one kind or another, again works are
specified, but as noted in Section 3, this usually requires public agency
site preparation before development can take place.

G. Management Policies

These refer to statements about the management practices of various local
authority departments or other public agencies whose activities are important
in the area. The most common of these relate to public housing management.
But they are also found in open land management plans, concerned with such
matters as the maintenance of meadows, or woodland areas. The DoE has
consistently advised that these should not be included in local plans,
although it can be argued that they provide an important support to other
policies in a plan, or that the public demand more knowledge of how the
authority proposes to manage itself.

H. Intentional and Advocacy Policies and Proposals

Such policies express what the local authority intends to do in respect of
issues relevant to the plan. Commonly, these are the policies which arise
from other council programmes (such as housing), or where the authority
cannot yet be precise about the level of expenditure or the details of a
programme. Farnworth treated these as "other supporting council policies".
Gloucester refers to its intentions to develop a housing improvement
programme. These policies may often go beyond the land use remit, but are
valuable for the authority to include within the plan either because they
strengthen the other plan policies (as in Farnworth) or because they
express at least the council's goodwill in respect of a problem, although
it may not know what it can do about it.

Advocacy policies occur where the authority seeks but has not necessarily
achieved the commitment of another public agency to particular policies.
Camden Borough Plan explicitly identifies these, particularly in the area
of employment and economic activity, where a London Borough short of land
has few direct powers:

   "Advocative industrial policies:

   (i)   The Council will continue to press for the abolition of IDC
         controls in Inner London.

(ii)   The Council will press for effective measures to give more
       assistance to industry in Inner London.

(iii) The Council will continue to press for the relaxation of
       restrictions on advertising for industry imposed on London
       Boroughs".

Horsham's policies about grubbing up of hedgerows should probably be
considered as advocative policies! More commonly, policies state that the
authority will seek to persuade the Gas Board, British Rail, the Education
Authority, the Health Authority, the Water Authority or Central Government
to provide a particular facility.

It is evident in this summary of the ways policies are expressed that local
plans reflect a much more sophisticated approach to the management of the
local planning authority's role in land use change than that exemplified in
the simple zonings of most old-style development plans. The most
significant shift has been from zoning land for particular uses and the
application of single value standards to control the amounts of uses, to
attempts to control the amount of activities in other ways than by control
of sites and bulk, to discriminate between users as well as uses, and to
locate land use policies in a wider context of the local authority's role
in land development and management. However, this developing
sophistication does not necessarily mean that policies are pursued more
effectively because of a different plan format. It is also more difficult
for an applicant, developer, local citizen or development control officer
to "read off" an authority's policy from its local plan. I will return to
this issue in Chapter 8. I will now consider what evidence there is within
the plans of how authorities envisage that their plans will be implemented.

4. THE IMPLEMENTATION OF POLICIES AND PROPOSALS

Statutory local plans are required by the regulations to consider resources.
Most have a section at the end of "implementation and resources", as if this
were yet another topic. Some of these sections say very little (e.g. two
paragraphs in the Farnworth plan). Others are little more than essays in
local government finance and powers (e.g. Gloucester). It is rare for there
to be any detailed costing of proposals or assessment of the financial
implications for the local authority and other agencies, although a
financial appraisal was undertaken for the Chandler's Ford plan to assess
the implications for the County Council of alternative development options
(Healey 1982c). Islington and Watford District Plans both include a review
of financial and land resources, indicating what action they propose to take
or to encourage to make both available.

In many plans, it is assumed that implementation will come about by the
investment of the private sector. Thus the Horsham plan has no section on
implementation. Yet one might expect an analysis of the way private
investment has been operating and is likely to operate in the area concerned.
Apart from some discussion of trends in building rates, with, in a few
recent plans, comments on the marketability of sites, there is no evidence
in most plans of any such analysis. Yet authorities are usually aware that
the land they allocate is held by owners, some more likely than others to
bring their land forward for development. This usually emerges at public
local inquiries which often contain interesting site histories, not usually
found in plans. In Newton-le-Willows and Farnworth, it is proposed to
acquire land where owners are not developing it. But little indication is
given as to whether these are likely to be major developers holding onto

their land banks, farmers who wish to continue in business, small property owners or large pension funds. I suspect the reason for this neglect in plans is not just that knowledge of land ownership and development intentions is partial. If too much is specified about the ownership of land, and about the way the land market is operating in a particular area, a local plan could give the impression of selectively favouring certain interests, thus distorting the appearance of demonstrating that plan policies are a reasonable calculation of the public interest. A fascinating exception to this generalization is a draft local plan for the area around the northern margin of Heathrow Airport which shows the ownership of green belt land which abuts the airport. Most of it is owned by airport-related companies or financial institutions (Heathrow Airport Local Plan, Hillingdon LB).

Where the public sector has a major role, as in inner city areas or opportunity sites, investment charts are common to indicate which agency will be investing when. Yet specificity is often difficult because of uncertainty affecting public expenditure programmes, as noted above. Where the local authority is the main landowner, it is easier to be more specific, but the authority may still be uncertain when sources of finance for development will become available. And although it was noted in Chapter 6 that plan preparation may influence public agency resource commitment, there is no certainty that it will continue to have that effect once prepared. As Byrne notes in connection with Beckton District Plan (Newham):

> "Local Plans are statutory documents, putting forward policies
> and proposals for a ten year horizon ... (Other planning systems)
> consist of general strategy statements accompanied by detailed
> short-term programmes of action, which are regularly reviewed
> and rolled forward ... (In attempting to interrelate the two,
> there are) two problems. Firstly, the programming information
> was immediately "bled off" into Service Plans as soon as it
> appeared in the draft version of the Local Plan. As a result,
> commitments have been made well in advance of the Local Plan
> being adopted. Secondly, the programming information dated
> quickly. To be of use, it should be annually updated as a whole.
> In practice, the only chance of updating was between the draft
> version of the Plan and the approved Plan for "deposit". Now
> that a statutory Local Plan is locked on the conveyor belt of
> deposit-public enquiry-adoption-modification, it becomes
> increasingly less useful as an input into the individual sectoral
> Service Plans" (Byrne 1978 pp.185-6).

Similarly, a few plans, such as Farnworth, express the hope that community initiatives will be encouraged to implement plan policies. But how this encouragement is to take place is not specified.

One is left with a curious impression, after reading plans and what is said within them about implementation, that local authorities have often not considered what the role of the plan itself will be in implementing the policies within it, except in so far as policies are defensible in appeals. It appears that authorities hope that several groups will be influenced by plans - potential investors, community groups, public agencies, constituents. Yet reading plans involves a reasonable degree of literacy. It also requires an ability to understand the various quirks of presentation. The reader in most cases has to work through the plan to select those policies and proposals which affect h/her interest, although a few plans provide helpful cross-referencing (e.g. Islington). If you are local, literate and have time, you can probably eventually get the hang of a plan. But if you are a speculative land purchaser, a developer looking for housing land, a firm seeking a new site or wondering how council policies affect an existing site, a house buyer, or an occupant concerned about possible development proposals, you may face a daunting prospect. In many plans, the intention is that local people and potential investors should "receive" the messages about policy intentions which the plan contains. Yet how far are those messages being blocked by the way in which plans are presented? Even sophisticated developers or their agents may find Islington's plan difficult to understand. Thus the way plans present policies may obscure rather than reveal local planning policies except to those with a sophisticated understanding of the planning system. One result of this is to encourage potential applicants to enter directly into discussion with local authorities. Both authority and developer may possibly prefer this negotiative style of operation, but it may well occur with development control officers who themselves may have difficulty in understanding the plan and its policies. This encourages the more selective use of policies than the plan appears to suggest. The consequence could be less policy consistency and less public accountability in the exercise of local authority planning powers.

5. CONCLUSIONS

Local plans, then, are primarily oriented to land use and development matters, and are aimed principally at facilitating private sector development in co-ordination with public sector investment. The objectives of this exercise may be to restrict development, (e.g. Southern Shire Counties), promote development selectively (e.g. London), or generally, to promote wholesale economic revitalization. Although the plans refer to social considerations, few of these are followed through directly into policies and proposals. Nor do any of the plans I have seen provide a clear statement of the social and economic impact of proposals. The content of local plans thus appears to confirm the general conclusions made about the planning system as a whole, as discussed in Chapter 2. Yet local plans are discretionary tools. Is it the collective exercise of planning authorities' own discretion which has produced this result? or has it been determined by the form of local plans as specified by the legislation, or by professional ideologies?

In the mid-1970s, some planners clearly imagined that local plans could be general expressions of social and economic policies of an area (see Chapter 5). Farnell's study confirms that plans with these purposes were begun. Yet there were no examples of such plans in my scan. One reason for this must be the effect of central government advice, which, as we have seen, has increasingly stressed that local plan policies and proposals should be limited in content to land use matters. In many instances, local planners have left out a number of social policies which either cannot be expressed in land use terms or are difficult to implement (e.g. local housing needs policies) as a result of DoE advice. In some cases this advice has been given directly. DoE officials have also visited local authorities and spoken at meetings of planning officers. Consequently, their views are likely to be well known to most local planners. DoE views on the appropriate content of plans also became clear through the modifications to structure plans. As was shown in Chapter 3, the social policies of South Yorkshire and Cambridgeshire structure plans were substantially modified. The policies restricting development to that for local needs only have been modified in a large number of plans, on the grounds of feasibility as well as over-restriction.

I conclude that central government through its interpretation of legislation
has played a major role in determining the content of local plan policies
and proposals, through limiting their scope, and has also influenced the
form of their expression. This effect has been produced not only in
deposited plans, but in most others. Yet if local plans are prepared at the
discretion of local authorities, and their form in theory is discretionary,
how has this come about? The legislative constraints on form and content
are actually very limited. What other powers can central government exert
to produce such a considerable degree of conformity in content? There are
two very important considerations here. Firstly, local plans must formally
be a development of structure plan policies. In so far as the latter are
limited to land use and development policies, so are local plans. However,
there is considerable interpretive leeway here, and local plans do not have
to be statutory. Secondly, for many authorities, a central reason for
preparing local plans is for use as support and justification for decisions
on planning applications, where the local authority's decisions could be
appealed to the Secretary of State.

In other words, local plans reflect central government advice on their form
and content because in many cases their primary purpose lies in a dialogue
between local authorities and central government over the validity of the
former's policies, mediated through the Inspectorate. The irritation that
local authority planners often express over having to conform to central
government advice thus partly reflects a sense of being in a weaker
position, and partly central government's lack of appreciation of the
problems of fitting a standard format to local circumstances. In addition,
as with other policy vehicles designed by central government to be
prepared by local authorities, authorities may also want to graft on other
purposes to local plans than that of defending their decisions to central
government. Because local plans have some standing outside the local
authority, authorities may use them for local political purposes (as an
expression of concern for the problems of an area), or to obtain some
co-ordination among public agencies, or to attract investment, both public
and private. However, to sustain that "standing", the format of plans must
not depart too far from that sought by central government.

In this interpretation, local plans appear as yet another mechanism through
which central government has been attempting to manage the behaviour of
local authorities. The special nature of local plans as policy vehicles
is that central government's influence is achieved not by its control over
resources, but indirectly, via structure plan policies and the appeal system.

Yet local authorities do not have to accept this limitation, especially
where the law is uncertain (as over "user" discrimination) or where few
appeals are likely (as in many areas with depressed economies). Consequently
there must also be locally-generated pressures to emphasize land use and
development matters. Two factors operate here, in addition to central
government advice; firstly, the powers which local planning authorities can
themselves wield, and secondly, the attitudes or ideologies of local
planners themselves. Although planners in the early seventies were
attracted by notions of urban social and economic management ("governance")
(see Chapter 2), they reacted in the later seventies to demands from
politicians and general public comment to produce visible physical products.
At the same time, other local authority departments were frequently
unwilling to admit the planning department to a substantial role in
allocating resources which they controlled. As a consequence, local
planners were forced back on using those powers within their area of
departmental concern, which primarily related to the Town and Country
Planning Acts and land use and development matters. The legislation provide

only limited powers for direct intervention in land purchase and assembly, and even fewer resources. Nor are there powers to enforce the co-ordination of public sector development investment. This sectoral limitation on the concerns of local planning authorities has been imposed on both central and local government. Yet local planners have been unwilling to give up their claim to a broader concern with the interests of other sectors, as is reflected in the review of broad objectives and problems common in the introduction to plans.

Both in their form of preparation and in the arrangement of most plans, it often appears as if the local authority has carried out a wide-ranging review, consulted all relevant parties, and produced policies and proposals which represent a considered view of the general interest in respect of the future use of land and development in an area. These introductory statements reflect, substantially in some cases but implicitly in others, the policy stance of the local authority concerned. Yet the proposals for allocating specific sites may not really result from this process. At Ashby Woulds, small land allocations were changed as a result of public discussion; in Gloucester, the major allocations for housing and industry were fixed by prior decisions to release land, and it is probable that this was also the case at Horsham. Detailed studies elsewhere in the South East suggest that few sites allocated in local plans in the 1970s had no previous history of development proposals (e.g. Healey *et al*. 1982). In other words, the plans, for all the appearance of producing proposals which conform to the general interest, are often merely rationalizing decisions already made. This has happened partly because so much land was released in the early seventies, which was consumed very slowly after the collapse of the property boom. Consequently, in reviewing policies in plans, authorities have been burdened by prior commitments. Yet this phenomenon probably happened before this and will continue to be common. During the seventies, planning authorities have become accustomed to negotiating directly with applicants, and expect to do so once plans are produced. As a result, new commitments have often been entered into while a plan is in preparation. This raises the question, for discussion in Chapter 8, of how far local plans are likely to guide such negotiations.

To conclude, the content of local plans has been substantially produced by the limited legislative powers available in respect of land and development, the sectoral habits of central and local government, and the way central government has developed its role in respect of structure and local plans, and appeals. The resultant plans then reflect the way the general format which these constraints provide has been fitted, by local planners, to the political and organizational characteristics of the local authority, the local political climate within which it operates, and local development commitments of various kinds.

Local plans may thus vary little in scope. Yet it is possible, by directing the way the authority exercises its planning powers, to affect different sets of interests through different policies. Thus several plans if implemented would benefit disadvantaged groups in one way or another. Some would protect them from dislocation through redevelopment (e.g. Waterloo District Plan, LB Lambeth), or provide environmental improvements and social facilities (e.g. Farnworth), or more job opportunities (e.g. Farnworth, Islington, Newton-le-Willows, Gloucester). In these cases, the intention of the plans is to produce such effects. In practice, because of difficulties in implementing the necessary discrimination, it may be difficult to avoid what has been called "gentrification" in the housing field, but could equally happen with industrial or commercial development. Here, policies to protect particular types of property for the disadvantaged

attract middle class occupants who displace poorer families, and
industries employing skilled workers or specialist craft workers rather
than the semi-skilled and unskilled.

Many more plans should benefit farmers by protecting land from development,
and by doing so preserving areas of countryside for the enjoyment of those
who live in these or can afford to buy their way into them. In this way,
local plans are merely confirming the tradition of containing and
concentrating development which has been a main plank of national urban
settlement policy since 1947. Only if a local authority owns land and has
the resources to develop it can it provide adequately for the housing
needs of the disadvantaged. Speculative developers may find some reduction
in the uncertainty affecting sites, and consequently fewer opportunity
sites for speculation. Most other residential developers, however, despite
their current complaints against restrictive policies in some areas, should
find a substantial amount of land allocated for them. The problem for
individual firms is, of course, that other firms may own or have options
on, the sites allocated. Finally, industrial and commercial investors will
find welcoming policies and proposals outside the south, and even here,
authorities are currently much more interested in attracting employment-
generating firms.

One might therefore conclude that those likely to gain from local plan
policies and proposals are all those who would benefit from co-ordinated
land release which ensured that the developed area was reasonably
concentrated and that the location of new development was reasonably
predictable. Hall *et al.* (1973) came to the same conclusion in their
study of the overall impact of the planning system in the two decades
after 1947. Yet this *de facto* national urban strategy was barely
articulated as a national policy after 1950. Rather, the policy of
containment was implemented through the articulation of the policy in each
county area and in successive and mostly routine development control
decisions. The 1968 Act claimed to introduce more concern with social and
economic policies into planning polcies, and the reorganization of local
government further fragmented the planning system. Yet the two results in
terms of local plan policies do not look very different. The important
point here is that while the economic climate and the format of plans have
changed, the powers to implement planning policies are substantially the
same as those available from the early 1950s onwards.

CHAPTER 8

Local Plans in Use

1. ASSESSING THE IMPACT OF LOCAL PLAN PRODUCTION AND USE

In Chapter 5, I suggested that most local plans have been produced for areas where significant changes in land use have been occurring, notably in the areas around the conurbations and in inner city areas. Chapter 6 showed how their production involves a cumbersome mixture of technical, consultative and semi-judicial procedures in which existing policies and proposals are reviewed and new ones sometimes brought forward. Chapter 7 concluded that these policies and proposals are predominantly concerned with land allocation and development change and with facilitating development. How have these local plans been used and what has been the impact of their production and use?

This apparently simple question is in practice very difficult to answer, even if we put aside the problem, faced throughout this account of local plans, of the wide variation of situations in which they are produced and used. One difficulty, noted above, is that the policies and proposals in plans are not necessarily initiated in the plan. Consequently it is necessary to identify not only the impact of the policies and proposals themselves, but whether their inclusion in a plan has in any way affected their impact. The important distinction here is between a local plan as a statement of the local planning authority's intentions, and the plan as a tool for implementing these intentions. The two are obviously related, although a plan may contain policy statements which the authority may have no real intention of implementing, and in its actions it may in effect be following a policy not articulated in a plan. Yet the existence of a plan in the first sense raises questions about the legitimacy of an authority's policies and proposals, and whether the authority actually adheres to its publicly-adopted plans. In the second sense, the central question is the effectiveness of the plan as a tool.

---

[72] My thinking in this chapter has developed from work undertaken at Oxford Polytechnic with Martin Elson, Paul McNamara, Shiela Terry, Margaret Wood and Julian Davis. See in particular Healey *et al.* 1982a and Healey 1982b.

There have been very few attempts to study directly the impacts or
implementation of a development plan. Hall's national study reviews the
consequences of local authority land allocations but provides only
circumstantial evidence on how the result, of contained dispersal, was
produced (Hall *et al*. 1973). Best's studies assessed the amount of land
allocated for development in plans, but did not assess what the effect of
this allocation was on development and land use change (Best and Champion
1969). Mandelker (1962) was able to show that green belt policies, which have
to be expressed in development plans, have been effective in restricting
development, although subsequent studies have cast doubt on whether they have
led to the positive use of land within green belts for farmland, or
recreational areas (Coleman 1976, SCLSERP 1976, Munton 1979).

Other studies on land availability for housing development show that except
for green belt allocation, a considerable amount of development has been
allowed on land not allocated in plans (e.g. Pearce and Tricker 1977).
Blacksell and Gilg (1977), Anderson (1981) and Preece (1981) investigate
development control in Areas of Outstanding Natural Beauty, and here find
no consistent pattern of exclusion of development. But this, of course,
was not the primary purpose of AONBs. There are a number of case studies of
town centre or housing redevelopment where the area concerned has been a
Comprehensive Development Area in an old-style development plan (Dennis
1970, Ambrose and Colenutt 1975). But few set out to compare some aspect
of a plan's proposals before and after development. A fascinating exception
is Anstey's study of land values before and after CDA designation and
development in the Barbican, London (Anstey 1965). Another interesting
study in London examines the implementation of the Covent Garden Action Area
Plan (Williams 1979), following through the progress of development on
particular sites since the plan's adoption. An interesting comparative
study of development in Oxford and Leiden, Netherlands, in relation to plans,
concluded that there was more deviation from plans in Leiden because of the
greater specificity of land allocations in Dutch plans and the smaller
amount of "flexibility" (administrative discretion) in the Dutch planning
system (Thomas *et al*. 1983). Recent work at the Building Research
Establishment (BRE) is attempting the difficult task of assessing development
control decisions against local plan proposals in a selection of local
plans. Their central concern is to assess whether a local plan helped to
reduce the delay in dealing with applications[73]. They found that on average
well over half of applications made conformed with plan policies and
proposals. A similar conclusion, of a substantial agreement between plan
policies and proposals and development control decisions, has been reached
in work on housing land allocation and employment-generating development
undertaken at Oxford Polytechnic for the Department of the Environment
(Healey *et al*. 1982a).

However, studies of the post-1968 British planning system illustrate the
problems of assessing the impact of the new-style local plans. The BRE
work found between 25% and 65% of applications were not covered by a
specific policy in a plan. As Chapter 7 illustrates, policies and
proposals are not necessarily site-related and often indicate the criteria
by which applications will be judged rather than specifying uses precisely.
Consequently, while it was possible to assess the conformance of development
with the land allocations of old-style development plans, development now
has to be assessed in terms of its performance in relation to a number of
criteria. In such cases, it is much more a matter of judgement whether the

---

[73]Per. comm. M. T. Pountney and P. W. Kingsbury.

plan is being followed or not. The situation is further complicated by the deliberate avoidance of specificity in a plan, either because conflicts could not be resolved or because the authority wished to preserve its discretion (see Chapter 6). Very few plans specify how the impact of the plan will be monitored. (The major exceptions here are those plans attempting to phase land release, e.g. Horsham District Plan).

Some people will argue that policies and proposals should be clearly specified in local plans, with a specification of what impact a policy is intended to have and how its achievement may be identified. Owen (1980) and Kingston (1981) provide useful ideas on how this might be done. However, even where this is provided, there are major methodological problems to be overcome in monitoring and assessing the effects of land use policies. The first arises from the fact that permitting or refusing an application, or encouraging a specific development, is rarely sought for its own sake. It is instrumental to a wider purpose, such as job creation or providing a range of housing to meet all needs. Yet making land available is usually a necessary, though not sufficient, condition for achieving that purpose. Secondly, the timescale over which development takes place may be longer than the life of a plan. The plans whose impact we can trace today may be those produced fifteen or twenty years ago. With the periodicity of the building and property development industry overlain by prolonged recession, and with cutbacks in public expenditure for development, it is probable that the lead times for development have become increasingly drawn out during the 1970s.

Thirdly, it is extremely difficult, as I indicated earlier, to disentangle the effects of a plan from those of the policies within it. Measures of conformity may show that a particular policy or zonation has been adhered to, but provide no means of telling whether this would have happened without a plan, or without planning policies. Green belt and containment policies are often blamed for high urban fringe land prices. Yet these might have been high and increasing anyway. A plan indicating where the green belt is may merely define which sites do and do not attract these prices. Comparative studies of long developed urban regions without green belts but with substantial private land ownership would be helpful here (see for example Clawson 1971, Archer 1973, and Brown et al. 1981).

To investigate the impact of plans directly, however, it is necessary to study the processes by which development occurs, and the extent to which the planning authority's action and its plans affect these processes. In only a very few cases is a local plan used so explicitly as a tool that its effectiveness can be identified precisely. In South Hampshire, a growth area defined in regional policy in the Strategic Plan for the South East 1970 (SEJPT 1970), substantial blocks of land were released in the late 1960s and early 1970s via an informal policy statement which specified sites, and indicated infrastructure constraints. The South Hampshire Structure Plan, completed by 1972, proposed that no further land should be released in the growth areas until local plans had been adopted. Unfortunately, the structure plan was not approved until 1977, and the first local plan, the Western Wards of Fareham Action Area Plan, was not adopted until 1979, although the structure plan intended land to be released here in 1976 (Healey 1982c). In effect in South Hampshire, implementation of policy was to be plan-based, following sequentially upon the preparation of structure and local plans. Yet as was suggested in Chapter 6, it is probably more common for implementation to proceed in parallel with the development of policy, a process which might be punctuated by the articulation of policies in a local plan.

There is no doubt that further work is urgently needed to identify the impact of planning policies, and the various tools used to further them, on the way the physical environment is produced, managed and changed. In this chapter I will attempt to review the limited evidence available on the role of local plans within the ongoing relationship between local planning authorities and the processes of land use and development change. This raises yet a further problem of how the relationship should be conceptualized. Traditionally, "planning" has been opposed to "the market", or the "public" sector to the "private" sector, the planning/public sector replacing and/or guiding the market/private sector. However, this conceptualization is inadequate on a number of grounds. On the one hand, there is no simple distinction between public and private sectors. Firstly, as I have shown, the planning authority's policies may reflect certain "private sector" or "market" interests, such as existing land allocations, or a concern to make adequate private sector housing land available, or to make conditions attractive to private investors. Secondly, many of those engaged in development processes are public sector agencies. Many older urban areas are currently substantially owned by their local authorities. The public sector not only provides infrastructure for development, but is a substantial developer in its own right. Thirdly, the structure of development opportunities perceived by private sector firms is in many cases dominated by considerations related to government policy, such as the effect of interest rates and mortgage availability on private housing demand.

On the other hand, local planning authorities as such are neither replacing "the land and property market", nor necessarily "guiding" development processes. They are required, as a result of the public ownership of development rights, to replace the market in the determination of whether land use and development initiatives proposed by "the market" should be allowed to go ahead. They may also exert some influence over public sector development initiatives. Local planning authorities thus find themselves in the formal position of "guiding" development processes according to some interpretation of the public interest, but with limited powers to direct development or ensure positive land management other than through their powers to permit or refuse particular development proposals.

Thus, planning authorities cannot necessarily achieve the allocation of physical space sought by policies, nor necessarily provide for the needs of those seeking space for their activities. Nor again can they ensure that the environment produced by the physical spaces and the activities within them is satisfactory to those who live in or "consume" the built environment. The power of regulation thus gives local planning authorities only an indirect means of affecting the provision and design of space. The distancing of local planning authority regulation from the users of space and the consumers of the environment is increased by the existence of a sector of the economy which specializes in the production of physical space, namely the building and property, or "development", industry. An important trend, first in the housing field, then in commercial property development and now in industrial property development, has been for the production of buildings to be taken out of the hands of users. As a result, the operation of development control typically involves local planning authorities and developers both debating on a proxy basis the needs of users of a specific development and the interests of those who consume the environment it will affect.

We may thus ask how far local plans and the policies expressed within them actually guide local planning authorities in their own decisions and discussions with developers and other applicants; how far the public and private institutions which make up the development industry are in turn

guided by local plans; and whether local plans as such have any impact on
those who use the development produced, and consume the resultant
environment. In this chapter, I examine each of these questions in turn.
Finally, I assess the importance of local plans as a mechanism for holding
the planning authority to account in the use of its discretion when making
decisions on the use and development of land.

2. LOCAL PLANS AND THE WORK OF LOCAL PLANNING AUTHORITIES

The organization and work of local planning authorities, even within a
similar area and under similar local government arrangements, may vary
substantially, as our work on the planning departments in the London Boroughs
showed (Healey and Underwood 1977). Several authorities do little more than
their statutory obligations in relation to development control. Others are
involved in a range of projects, such as housing and renewal projects in
cities, or countryside management projects in shire districts. In some the
emphasis of the work over and above development control is on design matters.
Elsewhere, the authority may provide an information service for the council
or the public. In a number of authorities, the planning department plays a
key role in land acquisition and disposal. In others, its role is central
to overall policy formulation within the council. The way a local plan is
used may be expected to vary with these different roles and activities. As
yet, however, we have little systematic evidence of the way plans are used
within departments (but see Fudge *et al.* 1982a). Yet if publically-
produced plans are supposed to provide a guide to local authority
intentions and future actions, it is important for their public credibility,
and for their value to developers as predictors of local authority
behaviour, that they do actually guide the local planning authority. To
try to assess whether they do, I consider first the role of local plans in
relation to the various developmental initiatives a local planning
authority may be involved with. I then turn to their most significant role,
in respect of development control decisions.

In old-style development plans, it was possible to define areas for
comprehensive development. These were areas where the authority expected to
undertake substantial redevelopment, either for housing purposes, to clear
slums and reduce excessive densities, or where areas were bombed or
otherwise rundown. As property development picked up during the 1950s, the
renewal of town centres became an attractive commercial proposition, and
many town centre schemes were initiated as revisions to development plans,
or as informal plans on the lines of the MHLG's Planning Bulletin No. 1
(MHLG 1962). It was these sorts of areas that were expected to be action
areas in the new development plan system. The important aspect of CDA's,
and of subsequent formal town map amendments, was that land could be
assembled for development by the planning authority using compulsory
purchase powers. It thus did not have to be purchased by a "service"
committee for a specific use. Until 1959, the authority could make such
purchases at existing use value. In town centres, CDA designation assisted
authorities in assembling sites for private development, usually in some
form of partnership between the authority and the developer (Marriott 1969,
Ambrose and Colenutt 1975). There is considerable circumstantial evidence
that development plans were important in these schemes in delineating the
area of the schemes, in providing a framework for the various investment
interests, in supporting land purchase, and in reserving sites for public
use. This latter benefit was in many cases in retrospect a disbenefit both
to those using the sites and the consumers of the relevant environment,
since as the public sector became increasingly starved of funds, those sites
which depended on public investment were blighted until such time as finance

for them could be found. The few case studies available (e.g. Elkin 1974,
Gough 1976) show that plans were frequently amended, as the various parties
involved changed their ideas. Highways authorities have been notorious for
indecision over actual roadlines. Developers have shifted the mixture of
uses in a development in response to changing market conditions. Planning
authorities have become increasingly sensitive to public comment and have
sought to obtain more financial and social benefits from schemes.

Yet despite such adjustment of planning frameworks, in cases where
substantial development is being initiated and followed through by a few
main interests, some kind of detailed site-specific development framework
is needed and used, since most of the development interests involved are
mutually dependent, and benefit from the co-ordination of the timing,
location and design of development. Such mutual benefits can also be
identified in large greenfield development projects, particularly where
several landowners and developers are involved (see for example, Lower
Earley in Central Berkshire, Davis 1982, Henry 1982). A development brief
may be as appropriate as a local plan for this purpose. The difference is
that whereas a local plan is prepared through consultation with a
potentially wide range of interests, development briefs are typically the
product of consideration of the interests of the developers and the local
authority.

Where few development interests are involved, as with slum clearance and
housing renewal schemes, authorities have typically proceeded on a site-by-
site basis, using internal project briefs to organize questions of
detailed design and layout. In this case, the dialogue was entirely
contained within the local authority. It is probable that many such
briefs lacked any relation to an overall view of the development of an
area. One may hypothesize that some of the environments of the publicly-
reconstructed parts of our cities are as apalling as they are because they
have lacked such an overall view.

Since the middle 1960s, however, because of recession, an over-provision of
central area retail space and cutbacks in public expenditure, there have
been many fewer large-scale redevelopment schemes, and those left over from
earlier periods have required substantial revision, not least because of
the shift of public investment away from road building and slum clearance.
Local authorities have turned increasingly to the use of development briefs
for complex sites of all kinds, and to a variety of promotional activities.
These include housing and environmental improvement, urban and rural
conservation measures, preservation of historic buildings and special
landscape features, countryside management projects, industrial promotion,
and the positive use of vacant and derelict land, to name but a few. Some
of these activities reflect longstanding local authority programmes which
are likely to be included in plans, though planning departments do not
necessarily have a central role in such activities. In a few cases, the
programmes might be generated by problems identified during a plan
preparation exercise. But the most common situation has been for new
programmes or interests to be engendered by the provision of a new piece of
enabling legislation (General Improvement Areas, Conservation Areas,
Housing Action Areas, Industrial Improvement Areas, Enterprise Zones),
or the provision of a new source of grant (derelict land grants,
environmental programmes (e.g. operation clean-up and eyesore), the urban
programme, Countryside Commission Country park and countryside management
experiments).

Although there is usually some connection between such national initiatives
and local circumstances, often mediated through professional debate, I have

little evidence of local plans actually guiding the way the opportunities
provided by these initiatives have been used. An interesting exception to
this are the river valley local plans in Greater Manchester where management
programmes and local plans are closely linked. An important element in
maintaining this link is the county's ability to disburse funds for
environmental improvement schemes in the valleys. Another exception already
referred to is the Wirral case, where local plans were used as the basis
of bids for urban programme aid. The significant point here is that these
initiatives are picked up by local authorities in relation to their own
evolving policies and programmes. If it should happen that the articulation
of policies in a local plan has been an important element in the way an
authority responds to new issues, or if for some reason a local plan has
just been prepared, then such initiatives may be "plan-based". Otherwise,
local plans are more likely to reflect them. In other words, the relation
of local plans to local authority development work will depend on their
timing and the way an authority evolves and articulates policy.

Apart from Comprehensive Development Areas, there is similarly little
evidence of local planning authorities making land purchases and disposals
in relation to plans. This is partly because as planning authorities,
local councils have had few resources with which to buy land. Local
authority land dealings are in any case usually the province of estates
departments rather than planning departments. In Section 3.1, I consider
how far the land transactions of other departments of local authorities and
other public agencies have been influenced by local plans. A few
authorities used or contemplated using Community Land Act powers to purchase
sites identified as significant within local plans (e.g. Fareham Western
Wards). The Land Authority for Wales set out to purchase land identified
for development in plans by planning authorities (Sant 1980). And of course
New Town Corporations and those authorities engaged in town expansion under
the Town Development Act 1952 bought land strategically for future needs in
line with plans. This generally low level of direct local planning
authority involvement in land purchase has to be qualified by the various
cases where local authorities have developed a considerable tradition of
land dealings, often thereby owning significant land banks (see Barrett
et al. 1978). Such reserves have enabled authorities to use land
strategically in relation to plan policies, as for example in pursuing local
housing need policies (Healey et al. 1980), although recently land sales have
been prompted more by financial considerations than planning policies.
Yet there has been very little research into the principles by which
authorities have purchased and sold land[74].

There are some interesting cases where planning policies have encouraged
strategic land purchases. Two examples are worth citing. The first concerns
Buckingham, a small market town in the north of Buckinghamshire which in
the 1960s was experiencing some decline and severe traffic congestion.
Various suggestions for substantial growth were put forward in the region,
finally settling upon Milton Keynes, but with outposts at three small towns
in North Bucks, including Buckingham. The county's chief architect and
planning officer of the time, Fred Pooley, conceived the idea that
development could be used to pay for a by-pass to relieve the congestion.
A sketch plan of an expanded area, housing sites and the by-pass line was
produced, a development company was set up, under the auspices of the county
council, and land was purchased reasonably cheaply. The land purchased has

---

[74]John Montgomery's PhD research at Oxford Polytechnic on local authority land
ownership and local planning should be of considerable interest here.

been sold off to various private developers, and bit by bit the by-pass is being built. By 1991 the town may be relieved of its congestion[75].

My second example is from South Hampshire. Here the county has attempted to follow the spirit of the PAG report, the 1968 Act and the Skeffington report. Growth areas designated in the regional strategy were developed into indicative amounts of development to be located in growth areas according to the structure plan, to be located specifically in local plans. As in Buckinghamshire, the county has been reluctant itself to cover the costs of infrastructure provision and has increasingly sought developers' contributions to these. In addition, Hampshire decided to make opportunity land purchases with the aid of the financiers, Hill Samuel. Regrettably, however, a substantial site was purchased before even the structure plan was approved, still less a local plan produced. Public participation in the local plan inquiry (Western Wards of Fareham), as described in Chapter 6, supported by the then district council and the Inspector, argued that there was less need for development and some land should be struck out of the plan, including the county council's site. As this land was bought just before the property boom of 1971-73 collapsed, the site is known locally as the most expensive piece of farmland in the country (Grant 1978).

Since the days of CDA's, then, local plans and their antecedents have probably had only a limited impact on the work of local planning authorities. This is partly a reflection of the considerably-reduced scale of development projects during the 1970s. Does the picture look any more encouraging when we turn to development control? As I noted earlier, if plans are to be any help to potential applicants as to the attitude a local authority will take to a proposal, then it is important that the authority follows its own plans. Yet the characteristic of the British planning system is that plans are only a guide to the local authority's views, to be weighed by the authority in the balance with "other material considerations". As with much of the planning system, we know very little about how development control officers (and their committees) set about constructing the inputs and the outputs of this balancing act.

McLoughlin (1973b) in his survey of development controllers in 17 local authorities, tried to assess the relative importance of what he calls "information inputs" into development control recommendations (see Diagram 8.1). This shows the importance of consultation with colleagues and applicants in framing the development controller's views. Among documents, case files and precedents were more important than development plan maps, and these maps were in turn more important than plan texts. McLoughlin's development controllers were of course working with the old-style development plans. It is sometimes suggested that control staff have more difficulty with the new-style plans, since these put more weight on the text than the maps. Yet Underwood's study of Haringey in 1975-76 suggests that development control officers at least in some authorities appreciate up-to-date guidelines, and have considerable understanding of the social and economic impacts of development decisions (1980 pp.117-18). In some authorities, plan preparation has proceeded in discussion with development control staff, so that as plan policies evolve, the policies used in development control recommendations also emerge. It is likely, though, that control staff in a large urban authority are more sophisticated in their approach than those in many a small shire district. Perhaps more important is the problem created by a large number of potentially-

---

[75]See Minns and Thornley 1978 for a brief note on this scheme.

INFORMATION INPUTS
for making recommendations

DOCUMENTS	Statutory Plan Map
	Non-statutory Plan Map
	Office Survey Maps
	Statutory Plan Texts
	Non-statutory Plan Texts
	Case Files/precedents
	Committee Resolutions/Reports
	Acts/Statutory Instruments/
	Ministry circulars
	Unpublished statistical information
	Ground photographs
	Air photographs
	Other documents*
COLLEAGUES	
	Planning Department
	Clerks Department
	Estates/Valuers Department
	Engineers/Surveyors Department
	Architects Department
	Housing Department
	Health/Welfare Department
	Education Department
	Other Departments/Authorities

SITE INSPECTION

CONSULTATION with applicant

CONSULTATION with general public

    * *This residual includes*
       — published statistical information
       — comprehensive policy document

Frequency of use/occurrence as percentage   0   50   100   % respondents

Source: McLoughlin 1973 p. 94

Diagram 8.1.   Information Inputs into Development
Controllers Decisions

conflicting policy statements in new-style development plans. What seems
to happen is that only some of the policies in plans are in fact implemented.
Some prove too difficult to implement, too contentious or apparently no
longer relevant. Thus the policies actually pursued by authorities through

development control are only a selection of the policies articulated in plans[76]

Evidence of the actual use of plan policies in planning decisions can be found in appeal cases, in the few studies of development control decisions, and can be inferred from the various studies of the conformity of control decisions with plan policies mentioned at the beginning of this chapter. These suggest that many applications are unproblematic, in line with the authority's policies, however these have been derived. Green belts have perhaps been the most successful of all planning policies in that few developments which are not permissible according to the policy are ever allowed. Few applications are granted on green belt land, and most refusals are upheld on appeal. Where problems arise, it is over definitions. Is a particular site in the green belt or not? The position in AONB's is of course much less clear, since the policy is not to resist development but to preserve the landscape. And as Preece shows, landscape preservation policies may run in parallel with those to increase job opportunities in declining rural areas (Preece 1979). There are also many cases where an application is turned down for reasons which are thought likely to be upheld by the Secretary of State or the courts on appeal, but which are not the real policy reason for refusal. An interesting case arose in LB Haringey, where a supermarket, because of potential employment loss, was refused permission to extend on to backland occupied by small cheap industrial units, although it was zoned for commercial uses. The applicant appealed, but his appeal was dismissed, not on the grounds of employment loss, but access!

However, our work at Oxford on the implementation of selected strategic policies in the outer South East shows that strategic policy reasons are often used in framing development control recommendations. In High Wycombe, where the concern was to restrict employment-generating development to that connected with the interests of existing firms and premises, extensive use was made of conditions restricting occupants to "local users" (Wood 1982). In Wokingham, where substantial growth was to be contained on a few large sites, residential development elsewhere was refused on the grounds that sufficient land had already been allocated (Davis 1982). We concluded from this study that where planning policies involved restricting the release of sites in some way, policies in plans were upheld except where there were doubts about whether they would be supported on appeal, as with the use of conditions to restrict housing occupancy to "locals". Yet it was not immediately clear from plans which policies were given most weight, and which were the ones most susceptible to challenge. In addition, development control officer recommendations were not necessarily accepted by councillors, who liked to preserve some freedom to make decisions which might not conform with policy statements they had earlier agreed to. As a result, applicants with a sophisticated knowledge of how the planning authority worked, including the attitudes of councillors had a considerable benefit over those with little such knowledge or understanding (Healey et al. 1982a).

How far does the Inspectorate and the Secretary of State support local authority planning decisions? There is regrettably no overview of appeal decisions. A review of all the appeals recorded in Planning Appeals and Planning suggests considerable use of plan policies and support for them by

---

[76]Elson and McNamara's work on the implementation of restraint policy in Hertfordshire provides some good examples of this (Elson 1982).

the Inspectorate and the Secretary of State. I scanned all appeals recorded in Ambit Publication's three volumes of *Planning Appeals*, which cover the period 1975-78, and those recorded in *Planning* from 1977-80, extracting all those which related in some way to development plan policies. Of the 61 cases found, 7 involved situations where plan policies were not clear. Eighteen related to prematurity arguments (land release delayed until a plan prepared). Of these, four fifths were upheld; of the remainder, 64% were upheld. Where appeals were allowed, it was usually because some special case applied; this picture is confirmed by our own work in the case studies already referred to.

My conclusion from this admittedly sketchy evidence is that many of the policies in plans are given considerable weight in development control decisions. However, this is partly because many plan policies merely articulate policies which have been used for many years in development control. As Harrison (1972) argues, policies about amenity, site considerations, and design are often deeply embedded in the office cultures of planning departments, reinforced by experience of what is politically desirable, and likely to be defensible when challenged at appeal. The point worth further investigation is how quickly development control reacts to demands for policy change. The preparation of a local plan may be an expression of the demand for such a change. In other situations, pressures for policy change may encourage development control decisions to drift away from policies articulated in local plans. In our studies in the outer South East, we noted such a drift occurring around 1980 as districts became more interested in accepting employment-generating development as the recession deepened. We thus concluded that development controllers would be likely to base their decisions on plans only where there was reasonable policy stability, a similar conclusion to that reached by the District Planning Officers' Society (DPOS 1978).

We also concluded that up-to-date statutory plans were probably only of importance in "guiding" development control decisions where central government demanded such backing for policies in appeal statements, or where a local authority had developed a style of articulating policy in publically-available policy statements. In these circumstances, where decisions are likely to be appealed, or where an authority's actions are closely monitored by a critical public, it is difficult for an authority's "policies-in-action" to drift away from their "policies-in-plans". However, it is unusual for the public at large, or even well-organized pressure groups, to monitor a planning authority's development control decisions. And with much less demand for development, authorities are refusing less development. Consequently, there is less external pressure on authorities to uphold their own policy statements.

If the findings from these studies are generally applicable it suggests that we cannot assume that a planning authority, in its development initiatives and in its regulatory activities, is necessarily following the policy guidance it has itself publically articulated in local plans. Statements in plans may be used as justification for a particular position adopted by an authority and in this sense can be considered as tools. The preparation of a plan may help to change the policies pursued in actual decisions by an authority. In the few cases where an authority is involved in development projects with other public and private interests, a plan may be used as a co-ordination programme. But only in a few instances can it be said that the actions of planning authorities are "plan-based".

3. LOCAL PLANS AND DEVELOPMENT PROCESSES

If the policies in local plans have any other purpose in relation to
development processes than rationalizing those processes already underway
as in the "public interest", then the planning authority must seek to
produce some modification in the behaviour of one or more individuals or
firms engaged in development. The nature of the behavioural change and the
agents who are to be affected will depend on the local authority's policy
ends and the particular pattern of development interests in an area. As
I have noted several times, plans are rarely specific about the precise
changes in development processes they are seeking. Some policies seek to
facilitate and attract development (to northern industrial regions and
inner cities), others to resist it (restraint areas in the South East
outside London). In several plans which allocate land for development, the
chief problem is infrastructure provision, involving phasing public
investment with private development. In areas where development is to be
"restrained", policies may seek to discriminate in favour of those
developers most likely to build for local needs and users. In areas of
economic decline, labour intensive activities may be encouraged (see
Chapter 7). As I have suggested earlier, this lack of specificity is *in
part* the result of lack of knowledge by planners about the characteristics
and dynamics of development processes. It also reflects a hesitancy to
discuss explicitly the differential pattern of gains and losses which
planning authority decisions may produce among development interests.

There is in any case a genuine problem for planning authorities in
distinguishing between different development interests. Applicants range
from householders to local building contractors, volume house builders
and multinational companies. We cannot assume that each uses or is
affected by plans in the same way. Furthermore, the nature and operation
of private development firms is volatile, changing in response to
prevailing opportunities. Public sector agencies may be more stable in
their basic functions, but vary in their activities in response to changing
flows of finance and shifts between priorities. Both public and private
firms may also differ in their interest in a development project, some
being more concerned with long-term investment, others having a short-term
interest in a particular project. As yet, we have no systematic account
of who is involved in development and how they relate to planning
authorities and to plans. In this section I briefly review what is
presently known about these relationships and how they vary.

3.1 *Public Sector Agencies and Local Plans*

Despite the shift to the private sector as the major developer during the
1950s, the public sector has been responsible for a substantial amount of
investment in making land available for development and in construction.
Yet represented within the public sector are a variety of development
interests, overlapping with each other in complex ways. This partly arises
because for most public agencies, engaging in land development or holding
an interest in land is instrumental to some other purpose, such as
providing schools, or power, roads or public housing. It also results from
the fragmentation of responsibilities within the public sector. The
sectoral divisions into departments characteristic of central and local
government organization are complicated in the development field by a range
of semi-autonomous agencies responsible for power, postal and
telecommunications, water, sewerage and drainage, and health. It is hardly
surprising that concepts of interorganizational networks have been
developed as an approach to co-ordinating public sector development

activities (for example, Friend *et al.* 1974; Hickling *et al.* 1980).

In order to understand how public agencies involved in land and development may relate to local plan policies, it is necessary first to consider their interest in land and development. Public sector developers may be grouped into three broad categories in this respect:

a) providers of community welfare services;

b) public corporations engaged in production and the provision of nationwide services;

c) infrastructure agencies, providing and maintaining basic service networks.

The providers of services to the community are concerned to manage those that they provide, and expand and alter the service as circumstances permit. In this latter activity they may wish to acquire sites and buildings, or sell them off. Where the services concerned are the responsibility of central government (e.g. social security services, employment offices) such development is managed by the Property Services Agency. Area Health Authorities undertake their own development, using central government grants. Housing, social services and education are under local authority control, though outside the metropolitan areas the last two are the responsibility of counties. Often the search for sites or discussion about the use of sites no longer required is undertaken by the local authority department concerned. But, site acquisition and disposal are frequently the responsibility of estates departments. In some cases (for examples see Underwood 1980, Healey 1982d), the planning department may play a role in site-finding, or discussions over disposal. It is also common for planning departments to be involved in working up development briefs for local authority sites. The provision of land and development needs of these services is usually arrived at by the interaction of local political priorities among councillors, professional views of the way the services should be provided and the availability of central government loans and grants.

In theory, some co-ordination of the various services in relation to the needs of the community as a whole might be expected, and local plans, being locality based, might provide a useful role in this. The interest in area management in the mid-1970s was an attempt to get more such co-ordination (Hambleton 1978). Haringey, during the mid-1970s, set out to use district plans to produce a site dimension to the authority's capital programme (Frith 1976, Underwood 1980). Special project implementation teams are also common, for complex housing or town centre schemes (as in Haringey). However, two interrelated problems arise in trying to co-ordinate the activities of these service agencies, let alone guide them, in line with planning policies. The first relates to priorities. Each agency or department is encouraged by the sectoral structure of central and local government to set its own priorities for expenditure. Secondly, the flow of finance to each service has been on a sectoral basis, in several cases organized through policy vehicles designed to systematize the bids from local government for central government grants (HIPs, social services and Education Department plans) (Hambleton 1981). In addition, in the current financial conditions each department may seek to use its own excess land and property to realize resources for maintaining a service. With financial flows increasingly difficult to predict, service agencies and departments have been reluctant to reduce their manoeuvrability by tying themselves to local plan priorities.

More fundamentally, the consumers of the services provided are rarely in a position to impose co-ordination on these various public sector service providers. The demand from local people in Fareham Western Wards that new amounts of development should not be allowed in the area until adequate services were available for the existing development was unusual in both the strength of the case made and its consequences for the phasing of new development in the local plan. The inner area studies of the mid-1970s came to gloomy conclusions about the prospects for welfare service co-ordination (DoE 1977b), and local planners report that agencies such as Area Health Authorities are the most difficult to co-ordinate with and the least likely to alter their investment programme to co-ordinate with development planning objectives.

The public corporations engaged in production and in running major services, i.e the National Coal Board, British Nuclear Fuels, the Gas Corporation, the CEGB, British Rail, British Telecom, British Airports Authority, and of course, the Ministry of Defence are all large bodies, with sources of finance directly from central government. When they are involved in land development, their activities in most cases lead to substantial projects which are considered to be in the national interest and are dealt with by major public inquiry. Local planning authorities can do little more than adjust to their projects and put a case forward at inquiries. Yet some of the smaller scale development activities of these authorities can have significant local impacts, such as NCB's policies about the management of its housing stock, or the closure of MoD operations and the sale of parts of bases or of MoD housing stock. Such corporations are also major land owners, and often impede the development of small area land management by holding on to large sites for future potential operating needs, or viewing unsympathetically local planners' arguments that they should consider the use of their excess sites against community as opposed to commercial criteria. Such corporations are encouraged to operate as commercial enterprises and therefore view their land and property holdings as assets to be realized to assist each corporation's financial viability. British Rail have been developing city centre stations with office, retail and hotel developments for some years. More recently, and under pressure from central government, they have been turning sites over for industrial use, storage and sometimes housing. As with private developers, the British Rail Property Board's interests are in short- and long-term investment returns. As was indicated in Chapter 6, planning authorities have great difficulty in obtaining information about development intentions from these corporations, and are in a difficult position in making them accept development control decisions since planning authorities are required to consult with them in policy formulations and know that the weight of central government lies behind the agencies.

By contrast, the infrastructure agencies, the Regional Water Authorities and County Highways Departments are required to provide a service network in line with demand within the locality. Structure plans and local plans should provide them with information on the future location of demand. However, this apparently simple dependent relationship is complicated by the way this demand is expressed. Water Authorities have to service new development. If they fail to do so, they can be "requisitioned" to do so by a developer. Consequently, Regional Water Authorities have an interest in co-ordinating with planning authorities to ensure that the latter do not release land that it will be difficult or costly to service. In the mid-1970s there was considerable concern over the co-ordination between planning and water authorities.

Yet more recent evidence suggests that relationships are usually quite good (see Chapter 6). It is possible that the concern was a reflection of the organizational disruption created by local government reorganization and the creation of the large water authorities from a wide variety of smaller, usually local authority controlled, organizations. What is significant, however, is that the co-ordination that occurs, though related to policies about land use, is rarely based on plans as such. It is much more a matter of ongoing consultation with planning authorities and negotiation with developers. An interesting example here is the Berkshire Development Programme, which exists as a document translating structure plan policies into a programme of public sector projects. In practice, it is not the document which is important, but the regular meeting of the various parties involved to review each other's progress (Patterson 1978, Hickling *et al.* 1980, Davis 1982).

In the case of County Highways, by contrast, the situation is very different. There are few problems about small-scale access, and those that arise can usually be negotiated away, although the road engineer's standards may affect the design of new development. But the existing road network has a considerable capacity to absorb expansion of demand. Meanwhile, there is considerable public demand for the improvement of the road network which is rarely heard in relation to water mains, sewers and drains. Thus Highways Departments are typically balancing the priorities for making the road network more efficient for strategic movements and the demand for by-passes and other adjustments to remove the costs of strategic traffic movements from particular communities. With reduced public expenditure, it is not surprising that getting agreement over road investments is one of the most difficult issues in many local plans. Planners often claim that County Highways Departments are deliberately obstructive to planning policies even when the two groups are linked in the same department. This may be so in some cases, but the difficulty between planning and highways departments is more likely to in the different interests which each considers in evolving its view of "the public interest".

Finally, it must be remembered that there are some public agencies who are primarily land and property developers as the term is understood in the private sector. The Property Services Agency is a property manager and developer for central government. Local Authority Estates Departments perform the same function for their authorities, and several of the agencies noted above have land development sections (as with the British Rail Property Board). Only the Land Authority for Wales is specifically charged with acting as a land assembler and developer, a successor in many ways of the Land Commission of 1967-70. As I have noted, LAW possibly pays more attention to planning authority policies and plans than many of the other agencies. Even within local authorities, estates departments are more likely these days to be selling land to realize short-term capital returns to ease their authorities over the present short term financial crises than to be safeguarding sites for future development (e.g. public housing, parks) in line with plans.

There is thus a major problem of co-ordinating the development activities of the public sector and hence of implementing planning policies where such development activities are significant. The public corporations are larger, command more resources and specialist expertise than district planners, and have traditions of independent operation. As has been pointed out in several studies, their planning and management styles operate on different principles and timescales to those of structure and local plans (Stewart 1977, Hickling *et al.* 1980). Yet some impact on these agencies can

be made by planning authorities. I discussed in Chapter 6 how consultation
with these agencies could bring out proposals for discussion and review.
Authorities can also act in a brokerage role in relation to infrastructure
provision, between public agency and developers, especially where
developers' contributions are involved. However, where co-ordination does
occur, it is unlikely that local plans have much to do with it, except
through the impetus for co-ordination that is sometimes created during
plan preparation.

3.2 Private Sector Development Interests and Local Plans

An enormous range of individuals, firms and other organizations make a
contribution to the way land is used and developed in an area. Only a
proportion of these come forward with proposals for development as
applicants for planning permission. Some modify the use of land and the
structure of buildings, but do not need planning permission. A few build
illegally, though this probably does not occur on a substantial scale in
the U.K. Others are merely managing and maintaining their land and
property, from farmers and those with substantial urban estates to small
householders, maintaining their dwellings and gardens. Among all these,
those which concern us in this section are the individuals and firms
whose primary interest is in the investment value of land and property,
and in particular with producing a change in the way land is used and
developed. It is these which in most cases require planning permission
before proceeding with their proposals. Planning authorities have no
direct effect on how most people and firms manage their land and premises,
although planning policies may affect the climate of land and property
values and opportunities within which people make decisions about land and
property management and development, and in a few instances are linked to
financial incentives to improve property (as in General Improvement and
Housing Action Areas).

Until recently, very little was known about how the mix of private sector
development interests varied between areas, how this was affected by
planning policies and whether there were significant differences in the
way different private sector interests related to planning authorities.
Most studies have concentrated on the relationship between planning
authorities and property developers in town centre redevelopment schemes,
in effect a form of private-public sector partnership (Elkin 1974, Ambrose
and Colenutt 1975, Gough 1976). In our work at Oxford on development in
the outer South East, however, we have found considerable evidence of the
effect of planning policies on the mix of private development interests
operating in an area, and have suggested that the relationship between the
planning authority and development interests varies with the nature of that
interest (Healey and Elson 1981, Healey et al. 1982a, McNamara 1982a).

Clearly, the type of development interests in an area reflects the
development opportunities in that locality, which are in turn a product of
the local economy and its evolution, the historical pattern of land and
property ownership, local attitudes to growth and development and the
national context of investment opportunities. Thus specialist commercial
property companies are likely to dominate central city development projects
in most larger cities and towns; volume house builders found opportunities
in the north and Scotland in the 1960s when there was a rapid expansion of
home ownership in these areas; smaller house building firms may dominate
the market in conurbation fringe areas where suburban development over many
years has meant a steady stream of work. In many industrial areas, a major
development interest has been industrial firms looking for expansion sites.

As a result of this variation, produced by the structure of local demand as related to investment opportunity, the mix of development interests is likely to vary significantly from area to area. I have already noted that there is as yet no satisfactory way of categorizing these differences, but important dimensions of differentiation are:

1. whether the development concern is with the use value, the exchange or investment value of the proposal;

2. the use to which the development is to be put, since development firms appear to vary significantly in their behaviour when dealing with different sectors of the market;

3. the interest the developer has in the land, which may be as a long term investment interest or to realize investment return in the short term by selling off the development;

4. the scale and range of activities the developer is engaged in (national, regional, local scale; concentrating on one sector of the market, or a wide range, or with development as only one activity in a large multi-activity company).

5. the degree of specialization within a firm in the process of development, from the small building firm which uses a range of small specialists to help it with designing, getting planning permission and selling, to the large company which internalizes all these processes within itself;

6. the source of finance being used for development investment, which can vary from a firm's own funds, or loans from local banks, to raising funds on the stock exchange, or a connection with the investment funds of the major financial institutions, particular insurance companies and pension funds[77].

Two points should be noted about these differences between development interests. Firstly, firms are operating in a very volatile situation. The nature of development opportunities themselves can change quite rapidly in response to changing economic conditions. Strawberry fields in South Hampshire which were seen as prime development land in the early 1970s, because of a booming land market and high labour costs for harvesting strawberries, were not developed in the late 1970s because with "pick-your-own" harvesting and a less certain property market, yields to landowners were higher from keeping the land in strawberry fields. Partly as a reflection of this, firms can appear and disappear rapidly in response to new development opportunities. A significant consequence of the collapse of the property boom in 1973 was the mopping up of a number of specialist development and property companies by national and multi-national building and contracting companies and by financial institutions. In other words, there has been some concentration within the development industry, in order to prevent the kind of financial destabilization which threatened when the collapse of land and property prices caused the bankruptcy of a considerable number of firms which had financially over-extended themselves in the property field (Ball 1982).

Secondly, the variation in the types of firms affects the way they come

---

[77] This list is a development of one produced in Healey and Elson 1981.

forward with development proposals to the planning authority, the way they
negotiate with planners, and the extent to which they are able to and are
interested in affecting the planning authority's policies and proposals.
As Drewett (1973) noted in his study of residential developers in the South
East, there are in effect two land markets in which a development firm may
operate, that in land with planning permission or a clear planning status,
and that without. He found that the speculative residential developers
of the late 1960s were typically operating in the second market, trying to
reap the development gains to be made from converting greenfield land to
development land. In our own studies in similar areas in the late 1970s,
after the property boom, we found historical evidence of the same
phenomenon. However, by this time, overall demand for new housing was less,
firms were more cautious and planning policy was clearer, with local
policies supported by central government. As a result, challenges to
planning policy were less likely to succeed.

We found a more complex situation in our work in the outer South East
(Healey *et al*. 1982a). Many development interests in fact acquired land
with planning permission or a clear planning status; in other words, at
development value. Several of these were small building firms, as well as
large volume builders, which in these areas came in to buy up the sites
owned by financially-shaky property firms around 1974. Much industrial
and commercial development was also undertaken by existing firms on sites
with a clear planning status. In such cases, discussions with the planning
authority concentrated on matters of detailed design and layout, not the
principle of development. Sometimes, as I have shown in Chapter 7, local
plans contain statements of the sorts of policies and standards the
authority will apply in these cases. Other authorities use statements of
"development control policies" to provide similar guidance. It is
difficult to assess how far such statements are helpful to applicants since
each development proposal is likely to raise unique questions. There is
some evidence that applicants make use of whatever documentation is
available, particularly in cases where the applying firm is skilled in
understanding planning documents but not necessarily knowledgeable about
the particular area (as with large housebuilding and property companies).
However, direct consultation with the planning authority appears to be much
more important than documents in framing development proposals,
particularly as authorities may use their own documents selectively, as
noted in Section 2.

It could be said that in the above cases, planning policies were "guiding"
the market, since development value is associated with the planning status
of sites. Which development interests challenged that policy and how far
have these challenges been contained by local plans? Here it is helpful
to separate out residential development from commercial and industrial
development. In the case of residential development, evidence from the
1960s suggests that a considerable amount of development was allowed which
was not allocated in plans, particularly "white" land (DoE 1975, Pearce and
Tricker 1977). One reason for this was that planning policy in the areas
under pressure for greenfield housing development was under review
throughout the 1960s. In the South East, it was not clarified until 1970,
and in the West Midlands not until 1973 (Saunders 1977). As a result,
development plan reviews put forward by counties were not approved, and
plan production was then held up by the change to new-style development
plans and local government reorganization. It has thus been suggested that
once the new system is in operation, fewer such "challenges" will be
successful.

To an extent, our studies in the South East support this conclusion. Few
challenges to planning policy succeeded, and those that did either
exploited interpretive loopholes in policies or were the outcome of
longstanding development interests in sites which the authorities for one
reason or another were inclined to favour. However, when we inquired
further into how these challenges were made, we were led to question how
robust policies were and whether their expression in plans was of much
importance. What we found was that nearly all planning applications which
contested the *principle* of development on a site were being brought forward
either by local sophisticated development agents of the kind described by
Stephens (1981), or by larger locally-based development firms, or, in a few
cases, by volume housebuilding firms with specialist planning staff. The
role of locally based development agents and planning consultants was of
particular interest. Such agents identified sites with development
potential, helped landowners bring them forward, found investors and
possible users of sites, and obtained planning permission. In effect, they
played a distinctive role in increasing the quantum of development land
with a clear planning status, and they did this by a good local knowledge,
both of development opportunities and the changing nuances of planning
policies. All the firms of such agents we found had a former member of the
planning authority on their staff (McNamara 1982b).

During the later 1970s in our study areas there was local political
agreement over planning policies. These were in turn upheld by central
government, but by 1980, this consistency was beginning to break apart.
Whereas in the mid-1970s, these sophisticated locally-based development
interests could only chip away at the margins of local planning policy,
they were alert to and likely to take up the opportunities created by any
shift in policy. We also suspected that because of the close negotiative
relationship which existed between the planning authorities and these
locally-based developers and development agents, the latter were able to
exercise some influence on the formulation of planning policies and
particularly, the identification of sites to be found in local plan
proposals. We also gained the impression that between them these interests
monopolized the local development land market. Other residential developers,
often small housebuilders and volume builders without a local base, then
found it difficult to get access to land except through the agents, which is
probably one of the reasons why the House Builders Federation has been so
preoccupied by land availability (see Hooper 1979 and 1980).

In the field of industrial and commercial development, challenges to the
principle of development have concentrated on the type of use and density
of redevelopment sites within the urban fabric as well as the use of
greenfield sites. The extent to which planning policy has been challenged
in these cases appears to relate to the extent to which the developer is
interested in short term realization of development value, the
attractiveness of the development opportunity and the extent to which
technological change has created a land-hungry demand for space. Office
development is usually a speculative investment undertaken by property
companies. Planning authorities during the 1970s have become increasingly
wary of such proposals, fearing empty new offices and/or more vacant
premises elsewhere. Industrial proposals have been treated in recent
years more favourably because they were seen as local firms creating local
jobs, although previously their image was one of polluting factories to be
restricted to segregated areas. However, industrial development itself is
now undertaken more by specialist property firms as speculative ventures,
providing multi-purpose factory units. This appears to be a response to
the substantial demand for new premises from firms introducing new
technologies. There is evidence that a very considerable amount of land
has been released outside urban areas for industrial purposes, whatever

planning policies had to say (Fothergill *et al.* 1982). Our own work
suggests that once again, development agents have been important in
identifying sites and obtaining planning permission for them, these agents
either being specialist property agents, usually London-based, or the same
locally-based agents who operate in the residential land market. In more
rural areas, it is possible also that agricultural land agents have played
a similar role.

We may thus conclude firstly that where local planning policy is operated
consistently and upheld by central government, development interests can
be said to be "guided" by these policies. Yet some development interests
are more capable of challenging the principles of this guidance than
others. Others again through their relationship with the planning
authority may be able to affect the content of this guidance, while others
do not. Some interests with links to central government, such as the
House Builders' Federation and the big building-contracting firms in the
present government, may be able to persuade central government to use its
powers to shift over-restrictive local authority policies. Local plans,
however, are probably not very important tools in managing this
relationship between planning authorities and development processes. Some
firms may use them to find out about planning policies if they do not
already know of these through contact with the planning authority. These
may be unexperienced small firms, or large national firms looking for
development opportunities. In a few cases where several developers are
involved in a major project, local plans may be useful co-ordination
devices, though development briefs are probably equally satisfactory. But
the most important way in which planning policy is conveyed to development
interests is via discussion and negotiation. Statements in plans may then
be used as justification for a position taken by the planning authority or
a developer in arguing a particular issue. Plans can thus be said to
provide a formal base line for negotiations, while statements within them
may be used as counters in bargaining situations. Statements in plans
are thus tools for specific eventualities, but they can hardly be said to
"guide" development.

If the relationship between planning authorities and most development
firms is typically a negotiative one rather than a plan-based one, why
have some development interests been calling for local plans to give
clearer and more specific guidance on authority's intentions? There appear
to be four reasons for this. Firstly, those firms who do not have the
benefit of a close negotiative relationship with the planning authority
may be disadvantaged in that they do not know what the planning authority
is likely to approve. Secondly, firms want to constrain the discretion of
authorities to evolve new policy ideas during the exercise of planning
control without the opportunity for public challenge which formal
expression in a plan provides. Design and layout considerations have been
typically subject to such an evolution. Thirdly, development firms are
operating in an uncertain investment climate and clear planning frameworks
might help to reduce their operating risks. Fourthly, development
interests may appreciate statements in local plans which suggest that the
character of an area will have particular qualities over a period of time.
This may help to define the status and hence development value of sites.

Yet while arguing for clearer and more specific planning guidance, many
development interests at the same time want the opportunity to negotiate
around their own proposal. In a climate of great uncertainty about future
economic investment opportunities, political priorities and public
investment programmes, neither development interests nor planning authority
can be too clear and specific about what sites should be used for and what

the design of developments should be. Thus the negotiative relationship
between planning authorities and development interests both benefits some
of these interests more than others and is difficult to avoid.

4.   THE USERS AND CONSUMERS OF THE PHYSICAL ENVIRONMENT

A family or firm may become interested in planning policies when they are
looking for a home or premises, and when considering the future of their
property or of the area within which their property is located. In their
capacity as citizens of an area, members of these families and firms may be
interested in what planning policies have to say about their area's future.
How far are local plans used in finding out about planning policies by these
people? There is little evidence to refute the conclusion that most people
know little about planning policies for their area and still less about
plans.

It might be expected that people are most concerned about what planning
policies imply for the future of an area and for the use and exchange value
of a property when people and firms are searching for property. Those local
plans seeking to attract investment are in part publicity brochures to
attract mobile investment. As part of the procedure for purchasing property,
local authorities are requested by solicitors to "search" their records to
identify any proposals which might affect a particular site. The proposals
involved could be for roads, schools or parks, compulsory purchase orders
for slum clearance, or notices declaring property to be unfit. The search
should indicate whether the property is in an area for special consideration
such as a conservation area or General Improvement Area. Searches however
reveal nothing about the area as a whole. Nor is it clear when a proposal
acquires the status of being revealed in searches. A proposal on a
statutory local plan will certainly be noted. But a draft clearance order
may not be revealed until formally approved by the relevant council. The
bottom-drawer plans used as working documents within planning departments
might similarly not be recorded. The significant link here is with blight.
Public authorities are now required to purchase properties blighted by their
proposals. This becomes evident when an owner is unable to sell his property
or can only sell it at a much reduced amount. It would be interesting to
study the connection between evolving public sector proposals, searches and
compensation for blight.

When firms and families are searching for property, however, very few are
likely to consult planning authorities or look at local plans. They may ask
estate agents and others about planning policies, though probably most make
a visual and subjective assessment of an area. It could be said that they
appreciate planning policies indirectly through the atmosphere of an area
and what people they meet happen to say about it. A few environmentally-
conscious families may go to the planning department for information and
advice. Firms looking for property may also consult planning authorities
about the availability of sites and properties. Planning officers in
Hertfordshire districts seeking to restrain employment-generating development
reported a stream of inquiries in the late 1970s from firms about premises
and considered that they made an important contribution to regional
industrial location policies through the advice they gave in response to
such inquiries. Firms may also seek advice from planning officers about
labour availability, housing support services and markets, and transport
problems, although in authorities which are actively promoting employment,
industrial development officers or industrial liason officers are more
likely points of contact with local authorities than the planning department.
This role has probably diminished where property companies have moved in to
undertake industrial development.

That some families and firms are interested in planning policies is
evident from the consultations surrounding structure and local plan
preparation. Although in most situations, as we have seen in Chapter 6, the
numbers who make representations about policies are few, it is clear that
households are very concerned about proposals which could adversely affect
not only their property investment, but the environment with which they are
familiar, or in which they have chosen to live. It is sometimes argued
that where people do not get involved in local plan preparation they are
not interested in environmental changes or are satisfied with plan
proposals. Yet reactions to actual proposals suggest this is by no means a
valid conclusion. Existing firms, in their turn, may have a significant
impact on the formulation of proposals, whether authorities are seeking to
encourage or limit investment. Local Chambers of Commerce and individual
firms may seek assurances that existing firms will be sustained rather than
impeded by planning policies. With the increased attention to job
protection and expansion, local authorities are of course more prepared to
assist them. It is only recently that it has been appreciated that a
variety of local authority policies have had the effect of closing firms or
encouraging them to emigrate in search of better sites and conditions.

Aware that this kind of blight can undermine productive operations and lead
to environmental dereliction as positive uses for sites are withdrawn,
authorities are now much more sensitive to the need to provide existing
users with a secure investment climate, whether these be inner city firms
or farms on the urban fringe. It is in the few areas where local people
are actively concerned with monitoring the local authority's activities in
relation both to services and facilities provided, and to its overall role
in managing the physical environment, that a local plan may be used most
directly. In some areas, such as Lapworth, Fareham Western Wards, Covent
Garden, Waterloo (Lambeth LB), or Wandsworth, a local plan has become an
important document within the context of local politics, embodying
statements of policies agreed between citiziens and local authorities about
an area, and sometimes providing the agenda for major political debate. In
these situations, deviations from plans may lead to intense local reactions,
as is evident in the Coin Street case (Waterloo District Plan), where major
office development schemes are explicitly opposed in local plan policies.
The strength of this policy is being fought over through a series of local
inquiries. At Covent Garden, local interests involved in plan
preparation took up the cudgels again in an action committee when the
planning authority deviated from the plan by allocating sites for different
purposes (Williams 1979). In High Wycombe, conservation societies monitor
all planning applications to ensure that they are in line with planning
policies. Their influence is so important that development agents
sometimes consult them about their attitude to development proposals. It
is the conservation groups here who demand greater specificity in plans,
not the development interests (Wood 1982).

Local plans, then, could be valuable publicity documents for those seeking
sites, for those assessing the investment future of their land and property,
and for those interested in the development of an area as a whole. Yet
they are only one of the ways planning authorities provide information about
areas and about policies, and it is difficult to assess whether the local
plan format has any advantages over direct advice, or a simple summary of
facts and policies for an area, or merely the stream of documents and
discussion that many planning offices produce. However, the High Wycombe
example suggests that what *is* important about local plans is their role in
keeping the discretion of local planning authorities in check.

5. LOCAL PLANS AND THE REVIEW OF ADMINISTRATIVE DISCRETION

Local planning authorities, in the exercise of their development control
powers and in the other initiatives they undertake, have very considerable
discretion to determine where the "public interest" lies. Formally, this
discretion is limited by accountability to councillors; by the existence
of statutory development plans conveying central government and county
policy attitudes as well as those articulated by the local authority; and
by the appeal system. Yet I have shown in this chapter that the activities
of planning authorities and public and private development interests can
hardly be said to be "plan-based". Planning policies may be furthered by
plans, but this is done through the interaction of the various interests
involved, the success of the planning authority in achieving its ends
depending on its power relationships with other development interests and
the support given to its policies by central government. This interaction
by its nature is difficult to scrutinize by any of the processes noted
above.

The model of hierarchical control which, as I have argued, lies behind the
design of the development plan system, assumes that "departures" from plans
will be referred to counties where structure plan issues are raised.
Central government may also call in planning applications if local
authorities appear to be likely to abuse their discretion. Counties and
districts have evolved various arrangements for dealing with planning
applications which raise issues relevant to structure plans or other
county policies. The real problem for counties is when a district intends
to permit an application which is contrary to the structure plan. Until
1980, the county had powers to direct refusal where an application was
referred to them as a "county matter". This itself could be a matter of
controversy. In one case in Oxfordshire, a district referred an application
to the county as contrary to the structure plan. The county directed
refusal. The district then decided it should not have been referred in the
first place, and granted planning permission. Counties have varied in their
use of direction powers, reflecting their relations with their districts.
For example, Hertfordshire have issued several, Berkshire very few.

The procedures for consultation and the disputes which sometimes arose was
one of the factors which led to changes in county powers in the 1980 Local
Government Planning and Land Act. Districts are now only required to
consult counties on applications which raise issues relevant to structure
plan policies. There is no requirement for districts to *accept* county
advice. The county can ask central government to use its powers to call in
applications for consideration, but these are rarely used. Yet there have
been several recent examples where counties have asked for central
government intervention to prevent districts on conurbation peripheries
granting applications for new development which would compromise policies
for encouraging the regeneration of inner city areas. In other words,
districts may use county support and structure plan policies where these
are convenient. They have the power to amend them or bypass them where
the district wishes to pursue a different policy, in general, or in respect
of a particular application.

It is in the county's interests to persuade the districts into adopting and
following statutory local plans, since these have to be certified as in
conformity with structure plans. The county planning officers' association
has until recently been firmly in favour of comprehensive coverage by local
plans. This would then put districts in the position of departing from
their own plans. Yet one reason for the reluctance to prepare statutory

local plans at district level is resistance to having the district
authority's discretion contained by county policies, or any policy document
for that matter. If an application which an authority wishes to permit is
a departure from the plan, then special departure procedures are supposed
to be used. These were necessary in the 1960s and 1970s when out-of-date
old-style development plans were still in use. As yet we know little about
how departures will be defined in relation to new-style plans, but our own
work suggests they will rarely be used, as the flexibility which the present
format of local plans allows gives more room for discretionary
interpretation by districts. If counties, and central government, wish to
check on whether districts are implementing structure and local plan
policies in which they have an interest, they will have to depend on
sophisticated monitoring procedures. Central government has no such
procedures, and counties and districts normally only develop them where the
information provided is useful in justifying their own case, as in disputes
over housing land availability.

Central government has powers to determine the outcome of planning
applications, firstly through its powers to call-in applications, and
secondly through the appeal system. I know of no systematic study of the
use of call-in powers, although the cases involved relate to major
developments (such as airports), large developments where councils may be
in a position to give themselves deemed planning permission, and projects
around which there is public controversy or the hint of corruption. The
numbers of applications called in is very small indeed. The impact of the
appeal system is much more important. Although in principle an
opportunity for the review of individual local decisions, the effect of the
precedents set by appeal decisions has a considerable influence on how
planning offices structure their decisions when refusing an application,
or justifying refusals at appeals. As I noted in Section 2, the
Inspectorate and the Secretary of State during the late seventies have
apparently upheld local plan and structure plan arguments more often than
not, although other policy documents have also been supported where
policies in them are reasonable and adopted by the council concerned. DoE
Circular 55/77 emphasized that adopted local plans would be given
considerable weight over informal local plans, unless the latter had been
through all the stages up to deposit (particularly consultation). It is
probable that the Inspectorate, who have to have regard to any circulars
when making their decision, have been advised by the Department to give
particular weight to local plans. This may be one factor encouraging local
authorities into the statutory local plan fold.

However, it has to be remembered that only a small proportion of applications
are refused, and of these only a few are taken to appeal[78]. And local
authorities have no means of assessing the implicit policies of the
Inspectorate other than by looking at past decisions as there is no policy
review of appeal decisions. Finally, in certain key decisions, the
Secretary of State has not necessarily upheld local plans. The Coin Street
inquiry is being studied with particular interest in this respect. Other
cases are known where local plan policies have been over-ridden on appeal
prior to formal adoption. If local plan policies are not systematically
upheld, the pressure for local authorities to prepare and uphold their own
local plan policies is clearly greatly diminished.

---

[78]In 1979-80 and 1980-81 only 14% of applications in England were not
    permitted (25% of "major" applications). See DoE development control
    data, unpublished.

These ways in which counties and the DoE can check whether local
authorities are maintaining the policies adopted in local plans are
essentially administrative reviews of administrative discretion. The role
of county councillors, and in most cases, government ministers, is purely
formal. Yet, were such political involvement to occur, it is more likely
to undermine plan policies than support them, as politicians tend to be
more concerned with the issues about a particular case as they relate to
all the considerations a politician has to weigh up at the time, than
with a case as part of a stream of decisions relating to a specified
policy. Inconsistency in the Secretary of State's decisions has already
been noted. Local councillors are accused by developers of further
inconsistency, in not upholding policies they have formally supported in
plans (e.g. Moor and Langton 1978, Wood 1982). It has to be remembered,
however, that what planning officers and applicants may perceive as
inconsistency may in reality represent a significant shift in policy as
well as the problems of resolving conflicting policy interests.

The only other ways of review of administrative discretion in planning
decisions are through the courts and by the action of citizens. The courts
in theory cannot review policy content. They may consider only whether
the considerations taken into account in making decisions, and the
procedures adopted for making them, are legitimate, rather than *ultra vires*.
There has been considerable recent discussion of the changing attitude of
the courts to the range of matters which can legitimately be considered in
relation to planning applications. Physical planning considerations such
as amenity, and access, have traditionally been allowed, but there has
been some debate over how far social and economic matters can be considered
(Harrison 1972, Loughlin 1980, see Chapters 4 and 6). Purdue (1977)
suggests that local plan policies could serve to establish more clearly
the legitimacy of social and economic considerations in planning decisions,
that is if such policies survive central government attempts to limit their
scope (see Chapters 6 and 7). However, there have been no cases where the
role of a local plan in relation to such policies has been tested.
McAuslan (1980) thinks that the courts might look with disfavour on any
widening of the scope of planning considerations, since he sees the current
role of the courts as essentially concerned with protecting private
property interests.

The review of local authority planning decisions is, then, substantially an
administrative matter, in which the Inspectorate, and behind them the
Secretary of State and the courts, play a considerable role. All have in
the past adopted a limited interpretation of the scope of planning, and,
except where the Secretary of State has sought to produce a general shift
in local authority policies (e.g. the recent pressure to give more support
for industry, or to make land available for housing), there has been little
attempt at policy review. We have as yet little evidence on whether local
plans have assisted any of these parties in reviewing local authority
decisions, or assisted the local authorities in establishing their position
more clearly when subjected to such review. And review concentrates on
local authority refusals, not permissions, though the latter make up the
bulk of decisions.

It is therefore up to citizens to monitor the activities of their
authorities. They can do this by commenting on planning applications
during the period necessary for advertizing the application. They can do
it politically by putting pressure on councillors, either directly in
relation to a case, or establishing a climate of local opinion which
councillors have to take account of. And if they can demonstrate misuse of

procedures, they can appeal to the local ombudsman[79]. Yet citizens use
the ombudsman in default of other mechanisms for expressing their concern.
The problem for them, whoever they are and whatever their interests may be,
is that their opportunity to review the way the local authority establishes
the "public interest" in relation to land use and development change in
their areas is provided through the preparation of local plans, and
indirectly as electors of their councillors. It is much more difficult for
them to review the implementation of plan policies and proposals, unless
they are very vigilant, checking and reacting to all applications. This is
a task undertaken by some parish councils, residents' groups, and
environmental or other specialist societies, as in the High Wycombe case
already noted, but even here there are problems of responding sufficiently
quickly. Because of the reliance in British local government on the model
of representative democracy, and in the British planning system on the
hierarchical and plan-based control of administrative decisions, the rights
of "third parties", (third as opposed to the applicant and the planning
authority) are limited.

6. CONCLUSIONS

From this admittedly sketchy review, the main uses of local plans emerge as
their role as a baseline for negotiations in the relationship between
planning authorities and development interests, their role in the
administrative review of administrative discretion and their role in
enabling citizens to review the activities of their planning authority. In
none of these roles are local plans particularly effective. Other roles
identified have been in co-ordinating major development projects in which
the planning authority had an interest, in changing policy as operated
through development control, and in helping define the long term status
and value of sites. There is little evidence that plans as such "guide"
the local authority or development interests, whether public or private.
Development decisions are rarely plan-based in the sense that policies are
followed *because* they are in the plan. Rather, development interests and
planning authorities are appraised of each other's interests and
intentions in various ways through an interactive process.

This confirms Barrett and Fudge's view that in many public organizations,
policy is an evolving phenomena, developing from and influencing ongoing
activities (Barrett and Fudge 1981). Local plans are statements at one
point in time of what these policies are, but can easily become outdated.
They reflect an authority's current policy stance, which is also
reflected in its other activities. These other activities are only likely
to be plan-based, in the sense that a considerable effort is made to keep
to the policies in the plan, where an authority is facing development
interests who will exploit the slightest weakness in its position or
where politically it must be seen to uphold its own policies. Thus as a
tool, local plans are not of great importance to local authorities except
where they will have to resist a significant amount of development
pressure. They are probably more important as accountability statements,
yet as such they are deficient because they do not necessarily keep up with
evolving policy. Meanwhile, the role of local plans as a tool in

[79]Planning matters are the largest single category of cases referred to the
ombudsman, which reflects the degree of concern about such matters,
although a number are also made by aggrieved citizens. The number of
cases where formal maladministration is found is small.

co-ordinating substantial new development and redevelopment, a task which
the PAG report considered of such importance, is now of limited significance
because there are so few such projects.

The fact that planning authorities' activities are not commonly plan-based,
and that the relationship between planning authorities and development
interests is primarily an interactive one, characterized by negotiation,
creates two key problems for the British planning system. Firstly, it
allows the lowest tier of local government to drift away from policy controls
which counties and central government may wish to impose. It could be
argued that local authorities should be left to work out their own policies
with no attempt to implement regional spatial strategies or national
policy. This argument can also be used to justify the removal of a county
role in planning. To some extent this position was encouraged by the 1979
Conservative government with the disbanding of the Regional Economic
Planning Councils and Boards, and the weakening of the county role. One
result would be that the public sector's response to large-scale shifts in
the location of investment would be highly fragmented. However, central
government is not at the present time following such a decentralist
approach. It is in practice leaning heavily on local authorities with all
the powers it has to ensure compliance with its policy interests. Because
local plans are not in practice a very effective tool for this, such
pressure is being exerted through a variety of channels.

Secondly, it is difficult to tell if the way local planning authorities
are exercising their powers over the way land is used and developed is
really in "the public interest", however this is defined. McAuslan (1980)
argues for a closer relation between development control and local plans
because he fears that left to their own devices, public agencies in the
environmental policy field emphasize administrator's interpretations of
efficient procedures rather than the policy ends that politicians and
citizens may be seeking. Yet many planners and developers will argue that
it is not possible to constrain development initiatives by tight criteria
specified in advance, particularly in the present climate where there is so
much uncertainty about both economic conditions, which affect the
possibility of meeting criteria, and political conditions, which affect the
continuing validity of such criteria.

The development plan provisions of the 1947 Act planning system were changed
to provide more appropriate policy guidance for the development conditions
of the 1960s. Local plans in this system were to be primarily a tool for
furthering strategic development objectives. Now it is being suggested by
many that the system as revised is inappropriate for the conditions of the
1980s. This is partly because some of the important questions about policy
guidance for a planning authority's role were not asked in 1947 or in 1968.
It is also partly because economic and political conditions are now very
different from those prevailing twenty years ago. Yet is it really
possible to provide publicly-available statements of what policies
planning authorities are actually following given the kind of planning system
we currently have?

In Part III, I attempt to answer the question of whether there is a
continuing relevance for local plans and if so in what form, by looking again
at the planning system as a whole. In Chapter 9, I attempt a theoretical
explanation of its current form and practice. On the basis of this, I
develop ideas about alternative directions in which it might be changed, and
the consequences of these for different interests.

PART III

CHAPTER 9

Towards Explanation

1. LOCAL PLANS, ADMINISTRATIVE DISCRETION AND THE "PUBLIC INTEREST"

This book has explored the development and interpretation of a particular administrative tool within the British land use planning system. As an administrative tool, statutory local plans have several peculiar characteristics. They are to some extent an internal management device, to direct the detailed work of a planning authority. They are also a tool for interorganizational control, "implementing" structure plan policies in which central government itself may have an interest. They are a mechanism whereby the principles by which planning decisions are made may be subject to public review, offering also the right of objection to those whose direct property interests are affected. In addition, as a site-specific guidance framework, they purport to be a tool for managing development. Finally, they reflect the values that planners, as a particular group of professional experts, have traditionally placed in small area frameworks, and more recently, in rationally-formulated policies and policy review.

The particular form of local plans reflects the design of development plans in 1947 in which professional ideas about the need for land allocation plans were combined with legislative concern to limit the potential interference of a new activity, planning, both in the sphere of other departments and in the sphere of private property interests. The 1968 Act then devised a hierarchy of plans to rid central government of an administrative burden, and provide professionals with apparently more flexible and relevant tools for the task of substantial urban renewal and expansion which seemed to lie ahead. On top of this were added provisions for public consultation which reflected a political response to increasing public concern about the extent to which planning policy-in-action was in a legitimate "public interest". Yet meanwhile this policy-in-action has become increasingly complex and "hidden" as both planning authorities and many development interests have become more sophisticated in their operations.

It is perhaps, therefore, not surprising to find that statutory local plans are procedurally complex, reflecting several of these different elements, or that they have been used with different emphases by different local authorities. Authorities were explicitly given the discretion to use

the device of the local plan to suit local circumstances as they saw them.
Part II has illustrated some of this variety. Yet, nevertheless, there is
considerable consistency in the way local plans have been produced and used.
Whether statutory or not, we find that they are used primarily for areas
where land use and development change is underway, notably for small towns
and villages under development pressure, town centres and inner city areas
or large urban complexes (Chapter 5). If we consider the policy content of
plans, we find that they contain primarily land allocation policies
(Chapter 7). Thus, despite professional rhetoric about rational multi-
sector policy planning, or multi-sector planning for social welfare ends,
local plans have been primarily concerned with land use and development
issues.

Many planners have bemoaned this result, blaming central government
officials for imposing a limitation on the content of development plans.
Yet the confrontation reflected in the debates over the scope and content
of plans summarized in Chapters 5 and 6 is not really between planning
professionals and government administrators. Rather it is between
professional ideals and ambitions, and the powers provided by government
for intervention in the way land is used and developed. Planners in
whatever country they are working typically stress the values of organized
physical development, of a co-ordinated relation between economic and
social programmes and their land and development needs, of a comprehensive
interrelation of activities and interests into an "optional" or "fair"
physical development programme. Because of their concern with such
interrelationships, they have continually sought to expand their sphere of
operations beyond land and development matters.

How successful they are in such ambitions depends on the particular context
in which they operate. In Britain, the limitations on the scope, content
and impact of development plans, and local plans in particular, is an
expression of the limitations on the planning system itself. This system,
in legislation, and supported in interpretation by central government and
the courts (McAuslan 1980), has treated land use and development matters as
a separate sector of government concern. Elaborate consultation procedures
have evolved which allow other government and public agency interests to
exercise a powerful influence over the content of planning policies and
decisions. The caution of the legislature when intervening in private
property rights has led to further consultation and objection procedures.
A preference for administrative powers and administrative flexibility has
provided a system of land use regulation which allows considerable
administrative discretion. Yet the above, combined with central government'
longstanding suspicion of the capacity of local authorities to operate
planning regulations effectively, has limited the scope of this discretion
to land use and development matters. Finally, those most directly affected
by planning regulations - developers, builders, property firms of various
kinds - have been quick to test out attempts by authorities to enlarge
the scope of "material considerations" in relation to planning decisions.

To some extent, planners have reinforced a narrow interpretation of the
content of the planning system, of planning decisions, and of plans, by
methodological habits which have not been in accord with their broader and
changing ideals. McAuslan (1975) suggested that planners might be much
more successful at local plan preparation than at structure plans since
their earlier experience was with detailed physical development plans. As
it has turned out, many local plan teams up and down the country in the mid-
1970s were young and inexperienced. They were formally much better
educated than their predecessors, the product of fulltime undergraduate and

postgraduate courses which had expanded substantially in the late 1960s and
early 1970s (Healey 1982a). These were in part influenced by the dominant
ideas within the planning field at this time, notably the role of
information and analysis, and rational planning by objectives. Yet these
generalized policy-planning ideas were united in an uneasy but unquestioned
combination with exercises in the strategic spatial allocation of
activities. Thus, producing spatial plans by complex methodologies was
part of the young planner's educational inheritance in the mid-1970s.
Analysis of the nature of the planning powers she/he would in practice be
manipulating was not. Still less was she/he likely to have experienced
any discussion of the way development plans related to these powers.

Yet it would be incorrect to assume that increasing the awareness among
planners of the processes in which they are engaged would remove the
difficulties and misunderstandings likely to be encountered in local plan
preparation and use. Not only are the powers for state intervention in the
use and development of land limited, but a number of interests seek to
influence the way local planning authorities, both planners and councillors,
exercise these powers. Thus although the legislation in effect goes for
over-kill in the attempt to ensure that planning policies and proposals
are demonstrably in "the public interest", this can by no means be
guaranteed, whatever definition of the public interest is taken.

Somewhat curiously there has been as yet little concern with monitoring
how far the decisions a local planning authority actually makes have been
in line with policies as enunciated in development plans. The evidence
discussed in Chapter 8 suggests that the likelihood of policies and
proposals in plans being achieved depends on whether they can be
implemented through planning powers and whether local authorities are really
committed to them. Local authorities can achieve more than this, but it
requires considerable political will and support both locally and
nationally. Further, since central government and local authorities are
not static in their interests, policies in plan documents may be over-
ridden by changes in intentions or circumstances. Consequently, the impact
of policies and proposals in local plans on land use change and development
may be small, depending on the relation of particular plan policies to
planning powers, and the relevance of plan documents to the contemporary
policy interests of a local planning authority (see Martin and Voorhees
1981, Healey et al. 1982a).

Nevertheless, central government and other interests attach sufficient
importance to development plans as a way of exercising control over a local
planning authority's policies-in-action that it expends some effort in
modifying structure plans and maintaining an over-view of local plan
production. In doing so, it is assuming that the hierarchical mode of
policy control embodied in the legislation, which reflects a sequential
notion of the relation between policy formulation and implementation, can
be made to work. Because central government can reinforce its views
through the development control process, this assumption is sometimes
justified, particularly where the implementation of planning policies
requires refusing development proposals, or where a planning authority
wants the support of central government (or a district of its county) in
furthering a policy. Yet central government's influence and the ideologies
of planners are not the only reasons why there is some consistency in the
content of local plans. Certain longstanding planning policies, enshrined
for many years not only in plans, but in the attitudes of planning officers,
councillors and many members of the public also define the limits of
acceptable or unacceptable proposals. These longstanding spatial ideas such
as contained settlement growth (rather than sprawl); the segregation of

major industrial developments from residential areas; areas of special
landscape protection and green belts, are so deeply embedded in the
consciousness of those with an interest in the operation of the planning
system that they hardly need to be stated in plans, although they are
sometimes redefined in central government advice. These essentially
cultural ideas provide an implicit framework for development in Britain.
Their origins lie in the culture and landscape of lowland England, though
imposed on other areas, such as the celtic fringes, with quite different
historically-developed settlement patterns.

Chapter 8 has shown that development plans as such rarely provide a
framework within which development interests operate, except for smaller
firms. Nevertheless, these longstanding and implicit landscape and
settlement policies, combined with the policy concerns of central
government and local authorities, do provide some sort of a framework, in
the sense that development interests can only seek to adjust them
marginally. This they do by seeking to influence both the formulation of
policies and detailed site proposals, and their implementation through
development control. As Chapter 6 shows, developers and landowners are
little in evidence in the formal processes for public consultation in plan
preparation. Their preference is for direct discussions between industrial
firms and planning authorities, combined with informal access to
politicians and officials via national and local elite networks, and the
use of inquiry procedures when these channels fail. It is only recently
that housebuilders have taken to organized lobbying to further their
interests, while local Chambers of Commerce can usually rely on routine
consultation procedures.

In effect, in exercising their influence on policy formulation, development
interests are merely extending their normal interaction with planning
authorities in relation to particular applications. A key part of the
expertise of the more successful developers is their knowledge of the
changing nuances of planning authority policies and central government
attitudes and their ability to challenge these, through negotiation and if
necessary, on appeal. In such negotiation, statements in development
plans may be used as a baseline for these negotiations where appropriate.
In other words, planning authorities and the larger development interests
can be seen as engaged in an often complex and extended game, in which
changing government attitudes and shifts in local planning authority
policies enter as counters which each side attempts to use to its
advantage. Other local authority departments, other central government
departments and the public service agencies enter into this game from time
to time, either with development projects of their own, or because the
planning authority or an applicant needs their help in providing
infrastructure and other services, or, as for example with MAFF, in
supporting their case. Less powerful participants, for example small
builders, small firms looking for sites, householders seeking an extension,
voluntary agencies with small projects, then have to fit themselves into
the interstices of the game. While the larger development interests are
sufficiently knowledgeable to treat development plans as a negotiative
counter, applicants with less experience of the development game may find
that for them, the plan becomes a framework within which they are required
to fit.

There has been much discussion recently of what is sometimes called
"negotiative" planning. Although it has probably been a feature of the
relationship between planning authorities and larger development firms for
many years, it is receiving more direct attention partly because many local

planning authorities are much more concerned to promote development, and because central government is urging authorities to assist developers. It is also possible that the increasing scale and sophistication of development firms (Boddy 1981) has changed the nature of the negotiation.

However, a further reason is that the ability of the public sector to determine the public interest is being more seriously questioned than before. Negotiative processes encourage the policy-in-action of planning authorities to become hidden from means of public scrutiny, and public control through development plans. Councillors and Ministers have to rely on the good faith of planning officers and government administrators to ensure that planning policies-in-action are in line with their current policy intentions. Citizens in turn have to rely on the good faith of both politicians and officials. The lack of confidence in this good faith is lacking in many quarters, not just faith in planning officials, but in public sector administrators and experts in general, is one reason for the active local interest taken in planning matters in some areas. This may produce a multiplicity of pressure groups, which swing into action whenever a planning authority discusses a contentious issue or considers a contentious application. In some cases, pressure groups may become a part of the negotiative process itself. The RTPI's recent proposals on public participation in effect propose that "Community Planning Councils" should articulate public interests and participate in negotiation with developers (RTPI 1982).

There can be little doubt that councillors and planning officers are very sensitive to articulate public pressure, which in certain areas effectively extends the range of participants involved in the development game. However, it seems likely that only certain sorts of participants become so actively involved, notably the articulate middle classes in attractive urban fringe areas and the few instances of well-organized protest against inner city redevelopment (see Chapter 8).

Local plans, despite their cumbersome preparation procedures are thus not particularly effective either in "structuring the development game" or in ensuring that planning authority policies, development initiatives and decisions are demonstrably in the public interest. This raises two questions. First, how far is the multi-faceted tool of a local plan relevant to the reality of contemporary relationships between state agencies, between the state and development interests, and the state and the citizen. Secondly, if the core of the planning system in practice can best be represented as a complex game *between* planning authorities and development interests, rather than planning authorities determining the form and rules of the game, what does structure the game? I will pursue these two questions in the following three sections which consider in turn, the general debate about state intervention and its relation to the land policy field; contemporary trends in the way land is used and developed, and the changing behaviour of the development industry; and the institutional and procedural arrangements in the land use planning field. What I attempt to do in this discussion is to explore possible explanations for the changing form and operation of the planning system which relate this form to the content or substance of these operations. Evidently, this will take the discussion some way from specific explanations of the form, content and use of local plans in Britain. However, as I have argued, such an administrative tool cannot be viewed in isolation from consideration of the purpose and form of government intervention in land use and development as a whole.

2. THE STATE AND LAND USE PLANNING

In Chapter 1, I considered the various purposes which public intervention
in land, its use and development might be designed to further. I concluded
that in a country such as Britain, it was to be expected that public land
policy would be directed at several such purposes, and that there was
potential for conflicts between purposes. As I discussed in Chapter 2, in
the early post-war years, such potential conflicts were concealed within
the ideology that government was capable of determining the public interest
in relation to land use and development, and that this public interest
itself was a unitary one, upon which there was broad national agreement.
Publicly-reviewed plans demonstrated the principles or rationale behind the
particular determination of the public interest in decisions about the use
and development of land, as well as providing for the right to a hearing of
those property interests adversely affected by the plan.

This comfortable consensus on the purpose of planning fell apart in the
1960s, as predicted by contemporary observers such as Foley (1960) and Glass
(1959). There was in any case little consensus on the closely-related
question of land values. This breakdown, and the consequences of separating
the regulation of rights to use and develop land, from regulation of land
value and the state's role in land assembly and infrastructure provision,
were quite inadequately represented in the Planning Advisory Group's 1965
report, which argued that "the planning system" could be made appropriate
to the changed circumstances of the 1960s by adjustments to the form of
development plans. As with many other areas of public policy at this
time, the difficulties emerging in the planning system were seen to be
resolvable by the application of improved technology, particularly in the
field of strategic planning. There was curiously very little analysis of
the economic processes producing the "obsolescence" of the existing built
environment and the need for its renewal and extension which the report
emphasizes. Similarly, there was a quite inadequate appreciation of the
scale of public interest in environmental issues, and of the declining
public confidence in the capacity of state bureaucracies to operate
efficiently and in the public interest. Given this naivity on the part
of influential planners involved in the design of the local plan tool, it
is not surprising to find difficulties in actually using it in planning
practice in the 1970s.

I have suggested that this planning practice has had the characteristics of
an often hidden and increasingly sophisticated game between planning
authorities and development interests. This game has often been treated as
if it was essentially local in its operations, with local development
interests interlocking with the local authority, the public agencies, and
with local pressure groups. Yet although the game is played out in a
specified locality, the interests each participant may have in the game and
the way each operates may well be related to political and economic
considerations on a quite different scale. The nature of the investment
opportunities for development firms in an area are likely to be related to
both particular local economic circumstances and the climate of investment
opportunities within which each firm operates. In addition, local
authorities, public agencies and development firms are all affected in
various ways by central government.

Thus, the "game" is neither necessarily local, nor isolatable from the
political and economic forces which structure state intervention in the land
policy field in general. In other words, one cannot just accept the "game"
at its face value and interpret its outcomes as the result of the interplay

between relatively independent participants, as many pluralists would do. The saga of events in any particular configuration of the game, which is the stuff of journalistic reporting of planning, and more rigorously of many student dissertations, must be related to these wider forces if we are to generalize about the operation of the planning system in total.

Any search for explanations of the form and operation of land use planning and the role of local plans within it which seeks to escape from the consensus assumptions which appear in the design of plans, and from the pluralist interpretations which mirror the reality of a development game but do not explain it, must move to the wider sphere of the nature and articulation of political and economic forces as they affect both central and local government; the operation of firms in general, and their development activities in a particular locality. Recently, there has been an explosion of work in this field, much of it associated with Marxist attempts at explanation of the role of the state in contemporary developed economies. Central to Marxist explanation is the notion of the capitalist mode of production, the product of a particular relation between an exploiting capital-accumulating class and an exploited working class, the value of whose labour is extracted by the capitalist class. Classes are thus interdependent. It is the demands for the sustenance of this relation and the conditions for capital accumulation which, in Marxist arguments, explain the particular form of state agencies and state programmes. Weberian interpretations, which also contribute to these debates, would by contrast see the existence of classes and the formation and operation of state agencies as related to structures of economic organization, but ultimately independent of them. Both basic directions of theorizing about the nature of social and political relations and structures have contributed to what is broadly known as the "political economy" approach to the contemporary role of the state, and analyses of particular sectors of production as they affect locational and land needs. I do not here provide general summaries of this work, since there are now a number of collections of contributions within this approach to the analysis of urban and regional planning[80]. I merely pick out of these ongoing debates those ideas which appear to contribute to explaining the form and operation of the British planning system.

It is evident that we have moved a long way from the discussion of local plans, illustrating one of the central methodological problems of the "political economy" approach to explaining the operation of particular state agencies. Coherent theoretical structures are at such a broad level of generality that they cannot be tested against actual events, while in investigating events, it is difficult to substantiate precisely the connections between these and wider forces, even though a good interpretive guess can be arrived at by assembling various forms of evidence. Thus, for example, in a particular "development game", we may find a planning authority faced with housing developers who in one year appear desperate to get more land, and a few years later are coming back for variations to planning permissions on the same land to make their proposals more marketable in a poor selling climate. It is not too difficult to relate this to mortgage availability and its effect on demand for new housing. But this in turn has to be related to the reasons for the episodic nature of mortgage availability, which lie in government policies towards interest rates and towards the role of clearing banks and building societies, and in

---

[80]For example, ed Pickvance 1976, ed Harloe 1977, ed Cox 1978, ed Tabb and Sawers 1978, ed Dear and Scott 1981, ed Harloe and Lebas 1981.

the pattern of alternative investment opportunities (see Boddy 1980).

My own view is that we have to locate any analysis of the operation of a
field of public policy within some understanding of the structure of a late
capitalist economy, in which the state has grown to play a very
significant and complex part. However, I do not think it is either
methodologically possible nor theoretically necessary to demonstrate every
link in the chain between this and the detailed object of analysis, in this
case local plans in the planning system. It is unlikely that individual
events are determined in this way. What is more helpful is to identify
general organizing ideas which suggest the key relations and tendencies
which affect detailed events. With these brief methodological provisos in
mind, I will now summarize those "organizing ideas" which provide some
insights into the state's contemporary role in land use planning. In this
section, I will concentrate on two points; firstly the increasing role of
state activities; secondly, the state's conflicting practices.

The dilemma for Marxist theorists is to explain the evident expansion in
the state's role in contemporary western economies while maintaining the
central thesis that the primary function of the state is to support the
conditions for capitalist accumulation. Originally, Marxists assumed that
the state's role was limited to maintaining law and order and thus the
legitimacy of the social relations on which the capitalist mode of
production depended. The growth of the state's economic and social role in
the twentieth century has meant that this simple assumption has required
reappraisal, just as the economic problems of the 1930s caused Keynes to
reappraise laissez-faire notions of the state's role in relation to the
economy. The Fabian social democratic tradition has of course maintained,
in Weberian manner, that the state can act independently of capitalist
classes to provide social welfare services to benefit the mass of the
people. Marxist explanation rejects this view on the grounds that the
state cannot act independently of classes in this way, nor can it favour one
class without thereby affecting that class's relations to other classes. It
is argued instead that the state is drawn into intervention in the economic
or production sphere, and in the provision of goods and services to support
the production sphere, due to the various crises to which capitalist
economies are subject. It is drawn into providing for and/or appearing to
provide for the needs of the working classes because of the growth of
challenges to the legitimacy of capitalist social relations. Thus, most
current Marxist analysis argues that the state becomes enmeshed in economic
and social life in a three-pronged effort; - the direct support of
capitalist enterprise; providing the investment and services to ensure the
inputs to capitalist production; and maintaining the support for the system
which capitalism represents.

Following this thinking, Cockburn (1977) in her account of corporate planning
and community development programmes in Lambeth, explains both initiatives
as part of an orchestrated attempt at ensuring the means of production and
reproduction of the capitalist mode of production. Roweis and Scott,
discussing the growing extent of state intervention, explain this as due to
the need to regulate economic cycles and underwrite the social costs of
capital (Roweis and Scott 1978). Each intervention then creates further
problems which can only be resolved by yet more intervention. This leads
them to argue, in relation to "the urban land question", that:

> "the palpable geometric increase in urban planning activities in
> recent decades is almost certain to continue unabated but with
> some altered modulations.... The state will undoubtedly continue
> to provide massive injections of public funds into physical urban

infrastructure, though in a more highly discriminating and
rationalized manner than has been the case in the recent past ...
(and) ... the state will, to an increasing degree, impose
administrative rules whereby the urban game is played. Zoning
regulations and urban general plans, for example, are only the
mildest apprehensions of this development" (Roweis and Scott,
1978 p.67).

Roweis and Scott are here referring to Canada and the United States, which
both witnessed increased government interest in urban land policy in the
early 1970s. Yet there is ample general evidence to argue that, as
economies get more complex, firms in general benefit from state provision of
certain services (transport, labour training, housing etc) and from state
regulation of adverse externality effects (for example, congestion costs,
pollution costs). This increased intervention in all areas of economic and
social life leads to demands that the state operate efficiently in its
activities, which is a reason sometimes given for the concern with both
planning and budgeting processes in public agencies, and the more effective
control of local authorities by central government. Some people, notably
Pahl and Winkler (1974), have also argued that as its activities have
expanded, the state increasingly operates as an entity independent of other
groupings in society, developing the notion of a corporate state, associated
with a qualitatively different state-managed mode of production. The
characteristic of a corporate state is that its operation is determined by
a three-way interaction between state agencies, corporate firms and organized
labour. This notion is challenged by those who argue that although
corporate firms and organized labour do exercise considerable influence
on how state agencies operate, the control of the economy remains in the
hands of capital, and working-class interests do not significantly gain
more (Westergaard 1977). Consequently, there is no qualitatively different
mode of production in operation. Rather "corporate" working relations are
a particular process evolved *within* a late capitalist mode of production.

Nevertheless, the growth of state activity, accompanied by a preoccupation
with management technologies, in which the notion of objective *planning* has
played a significant part (Watson 1975), has been a common experience in
most developed western economies. The ripples of these technologies have
found their way into aspects of the concept and preparation of local plans,
as I have shown (particularly in Chapter 6). However, both the Marxist
three-pronged model of state activity and the corporatist model can all too
readily fall into a simple assumption that what the state does at any point
in time is functional to specific requirements of the capitalist or
corporate mode of production. Yet this belies both the evidence of conflict
over planning priorities and the experience of ineffectual operation in many
parts of the planning system. Nor is it clear why any particular government
programme should *inevitably expand,* even though government intervention as
a whole may increase. Indeed, the 1979 Conservative government's
reorientation of state investment demonstrates the contrary. This suggests
that more complex processes are at work.

O'Connor, in his work on the financial problems of U.S. state and municipal
government, analyses state expenditure in relation to the two main functions
of the capitalist state, which, following Marxist analysis, he sees as
maintaining the conditions in which capital accumulation can continue, and
maintaining social harmony which provides political acceptance of the
capitalist system. These two functions, accumulation and legitimation,
produce two forms of social expenditure, social capital and social expenses.
But they are also potentially contradictory. Social capital itself is made

up of a further division into social investment and social consumption
expenditure. Thus O'Connor arrives at the following three categories,
reflecting the three-pronged role of the state:

"(i)   *Social investment*: projects and services that increase the
        productivity of labour,

(ii)   *social consumption*: projects and services that lower the
       reproduction costs of labour power,

(iii) *social expenses*: projects and services which are required
       to maintain social harmony - to fulfil the state's
       legitimation function" (O'Connor 1973, p.6).

O'Connor then argues that the state faces dilemmas over the amount of
expenditure to devote to each heading at any one time, this dilemma being
particularly acute in times of recession when the overall level of the
state's activities vis-á-vis private capital accumulation may be challenged.
In other words, he is arguing that the nature of capitalist social
relations creates *tendencies* for state expenditure, but that since the
capitalist system is *itself* based on a fundamental contradiction between
the interests of capital and the interests of labour, these tendencies are
themselves potentially contradictory. Thus the state is as likely to
reflect this contradiction in its operations as to be functional to the
particular needs of capital.

O'Connor's categories were developed for analytical purposes. They relate
to expenditure on programmes, and it is not necessarily possible to
allocate a particular programme to a particular category. Nevertheless
major transport projects could be considered as social investment, social
welfare programmes as social consumption and law and order programmes as
social expenses. Some programmes, then, can be readily slotted into a
single category. But are state housing programmes concerned with social
consumption or with social expenses (such as programmes for housing the
elderly); are education programmes to do with training the workforce
(social consumption) or sustaining support (social expenses)?

When we look at contemporary British land policy, we find not only that
various aspects within it can be found within each of O'Connor's categories,
but that since it is a largely regulatory programme rather than an
expenditure programme, it does not really belong in O'Connor's categories
at all. One possibility is that land use planning could be treated as a
form of social expenses, a regulatory programme of the same nature as law
and order programmes. Yet firms require serviced land and protection from
adverse externality effects (see the discussion in Chapter 1). Land is
equally needed for social consumption programmes, so in other words, land is
a resource required by all activities. To the extent that state regulation
of land use seeks to organize competing claims for land from them all, it
is a necessary input in all three of O'Connor's expenditure categories.
Thus, regulatory land use planning "rides across" O'Connor's categories.
Given that these categories themselves represent contradictory demands on
the state, then the British planning system is internally grappling with
the fundamental conflicts generated by a capitalist mode of production in a
way that many other policy areas are not. If one accepts this case, it goes
a long way to explaining both the difficulties in achieving coherent
outcomes to planning programmes, and the multi-faceted nature of development
plans.

However, it is again too simple to view a "capitalist" class and a "working" class as homogeneous and in permanent direct opposition. In practice there are many groupings of interest, even within what can be broadly identified as a capitalist class, reflecting both the historical legacy from previous modes of economic organization and differentiation within the production sphere. As Massey and Catalano (1978) have shown, there are still landowners who hold land as the economic base for a long-established way of life. Although these "feudal landowners" treat their land as a commodity when a particular financial opportunity arises, and in many cases are significant agricultural producers, they still often operate with an ethos that views land or "the environment" as an estate, to be husbanded and passed on from one generation to another. This value is upheld by very powerful lobbies both inside and outside Parliament. The sanctification of policies such as urban containment and rural restraint on development owes a great deal to their influence, supported by the demands of the middle classes who have moved into the landscapes protected by these policies and who wish to continue to consume them.

Massey and Catalano also highlight the conflict between enterprises seeking cheap sites and premises as an input to production and those engaged in land dealing and property production whose interest is in extracting a significant rate of return for themselves. Among property interests, the land and property speculator's activities are more at odds with those of firms directly engaged in production. Thus, Marxist analysis stresses that any land policy in contemporary Britain cannot escape addressing the fundamental conflicts of a late capitalist society, as well as the secondary conflicts between "fractions" of capital. Most non-Marxists would also today recognize these conflicts (as Foley did in 1960). They would differ from Marxists in how they assess their ultimate resolvability. Yet, whether one takes a Marxist view of the role of the state and the contradictions within society or not, making neat equations between particular structuring tendencies and the pattern of actual events produces mechanistic and functional hypotheses that are unlikely to stand up against evidence. Some commentators have argued, for example, that the mechanisms for "planning" associated with British land policy have been a deliberate mystification, to create the illusion that government intervention in land and development was in the public interest, when in fact it was in the interests of capital. This ignores the potential and actual limitations on certain capitalist interests which the planning system has had. And it deals in far too simple a way with the genuine problem of legitimizing a land regulation policy which will always adversely affect some powerful interests.

To summarize the argument so far, the analysis I have referred to stresses that the state is not independent of wider economic forces but responds in various ways to the demands generated by these forces. But though the state's responses are likely to express some of the contradictions of the economic system itself, they are not automatic. For historical reasons, because of the time lag between stimulus and response and because in the last instance individual action is not fully determined by external factors, it is unlikely that the form and content of state programmes can be "read off" from any particular configuration of economic interests. Nevertheless, by explaining the tendencies within the economic sphere and the various forms of state responses to these, we may come to some understanding of why particular state programmes evolve in the way they do.

The value of the Marxist analysis of the role of the state, and in particular O'Connor's categorization of the types of programmes the state may engage in, is that it allows us to recognize the tensions which may exist within state programmes. In particular, it encourages a distinction between the state's direct support for the production sphere (social investment), its activities within the consumption sphere (social consumption and social expenses), and its requirements to demonstrate that its activities are legitimate[81]. However, O'Connor's analysis tells us nothing about what produces the particular balance between production, consumption and legitimation activities at any particular point in time. As a categorization, it is both static and descriptive. It highlights the difficulties of the design of state programmes, such as land policy, and indicates the role that something like a local plan may have in legitimating that policy. However, it does not explain either the forces which produce particular interventions or which rearrange the balance between categories over time. Nor does it tell us anything about *how* the state organizes its interventions. For the former, we must look in more detail at the forces behind the way land is used and developed in Britain's recent history. For the second, we find ourselves returning in a different way to a discussion of modes of policy formation and implementation, familiar to planners in the guise of alternative decision-making models. The next two sections explore these two issues.

3. LAND, ITS USE AND DEVELOPMENT IN CONTEMPORARY BRITAIN

Land and premises are resources required for all activities in one way or another. Like finance, modern capitalist economies have developed specialist agencies and procedures for allocating land and premises to activities. In this country, these represent a mixture of market operations and state activities. However, while financial arrangements are a central management concern of all governments and major economic interests, land and premises are very much a peripheral concern. They tend to be the object of political concern only when land and property transactions threaten financial stability (as in the property collapse of 1973) or social harmony (usually as an aspect of major social programmes, for example current concern with inner city "regeneration"). Yet as noted in Chapter 2, the way we value land and property in this country is affected by historical traditions as well as the demands created by contemporary economic and social needs.

In current debate land and property are conceptualized in four ways, related to four broad interest groupings:

1. as resources to be activated according to demand, their value being determined by competing demands for particular sites and properties with specified locational characteristics; the users of such sites seek efficiency in their availability, i.e. sufficient supply at low cost;

2. as commodities, out of the production of which profits can be accumulated; for those engaged in such production, (land and property development), the maximization of return over outlay is the central concern, either in the short term as properties are passed on to consumers, or as investments, with consumers providing a long-term rental return;

---

[81] See Dunleavy 1980 and Saunders 1981 for a discussion of the concept of a distinctive state role in "collective consumption".

3. as a cultural heritage to be husbanded and conserved; because
of the value attached to situations which possess such heritage
characteristics, cultural value can be realized as a financial
gain by property developers;

4. as a resource which should be owned by communities and allocated
by them to specific needs, rather than as a marketable commodity.

The first two of these conceptualizations can be related to the two
categories of "production" interests discussed in the previous section,
i.e. the production of goods for consumption and the production of the
space and built form within which such production and consumption
activities takes place. The third relates to cultural traditions which can
only in part be related to contemporary economic preoccupations, yet where
it attaches to particular environments is itself something that can be
consumed. The fourth emphasizes consumption interests in that the
production of and access to space should be dependent on community needs
rather than the imperatives of production processes and capitalist
accumulation. Clearly, each leads to different attitudes to property rights,
the nature of rent and the role of state intervention. Clearly, also, if
these distinctions between production and consumption activities reflect
fundamental and secondary contradictions or tensions within a capitalist
economy, we may expect to find conflicts over how land and built form
should be provided and distributed, and what role the state should play, if
any.

What forces then may expose these conflicts, and what conceal them? Within
the burgeoning political economy literature on urban phenomena, there are
two strands of explanation for the emergence of conflicts over land, its
use and development. The first, represented most vigorously by Castells,
argues that the way land is used and developed is one outcome of class
conflict, with what he refers to as "urban social movements",
representing the working class, significantly changing the land using and
dealing behaviour of the capitalist class. He recognizes, as Roweis and
Scott do (see Section 2.2), the game-like nature of urban development
processes, (Castells 1976), but argues that this is the result of
institutional arrangements which express the particular state of play
between opposed working class and capitalist class interests, as well as
conflicts within the capitalist class. He stresses the role of urban
planning and plans in particular in legitimating the position reached in
the game. To repeat the question used at the end of Chapter 1:

> "Plans stamp all schemes with a double character: on the one hand,
> they come to be seen as 'reasonable', rational technical solutions
> to the problems posed, and, on the other, they appear to bring
> about a convergence of the various social groups and urban
> functions" (Castells 1977 p.76).

However, although all parties in the game may seek to use planning and plans
in this way:

> "planning is a privileged instrument of negotiation and
> mediation which each group present seeks to appropriate in order
> to give itself the appearance of social and technical
> neutrality" (p.76).

Thus, the dominant class has much more power and is therefore more likely
to achieve control over the planning machinery. Nevertheless, working
class social movements may use the arena of urban planning to challenge the

dominant class, producing urban crises which will be of national political significance.

Castells' view has been criticized for the assumption that the dominant classes will necessarily win control unless systematically challenged by working class groups, for the way he relates "urban" crises to fundamental crises of the capitalist system as a whole, and for his expectation that urban social movements as he defines them produce significant social changes (Pickvance 1976, Saunders 1981). Yet Castells' contribution is important since he emphasizes the role of *plans* in legitimating the appropriation by dominant classes of the state machinery organizing the way land is used and developed. The discussion in Part II has repeatedly stressed the role of development plans in demonstrating that the public sector is operating in the "public interest" in the planning field, as well as illustrating the various ways in which the more powerful interests seek to influence the determination of planning policies, in plans and in detailed decisions.

However, I suggested in Section 2 that it is not sufficient to treat "dominant classes" as homogeneous, nor are plans purely legitimating devices. Plans do not merely legitimate bargaining and negotiating over land and its development among different sections of the dominant class. They are also, as I have indicated in Chapter 1 and in the introduction to this chapter, a tool used as part of the productive process. Castells gives us little insight into this and, despite his recognition of the existence of a development game, provides little analysis of the forms it may take. For this we have to turn to the sorts of explanation developed by writers such as Lamarche, Lojkine, Harvey and Scott.

Lojkine (1976) and Scott (1980) develop their discussion of urban land problems from an analysis of the processes of urbanization in capitalist societies. Their analyses follow familiar lines, arguing that collective action to reduce externality costs and provide infrastructure support arises as production is increasingly concentrated in the face of the imperative of continued profit making. Scott stresses the importance of technological innovation replacing labour with capital in fuelling this concentration, which first leads to spatial concentration, and then dispersal enabled by transport technologies, to escape the dis-economies which increasingly surround central city sites. These dispersal tendencies are now recognized in all developed western economies (see Drewett and Rossi 1982). I have noted in Part II how a considerable proportion of local plans have been prepared in response to them. In Britain, the demands for a different form of "production space" located outside conurbation cores is being provided by large property companies closely related to financial institutions which consider property a valuable long-term investment.

In theory, these *industrial* dispersal tendencies within those sectors of the economy which are still investing should have come into direct conflict with the powerful lobbies defending agricultural land, environmental heritage and the right to consume attractive rural environments as a place to live. However, despite an undercurrent of hostility, overt conflict is rare. This situation has received little investigation, except in Flynn's analysis of the "incorporation" of industrial interests in the preparation of the Kent structure plan (Flynn 1979). However, it seems likely that industrial firms and industrial property development interests have managed their inroads into the shire counties by astute negotiation with planning authorities and a careful appreciation of the limits of public acceptability of modern industrial development.

The history of housing development pressures in the shire counties has by contrast been quite different in Britain. In particular, the allocation of land for large housing estates on greenfield sites around the conurbations has been bitterly opposed. It can be argued that one of the reasons for the high level of acceptability of the planning system in 1947 arose because it was a tool for controlling "sprawl" and containing housing development. To some extent, the explosion of private housing around the fringes of conurbations can be related to similar processes to those analysed by Harvey in the USA. He relates the major extension of home ownership there in the 1950s to federal subsidies promoting mortgage availability, which in turn was encouraged by the federal government seeking to stimulate consumption within the economy (Harvey 1981). The middle classes were encouraged to invest and reinvest in housing as a commodity. Cheaper but attractive sites were needed for this than could be provided in inner city locations. Consequently an ever-extending urban fringe has been encouraged. Land use regulation in the form of exclusionary zoning, keeping out lower value activities, has played a role in this process by assigning status to parcels of suburban land, thereby assisting the marketability of the product, suburban housing (Ashton 1978). There can be no doubt that many local plan exercises in this country fall into this category. Following Harvey, we could conclude that such plans, by establishing a particular status for sites, assist the producers of private housing to realize profits from house construction, and the consumers of such housing to realize their investment at some future date. Tensions over status may nevertheless result where the market considerations of housing producers and the investment ambitions of existing residents demand different densities and layouts, or the development of different sites.

Local plans, as site-specific guidance documents, thus may have a role in this suburbanization process not only to legitimate the accommodation reached among these conflicting interests, but as workable allocations of status and hence value to sites. Which sites become the object of development attention will reflect developers' assessments of the margins within which they can shift the embedded implicit planning policies noted in Section 1, as well as the sites individual firms can get access to. The acquisition of specific development value to these sites may occur by their allocation in a local plan as a result of technical assessments by planners. However, the evidence in Chapter 8 suggests it is much more likely in recent years in Britain that the larger sites allocated in plans will already have been the subject of discussion and negotiations between planning authority and developer. A local plan legitimates such assessments and provides a guarantee of long-term value. This is as important for housing developers looking to the marketability of their properties as for the financial institution seeking a secure long-term investment. Such a guarantee is not necessarily a *prediction* of long-term value, of course. The position of the development game may shift, producing a new alignment and new ideas about the status of sites. But the *appearance* of such a long-term guarantee serves short-term accounting needs, as well as a short-term political function. The role of local plans and of obtaining planning permission in establishing the book value of a company's land holdings is a recurrent theme in discussions with land holders.

However, as Hall's study clearly demonstrated (Hall *et al.* 1973), the consequence of using state regulation of land uses to guarantee the status of land is that the prices of development land are forced upwards. There has been considerable debate on whether the regulation of the use and

development of land of itself produces an increase in the value of
development land or whether land values are increasing anyway due to more
fundamental economic processes (Drewett 1973; Boddy 1980), echoing a
similar debate on whether financial operations create value (Revell 1973).
Nevertheless, state land use regulation, unless it is excessively generous
in the land allocated for development, concentrates value on specific
sites. This increases the possibility of conflict between those producing
sites and property and those using sites and property as inputs to
production. So long as the latter directly control the demand for the
former, in principle land and property inflation should not increase
production costs. In other words, where users of land and property control
supply, there is little opportunity for price inflation.

However, just as financial intermediaries have grown increasingly powerful
in managing the flow of money between firms wishing to invest and those
wishing to borrow, so intermediaries, the developers, property companies
and agents, have expanded in the land development field. In addition to
the effect of the planning system in reducing land supply, this has had
the effect of distancing suppliers of land and property from users. Even
the provision of industrial property, once dominated by users, has now
become the province of industrial developers. Both government and
financial institutions have periodically encouraged the expansion of this
sector by their influence on the demand for property. As in the US, the
British government has from time to time adopted financial policies which
have had a significant effect on mortgage availability and hence on the
demand for new housing. Financial institutions have invested in land and
property to widen their spread of investments, and to some extent because
of the greater attractiveness of land and property against industrial
investment in a time of recession. Although financial institutions are
interested in long-term trends in demands and needs, in order to secure
their investments in the long term, their involvement in land and property
increasingly removes control over this input of production from users.

Some authors have identified a particular sector, property capital, as
distinct from industrial and banking capital (Lamarche 1976). This implies
that those investing in land and development are distinct and separable
from those involved in industry or the financial institutions. However,
this does not seem to be the case. Harvey (1981) and Boddy (1981) provide
analyses of "circuits of capital" which both illustrate the way different
types of capital are interrelated in the production of property and provide
ideas on how and why the flows of capital through different circuits change
over time. Harvey attempts to relate the changing flows of investment into
land and property development to "long waves" of capitalist development,
i.e. the various stages of economic organization since the nineteenth
century and their reflection in investment in infrastructure and premises.
Boddy concentrates on the more immediate history of property investment in
Britain in the 1970s. He notes the increasing involvement of financial
institutions in the property sector, leading to concern over the management
of property development to avoid booms and slumps which could "destabilize"
the operations of financial capital. He also uses this analysis to highlight
the potential for conflict between financial and industrial capital over the
costs of land and property, and the changed "structure of opposition" which
the involvement of financial institutions produces for state involvement in
controlling development gain, intervening in the development process or
nationalizing land. In an analysis of the housebuilding industry, Ball
(1982) emphasizes the operation of similar processes, stressing the
increasing concentration of production in this field.

Analyses such as these chart the development of a specialist property
development sector within the British economy and the increasing take-over
of this sector by large multi-national firms with close links to
financial institutions. I have suggested that this increases the potential
for conflict between the needs of firms for land and property as an input
to production, and the opportunity for capital accumulation through land
and property itself. However, the present tendencies to concentration and
the involvement of the financial institutions can be seen as a stabilizing
force, following the excessive price inflation and collapse associated with
the property boom of the early 1970s. To an extent then, this conflict is
in the long term self-regulating. Yet, as Roweis and Scott note for
Canada and the US, public intervention in this sphere is increasing.

I have argued that a state role in regulating the way land is used and
developed has assisted property interests through providing certainty about
value. In effect, it organizes land values and confines speculation to
margins of value and to "big" risks (such as the ultimate release of a
site from the green belt). If there was a long-term prospect of rising
demand for all types of development in any location, such an organizing
framework would have little benefit to property production interests.
However, this has not been the case for many years in Britain and is
probably only present in capitalist economies during relatively short
periods of rapid urbanization. Clawson (1971) notes the disbenefits of
unregulated speculative housebuilding for the firms themselves in the US.
However, when the property sector is affected by recession, as at present
in the UK, it demands further support from the state. The discussion of
housing land availability illustrates shifting concerns from merely
obtaining access to land via adjustments to plans, to ensuring land
allocated for development was adequately serviced, to a focus on those
sites where houses would still sell despite the difficulty marketting
conditions around 1980, to pressure on the public sector to provide cheap
land (see Hooper 1979, 1980).

In other words, the more difficult the economic conditions, the more direct
intervention from the state is sought in the business of property
production, as in other sectors of the economy. Thus after the war, the
building and property sector was in such difficult circumstances that it
could not have undertaken the renewal of bomb-damaged cities without state
help which initially supported the recovery of the building industry
through public development programmes. During the boom period of the 1950s,
state assistance was limited to removing constraints (land assembly in
areas of multiple ownership), and organizing public infrastructure, with
programmes of more broadly-based support (cheap land and premises,
clearance of sites, advance servicing of sites) developing in the
depressed industrial regions. By the 1980s, this kind of support was being
extended to large parts of the country, encouraged by central government.

However, in addition to the state's support for production interests
through the regulation of land use and development, and through direct
inputs into the production process, it also plays a major role in mediating
the conflicts between those whose interests are primarily in development
and those concerned to resist it. As I have indicated, these are a
mixture of those involved in the business of agriculture, those anxious to
preserve for their continued consumption the landscapes they have bought
their way into and those genuinely concerned to conserve for future
generations elements of our built environment, landscape and ecology as
heritage. Given the increasing scale of public objection to large-scale
development proposals such as highways and power stations, it must be

concluded that the planning system has played a significant role in
providing an arena for and often defusing such conflict.

Thus it can be argued that the state regulation of development still has a
role in the conditions which currently prevail in Britain. Although the
amount of development occurring is much less than twenty years ago, it
still provides a valuable service to production interests in organizing land
values and in mediating conflicts between competing interests, particularly
between development and conservation interests. For both purposes,
publicly-prepared plans have some value. However, there are two reasons why
site-specific guidance frameworks may be of less use than they were.
Firstly, as property firms seek more direct support from the public sector
and as their cost margins are squeezed by continuing recession, the
relation between property firms and planning authorities becomes
increasingly a negotiative one, rather than a plan-based one. Secondly,
as property firms, and of course firms in other sectors of the economy,
are now much larger, the notion of the *local* determination of the way land
is to be released for development is increasingly challenged.

The fragmentation of the state's activity in regulating land use and
development among hundreds of districts means that large development firms
have to expend considerable effort in monitoring their interests both in
plan production and development control, which is one reason for the growth
in specialist planning sections of large development companies and property
firms, and of specialist development and planning consultancies (Stephens
1981, McNamara 1982b). The tension between large development firms and
small districts probably also explains the increasing role of central
government in monitoring the exercise of planning control. Yet there are
also advantages in the fragmentation, since it localizes the conflicts that
arise. In addition, the present form of the planning system encourages
such conflicts to be focused around plan preparation. Development firms
can affect this through consultation procedures, while continuing to
negotiate around proposals. Meanwhile the trends that these proposals
represent are often appreciated by districts as local peculiarities to which
they have to adjust. These trends, such as industrial dispersal into
shire counties, might be much more rapidly recognized by effective
monitoring at regional and county level.

In the next section, I examine in more detail the significance of the way
the regulation of land use and development is organized. Before doing so,
one final point should be made. Although the planning system does
accommodate "community needs" in so far as the main service departments
demand the reservation of sites for their programmes, and planners make
assessments of needs and propose projects and sites to meet them, there is
very little evidence of the political articulation of community needs in
relation to land and development, except ideologically in the discussion at
national level on the land value issue. The exceptions are the few cases
within inner city areas where protest groups, often stimulated by community
activists with specialist knowledge, have opposed slum clearance and office
redevelopment schemes. As Dunleavy notes (1980), these are much less
common than Castells' arguments would indicate. We may suggest that in
Britain, at least, the state's key legitimation problem in regulating land
use and development has not been to ensure acceptability to working class
interests. This acceptability has rarely been a problem. The central
difficulty is to ensure the legitimacy of the compromise reached between
the firms who are users of property, the producers of property and those
concerned to limit the overall amount of development in order to pressure
the environment.

In other words, to use the Marxist vocabulary, the secondary conflicts of a capitalist economy are much more evident in the land use planning field than the fundamental ones. This is perhaps hard for planners, with their mix of public interest and social welfare concerns, to grasp. However, such a conclusion suggests a possible explanation for the persistent separation of land use regulation from the state's role in land ownership. A land policy which explicitly deals with both elements will "ride across" both fundamental and secondary conflicts. By separating them, the state's mediation role and the legitimacy of this can be confined to secondary conflicts among the more powerful interests in society. Until organized labour takes a sustained interest in land and development issues, this is likely to remain the case.

4. "LOCAL" PLANNING AND MODES OF STATE OPERATION

In the previous section I have examined very generally the economic forces which have affected the state's activities in the land and development field and how these have changed over time. I conclude that state regulation of land use, and some mechanism for establishing the legitimacy of the compromises reached between conflicting interests in the way land is used and developed, remain relevant and probably necessary interventions in the contemporary UK. Yet how far is the way these interventions are organized by the state equally relevant? In Part II, I stressed the complexity of the procedural arrangements surrounding local plan preparation, and the widespread involvement of different levels of government. Few other fields of public policy have such complex arrangements. Are they merely a quirk of history or are there ways in which they can be explained which will cast light on their continuing relevance?

Until recently, there has been little discussion of the possible relationships between the economic and political tendencies encouraging state intervention in the land and development field, and the institutional form which that intervention has actually taken. The criticisms of public consultation arrangements have gone little further than to demonstrate that such arrangements are not likely to encourage "participatory democracy" (McAuslan 1980, Hill 1980). Cawson (1977), Simmie (1981) and Reade (1980, 1982) in various ways suggest that land use planning operates in "corporatist" ways, linking this to dominant interest groups.

Meanwhile the critics of rational decision-making methodologies note that these stress the status quo and hence dominant groups rather than the needs of all interests, which they purport to do (Thomas 1979). Recently, however, Flynn (1979), Blowers (1980) and Darke (1982) have discussed the processes by which interests are mediated in the preparation of structure plans. Flynn and Blowers discuss how, through negotiation and, in the case of the industrial interests described by Flynn, "incorporation", a consensus is reached on the policy content of structure plans. Darke shows revealingly how in the process of arriving at the content of South Yorkshire structure plan, the mode of policy-making shifted between what he calls bureaucratic, rationalistic, public and political forms. He notes in particular that the different modes affected the *content* of policy, bureaucratic modes emphasizing "routine matters"; rationalistic ones "trend-following"; public modes "incremental change"; and political ones, "political principle".

In making these relationships, Darke is drawing on the work of Offe who has made valuable suggestions as to the way the state operates in capitalist

societies. He argues that initially, the state was primarily concerned
with *allocating* the resources owned by the state. It was thus primarily
concerned with its own internal management, for which a "bureaucratic" mode
was sufficient. By this, Offe means the allocation of resources
according to "predetermined rules through a hierarchical structure of
'neutral' officials" (Offe 1977 p.136). However, Offe argues that the
growth of state activities in the production sphere, as discussed in the
previous section, has led to the development of alternative modes of
operation. The first he calls the "purposive-rational mode", equivalent
to the rational decision-making method, and any mode of policy formation
which is based on informed objective assessment. But Offe argues that
this mode is ineffective except where goals are clear, "uncontroversial
and operational", the environment is stable, externalities are unimportant
and there are no fiscal constraints (p.137). Given that this is not
always the case, as the critics of rational planning methods have
repeatedly pointed out, a second mode of operation is attempted, "a
highly decentralized process of political conflict and consensus to
determine the production process". (p.137). Here the clientele of an
agency would decide what should be done. This is not so much the
incremental model of "partisan mutual adjustment" advocated by Lindblom
(1965) so much as the approach advocated by those seeking a participatory
democracy in a pluralist society.

As with models of decision-making, there is clearly a potential for endless
extensions and re-classifications of "modes of policy-making". The key
point however, is not the devising of typologies, but explaining why one or
another or several are adopted in a particular context. Offe's explanation
is clear. Since the capitalist state is engaged in contradictory functions,
as discussed in Section 2,

> "it is hard to imagine that any state in capitalist society could
> succeed to perform the functions that are part of this definition
> simultaneously and successfully for any length of time ... (it
> engages in a) constant attempt to reconcile and make compatible
> these various functions with its internal structure, or mode of
> operation. But ... there is neither a visible nor to be anticipated
> a strategy that actually *does* reconcile these functions
> and thus achieve a balanced integration of the state and the
> accumulation process, that is, a reliable and workable strategy
> of "systems maintenance" (Offe 1977, p.144).

Offe's analysis would suggest that where a state activity is involved in an
area of the economy where conflicts are difficult to suppress, persistent
attempts to revise the mode of operation of the state's interventions may
be expected. To an extent, the search for improved methodologies in land
use planning in Britain may be interpreted in this light. Yet the
procedural arrangements for local plan preparation are more than merely
the result of a history of unfulfillable attempts to achieve a satisfactory
mode of operation in a particular part of the planning system. Local plan
production involves different methods for the determination of "the public
interest" because different sorts of interests have to be mediated to
arrive at legitimate "planning policies", the mix between interests varying
from place to place. Is it possible to develop the argument further and
relate different interests to different modes of policy formation, a link
evident in a general way in Offe's discussion and hinted at in Darke's
analysis?

It is here that the ideas developed recently by Saunders are of considerable
interest. He sets out (Saunders 1981) to link economic interests to the

modes of operation of state agencies and the levels of government at which
different state activities are located. Firstly, he considers state
expenditures as broadly relating to either the demands of a production
sphere, or of a consumption sphere. This consumption sphere, as noted at
the end of Section 1, is a product of collapsing O'Connor's categories of
social consumption and social expenses. Saunders in effect argues that
state activities in these two spheres can be analytically separated,
although in grouping O'Connor's categories in this way he obscures what
O'Connor considers as a significant potential contradiction. Similarly,
my discussion in Section 3 would suggest that a production/consumption
dichotomy conceals significant internal conflicts although Saunders did not
intend his categorization to apply to state regulatory activities[82].

Nevertheless, using these categories, the second stage in Saunders' argument
is to relate the nature of state involvement (production support,
consumption support) to the mode of operation of state agencies. He argues
that to cope with the fundamental conflicts between production and
consumption spheres, the state's interventions in these two spheres are
separated out through different modes of operation and different levels of
government. Thus where production support is involved, the state develops
"corporatist" mechanisms for mediating interests:

> "State intervention in the economy is thus increasingly the product
> of negotiation between large capital, organized labour and the
> state ... this enables the state both to mould its policies more
> accurately to the needs of large companies, and (to some extent)
> to regulate economic class struggles by co-opting trade union
> leaders into a strategy whose purpose is to ensure the continued
> profitability of the most significant sections of private capital"
> (Saunders 1981 p.263).

By contrast, interventions in the consumption sphere use "competitive
politics" to mediate between different interests, by which he means:

> "the traditional institutions of representative democracy
> (notably elections, pressure group lobbying, demonstrations,
> petitions and so on) ... (which) ... function primarily as a forum
> of non-incorporated interests such as small business, welfare
> state clients, consumers and so on to press their demands"
> (Saunders 1981 p.264).

Saunders' third step is to associate production interventions and
"corporatist politics" with *central* government's activities and consumption
interventions and "competitive politics" with *local* government, which he
refers to as "the local state". In making these associations Saunders is
not presenting a mechanistic scheme. He puts forward a series of ideal
types to illustrate what he considers to be tendencies in the organization
of state activities. In particular, he is seeking to define a specific
area of concern for urban sociology, which need not detain us here; and to
propose that the production and consumption spheres can best be analysed
by using different theoretical modes, a marxist mode for production and a
pluralist mode for consumption activities. This distinction is
theoretically difficult to support, and masks some of the important
connections between production and consumption arenas so evident in the
land use planning field.

---

[82] Personal communication.

Saunders' typology as it stands is evidently too crude to apply to state intervention in this field. In addition to masking the distinction within and between production and consumption spheres, the two modes of interest mediation, "corporatist" and "competitive" do not reveal the range of modes evident, for example, in Darke's work. There is a significant distinction between rational/technical assessment and the kind of negotiation which characterizes much of the relations between planning authorities and development interests. Nor are these relations strictly "corporatist" in the sense that Saunders' defines them since there is no evidence of the involvement of organized labour. It would thus be wrong to equate this negotiation and consultation with the larger public sector interests and development firms as "corporatist" as this term is commonly understood. Yet this "mode" *is* typically dominated by production interests. Similarly, "competitive politics" conceals significant differences between strictly working-class groups, and those whose main concern is the defence of the environment.

In addition, in the land policy field, production and consumption spheres are interrelated in the work of *local* planning authorities. It is possible to make a case that there are tendencies towards centralization, and that these are fuelled by production interests. Examples here might be the reorganization of infrastructure provision into the regional water authorities; the creation of Urban Development Corporations and recent attempts to limit the ability of local authorities to undertake their own economic initiatives. Central government's own interventions in the planning system, particularly its attempts to restrict the scope of matters of planning concern, and its advisory circulars and modifications to structure plans, could be interpreted as furthering production interests. It could even be argued that the separation of "strategic" policy from "local" matters into structure and local plan arenas in the 1968 Act was an attempt to separate production from consumption spheres. If intended, this separation has certainly not been successful.

This is not just because, following Saunders' arguments, consumption interests are likely to challenge production interests if their articulation in structure plans imposes unwanted development on localities. The "legitimation crises" faced by Hampshire County Council at Fareham Western Wards is a case in point (see Chapter 6). It also happens because firstly, county structure plans may just as readily articulate "consumption" interests, for example in the structure plans in the shire counties which tightly restrain development. Secondly, as I have shown in the previous section, since ultimately development is about building on specific sites, production activities have an interest in the local articulation of planning policies. Despite apparent inefficiencies, it may be easier and quicker to negotiate proposals through small and often isolated district council planning authorities than large sophisticated counties. In addition, since site development currently involves attempts at co-ordinating land availability and infrastructure provision, as well as reducing adverse externalities, it is probably beneficial to productive interests if this activity is carried out by agencies with considerable local knowledge - of sites and of the local activities of other government agencies. In addition, site-specific development guidance is helpful to certain production interests, for example, in establishing land values.

I would therefore agree with Saunders that in analysing the form and operation of the British land use planning system, we should seek to relate the way the state actually operates and what the role of different parts of the state is at any point in time and in any locality, to interests broadly linked to the economic tendencies of a late capitalist economy and the political demands this creates. In exploring these

possibilities in empirical studies, we may discover systematic connections.
For example, I think it may not be too wide of the mark to suggest that
production interests tend to use and create opportunities for relatively
hidden negotiation over the release of land for development projects, while
consumption interests make more use of plans (Healey 1982c). Because plans
may constrain development opportunities, production interests seek to
influence their formulation. Meanwhile, consumption interests may
appreciate that if they are to constrain production interests, they must
enter the negotiative processes, as the RTPI proposes in its recent report
on public participation (RTPI 1982).

Yet over-categorization before we have adequate empirical evidence or
interpreted what already exists will merely stultify inquiry. I will
therefore conclude by summarizing the main organizing ideas which in my
view would be worth exploring in such inquiry, bearing in mind that they
should be considered only as broad structuring tendencies. In any
particular situation, due to peculiar historical and locational
characteristics, whether these tendencies are present and if so, what their
form and consequences are, can only be determined by detailed research.
For this reason, this present investigation of local plans can only
suggest some of the conclusions such research might lead to, since it is
necessary to examine in depth how the production of a local plan has been
used to pursue, and has actually benefited, specific interests.

I suggest, then, the following six organizing ideas. Firstly, any state
intervention in land ownership, its use and development has to take account
of demands for land for production of goods, and demands for space for
social needs. Secondly, these demands are likely to be in potential
conflict in a society organized on capitalist lines (and possibly elsewhere).
Thirdly, in the UK, the demands for land created by the existence of a
specialist housebuilding and property development sector, and the existence
of a powerful cultural tradition which stresses the value of certain
buildings and landscapes as cultural heritage, creates further significant
potential for conflict. Fourthly, the firms producing goods, firms
producing property, the interests of those protecting and conserving the
environment, and of the community benefiting from social services and
facilities, all benefit to some degree from state regulation of development.
In varying degrees also, they benefit from more direct intervention by the
state in providing and servicing land and buildings. Fifthly, because in
such interventions, the state's actions have to appear legitimate to all
these interests - it has to face all ways at once - procedural devices are
likely to emerge to demonstrate that the way the state exercises its role
is in the general public interest. However, the more powerful interests
(including here the more knowledgeable) will seek in various ways to ensure
their control over the determination of what this means. This may create
new procedures, both formal (e.g. consultation procedures) and informal
(e.g. negotiating practices) and, where conflicts are acute, lead to overt
long-running disputes. Sixthly, because the way land is used and developed
is a consequence of economic and social activities, including state
policies; and because, where these activities require space this involves
the consideration of specific sites and specific localities, it is unlikely
that state land policies can operate effectively by attempts at
institutional isolation, either as distinct *sectors* of state activity or
at particular *levels* within the state.

I suggest that these ideas provide us with a more sophisticated means of
understanding the nature of the local plan tool in British land use planning
and the ways it has been used than the simple recognition of conflicting

interests acknowledged in Chapter 1. They emphasize the persistent tension, in both the procedures for plan preparation and the practices of preparation, between the functional use of plans, to manage development as part of a co-operative exercise between the public sector and those engaged in development, and the need to legitimate the state's actions in the planning field. There can be no doubt that development plans were designed to have, and to an extent have had, an important role in both tasks. Because of the significance of these tasks, and because of the need for some part of them to be carried out at the local level, development plans have also been important in central government's continuing effort to control the exercise of local authority discretion, for fear localities would allow too much leeway to consumption interests, whether environmental ones or welfare ones. Yet if it is widely recognized that local plan preparation is a cumbersome process, which produces policy statements which do not necessarily relate to what a planning authority is actually doing, local plans can hardly remain either a satisfactory legitimizing mechanism or an adequate control device. Nor are they particularly effective in managing development either. Is this an inevitable product of unresolvable tensions, or is the form of development plans no longer relevant to contemporary role of the state in the use and development of land in Britain?

In Chapter 10, I develop the ideas discussed in this chapter in a speculative way by considering what the future shape of the planning system might be if dominated by each of the four broad groupings of interests noted at the start of Section 2. In this way, I attempt to identify the tendencies already developing with respect to the state's role in land policy and what kind of institutional structure, tools and mode of operation might result. Finally, I comment on the relevance of this analysis of the British planning system to understanding the form and content of land policy in other contexts.

CHAPTER 10

Towards Reform

1. REFORMING THE PLANNING SYSTEM, NOT LOCAL PLANS

I argued in Chapter 2 that the British land planning system as we currently
have it is little more than a remnant of the conception expressed in the
1947 Act. We have seen major swings in the degree of public intervention
over land ownership and values. We have seen bouts of tinkering with the
land use elements of the system; development plans receiving particular
attention in the 1960s, and development control in the mid-1970s,
culminating in a series of minor changes around 1980. However, since the
1940s there has been no comprehensive review of the operation of the
planning system[83]. Nor has there been any comprehensive political statement
on land policy, "land" typically being separated from "planning" in
political manifestoes and policy discussions. The 1979 Conservative
government reconnected them in its all-embracing Local Government, Planning
and Land Act 1980. However, there is little evidence that this association
had anything to do with a coherent rethinking of the role of government in
land and development issues. Rather, it is a response to those articulate
lobbies which the government felt it had to acknowledge, with a few
projects of symbolic value to the government's strong ideological commitment
to monetarist policies, combined with a whole number of minor changes which
civil servants sought as a result of experience in administration.

It is quite likely that the tinkering will continue, as new governments
respond to new lobbies and add their own symbols, and civil servants modify
a few more procedures. However, as Chapter 2 described, government
intervention in land, its use and development, is now much more
politically contentious than it was twenty years ago. Then, changes to the
development plan system were largely the result of professional
articulation of the various pressures for change. Now, each lobby has its
own ideas for the form of change as well as the need for change. If anything,
the incoherent and indiscriminate grapeshot which the 1979 government

---

[83]Hall's study (Hall *et al.* 1973) took a very general view and did not
consider in any detail the way public agencies were using the various
powers, tools and resources available to them.

directed at the planning system has encouraged political organizations, development interests and conservation groups to articulate more coherently both the philosophy that should underly the system and what this means in terms of purposes, institutional arrangements and operating procedures.

During the 1980s, we are therefore likely to see more overtly ideological debates about the whole field of British land policy than we have seen for forty years. This will not of course make the resolution of them in the form of legislative change any easier. As I have stressed in Chapter 9, the design of state intervention in the land and development field is inherently difficult because it "rides across" fundamental tensions in the state's role in late capitalist economies. As the problems of economic and political management as a whole have become more acute, particularly since the mid-1960s, so the expression of these tensions in the land and development field has become more evident. However, debates about the present state and future possibilities for land policy are still characterized by simplistic connections between political philosophies and legislative tools, and superficial analyses of the likely consequence of specific changes.

It would therefore be quite inappropriate for me to conclude this book with proposals for reforming the way local plans are produced, or with a discussion of alternative ways of providing site-specific policy guidance within the planning system. The aim of this chapter is to set the discussion of changes to *elements* of the planning system within the broader context of the evolution of land policy in Britain as a whole, and its relation to the demands and needs of the different interest groupings as suggested in Chapter 9. First, to illustrate the operations of the tendencies discussed in the previous chapter, I re-examine in Section 2 the recent history of the planning system, emphasizing the impact of different interests on the form and content of the planning system. This contrasts with the treatment in Chapter 2 which emphasized the role of the interplay of levels of government in the evolution of that system. In Section 3, I explore the possible directions that further evolution might take, depending on the interests which are given most weight. Rather than predict alternative future scenarios here, I construct ideal types to illustrate the internal logic of a strategy which favoured one interest group over others. I do this in an attempt to make explicit how different interests actually benefit from different sorts of government interventions and modes of operation. I then consider the direction which in my view the development of land policy should take in this country. Finally, for those overseas readers who have struggled through this detailed account of the operation of a part of the British planning system, I make some comment on the implications of this study of local plans and British land policy for other countries.

2. CHANGING EMPHASES IN THE PLANNING SYSTEM: 1970-80

The period 1970-80 covers the years of two Conservative and one Labour government. However, the policies actually pursued by these governments in the land and development field, as in other fields, were not substantially different from each other or from their predecessors in the 1960s. Differences have related to expectations as to the scale of development and to ideological commitments to certain types of intervention rather than others. National government has nevertheless, throughout, pursued policies which encouraged local authorities to make adequate development land available to production interests, both industrial

production and property production. It has also encouraged authorities to
assist private interests in overcoming land assembly, land supply and
infrastructure problems. The decade as a whole witnessed a halt to rising
local government expenditure, with an increasing emphasis on private
provision of property and private contributions to public infrastructure
projects. Periodic concern with the social and economic problems of inner
city areas has not altered this. Rather, it has encouraged policies to
attract more private investment into inner cities.

During the 1960s, central government directly and through various regional
initiatives, sought to cope with the consequences of substantial economic
growth, with related population growth and increasing affluence. The need
to allocate sufficient space for the restructing of industrial production
was an important factor underlying regional policy (Massey and Meegan 1979),
and the planning system was encouraged, through regional and subregional
studies, to allocate sufficient land to accommodate this growth. Town
centre redevelopment was meanwhile facilitated by both national and local
planning policies, thus providing investment opportunities for office and
commercial property development. Speculative housebuilders, however,
operating particularly on greenfield sites around the conurbations, found
their opportunities constrained as the allocations of the development plans
of the 1950s were used up. They therefore put pressure on local
authorities to release more land, which the latter were reluctant to do.
Their local constituents were beginning to complain about the impact of
growth on their areas, in terms of their perception of their way of life,
the quality of their increasingly over-stretched services and the value of
their own properties. In other words, local authorities on the periphery
of the expanding conurbations tended to resist further land allocations
because of the weight they were encouraged to put on consumption interests
(the provision of social facilities for new development and the
protection of the rural landscape). Meanwhile, in town centres,
legitimation problems were occurring as people complained about the
disruption of the environment produced by urban renewal and then about
the quality of what was built, both in social and environmental terms.

The two main legislative changes of the Labour administration 1964-70
emphasized by contrast production interests, namely the emphasis on
strategic planning, dissociating broad principles of land allocation from
the detail of its local expression, and the Land Commission which again
reduced the role of local authorities by providing an autonomous agency
which engaged in land assembly. There can be no doubt that the Land
Commission reflected closely the housebuilders' belief that the problem
of rising land prices during the 1960s was due to local authority
reluctance to release land for development. The Land Commission maintained
this argument in lobbying the MHLG, which in turn continued pressure on
local authorities to release land (see Chapter 2, Section 3).

During the late 1960s, faced with this pressure, many local authorities had
little option but to release land, which they tended to do in large sites,
in the hope that they could thereby retain some control over phasing and
design. One result of this was that land assembly and the provision of
infrastructure became important questions, since sites allocated in plans
for development were not always available for development. Nor did they
necessarily have adequate road access, water supply, or sewage and drainage
provision. Access often also meant acquisition of key small sites, which
owners might refuse to sell. By 1970, housebuilders and local authorities
were as much concerned about infrastructure and land assembly as with
overall land availability. Nevertheless, the Conservative government of
1970, while continuing the previous administration's emphasis on releasing

more land, abolished the Land Commission though this could have been a
useful tool for making land available to private sector developers. In
its place, they combined exhortation with a special fund available to local
authorities for land assembly purposes, and key sector loan sanction for
infrastructure works in advance of development. Certainly in the South
East, the amount of land given planning permission for housebuilding shot
up, and there is some evidence that considerable advance infrastructure
was provided[84a].

The Conservative government gave a significant boost to the production of
property by these measures and by its financial policies which encouraged
the demand for property. This disadvantaged industrial firms which had
to pay consequential high land and property costs, and often that element
of house prices transferred in labour costs. Having abolished the Land
Commission, central government had to work through the local authorities
to achieve this end. But their main political supporters here were the
very counties and districts within which opposition to the operations of
housebuilders was likely to be strongest. Local authorities were encouraged
to engage in negotiation with private developers to assist with
infrastructure provision, using development briefs and Section 52
agreements, and "partnership" with the private sector was encouraged (DoE
1972). There can be little doubt that even without the excessive land and
property inflation consequent upon the government's financial, housing and
land policies, the government was heading into a major legitimation crisis
with its own supporters, particularly in the South East, on the grounds of
inadequate attention to service provision and environmental protection. In
addition, the property boom was having a destabilizing effect on the
financial system, a key element of any capitalist economy, and undermining
industrial investment still further, not only by its inflationery effects
but by its relative attraction as an investment outlet.

Not surprisingly, the Conservative administration was already reviewing
land policy measures by the end of 1973, having contributed to the property
collapse by regaining control of the mortgage supply. Land and property
development was a major item on the agenda of both parties in 1974. There
was also considerable general discussion of the "land question" at this
time, with civil servants, professional associations and academics working
up ideas of their own. This debate echoed in several ways that which had
preceded the Labour government's proposals for a Land Commission and
betterment tax, and the positions taken by significant interests at this
time have been sustained and developed during the later 1970s. Although a
few property interests still argued for the abolition of all forms of
planning regulation as the *cause* of high land prices, most had recognized
the need for some kind of partnership in which the state supported the
development industry (Denman 1974). This significant reorientation
occurred firstly because the typical developer of the pre-war and early
post-war periods, who took risks on the viability of a project, had
effectively been squeezed out by the property collapse and the strategies
of financial institutions (Spinney 1978). Secondly, the cost margins of
many property and construction firms were sufficiently affected by the
deepening recession to make it difficult to cover infrastructure costs
internally. The British Property Federation (1976) was therefore arguing
in 1976 for some form of development taxation to help pay for infrastructure

---

[84a] There has been no systematic study of infrastructure investment patterns
      over time. It is therefore necessary to rely on case studies. See for
      example Davis 1982 and Healey 1982c.

and services, although they were critical of some aspects of both the Conservative's Development Gains Tax and Labour's Development Land Tax.

Labour party debate meanwhile confronted the possibility of land nationalization, progressively drawing back from this ideological symbol to the half-hearted two stage nationalization of development land which became the Community Land Act. In conception at least, both land nationalization and the Community Land Scheme gave support to consumption activities. The cost of land to the public sector for services was to be cheaper than to private firms, reviving the differential abolished in 1959. Had public expenditure continued to increase and more money been allocated to the Community Land Scheme, local authorities might have been in a position both to improve the provision of land and property for consumption activities, and to assist both the production of property and industrial production by making cheap land available. As Massey and Catalano (1978) have pointed out, with the land speculator squeezed out of the running, there could have been widespread support for the scheme. Central government advice and financial arrangements, and actual practices as they developed in local authorities, treated the scheme as more or less separate from other activities, with direct negotiation encouraged between landowners, developers and local authority (see Barrett *et al.* 1978). These negotiations were not readily available for public scrutiny, and I am inclined to think that whatever the intentions may have been, the practice of the Community Land Scheme could best be described as another example of hidden negotiative forms of interest mediation.

Meanwhile, criticism of the land use elements of land policy was mounting. To some extent, this was part of a general criticism of the failure by the state to provide adequate social services and facilities generally. In addition, land use planning was criticized for being "negative" rather than "positive", although given the powers available, the capacity of the planning system to ensure development in response to needs and demands is clearly limited. The planning system was also criticized for the poor quality of the physical environment, for inefficiency and heavy-handed bureaucracy, and for lack of accountability, as studies showed how much land had been given planning permission which was never allocated in plans. It could be said that local planning authorities have sailed into the legitimation crisis produced by central government's emphasis on the role of land policy in aiding the production of land and buildings. Social and environmental interests have increasingly challenged planning authorities to declare their policies and actions, and to relate their actions to democratically-produced policies. Many representatives of these interests are in fact demanding that the negotiative relationship between the state and development interests should be obviously located within a framework publicly arrived at through debate with all interests, the implementation of which is publicly monitored.

Yet the Labour administration paid little real attention to these challenges to the legitimacy of land policies. Minor changes to the development control system as advocated in the Dobry Report (DoE 1975) were never followed up. Changes to the General Development Order to relax the lower limits of planning control were proposed but never pursued[84b]. Instead, increasingly sensitive to the consequences of the country's declining industrial base, the government's preoccupation in the land policy field

---

[84b]An amendment to the GDO (1977 No. 1781) was laid before Parliament in late 1977 but was withdrawn as the result of objections.

once again settled on the land availability question both in relation to
inner city land use and land values and in the suburban areas. This was
partly because local authorities, in preparing their structure plans and
influenced by the downward revision of estimates of population and economic
growth, had cut back substantially on land release since the heady days of
the early 1970s. In any case, many of these land allocations were being
only slowly developed, if at all. Meanwhile developers were finding that
sites which would have produced marketable properties in the early 1970s
were no longer commercially viable. Consequently, they sought to define
land availability in terms of marketability, while local authorities,
sensitive in many cases to often vociferous environmental lobbies,
preferred to define them in terms of needs, and local ones at that. More
sophisticated land availability reviews were therefore encouraged, with
further calls for co-operation and partnership between private interests
and the planning authority. In addition, faced with falling rate bases and
rising unemployment, both local authorities and central government encouraged
support for industry, beginning the progressive dismantling of regional
policy controls which culminated in the abolition of Industrial Development
Certificates at tne end of 1981.

Yet the legitimacy of this approach continued to be questioned. By the
late 1970s, a wide range of interests was putting considerable stress on
development plans and other public policy statements as mechanisms to
encourage greater accountability of the operations of local planning
authorities. The Countryside Review Committee (1979) and the CPRE (1981)
have stressed the need for prompt preparation of local plans, and their
support once prepared. The House Builders Federation (1977) were arguing
for regularly-updated Land Policy Statements in 1977 as a mechanism to
force local authorities to release sufficient land. The Confederation of
British Industy (1980) also welcomes development plans, although asking
that these reflect the concerns of industry. Meanwhile, as has become
particularly evident since the arrival of the 1979 Conservative
administration, central government has used development plans to force its
land release policies on local authorities. As it has become increasingly
difficult to maintain the legitimacy of any direction in land policy, the
legitimating role of the plan has increased in significance to all those
parties with an interest in government land policies but without a direct
assurance that their views will be upheld by central and local government.
The HBF and CBI want plans to tie local authorities to policies agreed with
central government. Local environmental groups want plans almost for the
reverse. Put crudely, development interests are probably satisfied with
a negotiative relationship with local planning authorities so far as their
own dealings are concerned. But they are very suspicious of the
negotiations that other firms may be engaged in and of the "inconsistencies"
of local councillors. Thus, in addition to an increasing presence in
public consultation exercises and at local plan inquiries, the HBF in
particular has adopted pressure group tactics at national and local level
to pursue its interests.

The 1979 Conservative government was distinguished by a central ideological
commitment to less government direct intervention and regulation. In the
land and development field, this commitment was translated into an attack
on bureaucratic inefficiency which was pursued with some vigour. Planning
was to be carried out more quickly, with fewer resources. Development
Control decisions were to be made more quickly, and survey work and
consultation were to be reduced in importance, thus speeding up plan
production. In other words, the technical and participatory elements of
plan preparation, and the production of unnecessary plans, were to be

curtailed (see Chapter 4 and 6). Not unexpectedly, given its ideological
association with land nationalization, the Community Land Act was abolished.

Nevertheless, in the land and development field, as elsewhere, the
government has been caught in something of a dilemma. In the interests of
support for production, it has emphasized privatization where possible,
the reduction of regulations, including, in the planning field, a
relaxation of the General Development Order and regulation-free Enterprise
Zones. Yet the House Builders Federation, who have had the ear of
ministers in this administration more than ever before, want not merely
more limited and faster-operating procedures for allocating development
land. They also want *more* help with infrastructure and land assembly
than they did in 1970, given the much more uncertain economic climate.
Although they have been shifting their operations onto smaller sites with
fewer infrastructure problems, their cost margins are more vulnerable,
while public capital expenditure has dried to a trickle. Builders are
also now suffering from the loss of public sector projects and high
interest rates, while unemployment affects demand.

In many ways, by abolishing the Community Land Act for ideological
reasons, as with the Land Commission in 1970, the Conservative government
have removed a power that could have helped them support production
interests at a time of deepening economic recession. However, faced with
the intractable problems of inner city areas, the government has introduced
a variety of land policy initiatives which in effect shift the balance of
intervention towards financial and other direct support for both
industries and property development. Significant examples are the Urban
Development Corporations, the recently proposed Urban Development Grant,
the financial subsidies associated with Enterprise Zones and with the
encouragement to local authority land sales at less than market prices.
The logic of the present government's stance on land and planning,
providing moral support for production activity but little direct
intervention, would be to remove regulation altogether. Yet its practice
departs considerably from its ideology in the land policy field, reflecting
the demands of both the property sector, faced with deepening recession,
and the political requirement for some action on the inner city front.
In many ways, its strategy is little different from that of the previous
Conservative administration. Yet land use regulation has stayed more or
less intact in both administrations and local government remains the main
implementor of the planning system, UDC's notwithstanding.

The reason for these anomalies lies in the traditional Conservative support
among the shire counties. This support combines a concern to preserve the
attractive environments in which they live and a commitment to local
democracy at the smallest scale. The 1972 Local Government Act ensured
continuing Conservative control of suburban and rural areas. Conservative
governments thus face a dilemma. At national level they may be
concerned to shift land policies more towards production than consumption
purposes. Yet they must not lose the support of the environmental lobby
or local Conservative councillors. In other words, the ideology of
limited intervention which the current Conservative administration espouses
sits uneasily with its need to respond to the demands of industrial and
property production and to those for environmental conservation and local
control over land policy. Secretary of State Heseltine claimed that it
was necessary to find a balance between these competing interests, implying
that this is a simple matter (Heseltine 1979). The evidence from Chapter 6
illustrates that it is not and the discussion in Chapter 9 explains why it
is not.

To conclude, government land policies during the 1970s have followed familiar channels. Apart from a short period in the mid-1970s, the emphasis has been on support for production activities, particularly the property development sector. However, this support has not been seen as particularly effective by either industrial firms or property firms. Both would like to see government take a more interventionist stance on their behalf, with a financial contribution to land clearance, land assembly and infrastructure provision, perhaps paid for out of some form of development charge, and organized more efficiently than is possible when planning regulation is administered by over 300 district councils. Meanwhile the problems of legitimizing this stance have become increasingly difficult. While low income residents of inner city areas challenge the systematic neglect which has left them in decaying or derelict environments with limited employment prospects, those in the suburbanized countryside defend ever more vociferously the environments they have been brought up in or bought their way into.

The political organization of local government itself, and the formal requirements for publicity and inquiries in plan-preparation and development control, provide arenas for both types of challenge and receive support from the advocates of a decentralized, participatory democracy (even if in practice many local authorities are closed paternalistic hierarchies). Yet the environmental lobby at least has expressed dissatisfaction both with the amount of administrative discretion within the planning system and the capacity of local authorities and/or central government to determine the public interest in any case. The "Land Decade" and the debate on the Wildlife and Countryside Protection Act 1981 provide evidence of the powerful interests which continue to support countryside protection. As articulated in particular by the Town and Country Planning Association, it puts more emphasis on probing independent inquiries and on binding administrative discretion by plans. So far, government has paid very little real attention to this lobby. Yet if the underlying direction of economic change is towards ever more severe economic problems, it may be that the power of the cultural heritage will diminish. There may come a time when protected countryside, green belts and contained towns and villages are less important to us than widepsread evidence of new productive enterprises. There are signs that this has already happened in some of the older industrial conurbations.

This section set out to illustrate through the recent history of the planning system, the effect of the tendencies examined in Chapter 9 on the institutional form and actual operation of British land policy. Three points stand out from this analysis; the persistant influence of the property production sector on the form and practice of land policy; the continuity of government land policy during the 1970s and early 1980s; and the increasing problems of sustaining public acceptability for that policy. In effect, the consensus over land policy of the early postwar period has broken apart to such an extent that the notion that the state can act in this arena in the general public interest is no longer credible. This explains why each interest is now articulating its own strategy. It also means that no government can articulate a coherent strategy without demonstrating which interests it seeks to advance and which to disadvantage. Even if this is not made explicit in formal policy statements or ideas for legislature change, it is readily discernible in the detail of any strategy, its powers, its modes of operation and the levels of government which are to be involved. To illustrate this, and as a basis for a more informed debate about future land policy, the next section examines alternative directions which land policy might take, depending upon which interests government policy seeks to promote.

3. DIRECTIONS FOR CHANGE

Several planners writing recently about likely changes in land use planning
in the 1980s have made predictions arising from the present conditions of
planning practice, the inadequacies of development plans, the emphasis on
"getting things done", and the increasing apparent variety in planning
practice[85]. A few are attempting to work up the economic implications of
the Labour Party's alternative economic strategy proposals (Thompson 1981).
Davies (1982) constructs four scenarios for planning based on degrees of
economic growth and the extent of government intervention. Broadbent's
approach possibly comes nearest to the one I discuss here (Broadbent 1979).
He presents two main "political" options for government, withdrawing further
from the market, or intervening further. In the latter case, he suggests
two alternatives, more active support for the private sector ("planning for
production"), or a "collectivist style of planning, placing first priority
on direct social provision" (p.23).

Although both Davies and Broadbent present their "scenarios" and "options"
as the basis for discussion only, they give inadequate consideration to
the conflicting demands on government in respect of its interventions in
land and development, and the need for any programme which favours certain
interests to be accepted as legitimate to other major groups. In addition,
both assume that government intervention will vary in *extent*, depending on
political philosophy. Yet I have suggested that it is more likely to vary
in *type*, depending on the weight given to different interests. I therefore
present four "ideal types" or directions which land policy might take, each
type deriving from one of the four main interest groupings identified in
Chapter 9; namely those concerned with industrial production, those
concerned with the production of property, those concerned with the
consumption of goods and services, and those concerned with the consumption
of and protection of "environmental heritage". In each case, following the
discussion in Chapter 9, I examine both what actions of government would
contribute to furthering the interests concerned and what additional actions
or arrangements might be needed to legitimate such a strategy to both the
interest group itself, since its members will need to be reassured that the
state is operating on behalf, and to the other three interest groupings.

For each ideal type, I consider the rationale for government intervention,
what this implies for a strategy of intervention and how this might be
realized into institutional arrangements and modes of operation. In effect,
I am relating in a more direct way than in Chapter 1 the ends and means of
land policy. More specifically, I relate the *form* of institutional
arrangements and procedures to the *content* of policy in terms of the
interests and activities government intervention is expected to benefit.

Before discussing each ideal type, one final comment is in order. I make a
basic assumption that the context within which each ideal type will operate
is that of the British version of a late capitalist economy. In other
words, the ideal types are historically specific. I do not think that
land policy measures, even those as apparently radical as public land
ownership, are likely in themselves to effect any radical change towards a
different form of political economy. And if a new form of political
economy did emerge in this country, land policies would have to be examined
afresh in the light of the political and economic demands which such a new
economy might create. In what follows, I am merely drawing out the

---

[85] See *The Planner* January/February 1981, *Town Planning Review* April 1980.

tendencies which are already present in the demands being made on the state
in the arena of land policy.

A. *Land Policies to Support Industrial Production*

The justification for intervention here lies in the needs of firms for low
cost provision of production space, the need for protection from adverse
externalities which their collective operations may create, and the need for
the provision of collectively provided services such as transport and
environmental quality which firms by themselves cannot organize (see
justification 2, Chapter 1). These externality costs and benefits persist
through the lifetime of a firm, although their significance compared to
other costs and benefits varies with the type and scale of the enterprise
and is probably often insignificant. This may well be because of
longstanding policies to ensure that this is the case. From time to time,
however, as firms expand the scale of their production or introduce new
technology, new space is sought. Locational and cost considerations then
become important, though again varying with the type of firm. Such
investment in space may constitute a critical decision for the future of
firms, a decision which may need to be made quickly and, for larger
specialist firms, with the specific requirements of the firm in mind. As
Fothergill and Gudgin argue (1982), space for expansion has become a
critical factor for many firms as labour is replaced by more capital-
intensive and space-consuming technology.

Given the general vulnerability of productive activities in the UK at the
present time, a strategy which would assist them should be capable of
providing serviced sites in preferred locations efficiently (at low cost),
quickly and in response to demand. Currently, this is what most local
authorities up and down the land are claiming to do. However, they are
limited in their effort by its very diffusion, which affects the flow of
information about sites and the availability of expertise to predict the
needs of firms, and by the lack of public finance for land assembly,
clearance and infrastructure provision, costs which many firms would find
difficulty in internalizing. Central government was certainly hesitant in
giving further support to local authority economic initiatives as encouraged
by the Burns report[86]. At one time, central government contemplated
restricting local authority action to less than the product of a 2p rate,
which is the normal discretionary limit. The interests of industry might
better be served by some form of land development agency with the capacity
for land acquisition, combined with financial resources for clearance and
infrastructure provision, and a capacity to lease premises to firms and
provide mortgage finance for purchase. Such an agency would thus resemble
in several respects the Industrial or Regional Development Agencies of
many third world countries. Their mode of operation would be a combination
of technical work, assessing demands and needs of firms, project
assessment and project management, and consultation with firms. To be
effective in relating firm's demands to sites, such agencies would probably
be most effective at the regional scale, and would need the autonomy of a
QUAGO or QUANGO. Given the specific problems of firms operating in
particular areas, a regional organization would be necessary, but such
regional agencies would need to be closely linked with the national economic
strategy. An organizational structure such as that established for the

---

[86]Report by the Chief planner at the DoE on local authority economic
initiatives.

Water Authorities might be appropriate, with a regional structure and
nominated boards including representatives of industry as well as government.
The style of these arrangements would thus be technical and negotiative,
not unlike what Saunders' refers to as "corporatist". It is possible to
envisage such agencies providing land and infrastructure for consumption
activities as well, such as major housing, hospital and school sites.
Local authorities could then be left with small-scale environmental
management tasks. The Land Authority for Wales could be considered as a
partial prototype for such agencies.

Development plans indicating the amount and general location of land for
industrial activity would not be necessary to support the work of such
agencies, since they would be aiming to match demand and sites, and would
effectively have a major role in infrastructure provision. However, these
agencies would be public bureaucracies and would need to be evidently
accountable at least to production interests as a whole. To legitimate its
activities, therefore, we might expect agencies to produce annual
statements of policies to accompany statements of accounts. To manage
particular projects, however, site-specific development guidance such as
some form of local plan or development brief would often prove useful.

A LAND POLICY FOR INDUSTRIAL DEVELOPMENT

Rationale for intervention	The need to make low-cost land and premises available for industrial production; ameliorating adverse externality costs and encouraging benefits.
Intervention strategy	The state to provide sites efficiently, quickly and in response to demand, with financial and infrastructure support as necessary; public ownership of development land.
Institutional arrangements	Regional Land Development Agencies, with powers to acquire, sell and lease land, and resources for land purchase and clearance, infrastructure provision (on site and strategic), and powers to provide advice and financial assistance to firms in site search and purchase/leasing. Agencies to consist of appointed boards with representatives of industry as significant members.
Mode of operation	Technical teams providing R & I services; assessment of projects; project management. Consultation and negotiation over specific proposals between the agency and firms.
Legitimation problems	Challenges from: consumption interests and environmentalists; LDA's could provide cheap land for consumption activities; publicly-prepared plans and inquiries might be demanded to reduce over-emphasis on production. Production of property would be reduced to building/ construction as opposed to land development activities.

This strategy would face two major problems. The first would relate to the cost of land. So long as development land remained in private ownership, such agencies would tend to channel funds into the hands of those who owned the sites which the agency purchased. This in turn would militate against providing low-cost sites. Agencies would either have to receive significant subsidies for land purchase, or be in a position to purchase land cheaply. A more radical but possibly more effective alternative would be to revive the provisions of the Community Land Act for the public ownership of development land. The Land Development Agencies could then play a key role in implementing these provisions.

Such a strategy would be antipathetic to many of those engaged in the production of property. In effect, the Land Development Agency would be taking over the functions of developers, property companies and development agents. Firm measures to prevent these withholding land until a change of government occurred would be needed. But the strategy would also be suspected by those requiring land and property for social purposes and by those anxious to conserve the environment. In other words, the strategy would face a considerable legitimation problem. This could be reduced by attempting to construct common ground with "social consumption" interests, notably space for housing, social and community facilities and recreational facilities. Land Development Agencies could possibly extend their role to providing land and premises for consumption as well as production purposes which would be considerably assisted by public development land ownership. However, there would always be suspicion as to the weight given in agency expenditure to consumption over production interests, and to different localities. The accountability of agencies would thus be a contentious issue, with demands for consultation over policies and programme. In these demands, formal statements of policies and programmes might come to play a significant legitimating role. To both social consumption interests, and the environmentalists, a technical and negotiative mode of operation might be open to considerable criticism as its "hidden" nature would make it difficult to monitor the way their interests were protected. Attention might come to focus on decisions about the location and design of larger industrial projects, which could lead to requirements for environmental impact statements and a public inquiry for every such project. In other words, the construction of the public interest might have to take place on a case-by-case basis, and in public (see Chapter 2). This would, of course, reduce the capacity of agencies to be responsive to the needs of firms.

This ideal type thus involves the state in a substantial role in land development itself, operating largely through technical and negotiative arrangements, but with some acknowledgement of the need to legitimize the state's activities by public discussion of policy, and semi-judicial inquiries into projects. Local authorities might be left with a residual development control function, dealing with small scale externalities (justification 1, Chapter 1). The main losers in these arrangements would be those engaged in the production of property.

B. *Land Policies to Support the Production of Property*

It could be argued that the best state strategy to support property development is the removal of all intervention. Yet most property interests do not argue for this, and I have presented in Chapter 9 some reasons why regulation may actually benefit those with property development interests. What these interests appear to demand is government help with land assembly and infrastructure provision, and a locational framework which makes

A LAND POLICY TO SUPPORT PROPERTY PRODUCTION

Rationale for intervention	The provision of infrastructure, assistance with land assembly, and provision of a framework which allocates development status to land.
Intervention strategy	Finance for infrastructure provision, powers and finance for land assembly; development plans and/ or zoning ordinances to provide the regulative framework; possibly taxation of development to finance the above.
Institutional arrangements	Regional planning and development agencies, with powers and finance for land assembly and infrastructure provision, and a requirement to prepare plans in consultation with developers. Appointed boards, with strong development interest representation.
Mode of operation	Consultative, with property firms advising the boards on general policy, and consulting over specific projects.
Legitimation problems	Suspicion by industrial production and consumption interests that property firms were accumulating too much profit to themselves rather than providing low-cost land/premises. Environmentalists would suspect the emphasis on development *per se*. Consequently, there would be demands for public consultation and participation in plan preparation. This strategy is unlikely to succeed unless "hidden" within other arrangements.

generous allocations of land for development, but yet does not leave the task of determining the development status of land to the uncertainty of the market. It is likely that such interests would welcome regional agencies which both draw up such frameworks, development plans perhaps, in close consultation with property development firms, and had the resources for land assembly and infrastructure provision. Regional agencies would be favoured to ensure greater efficiency, and to avoid the influence of local interests which might take an antagonistic position towards property firms.

Some building and construction firms might accept the kind of arrangements outlined in (A) since these would inevitably create work for them. However, those firms engaged in bringing land forward for development, or transforming land and property from one form of development to another would be eliminated by the sort of land development agencies I have described. These interests would argue that public agencies do not have the experience and flexibility to respond to market conditions which their own operations in their view possess. Regional land planning agencies linked to a land servicing role would probably be acceptable, as well as some form of tax on development gain. The British Property Federation (1976) argued for this so long as the proceeds were spent directly on land servicing, a more formalized arrangement for developers' contributions. However, the House Builders Federation (1977) argue that this cost should fall on taxpayers in general, since the country benefits from "development".

This type then has a regulative form, backed by resources for infrastructure, and operated by regional agencies. These agencies would have a close relationship with property development firms, although with some autonomy since firms are in competition with each other both within and between regions. Their style, however, would be consultative, with assessments of demand and land allocation requirements made by drawing on the expertise of private firms rather than attempting technical assessments of market trends. It is possible that such agencies could develop an information role in demand analysis and marketing for property firms. Some kind of organizing spatial framework might be required to supplement the regulatory function, its main purpose being to prevent the land planning agencies from exercising too much discretion on their own account. Planning frameworks similar to US zoning ordinances might be desirable, giving firms the right to develop once land has been allocated in principle. As in the US, and other situations where definitive legal allocations are made, it is likely that few developments would in the end fit precisely the allocations made, with considerable further negotiation a common practice, depending on the specificity of the regulative framework. Another alternative might be local plans such as we now have them giving clear zonings for major uses, with special development orders to allow the developer discretion in how the sites are actually developed, as suggested in the DoE's discussion note on special development orders in 1981[87]. However, the pressure for simplification of any necessary bureaucratic procedures would probably be a constant in this sort of arrangement, with individual firms seeking flexibility within a framework which they themselves support for the collectivity of firms.

Property development firms will always argue that their role is instrumental to industrial production and consumption activities and that they provide a necessary service. Their critics accuse them of manipulating market demand for land and property into channels most profitable to themselves. In other words, the wrong sort of property is being provided in the wrong places at the wrong times at excessive cost. Of course, this could never be entirely true as property development firms would go out of business. Yet at various times their operations have contributed to land price inflation, which is then passed on in property prices. Firms have also tended to concentrate on what in the short term has seemed to be the most profitable type of property, the mass production of houses and premises which may be obsolete in a few years' time. This has arisen increasingly as property firms have developed speculatively, rather than for specific occupants, often leading to the over-production of particular types of space. Firms rarely have to pay the costs of this, since vacant space concentrates in the existing rather than new stock. As a result, the legitimacy of this type of land policy is likely to be vigorously challenged by other production and consumption lobbies and environmentalists. To some extent, property interests have been able to "hide" the pursuance of their interests within the operations of local planning authorities, which purport to balance different interests to achieve a public interest calculus. However, the challenges to the legitimacy of a state strategy of land intervention which primarily supported property development would probably be so great that only a government which sought to regenerate the economy through property development could contemplate it. Thus, the interests of property development may either continue to "hide" within whatever arrangements are established for other purposes, or be effectively squeezed into a genuinely instrumentalist role.

---

[87]In a letter to local authorities of 10 June 1981.

A LAND POLICY FOR CONSUMPTION ACTIVITIES

Rationale for intervention	The provision of land and premises for activities and services which provide for the material and cultural needs of individuals.
Intervention strategy	The provision of cheap land and premises; a mechanism for allocating land and premises among competing interests; a mechanism for ensuring positive use of all land; public ownership of development land.
Institutional arrangements	Local authorities (districts) with powers and finance to engage in "community estate management". Possibly also provides infrastructure, or may use regional agencies. Central government may provide differential subsidy from general taxation.
Mode of operation	Political articulation by local councils, supplemented by pressure groups, or in favourable circumstances, "participatory" politics; technical staff skilled in working with local groups to realize their ideas. Plans to express agreed compromises.
Legitimation problems	Industrial production interests would increase the efficiency with which their needs were satisfied; environmentalist would suspect the extent to which environmental conservation was given priority. Property production interests would oppose generally and make accusations of inefficiency.

However, the property business is not by any means static in its organization and ways of operating, as recent history has shown. Recently, two significant and related tendencies are emerging which could alter the demands this sector might put on government agencies. The first is the increasing concentration within the industry, with property production being absorbed as one activity within large multi-sector international companies. The second is the growing involvement of financial institutions in the property business. As a result, the medium-sized builder-developers which dominated the building industry some years ago, appear to be being squeezed out (Ball 1982). Large companies and the financial institutions are more interested in long-term returns than short-term profitability. It may be that the conflict between those wanting cheap sites and those seeking to maximize returns in property production will be removed by these trends. This is unlikely to happen so long as land and property carry investment attractions which are not directly relatable to the short term demand for space.

C. *Land Policies to Support Consumption Activities*

The justification for government intervention here is to ensure that land and premises are available for all the various activities and services which provide for people's needs and make up their living environment (see justification 4, Chapter 1). The extent of the state's role in this consumption sphere and the priorities within it will depend on the overall emphasis on consumption activities in any state strategy. Whatever the strategy, however, its realization will be greatly assisted by access to cheap sites and help with site servicing. There can be no doubt that access to cheap land has been a significant constraint on public housing programmes in the past, on the provision of many other facilities, including recreation and amenity space. In the competition for sites which currently occurs, consumption activities tend to get relegated to residual sites, unless a local authority has a long history of land banking. Even then, the ownership by authorities of large development sites often leads to concentrations of public development which, in a mixed economy, may itself create disadvantages for those who live there.

I have suggested, under strategy (A), that some form of public ownership of development land would ease the problem of land costs, though it would not necessarily produce cheap property as land values would become absorbed into property values. For many small-scale community purposes, it is access to premises rather than land which is most important. There is also the problem of determining priorities among a multitude of consumption activities, the demand for which is in any case mediated by government at present through the flow of finance to them as part of state programmes for housing, health, education and social welfare.

Combined with public ownership of development land, some form of community management of land and premises would be desirable. Such a capacity for *community estate management* might help to ensure that land and premises could be found for activities of all kinds, without the blighting effects of reserving sites for particular but unpredictable funded needs. The role of community estate management would be to find sites for community needs, provide buildings and spaces needed for collective activities to undertake environmental improvement works as necessary and ensure infrastructure provision. Just as the major social services programmes are subsidized, the money currently flowing into derelict land and environmental improvement programmes could be merged into a subsidized estate management budget. Such an activity could be an arm of the regional land development agencies discussed under (A). However, much of the detailed allocation of space to activities in localities involves the kind of detailed and sympathetic local knowledge more appropriate to neighbourhood and parish councils than regional agencies. It is possible that a land and environment budget, as well as the development of large projects, could be allocated to the regional level. However, community estate management probably operates more effectively at the level of local authority districts or smaller. Communities can then determine priorities between activities and the balance between technical assessment of ideas and schemes, bureaucratic provision and the involvement of community groups and individuals.

I am thus suggesting that the support of consumption activities leads to local programmes for providing land and premises for the various, often-competing community interests, but with more coherence than is provided by the present sectoral divisions within local authorities which separate planning departments from estates departments and which divide a local authority's view of its landholdings into separate activity categories. This coherence is what many local plans attempt to provide but without the powers to produce it. Probably the only way to do this is by combining the planning function, in the sense of developing a coherent view of the community estate, with the acquisition and disposal of land for the authority as a whole, and with funds for improvement works.

However, any such land and planning function, or planning and estate management function, would be inevitably criticized on different grounds by

each of the competing community interests. The agency or local authority
department performing this function would have to demonstrate to them that
its interpretation of the collective community interest was legitimate. A
technical input to this determination might have some role, but at this
level, local citizens are as likely to have good ideas on needs and how
they could be met as experts. The kind of expertise needed, if any, is more
likely to be assisting individuals and groups to realize projects and ideas,
than skills in analysis or the management of large development projects; a
kind of environmental social worker rather than an analyst or project
manager.

It may be argued that the normal operation of representative democracy as
evident in British local government provides the only way to establish the
legitimacy of community estate management of this type. However, this may
be challenged by those who seek more direct involvement of citizens in
their communities, as opposed to the articulation of their interests in a
local political party and pressure groups. It is here that we begin to
arrive at the image of participation which attracted the more radical of
planners in the late 1960s, and those arguing for more decentralization
away from large state bureaucracies in the late 1970s. Some people will
always argue that there should be no formal organizational structure for
articulating interests at this scale, allowing individuals freedom from
organization. However, it is difficult to avoid recognizing the need for
some form of interest articulation in all but the smallest units of
social relations. The key argument is likely to be whether this
articulation should relate to interest groups, or to areas (as in
proposals for strengthening parish councils, e.g. SDP 1982), or both.

However, a local community estate management function, though attractive to
many in favour of decentralization and an escape from bureaucracy, would
suffer not only from internal conflicts as different interests attempted to
establish their priorities as the basis for community programmes. It would
also be threatened on the one hand by production interests who would
challenge the efficiency of decision-making in such a participatory-
consultative way and on the other by environmentalists who might contend
that the cultural heritage was not something which could be weighed in the
balance with other priorities in a utilitarian way (see Allison 1975). In
effect both production and environmentalist interests would argue that, in
the national interest, or the interest of particular values such as the
need for a sound productive base to the economy or the conservation of a
cultural heritage, local discretion to establish priorities would have to
be constrained. In addition, it could be argued that in order to protect
the consumption interests in one area, perhaps with limited resources, the
discretion of those in another area should be limited, (although it might
be possible to deal with this problem by differential subsidies to
localities). In effect, this would re-impose those constraints which are
currently pursued in part and ineffectively through the medium of structure
and local plans. An alternative, if for example weight were to be given
to industrial and production interests, would be to deal with production
projects through the means of a regional land development agency as in (A),
with both public inquiries into projects at which local communities could
make strong representation, and a system of compensation for any losses
the community might incur through being asked to accept major projects for
non-local interests.

D. *Land Policy for Environmental Conservation*

As O'Riordan (1977) and Stretton (1976) have pointed out, the environmental
movement, although rooted in the middle classes in western economies,

A LAND POLICY FOR ENVIRONMENTAL PROTECTION

Rationale for intervention	To conserve the country's urban and rural architectural, archaeological, landscape and wildlife heritage.
Intervention strategy	Regulation of development to protect the heritage; finance for maintaining it.
Institutional arrangements	National specialist bodies, with finance for conservation purposes. Development plans/zoning ordinances drawn up by regional planning boards in consultation with national bodies. Local authorities to implement the plans. Individuals to seek grants from national bodies, with regional bodies with powers to impose maintenance requirements.
Mode of operation	Elitist and technical in the national bodies and regional boards; bureaucratic in local authorities.
Legitimation problems	Production and consumption interests would resist: a) any absolute limitation on space requirements; b) resultant cost of land; c) location of specific sites/projects consequent upon giving environmental values high priority.

includes ideological positions which co-exist uncomfortably. Some support the need for local community control of the environment on the lines suggested in (C). Others are seeking for the long-term conservation of resources to ensure their availability for production in the future, which links them to (A). Meanwhile, those stressing the need to conserve a cultural heritage, a form of large-scale management of our national estate in its traditional form, look to the involvement of national bodies which enshrine the values which express this culture. These ideas could lead to the widespread definition of zones of special cultural, landscape, historic or architectural protection supplemented by specification of sites and buildings for protection, with national bodies such as the Council for the Preservation of Rural England, Historic Buildings Society, Victorian Society, the Georgian Society and others playing a major role in their definition.

This might be supplemented by a system of grants to ensure maintenance and positive use of the sites, buildings and environment thus protected. On the principle that advice is more powerful when backed by resources, the national bodies could become the dispensers of grants to individual land and property owners. It could be argued that the latter should maintain their property themselves. Past experience has shown this to be an often vain hope. If a government wished to give special weight to heritage conservation, it should be prepared to subsidize private individuals for the costs such conservation involves, and to enforce maintenance where necessary, unless of course our major economic activity became the "production" of heritage for the world to enjoy. In such a case, the task of "provision" and recovery of the income so generated might be divided between individuals and the state. Elements of all the above can be found in the present ways in which heritage sites, buildings and environments are protected and managed.

Clearly, some form of regulation of development and demolition proposals
would be needed to ensure compliance with the zonings of environments and
specifications of sites. Clear plans specifying the zonings and sites would
provide a basis for such regulation. Such plans should have the effect of
limiting the discretion of the regulating agencies so that other interests
could not distort the principles and policies devised for environmental
protection. It is possible that U.S.-style zoning ordinances with their
appearance of legal certainty might be preferred to the present British
discretionery arrangements, so long as the kind of hidden flexibility in
zoning ordinances via innumerable variations could be resisted. In this
context, it is of interest that the extension of planning and zoning
ordinances in the U.S. in the past decade has been associated with the
growth of concern with environmental conservation. Conservation groups in
this country have similarly stressed the importance of local (i.e. detailed)
land allocation plans (e.g. CPRE 1981; Countryside Review Committee 1979).

As noted under (C), some hesitancy might be expected in allocating the role
of preparing such plans and exercising regulatory powers to small
localities, since these might not necessarily have the competence to assess
cultural heritage priorities or the political will to give them sufficient
weight. As suggested above, they might also be vulnerable to corruption.
A possible way out of this would be to have regional planning boards which
draw up plans in consultation with the national bodies, and which exercised
directly, or through smaller boards, powers to regulate development. For
natural justice purposes, inquiries against refusals to allow development
might be retained. Equally, for larger developments, inquiries might be
held to assess the environmental impact of proposals, with third parties
able to make formal objections. National bodies might then regularly enter
the arena of detailed decision-making as third parties (as they do in Eire).
In other words, local authorities would require close monitoring to ensure
they acted as effective agents of the environmental interest in plan
implementation.

This is essentially an elitist, paternalist form of interest mediation, in
which particular sorts of cultural heritage experts would in practice define
the content of land policy, by providing definitive interpretation of what
constituted the heritage to be protected. It would constrain both the
negotiative consultation of productive activities and intergroup consultation
of consumption activities. Consequently, it would be challenged by both.
However, it is possible to envisage some form of accommodation between the
principles of this type, and types (A) and (C), essentially by limiting the
scale of zonings, and of site and building specifications. In judgements
relating to these specified zones and sites, specialist national judgements
would be applied. Outside, they might be weighed in the balance with other
factors. To some extent, this two-tier system has been encouraged by the
present government's amendments to the General Development Order, which
makes regulation more restrictive in special environmental areas, while
attempting to limit the numbers of these. Elsewhere, regulation has been
made less restrictive.

4. A LAND POLICY FOR ECONOMIC REVIVAL?

The ideal types I have presented are obviously gross over-simplifications
both of the demands of the different interest groups and the way these might
be realized in a land policy. They may also reflect the bias in my own
knowledge towards southern Britain. Nevertheless, they illustrate a way of

thinking about land strategies which in my view would lead to more productive debate on land policy and land use planning than we have had in recent years.

There are several points of overlap between the different strategies arising partly because common interests may exist between the different groups represented by the ideal types, and partly because of the legitimation needs of each strategy. Thus I suggest that both types of production-based strategy emphasize regional agencies and a negotiative/consultative mode of operation. Only the social consumption strategy develops a strong emphasis on local involvement in defining and implementing policies and priorities. In contrast, the emphasis in the strategies for industrial production and social consumption are on direct public investment in the provision of facilities, while for property production the public sector's direct investment role is limited to the provision of serviced land. In effect, the industrial production and social consumption strategies would benefit by the nationalization not only of development land but of the property development business, squeezing out the property developer. Finally, mechanisms to ensure adequate accountability are necessary for all the strategies, although the form and purpose of these varies.

Publicly-available development plans, as noted in Chapter 1, are a multi-functional tool. Thus in the industrial production strategy, their role is for accountability purposes. Development briefs might be more appropriate for the management of specific projects. In the property production strategy, development plans would be prepared in consultation with developers, though for legitimation purposes token exercises in wider consultation might be necessary. The social consumption strategy involves the articulation of a wide variety of different interests. The collective preparation of a plan could provide a mechanism to articulate these. For environmental protection, a clear site-specific plan would be essential to define sites, buildings and areas to be protected. I conclude therefore that public development plans are likely to be a feature of any land policy in Britain in the future. But what their form should be and what procedures should surround their preparation will depend on the direction of land policy as a whole.

So what might this direction be? One possibility is a continuation of the tendencies in the past ten years which have *in practice* emphasized facilitating property production. The present Conservative government's strategy of adapting the regulatory powers of the planning system to support the property industry, while attempting to legitimate it to environmental interests is in effect the established land policy of this country. Yet it is a strategy which presupposes continuing economic growth to sustain the demand for property, and its relevance is now probably limited to the non-conurbation areas of southern Britain. Even the present government is having to invent different policies for areas of severe economic decline, and to support a property industry which is itself suffering from recession.

The other parties have given little coherent attention recently to the land policy field as a whole. The Labour Party appears at last to be relating land and planning together again, possibly, in response to the 1980 Local Government, Planning and Land Act. A recent discussion paper emphasizes the need for "comprehensive" planning, relating economic, social and physical policy at all levels of government; the importance of "maximum" public

involvement in all planning decisions and the public accountability of all
public sector organizations; the need for more provision by the public
sector in social services and facilities ("community infrastructure"); and
ensuring that land and property are not regarded as "commodities" but as
"opportunities" with which to meet community needs. Exactly what sort of
land ownership policy is needed to achieve this has not yet been determined.
There is no suggestion that the system of development plans should be
altered however, although supplemented at the strategic level by regional
plans, and at the local level by finance linked to local plan proposals and
"programme statements" to indicate priorities and responsibilities, a form
of implementation schedule[88].

The rhetoric of this approach is similar to my own social consumption
strategy, but there is little sign that there has been as yet any real
review of the land use elements of a land policy. The Social Democrats
similarly appear to be taking much of the "town and country planning" area
for granted. Their recent discussion paper on *Decentralising Government*
(SDP 1982) proposes the introduction of elected regional authorities to take
over many of central government's functions in the economic and social
spheres, including town and country planning. It suggests that these are
supplemented by regional development corporations, which might have town and
country planning functions delegated to them. These are comparable to my
suggested regional land development agencies. Below the regional
authorities, a single tier of local government would replace the two-tier
arrangements, with a substructure of community councils developing out of
the present parish council role. The present bits of the planning system
are thus to be shuffled among revised levels of government. My conclusion
is that this approach is not dissimilar to the two of my ideal types which
support production interests, with a nod in the direction of "public
involvement".

In my view, this continued tinkering around the edges of land policy is
not enough. Our economy is now very different from that of the 1940s when
the planning system as we now have it was designed. None of the changes
to it have adequately reflected the economic and social changes that have
taken place since the war in terms of their implications for demands and
needs for land. As a result, it has not been difficult for those with a
direct interest in land, its use and development, i.e. the property
industry, to exercise a pervasive influence on the practice of planning.
As a result of this, and of the weakened capacity for direct state
involvement in the provision of land and buildings, the users and consumers
of space, industrial production and social consumption interests have been
distanced from control over the location, price and design of that space.

This state of affairs is not conducive to economic revival or social
harmony. As public sector efforts flow into providing serviced land on
which new industrial units can be built, financed by investment companies,
many small firms starting up can still not find cheap enough premises. As
assistance is given to the private housebuilder, environmental and social
welfare groups challenge policies which neither protect environmental
heritage adequately nor provide cheap enough housing. Interest groups and
political parties recognize this but fail to appreciate that to alter the
planning system requires not only alterations to levels of government
responsibility and formal accountability mechanisms but a radical review of

---

[88]See the discussion document *Labour's Programme* published in Labour Weekly
June 1982, as summarized in *Planning* Newspaper No. 476, 9.7.82.

the mode of operation of the planning system, and in particular, how the considerable administrative discretion within it is actually used.

There can be no doubt that the political priority of national, regional and local governments for the rest of this century is going to be on economic revival. For this reason, developing a land policy to support industrial production should be a priority. My ideal type (A) suggests the direction, both in content and institutional arrangements and procedures, which such a policy might take. Exactly how land policy develops to support industrial production will of course depend on the specific approach taken to economic revival. Significant variations in the weight given to the economic sectors given priority, the type and size of firms encouraged, whether the state engages in industrial production itself or provides various sorts of financial incentives and the extent of spatial discrimination within and between regions could lead to differences in what the state does in the land policy field and how its initiatives are organized.

However, ultimately, the purpose of any economic revival in a democracy is to provide the conditions in which everyone can have a reasonable existence. Economic revival by itself will not ensure this, as dominant classes will appropriate the wealth created to themselves. Whether and how such an outcome is avoided will depend on who controls government. In my view, it will be essential to construct a land policy which both *supports* industrial production and *ensures* the provision of the infrastructure of land and buildings needed to support the variety of social consumption activities which people need and are entitled to have access to. Bearing in mind that some social consumption expenditure is in any case necessary to support the labour force involved in industrial production (see Chapter 9), it will be important to guarantee that both "social capital" and "social expenses" consumption is allowed for. I suggest that local community estate management on the lines of ideal type (C) might be worth considering in this context, as an adjunct to strategies for promoting industrial production.

These two tendencies, to support industrial production *and* social consumption, already exist in British land policy. If the explanations offered in Chapter 9 for the form and content of land policy are valid, such tendencies would in any case be expected. My argument is that within the land policy area in Britain we have for many years given far too much attention, firstly to the environmental lobby, and secondly, and more seriously, to the property interest. There can be no doubt that our environmental heritage is an asset both in material and non-material terms. But it is unacceptable that the protection of this heritage should allow class divisions to manifest themselves so clearly between those who can get access to such heritage environments, and those who cannot[89]. Some degree of environmental protection is justifiable in the national interest, but local extensions of these to protect middle class enclaves are not.

Finally, I have little sympathy with the special treatment that the property developer has received in the operation of the planning system in recent years, nor with the need for double protection of the interests of those with property, who can object both to general proposals which affect their property and to specific projects. The rights of individuals with

---

[89]I can claim such access, for example, living in a village in South Oxfordshire near the Thames, a conserved small town and with a view over an AONB.

property interests, which would still exist as occupancy rights even if land
and property were nationalized, could be adequately protected by a system
of inquiries into projects and a right to compensation up to a certain
limit where owners are adversely affected by a project.

There seems no reason to suppose that public property development could not
be as effective as private development, despite the vociferous claims to
the contrary by the property lobby. Ideally, it could be both more effective
and cheaper; the property sector in any case has an organization and
history which is specific to the historical circumstances of this country
and its structure is very responsive to changes in economic
opportunities and government policy. It is currently changing in response
to the increasing role within it of multi-national companies and the
financial institutions. A major reform of the way we organize property
development in this country, with a much stronger role for the public
sector, may well be an attractive prospect to these multi-nationals if it
could contribute to drawing Britain out of prolonged recession. Just as
Massey and Catalano (1978) concluded that few interests really stood to lose
by the Community Land Act, so the squeezing out of the property sector's
development role could benefit many interests at the present time.

5. THE WIDER RELEVANCE OF THE BRITISH EXPERIENCE OF LAND POLICY

Britain has a very considerable reputation internationally for its
initiatives in the land policy field, both for the radical nature of the
legislation embodied in the 1947 Act (see Chapter 2) and for the new town's
programme. For this reason, and because many former colonies have
legislation in the planning field based on the British model, this
country still attracts people from overseas who wish to learn from our
planning experience. Yet in this account of local plans in the British
land use planning system, I have stressed that little is left of the
radical legislation and that in any case its particular form and the mode
of operation is *historically specific* to Britain in the second half of the
twentieth century. Although certain general tendencies in land policy
which might be expected in developed western economies can be identified
(see Chapter 9), the form in which they are realized is specific to
Britain's distinctive economic and political history and its cultural
traditions. Reflecting this distinctiveness, among the peculiar
characteristics of British land policy are the significant role for both
central and local government, the degree of administrative discretion in the
planning system, the size and scale of the property development industry,
and the strength of the concern to preserve particular types of urban and
rural landscape. This book should therefore encourage skepticism about the
relevance to anywhere else of any method or procedure developed in the
British context. The discussion in this chapter in any case suggests that
many of the methods and procedures currently used in Britain have lost any
relevance they may have had. I would suggest, however, that this study
offers more than just a warning against the naive transfer of ideas.

Firstly, it is of value as a case study, to be contrasted with examples of
the operation of land policies in other western capitalist economies.
There is now considerable interest in such comparative studies as academics
and policy-makers seek to understand the nature of the fundamental changes
which such economies are experiencing[90]. However, although interesting as

90 See for example Clawson and Hall 1973; ed Hayward and Watson 1975, ed
   Roberts 1977, ed Koenigsberger and Groak 1980, ed Cullen and Wooley 1982,
   and Lichfield and Darin-Drabkin 1980 (appendix).

descriptive accounts, these comparisons rarely do more than highlight similarities and differences. In other words, they lack a framework within which to identify and analyse the distinctive characteristics of each country's experience and the reasons for these.

The second contribution of this book has therefore been to provide such a framework, in three ways. Firstly, I have argued that we need to locate accounts of the operation of any part of a land policy within an appreciation of its purposes, and its powers, procedures and modes of operation (Chapter 1), and how these have evolved over time (Chapter 2). Secondly, I have stressed that to develop such an appreciation it is not enough to examine formally-expressed intentions (Chapters 3 and 4). It is essential to examine how powers and procedures are actually used, and what their outcome has been (Part III). Thirdly, I offer in Chapter 9 some ideas about the processes which underlie the form and content of British land policy.

As already noted, some of the tendencies identified are likely to be found operating in other developed capitalist economies. The third contribution of this book, therefore, lies in its approach to explanation. Although, as I noted in Chapter 9, there is an expanding literature on the role of the state in the urban and regional development field, these are either general accounts or case studies. There have been few accounts of the operation of land policy powers and procedures, either in this country or elsewhere, which have been related to the theoretical developments in the political economy field. However, I have tried to show in Chapter 9 that valuable insights into the problem of developing and complementing land policies can be developed by this form of analysis, and in Chapter 10 I illustrate how analysis can be used as a basis for prescription, although clearly the interest groupings and the strategies I suggest are specific to Britain.

Finally, in the course of discussing the way local plans are prepared and used, I raise a number of methodological points which are likely to recur in the land-policy field. Examples include the ways in which development processes, needs and opportunities are analysed; the ways in which social and economic processes are related to space requirements and sites; the problems of constructing site-specific policy guidance which allows both public review of policy and flexibility to accommodate the individuality of development initiatives. Although methodological and procedural questions of this kind dominated the discussion of planning, both in Britain and many other countries, it was conducted at an institutionally-abstract level. There has been much less detailed guidance on how to address these methodological questions in specific institutional contexts. Further detailed studies of this kind could provide a basis for more relevant methodological generalizations in the land policy field than have so far been available.

To conclude, I present this book not only as a contribution to the evaluation of British land policy practice and to discussion about its future, but as a model of the sort of historically-specific investigation that is needed in the land policy field generally, and as a contribution to the development of theoretically-based explanation and prescription within this area of public policy.

Structure Plan Functions and Content: Official Statements

1. PAG REPORT: THE FUTURE OF DEVELOPMENT PLANS (MHLG 1965) (PARA 2.6)

The Purpose of an "Urban Plan"

"(1) set out the local planning authority's main objectives and policies for the development and redevelopment of the town, and bring these before the public and the Minister;

(2) clarify the physical structure of the town, with special emphasis on the communications network and main traffic generators, the grouping of environmental areas and the general form and direction of the town's future growth and renewal, including the policy for the town centre;

(3) define the transport policy for the town, including the relationship between public and private transport and the reconciliation of accessibility and environmental standards;

(4) concentrate on these elements to the exclusion of less essential detail, and to present to the Minister for approval only those policies and proposals that are of real significance and importance.

(5) provide a realistic basis for detailed planning in the areas where major changes are intended over the next ten years or so;

(6) provide a policy framework for development control;

(7) be in a form which facilitates its preparation, approval, continuous revision and amendment."

2. THE DEVELOPMENT PLANS MANUAL (DoE 1970) (PARA 3.10)

"Structure plans: functions

3.10 The structure plan performs the seven closely-related functions

set out below; what they mean for form, content and presentation
is dealt with later in the manual:

1. Interpreting national and regional policies
   Structure plans must be prepared within the framework set by
   national and regional policies. They interpret these policies
   in terms appropriate to the area in question (4.4-4.5)

2. Establishing aims, policies and general proposals
   The structure plan should contain a statement of the planning
   authority's aims for the area (4.11), and the strategy,
   policies and general proposals which are designed to achieve
   these aims (4.12-4.17).

3. Providing framework for local plans
   Just as structure plans are prepared within the context of
   national and regional policies, so they set the context within
   which local plans must be prepared. Thus the broad policies
   and proposals in the structure plans form a framework for the
   more detailed policies and proposals in local plans.

4. Indicating action areas
   In particular, the structure plan should indicate the action
   areas and the nature of their treatment. These are the priority
   areas for intensive action. Like other local plans, action area
   plans cannot be put on deposit or adopted, though they can be
   prepared, before the Minister has approved the structure plan.
   But the procedure differs from that for other local plans in
   that the authority's general proposals for comprehensive
   treatment must have been included in the approved structure
   plan, or in an approved amendment to it; the preparation of
   the action area plan is then obligatory (4.21-4.22).

5. Providing guidance for development control
   Local plans provide detailed guidance on development control.
   But a universal coverage of local plans is likely to take many
   years to achieve and may even be unnecessary. In these parts
   of the area not covered, or not yet covered, by a local plan,
   the structure plan will provide the basis for development
   control (3.14) (in association with the 1962 Act development
   plan whilst that is continued in force as a transitional
   measure).

6. Providing basis for co-ordinating decisions
   The preparatory stages of the plan will provide a forum for
   discussion between the various committees of the planning
   authority and district councils who deal with, for example,
   housing, roads and open spaces; they will also offer an
   opportunity to bring together, through consultation and
   negotiation, other public bodies such as statutory undertakers,
   river authorities and regional hospital boards, who are likely
   to be concerned with important aspects of the plan. Later,
   the structure plan itself will provide a co-ordinated basis
   upon which these various interests can develop the individual
   programmes of work for which they have executive responsibility.

7. Bringing main planning issues and decisions before Minister and
   public
   The structure plan will be the means of bringing the authority's

intentions, and the reasoning behind those intentions (3.12) to
the attention of the Minister and the public."

3. DoE CIRCULAR 98/74 STRUCTURE PLANS (PARA 3)

"The Functions of Structure Plans

3. Structure plans have three main functions:

a. To state and justify, to the public and to the Secretary of State,
the authority's policies and general proposals for the development
and other use of land in the area concerned (including measures for
the improvement of the physical environment and the management of
traffic), and thus provide guidance for development (including
development control) on issues of structural importance.

An issue is a matter which requires a choice between two or more
possible policies (e.g. concentration v dispersal): an issue of
structural importance is a matter on which the choice made will
affect either the whole, or a substantial part, of the area
concerned.

b. To interpret national and regional policies in terms of physical
and environmental planning for the area concerned.

National and regional policies tend to be primarily economic and
social (though they also include an important physical and
environmental content): structure plans represent the stage in
planning at which such policies are integrated with the economic
social and environmental policies of the county and expressed in
terms of their effect on land use, environmental development and
the associated transportation system. (The material on economic
and social policies in the written statement should therefore be
limited to those policies which have implications for land use,
environmental development or transportation.)

c. To provide the framework and statutory basis for local plans, which
then in turn provide the necessary further guidance for development
control at the more detailed, local level.

Without a background of up-to-date structure and local plans,
development control can deteriorate into a series of confusing
ad hoc and unrelated decisions. Conversely, up-to-date plans
would give developers clear guidance, and save much unnecessary
work for both developers and local authorities on planning
applications."

4. 1974 STRUCTURE AND LOCAL PLAN REGULATIONS (DoE 1974 SI No.1486)
   (Schedule 1)

"Part I: Matters to Which Policy is Required to Relate by Regulation 9(1)

The matters to which the policy formulated in a structure plan written
statement is required to relate by regulation 9(1) are such of the following
matters as the county planning authority may think appropriate:

(i)   Distribution of population and employment

(ii)   Housing

(iii)   Industry and commerce

(iv)   Transportation

(v)   Shopping

(vi)   Education

(vii)   Other social and community services

(viii) Recreation and leisure

(ix)   Conservation, townscape and landscape

(x)   Utility services

(xi)   Any other relevant matters

Part II: Matters Required by Regulation 10 to be Contained in Written Statement

The matters required by regulation 10 to be contained in a structure plan written statement are such indications as the county planning authority may think appropriate of the following:

(i)   The existing structure of the area to which the plan relates and the present needs and opportunities for change.

(ii)   Any changes already projected, or likely to occur, which may materially affect matters dealt with in the plan, and the effect those changes are likely to have.

(iii)   The effect (if any) on the area of the plan of any proposal to make an order under section 1 of the New Towns Act 1965 (designation of sites of new towns) or of any order made or having effect as if made under section 1 of the New Towns Act 1965 or of any known intentions of a development corporation established in pursuance of such an order.

(iv)   The extent (if any) to which town development within the meaning of the Town Development Act 1952 is being, or is to be, carried out in the area to which the plan relates.

(v)   The existing size, composition and distribution of population and state of employment in the area to which the plan relates, and estimates of these matters at such future times as the county planning authority think relevant in formulating the policies of the plan, together with the assumption on which the estimates are based.

(vi)   The regard the county planning authority have had to the current policies with respect to the economic planning and development of the region as a whole.

(vii)   The regard the county planning authority have had to social policies and considerations.

(viii) The regard the county planning authority have had to the

2

resources likely to be available for carrying out the policy and general proposals formulated in the plan.

(ix)   The broad criteria to be applied as respects the control of development in the area, or any part of the area, to which the plan relates.

(x)   The extent and nature of the relationship between the policies formulated in the plan.

(xi)   The considerations underlying any major items of policy formulated in the plan as respects matters of common interest to the county planning authority by whom the plan is prepared and the county planning authorities for neighbouring areas, and the extent to which those major items have been agreed by the authorities concerned.

(xii) Any other relevant matters."

5. DoE CIRCULAR 4/79: MEMORANDUM ON STRUCTURE AND LOCAL PLANS (PARA 2.1)

"The Structure Plan Functions

2.1 The structure plan has three main functions:

(a) to state and justify the county planning authority's policies and general proposals for the development and other use of land in the area concerned (including measures for the improvement of the physical environment and the management of traffic). It should therefore provide guidance for development and development control on matters of structural importance. Structural matters:

   (i)   either

      (a) affect the whole or a substantial part of the structure plan area;

      or

      (b) influence the development of the area in a significant way;

      and

   (ii) are proposals of the county planning authority which are subject to statutory approval by the Secretary of State;

(b) to interpret national and regional policies in terms of physical and environmental planning for the area concerned. National and regional policies tend to be primarily economic and social. The structure plan is the stage in the planning system when these policies are integrated with the economic, social and environmental policies of the area and expressed in terms of the effect on land use, the environment and the transport system; and

(c) to provide the framework for the local plans, which then in turn provide more definitive guidance for development and development control."

6. 1982 STRUCTURE AND LOCAL PLAN REGULATIONS

Part IV Section 9

"Matters to be contained in explanatory memorandum

9.   The prescribed matters to be contained in an explanatory memorandum (in
addition to the other contents required by section 7(6A) of the Act) shall
be such indications as the county planning authority may think appropriate
of the regard they have had to the following matters:

    (a) current national and regional policies;

    (b) social considerations; and

    (c) the resources likely to be available for carrying out the
        policy and general proposals formulated in the structure plan."

7. NEW MEMORANDUM ON STRUCTURE AND LOCAL PLANS

A new memorandum to replace Circular 4/79 is in preparation and is likely
to be produced in late 1982 or early 1983. It brings together the
legislative changes since 1979 and reflects the DoE's experience and
concern over the operation of the development plan system. Significant
changes are likely compared to 4/79, reflecting the development of the DoE's
thinking.

APPENDIX 2: List of Plans Referred to in the Text

The dates given for deposit and adoption are correct to 31.12.1981

Name of plan	Preparing authority	County	Size	Statutory (/) or not (x)	Deposit date	Adoption date
Abbey district plan	Leicester DC	Leicestershire	Large area	/	May 1977	September 1978
Ashby Woulds district plan	North West Leicester DC	Leicestershire	Small area	/	August 1980	
Ashford district plan	Ashford DC	Kent	Large area			
Askam and Ireleth district plan	Barrow-in-Furness DC	Cumbria	Small area			
Atherstone district plan	North Warwickshire DC	Warwickshire	Large area	/	January 1980	August 1981
Bakewell district plan	Peak Park Joint Planning Board		Small area	/	September 1980	
Banbury Town district plan	Cherwell DC	Oxfordshire	Small area	/	October 1979	November 1980
Bardon industrial action area plan	North West Leicestershire	Leicestershire	Small area	/	October 1980	
Barnsley Town Centre plan	Barnsley MD	South Yorkshire	Small area			
Basford/Forest Fields district plan	Nottingham DC	Nottinghamshire	Large area	/	August 1980 (IVV Act)	

Plan	Authority	Region	Size		Date	Date
Beckermet, Egremont and St Bees village plans	Copeland DC	Cumbria	Small area			
Beckton district plan	LB Newham	Greater London	Small area		March 1978	March 1980
Belbroughton district plan	Bromsgrove DC	Hereford and Worcestershire		/	July 1978	November 1980
Bexleyheath action area plan	LB Bexley	GLC	Small area		May 1980	
Bickenhill/Marston Green district plan	West Midlands CC	West Midlands				
Birkenhead central area local plan	Wirral MD	Merseyside	Small area	X		
Bishops Itchington district plan	Stratford-upon-Avon DC	Warwickshire		/	August 1978	October 1978
Bristol Docks local plan	Bristol DC	Avon	Small area			
Broughton Astley central area action area plan	Marborough DC	Leicestershire	Small area	/	November 1980	
Brunswick district plan	Salford MB	Greater Manchester	Small area	/	January 1979 (IVV Act)	May 1980
Brunswick Town district plan	Hove DC	East Sussex	Small area	/	October 1979	October 1980
Buckingham town plan	Aylesbury Vale DC	Buckinghamshire	Small area	X		
Buckinghamshire minerals subject plan	Buckinghamshire CC	Buckinghamshire	Large area	/	June 1980	
Camden Borough plan	LB Camden	GLC	All area	/	May 1977	January 1979
Chandlers Ford	Hampshire CC	Hampshire	Large area	/	February 1980	October 1981

Plan	Authority	County/Region	Area		Date 1	Date 2
Cheltenham central area district plan	Cheltenham DC	Gloucestershire	Small area	X		July 1981
Chineham district plan	Hampshire CC	Hampshire		/		
Church district plan	Hyndburn DC	Lancashire	Small area	/	August 1980	
Clough St. action area plan	Burnley DC	Lancashire	Small area	X		October 1977
Coleorton district plan	North West Leicestershire DC	Leicestershire	Small area	/	January 1977	
Covent Garden action area plan	GLC	GLC	Small area	/	November 1976	January 1976
Dacorum district plan	Dacorum DC	Hertfordshire	All area	/	January 1981	
Darlaston district plan	Walsall MB	West Midlands	Small area		July 1979	June 1980
Didcot interim local plan	South Oxfordshire DC	Oxfordshire	Small area	/		
Dungeness countryside subject plan for agriculture and conservation	Kent CC	Kent	Large area	/	October 1980	
Eagle St. action area plan	Coventry MB	West Midlands	Small area	/	July 1975	February 1977
East Hertfordshire district plan	East Hertfordshire DC	Hertfordshire	All area	/	August 1980	November 1981
East Moors district plan	Cardiff DC	South Glamorgan				
Eastwood district plan	Broxtowe DC	Nottinghamshire	Small area			
Eden Street action area plan	Coventry MB	West Midlands	Small area	/	July 1975	December 1975

Plan	Authority	Region	Area			
Elmdon Heath, Lugtrout Lane, Wheretts Well Lane action area plan	Solihull MB	West Midlands	Small area		May 1977	October 1977
Enderby/Narborough district plan	Blaby DC	Leicestershire	Small area	/	October 1980	
Fareham Western Wards	Hampshire CC	Hampshire	Large area	/	March 1977	March 1979
Farnworth district plan	Bolton MB	Greater Manchester	Small area	/	October 1980	June 1981
Featherstone district plan	Wakefield MD	West Yorkshire	Small area			
Foleshill policy guide	Coventry MD	West Midlands	Large area	/		
Glenfield district plan	Blaby DC	Leicestershire	Small area		November 1976	May 1978
Gloucester city local plan	Gloucester CD	Gloucestershire	All area			
Greater Chester district plan	Chester DC	Cheshire				
Greater Manchester green belt subject plan	Greater Manchester MC	Greater Manchester	Large area	/	April 1981	
Grimsby/Cleethorpes population and housing subject plan	Grimsby DC	Humberside	Large area	X		
Groby district plan	Hinkley and Bosworth BC	Leicestershire	Small area	/	January 1977	June 1978
Hadleigh district plan	Blabergh DC	Suffolk	Small area	/	December 1980	
Hammersmith and Fulham borough plan	LB Hammersmith and Fulham	GLC	All area		June 1980	December 1981

Plan	Authority	County/Region	Area	Adopted	Date	Date
Heathrow Airport local plan	LB Hillingdon	GLC	Small area	/		
Hemel Hempstead town centre plan	Dacorum DC	Hertfordshire	Small area	X		
High Wycombe area district plan	Wycombe DC	Buckinghamshire	Large area			
Holme action area plan	Scunthorpe DC	Humberside	Small area	X		
Horsham area district plan	Horsham DC	West Sussex	All area	/	October 1980	
Hove residential subject plan	Hove DC	East Sussex	Large area	X		
Hoyle district plan	Penwith DC	Cornwall	Small area	X		
Humberside coastal caravan and camping subject plan	Humberside CC	Humberside	Large area	/	December 1979	July 1981
Intensive livestock units subject plan	Humberside CC	Humberside	Large area	/	November 1979	
Islington borough plan	LB Islington	GLC	All area	/	September 1980	
Kensington and Chelsea borough plan	LB Kensington and Chelsea	GLC	All area	/	November 1979	
Kimberley district plan	Broxtowe DC	Nottinghamshire	Small area	/		
Lambeth borough plan	LB Lambeth	GLC	Large area	/	September 1981	
Lapworth district plan	Warwick DC	Warwickshire	Small area	/	September 1978	March 1980
Town of Lewes district plan	Lewes DC	East Sussex	Large area	/	May 1978	August 1979

Plan	Authority	County / Region	Area	Mark	Date	Date
Lewisham employment subject plan	LB Lewisham	GLC	All area	X		
Development on the Lincolnshire coast subject plan	Lincolnshire CC	Lincolnshire	Large area	/		
Longford action area plan	Coventry M	West Midlands	Small area		September 1977	December 1978
Loose Valley draft district plan	Maidstone DC	Kent	Small area			
Markfield district plan	Hinkley and Bosworth DC	Leicestershire	Small area		March 1979	August 1979
Medlock Valley subject plan	Greater Manchester MCC/transferred to districts	Greater Manchester	Large area	/		
Melbourn village plan	South Cambridgeshire DC	Cambridgeshire	Small area	X		
Mersey valley subject plan	Greater Manchester MCC	Greater Manchester	Large area	/		
Moorfield action area plan	Liverpool MD	Merseyside	Small area	X		
Morley local plan	Leeds MD	West Yorkshire	?		June 1982	
Mundford village plan and Dereham policy review	Breckland DC	Norfolk	Small area	/		
Newburn district plan	Newcastle MD	Tyne and Wear	Small area			
Newton-le-Willows local plan	St. Helens MB	Merseyside	Large area		December 1980	
North Birkenhead local plan	Wirral MD	Merseyside	Small area	X		
North Southwark …	LB Southwark	GLC	Large area	/		

Plan	Authority	County	Size		Date 1	Date 2
Norwich central area local plan	Norfolk CC/Norwich CD	Norfolk	Small area			
Oldbury with Langley district plan	Sandwell MB	West Midlands	Small area	/	July 1979	December 1980
Queens Road area district plan	Epping Forest DC	Essex	Small area	/		
Ratby district plan	Hinckley and Bosworth DC	Leicestershire	Small area	/	May 1979	December 1979
River Tees subject plan	Cleveland CC	Cleveland	Large area	/	August 1978	December 1980
Rixton brickworks subject plan	Warrington DC	Cheshire	Small area	/	May 1980	October 1980
Rochdale town centre district plan	Rochdale MB	Greater Manchester	Small area	/	February 1980	October 1980
Rossendale district plan	Rossendale DC	Lancashire	All area	/	July 1980	
Rytons/Greenside quarries subject plan	Tyne and Wear MC	Tyne and Wear		/		
Seacombe local plan	Wirral MD	Merseyside	Small area	X		
Seven Gorge district plan	Shropshire CC	Shropshire	Small area	/	August 1980	
Skippendale action area plan	Scunthorpe DC	Humberside	Small area	/	1979	October 1979
Solihull green belt subject plan	Solihull MD	West Midlands	Large area	/	May 1977	December 1977
Local plan for South Oxford	Oxford City DC	Oxfordshire	Small area	X		
Southam district plan	Stratford-upon-Avon DC	Warwickshire	Small area	/	November 1978	March 1979
Stone district plan	Stafford DC	Staffordshire	Small area	/	July 1978	September 1980

Plan	Authority	County	Area		Date	Date
Stratford-upon-Avon Leisure-in-the-valley subject plan	Stratford-upon-Avon DC	Warwickshire	Large area	/	November 1978	April 1980
Sutton Coldfield district plan	Birmingham MB	West Midlands		/	January 1976	April 1978
Swinefleet district plan	Boothberry DC	Humberside	Small area	/	May 1980	
Tamworth district plan	Tamworth DC	Staffordshire	All area	/	May 1980	
Thornhill district plan	Cardiff DC	South Glamorgan	Small area	X		
Totton district plan	Hampshire CC	Hampshire	Small area	/	February 1979	November 1980
Tranmere and Rock Ferry district plan	Wirral MB	Merseyside	Small area	X		
Uttlesford rural areas district plan	Uttlesford DC	Essex	Large area			
Waltham Forest borough plan	LB Waltham Forest	GLC	All area	/	May 1978	April 1980
Walton-Fazakerly district plan	Liverpool MB	Merseyside	Large area	X		
Walton Park subject plan	Warrington DC	Cheshire	Small area	/	October 1980	
Wandsworth borough plan	LB Wandsworth	GLC	All area	/	November 1980	
Wapping local plan	LB Tower Hamlets	GLC	Small area	X		
Warwickshire green belt subject plan	Warwickshire CC	Warwickshire	Large area	/	April 1977	
Waterloo district plan	LB Lambeth	GLC	Small area	/		September 1977

Plan	Authority	County	Area		Date
Watford borough plan	Watford DC	Hertfordshire	All area	/	November 1979 / January 1981
Westminster borough plan	LB Westminster	GLC	All area	/	April 1978
Widcombe priority area	Bath DC	Avon	Small area	X	
Wigston district plan	Oadby and Wigston DC	Leicestershire	Small area		March 1979
Wrekin rural areas district plan	Wrekin DC	Shropshire	Large area	/	August 1980
Wycombe housing subject plan	Wycombe DC	Buckinghamshire	Large area	X	

REFERENCES

Adamson, G.R. 1975. Local Planning Practice: The Plan-Making Process - The Sheffield Experience, *Structure Planning Practice and Local Planning Practice*. PTRC, London, pp.92-115.

Adcock, B. 1979. The effectiveness of local plans in the inner urban areas, *Local Planning Practice*. Proceedings of PTRC Summer Meeting Seminar E, PTRC.

Allison, L. 1975. *Environmental Planning*. Allen & Unwin, London.

Ambrose, P. and Colenutt, B. 1975. *The Property Machine*. Penguin, Harmondsworth.

Amos, F. 1982. *Manpower Requirements for Physical Planning*. INLOGOV, Birmingham.

Anderson, M. 1981. Planning policies and development control in the Sussex Downs AONB. *Town Planning Review*, Vol. 52(1), pp.5-25.

Anstey, B. 1965. A study of certain changes in land values in the London Area in the period 1950-1964. ed. Hall, P., *Land Values*. Sweet and Maxwell, London.

Archer, R.W. 1973. Land Speculation and Scattered Development: Failures in the Urban Fringe Land Market. *Urban Studies*, Vol 10 (3), pp.367-72.

Ashton, P.J. 1978. The political economy of suburban development. In ed. Tabb, W.K. and Sawers, L., *Marxism and the Metropolis*. OUP, New York.

Avis, M. 1976. *The Acquisition, Development and Control of Land in Kumasi: an explanatory booklet*. Land Administration Research Centre, U.S.T., Kumasi, Ghana. Mimeo.

Backwell, J. and Dickens, P. 1978. *Town Planning, Mass Loyalty and the Restructuring of Capital*. Urban and Regional Studies Working Paper 11, University of Sussex.

Bailey, J. 1975. *Social Theory for Planning*. Routledge and Kegan Paul, London.

Bainbridge, C. 1978. *Distributional policies and structure plans*. Diploma thesis, Town Planning Department, Oxford Polytechnic.

Ball, M. 1982. The speculative housebuilding industry. *The Production of the Built Environment: Third Bartlett Summer School Papers*. Bartlett, UCL, London, pp.31-51.

Banfield, E.C. 1959. Ends and means in planning. *International Social Science Journal*, Vol XI, pp.361-68

Barnard, T. 1981. A review of local plans. In ed. Fudge, C., *Approaches to Local Planning 2*. SAUS Working Paper No.17, School of Advanced Urban

Studies, Bristol.

Baron, T. 1980. Planning's biggest and least satisfied customer, *Town and Country Planning Summer School Proceedings*. RTPI, London, pp.34-40.

Barker, A. 1979. *Public Participation in Britain: a classified bibliography*. Bedford Square Press/RTPI, London.

Barras, R. and Broadbent, T.A. 1979. The analysis in English structure plans. *Urban Studies*, Vol 16 (1), pp.1-18.

Barrett, S.M. 1980. Perspective on Implementation. Paper prepared for the *SSRC Conference on Central-Local Government Relationships*, INLOGOV, Birmingham.

Barrett, S.M. 1981. Local Authorities and the Community Land Scheme. In ed. Barrett, S.M. and Fudge, C. *Policy and Action*. Methuen, London.

Barrett, S.M. and Fudge, C. 1981. Examining the policy-action relationship. In ed. Barrett, S.M. and Fudge, C., *Policy and Action*. Methuen, London, pp.3-32.

Barrett, S.M. and Fudge, C. ed. 1981. *Policy and Action* Methuen, London.

Barrett, S.M., Boddy, M. and Stewart, M. 1978. *Implementation of the Communit Land Scheme*, SAUS Occasional Paper No. 3. School of Advanced Urban Studies, Bristol.

Batey, P.W.J. and Breheny, M.J. ed. 1978. Systematic Methods in British Planning Practice. *Town Planning Review*, Vol 49 (3), (Part 1), (4) (Part II).

Bather, N.J., Sutton, A. and Williams, C. 1975. A strategic choice approach to structure planning. *Structure Planning Practice and Local Planning Practice*. PTRC, London.

Bayliss, D. 1975. TPP's and structure plans. *The Planner*, Vol 61 (9), pp.334-5.

Best, R.H. and Champion, A.G. 1969. *Regional Conversion of Agricultural Land to Urban Use in England and Wales 1945-1967*. Centre for Environmental Studies, London.

Bishop, A.S. 1980. *Institutional Obstacles to the Implementation of Development Plans*. University of London, M. Phil. thesis.

Blacksell, M. and Gilg, A.W. 1977. Planning Control in an Area of Outstanding Beauty. *Social and Economic Administration*, Vol. 11 (3).

Blowers, A. 1980. *The Limits of Power. The Politics of Local Planning Policy*. Pergamon, Oxford.

Boaden, N., Goldsmith, M., Hampton, W., Stringer, P. 1979. Public Participation in Planning Within a Representative Local Democracy. *Policy and Politics*, Vol 7, pp.55-67.

Boddy, M. 1980. *The Building Societies*. MacMillan, London.

Boddy, M. 1981. The property sector in late capitalism: the case of Britain. In ed. Dear, M. and Scott, A.J. *Urbanization and Urban Planning in Capitalist Society*. Methuen, London, pp.268-86.

Booth, C. and Edwards, J. 1981. Barnsley's Approach to Local Planning. In ed. Fudge, C. *Approaches to Local Planning 2*. SAUS Working Paper 17, SAUS, Bristol.

Bowen, E. and Yates, S. 1974. Comments. *The Planner*, Vol 60 (1), p.502.

Bridges, L. and Vielba, C. 1976. *Structure Plans Examinations in Public: A Descriptive Analysis*. Institute of Judicial Administration, University of Birmingham.

Briscoe, B. 1978. The Implementation of Economic Policies in the West Yorkshire Structure Plan. *Structure and Regional Planning Practice and Local Planning Practice*. PTRC London, pp.11-27.

British Property Federation, 1976. *Policy for Land*. BPF, London.

Broadbent, T.A. 1977. *Planning and Profit in the Urban Economy*. Methuen, London.

Broadbent, T.A. 1979. *Options for Planning: a discussion document*. CES, London.

Brown, J.H., Phillips, R.S. and Roberts, N.A. 1981. Land Markets and the
    Urban Fringe: New Insights for Policy Makers. *Journal American
    Planning Association*, Vol 47 (2).
Brown, R. 1974. Linking Local Planning with Structure Planning. *The
    Planner*, Vol 60 (1), pp.505-6.
Bruce, A. 1980. Structure plan amendments show centralist tendencies.
    Planning, 394, 14.11.80
Bruton, M.J. 1980a. The Future of Development Plans: PAG revisited. *Town
    Planning Review*, Vol 51 (2) pp.134-44.
Bruton, M.J. 1980b. Public Participation, Local Planning and Conflicts of
    Interest. *Policy and Politics*, Vol 8 (4), pp.423-42.
Bruton, M.J. and Lightbody, A.J. 1979. *Public Participation in Local
    Planning: Publicity and Communication*. School of Planning Working Paper
    No. 7, (City of Birmingham Polytechnic).
Bruton, M.J., Crispin, G., Fidler, P.M. and Hill, E.A. 1981. Public Inquiries
    for Local Plans. *Town and Country Planning*, Vol 50 (8), pp.231-3.
Bruton, M.J., Crispin, G., Fidler, P.M. and Hill, E.A. 1982a. Local Plan
    Public Inquiries in Practice 2. *The Planner*, March/April 1982.
Bruton, M.J., Crispin, G., Fidler, P.M. and Hill, E.A. 1982b. Local Plan
    Public Local Inquiries in Practice 1. *The Planner*, January/February
    1982.
Buchanan, C. 1963. *Traffic in Towns*. HMSO, London.
Buchanan, C. 1972. *The State of Britain*. Faber, London.
Burns, W. 1980. The plan-making process. In proceedings 1979. *Town and
    Country Planning Summer School*. RTPI, London.
Burrows, J. 1978. Vacant Urban Land. *The Planner*, Vol 64 (1), pp.7-9
Byrne, D.F. 1978. The Need for a Comprehensive Approach to Local Planning.
    Structure and Regional Planning Practice and Local Planning Practice.
    PTRC, London, pp.181-91.
Caddy, C. 1981. Local planning in an area of restraint. In ed Fudge, C.
    Approaches to Local Planning 2. SAUS Working Paper No. 17. School of
    Advanced Urban Studies, Bristol.
Castells, M. 1976. Theoretical propositions for an experimental study of
    urban social movements. In ed. Pickvance, C., *Urban Sociology*.
    Tavistock, London.
Castells, M. 1977. Towards a political urban sociology. In ed Harloe, M.,
    Captive Cities. Wiley, London, pp.61-78.
Cawson, A. 1977. *Environmental Planning and the Politics of Corporatism*,
    Working Paper 7. Urban and Regional Studies, University of Sussex.
CES Working Party 1973. *Education for Planning: The Development of
    Knowledge and Capability for Urban Governance*. Progress in Planning,
    Vol 1, Part 1. Pergamon, Oxford.
Chadwick, G. 1971. *A Systems View of Planning*. Pergamon, Oxford
Cherry, G.E. 1974. *The Evolution of British Town Planning*. Leonard Hill,
    Leighton Buzzard.
Clawson, M. 1971. *Suburban land conversion in the United States: An Economic
    and Governmental Process*. John Hopkins University Press, Baltimore.
Clawson, M. and Hall, P. 1973. *Planning and Urban Growth: an Anglo-American
    Comparison*. Resources for the Future, Inc.
Cloke, P.J. 1979. *Key settlements in Rural Areas*. Methuen, London.
Cockburn, C. 1977. *The Local State*. Pluto Press, London.
Coleman, A. 1976. Is Planning Really Necessary? *Geographical Journal*, Vol
    142, pp.411-37.
Collins, J. 1980. The planning system - how will it look in the eighties?
    Proceedings 1979 *Town and Country Planning Summer School*. RTPI, London.
Confederation of British Industry 1980. *British Industry and the Development
    Control System*. CBI, London.
Couch, C. 1978. Local Planning Practice. *Planning Newsletter No. 289*,
    13 October p.8-13.

Council for the Preservation of Rural England 1981. *Planning: Friend or Foe?* CPRE, London.

Countryside Review Committee 1979. *Conservation and the Countryside Heritage: a discussion paper.* HMSO, London.

Cowling, T.H. and Steeley, G.C. 1973. *Sub-regional planning studies: an evaluation.* Pergamon, London.

Cox, K. (ed) 1978. *Urbanization and Conflict in Market Societies.* Methuen, London.

Cox, A. 1980. The limits of central government intervention in the land and development market: the case of the Land Commission. *Policy and Politics,* Vol 8 (3).

Cullen, M. and Woolery, S. (ed) 1982. *World Congress on Land Policy.* Lexington (DC Heath), Massachusetts.

Cullingworth, J.B. 1972. *Town and Country Planning in Britain* (revised fourth editions). Allen and Unwin, London.

Cullingworth, J.B. 1975. *Reconstruction and Land Use Planning 1939-1947. Environmental History,* Vol 1. HMSO, London.

Cullingworth, J.B. 1980. *Environmental Planning 1939-1969. Vol IV, Land Values, Compensation and Betterment.* HMSO, London.

Damer, S. and Hague, C. 1971. Public Participation in Planning: Evolution and Problems. *Town Planning Review,* Vol 42, pp.217-32.

Darin-Drabkin, H. 1977. *Land Policy and Urban Growth.* Pergamon, Oxford.

Darke, R. 1979. Public participation and State Power: the case of South Yorkshire. *Policy and Politics,* Vol 7 (4), pp.337-55.

Darke, R. 1982. The Dialectics of Policy-Making: Form and Content. In ed Healey, P., McDougall, G. and Thomas, M.J., *Planning Theory: Prospects for the 1980s.* Pergamon, Oxford.

Davidoff, P. 1965. Advocacy and pluralism in planning. *Journal American Institute Planning,* Vol 31 (4), pp.331-8.

Davies, C. 1975. *Structure Plans: Theory and Practice.* Midlands New Towns Society.

Davies, H.W.E. 1980. The relevance of development control. *Town Planning Review,* Vol 51 (1), pp.7-17.

Davies, H.W.E. 1982. *Planning Practice.* Report for the SSRC. SSRC, London.

Davies, R. and Hall, P. 1978. *Issues in Urban Society.* Penguin, Harmondsworth.

Davis, J. 1982. *Wokingham: The Implementation of Strategic Planning Policy in a growth area in the South East.* Background Paper No. 3, for the DoE financed Implementation of Development Plans project. Oxford Polytechnic.

Dear, M. and Scott, A.J. (ed) 1981. *Urbanization and Urban Planning in Capitalist Society.* Methuen, London.

Dearlove, J. 1979. *The Reorganization of British Local Government.* Cambridge University Press, Cambridge.

Denman, D.R. 1974. Land Nationalization - A way out? In IEA *Government and the Land.* IEA Readings 13, IEA, London.

Dennis, N. 1970. *People and Planning.* Faber, London.

Department of Environment 1972. Circular 102/72, *Land Availability for Housing.* HMSO, London.

Department of Environment 1972. *Report of the Working Party on Local Authority/Private Enterprise Partnership Schemes* (Sheaf Report). HMSO, London.

Department of Environment 1973. Circular 74/73, *Local Government Act 1972 - Town and Country Planning: Co-operation between Authorities.* HMSO, London.

Department of Environment 1973. Circular 104/73, *Local Transport Grants.* HMSO, London.

Department of Environment 1973. Circular 122/73, *Land Availability for Housing.* HMSO, London.

Department of Environment 1973a. *Structure Plans: The Examination in Public.*
HMSO, London.
Department of Environment 1973b. *Structure Plans Note 7/73: Social Aspects
of Development Plans.* DoE, London.
Department of Environment 1973c. *Making Towns Better: The Sunderland Study.*
HMSO, London.
Department of Environment 1974. Circular 58/74, *Local Government Act 1972 -
Town and Country Planning: Development Plan Provisions.* HMSO, London.
Department of Environment 1974. Circular 98/74, *Structure Plans.* HMSO,
London.
Department of Environment 1975. Circular 121/75, *Community Land - Circular
1: General Introduction and Priorities.* HMSO, London.
Department of Environment 1975. *Review of the Development Control System.*
HMSO, London.
Department of Environment 1976. *Development Plan Schemes and Local Plans,*
Local Plans Note 1/76. DoE, London.
Department of Environment 1977. Circular 55/77, *The Town and Country
Planning Act 1971. (Part II as Amended by the Town and Country Planning
(Amendment) Act 1972 and the Local Government Act 1972); Memorandum on
Structure and Local Plans.* HMSO, London.
Department of Environment 1977. Circular 71/77, *Local Government and the
Industrial Strategy.* HMSO, London.
Department of Environment 1977a. *Local Plans: Public Local Inquiries.*
HMSO, London.
Department of Environment 1977b. *Inner Area Studies: Summaries of
Consultants Final Reports.* HMSO, London.
Department of Environment 1978. Circular 44/78, *Private Sector Land:
Requirements and Supply.* HMSO, London.
Department of Environment 1978a. *Form and Content of Local Plans,* Local
Plans Note LP1/78. DoE, London.
Department of Environment 1978b. *Strategic Plan for the South East. Review.
Government Statement.* HMSO, London.
Department of Environment 1979. Circular 4/79, *The Town and Country
Planning Act 1971 (Part II as Amended by the Town and Country Planning
(Amendment) Act 1972, the Local Government Act 1972 and the Inner Urban
Areas Act 1978): Memorandum on Structure and Local Plans.* HMSO, London.
Department of Environment 1979. *Central Government Controls over Local
Authorities,* White Paper, Cmnd 7634. HMSO, London.
Department of Environment 1980. Circular 9/80, *Land for Private
Housebuilding.* HMSO, London.
Department of Environment 1980. Circular 22/80, *Development Control Policy
and Practice.* HMSO, London.
Department of Environment 1980. *Structure and Activity of the Development
Industry.* Report of the Property Advisory Group. HMSO, London.
Department of Environment 1981. Circular 23/81, *Local Government, Planning
and Land Act 1980: Town and Country Planning: Development Plans.* HMSO,
London.
Department of Environment/House Builders Federation 1979. *Study of the
availability of private housebuilding land in Greater Manchester 1978-1981.*
DoE, London.
Diamond, D. 1979. The uses of strategic planning: The example of the
National Planning Guidelines in Scotland. *Town Planning Review,* Vol 50
(1), pp.18-25.
Dimitriou, B., Faludi, A., McDougall, G. and Silvester, M. 1972. *The
Systems View of Planning.* Oxford Working Paper No. 9. Department of
Town Planning, Oxford Polytechnic.
District Planning Officers' Society 1978. *Local Plans* DPOS.
District Planning Officers' Society. 1982. *Local Plans: the need for radical
change.* DPOS.

Donnison, D. 1977. Against discretion. *New Society* (London), 15/9/77.

Drake, M. 1975. Aims, objectives and problems in structure planning methodology. In Drake *et al.*, *Aspects of Structure Planning*. CES RP 20. Centre for Environmental Studies, London.

Drake, M. and Thornley, J. 1975. Public Participation in Structure Planning. In Drake *et al.*, *Aspects of Structure Planning*. CES RP 20. Centre for Environmental Studies, London.

Drake, M., McLoughlin, B., Thompson, R. and Thornley, J. 1975. *Aspects of Structure Planning*. CES RP 20. Centre for Environmental Studies, London.

Drewett, R. 1973. The Developers: Decision Processes, and Land Vaulues and the Suburban Land Market. Chapters.6 and 7. In ed. Hall, P., *The Containment of Urban England*, Vol II. George, Allen and Unwin, London.

Drewett, R. and Rossi, A. 1982. *Urban Europe: Structure and Change 1950-1980*. Urban Europe, Vol 3. Pergamon, Oxford.

Duerden, B. 1979. Local Planning in Liverpool. In ed Fudge, C., *Approaches to Local Planning*. SAUS Working Paper No. 3, 3. School of Advanced Urban Studies, Bristol.

Dunham, A. 1964. Property, city planning and liberty. In ed Haar, C.M. *Law and Land*. Harwood UP and M.I.T., Massachusetts. pp.28-43. Also in ed M. Stewart 1972 *The City*. Penguin, Harmondsworth.

Dunkerley, H.B. 1978. Urban Land Policies and Opportunities: an Overview. In Dunkerley *et al.*. *Urban Land Policies and Opportunities*. World Bank, New York.

Dunkerley, H.B., Walters, A.A., Courtney, J.M., Doebele, W.A., Sharp, D.C. and Rivkin, M.D. 1978. *Urban Land Policies and Opportunities*. World Bank, New York.

Dunleavy, P. 1977. Protest and Quiescence in Urban Politics: A Critique of Some Pluralist and Structuralist Myths. *Internat. Jnl. of Urban and Reg. Research*, Vol 1 (2), pp.193-218.

Dunleavy, P. 1980. *Urban Political Analysis*. MacMillan, London.

Dunlop, J. 1976. The Examination in Public of Structure Plans - An Emerging Procedure - 2. *Journal of Planning and Environmental Law* (February), pp.75-85.

Economist Intelligence Unit Ltd 1975. *Housing Land Availability in the South East*. Final Report for the DoE and the Housing Research Foundation. DoE, London.

Eddison, T. 1968. The wider role of the development plan. *Journal of the Town Planning Institute*, Vol 54 (10), pp.465-7.

Edwards, J. 1974. Organization. *The Planner*, Vol 60 (1), p.498.

Edwards, M. 1980. Notes for the Analysis of Land Use Planning. *Bartlett 1979 Summer School Proceedings*. UCL, London.

Eke, J.F. 1977. Structure Plans. *Public Finance and Accoutancy*. Vol 4 (5) pp.149-150.

Elkin, S.L. 1974. *Politics and Land Use Planning: The London Experience*. Cambridge University Press, London.

Elson, M. (ed) 1979. *Perspectives on Green Belt Local Plans*. Oxford Working Paper No. 38, Department of Town Planning, Oxford Polytechnic.

Elson, M. 1982. *Land Release and Development in Areas of Restraint: An Investigation of Local Needs Policies*. End-of-Grant Report to the SSRC Department of Town Planning, Oxford Polytechnic.

Etzioni, A. 1973. Mixed-Scanning: A "Third" Approach to Decision-Making. In ed Faludi, A., *A Reader in Planning Theory*. Pergamon, Oxford, pp. 217-29.

Eversley, D. 1973. *The Planner in Society*. Faber, London.

Faludi, A. 1973. *A Reader in Planning Theory*. Pergamon, Oxford.

Farnell, R. 1981. *Local Planning: An investigation into substantive concerns*. M. Phil Thesis, Coventry Polytechnic.

Finney, J. and Kenyon, S. 1976. Relationship between structure planning and
    local plans in a metropolitan area. *Structure Planning Practice and
    Local Planning Practice*. PTRC, London, pp.57-64.
Fisher, E.A. 1980. The Future of Development Plans: PAG Revisited. *Town
    Planning Review*, Vol 51 (2), pp.144-51.
Flynn, R. 1979. Managing Consensus: The Infrastructure of Policy-making
    in Planning. CES Conference: *Urban Change and Conflict*, Nottingham.
Fogarty, M.F. 1948. *Town and Country Planning*. Hutchinson, London.
Foley, D.L. 1960. British Town Planning: One Ideology or Three? *British
    Journal of Sociology*, Vol II pp.211-31 (also in ed Faludi, A. 1973, A
    Reader in Planning Theory. Pergamon, London.
Foster, A. 1975. The timing and implementation of desirable development in
    a South East Growth Area: 2. PTRC Conference, *Local Planning, Structure
    Planning and Planning Games* (PTRC).
Fothergill, S. and Gudgin, G. 1982. *Unequal Growth*. Heinemann, London.
Fothergill, S., Kitson, M. and Monk, S. 1982. *The role of capital
    investment in the Urban-Rural Shift in Manufacturing Industry*. Dept. of
    Land Economy Working Paper, University of Cambridge.
Friend, J.K. and Jessop, W.N. 1969. *Local Government and Strategic Choice*.
    Tavistock, London.
Friend, J.K., Norris, M. and Carter, K. 1978. *Regional Planning and Policy
    Change*. DoE, London.
Friend, J.K., Power, J.M. and Yewlett, C.J.L. 1974. *Public planning: the
    Intercorporate Diversion*. Tavistock, London.
Frith, D.W. 1976. District Planning. *Structure Planning Practice and Local
    Planning Practice*. PTRC, London, pp.42-46.
Fudge, C. 1976. Local Plans, Structure Plans and Policy Planning. *The
    Planner*, Vol 62 (6), September 1976.
Fudge, C. (ed) 1979. *Approaches to local planning*. School of Advanced
    Urban Studies Working Paper No. 3, University of Bristol.
Fudge, C. 1982. Local Planning in Practice: Camden. In Fudge, C. and
    Healey, P., *Local Planning in Practice 3*. School of Advanced Urban
    Studies Working Paper, SAUS, Bristol.
Fudge, C., Healey, P., Lambert, C. and Underwood, J. 1982a. *Speed, economy
    and effectiveness in local plan preparation and adoption*. Final Report
    on Research to the DoE. SAUS, Bristol.
Fudge, C., Lambert, C. and Underwood, J. 1982b. Local Plans: Approaches,
    Preparation and Adoption. *The Planner*, Vol 68 (2), pp.52-53.
Gans, H.J. 1968. *People and Plans*. Basic Books, New York.
Gault, H.I. 1981. *Green Belt Policies in Development Plans*. Oxford Working
    Paper No. 41. Department of Town Planning, Oxford Polytechnic.
George, V. and Wilding, P. 1976. *Ideology and Social Welfare*. Routledge
    and Kegan Paul, London.
Glass, R. 1959. The evaluation of planning: some sociological
    considerations. *International Social Science Journal*, Vol II, pp.383-409.
    (Also in ed. Faludi, A. 1973, A *Reader in Planning Theory*. Pergamon,
    London).
Gough, A.J. 1976. *Town Centre Redevelopment and Local Authorities*. M. Phil
    Thesis, University of London. Unpublished.
Gough, I. 1979. *The Political Economy of the Welfare State*. MacMillan,
    London.
Gower, Davies, J. 1972. *The Evangelistic Bureaucrat*. Tavistock, London.
Grant, M. 1978. Community Land? *CES Urban Law Conference*, Oxford.
Greater London Council 1976. *Approved Greater London Development Plan*.
    GLC, London.
Gregory, D. 1970. *Green Belts and Development Control*, Occasional Paper No.
    30. CURS, Birmingham.
Griffiths, J. 1979. Planning for Hertfordshire. In ed Fudge, C., *Approaches*

to Local Planning. Working Party No. 3, School of Advanced Urban Studies, Bristol.

Gwilliam, G. 1978. The Local Government Viewpoint. In ed Hammersley, R. *Development Plan Inquiries.* Sheffield Polytechnic.

Haar, C.M. 1951. *Land Planning in a Free Society.* Harvard University Press, Massachusetts.

Hack, J.S. and Pailing, K.B. 1972. The development plan system and corporate planning. *Local Government Finance,* Vol 12, pp.433-7.

Hagman, D. and Misczynski, D. 1978. *Windfalls and Wipeouts: Land Value Capture and Compensations.* Chicago: American Society of Planning Officials.

Hall, P., Gracey, H., Drewett, R., Thomas, R. 1973. *The Containment of Urban England.* Allen and Unwin, London.

Hallett, G. 1979. *Urban Land Economics.* MacMillan, London.

Hambleton, R. 1976. Local planning and area management. *The Planner,* Vol 62 (6), pp.176-9.

Hambleton, R. 1978. *Policy Planning and Local Government.* Hutchinson, London.

Hambleton, R. 1981. *Policy Planning Systems and Implementation: Some Implications for Planning Theory.* Paper for Conference: Planning theory in the 1980s, Oxford.

Hamdani, D.H. 1980. Concepts of land, urbanization and Islamic ethics. *Ekistics,* 280 January/February, pp.18-21.

Hamilton, R.N.D. 1977. Legal issues on the preparation of structure and local plans - 1. *Local Government Chronicle,* No. 5747, 20 May, pp.417-9.

Harloe, M. (ed) 1977. *Captive Cities.* Wiley, London.

Harloe, M. and Lebas, E. (eds) 1981. *City, Class and Capital.* Edward Arnold, London.

Harrison, A.J. 1977. *The Economics of Land Use Planning.* Croom Helm, London.

Harrison, A., Tranter, R.B. and Gibbs, R.S. 1977. *Land Ownership by Public and Semi-public Institutions in the UK.* Centre for Agricultural Strategy Paper 3, University of Reading.

Harrison, M.L. 1972. Development control: the influence of political, legal and ideological factors. *Town Planning Review,* Vol 43 (3), pp.255-74.

Harrison, M.L. 1979. *Land Planning and Development Control Aspects of Development Control Policy, Politics and Practice in England and Wales 1947-1972.* Department of Social Policy and Administration. Records Monograph, University of Leeds.

Harvey, D. 1973. *Social Justice and the City.* Edward Arnold, London.

Harvey, D. 1981. The Urban Process Under Capitalism: a Framework for Analysis. In ed Dear, M. and Scott, A.J., *Urbanization and Urban Planning in Capitalist Societies.* Methuen, London.

Hayek, von F. 1944. *The Road to Serfdom.* Routledge and Kegan Paul, London.

Hayward, J. 1975. Change and Choice: the Agenda of Planning. In ed Hayward and Watson, *Planning Politics and Public Policy,* C.V.P. 1975.

Hayward, J. and Watson, M. (ed) 1975. *Planning, Politics and Public Policy.* Cambridge University Press.

Healey, P. 1973. *Urban Planning Under Conditions of Rapid Urban Growth.* Thesis submitted for the degree of PhD of the University of London.

Healey, P. 1977. The Work of Policy Teams. In ed Healey, P. and Underwood, J. *The Organization and Work of Planning Departments in the London Boroughs,* CES CP 18 CES, London, pp.40-58.

Healey, P. 1979a. *Statutory local plans - their evolution in legislation and administrative interpretation.* Oxford Working Paper No. 36, Department of Town Planning, Oxford Polytechnic.

Healey, P. 1979b. Central-local Relations in Green Belt Local Plans. In ed Elson, M. *Perspectives on Green Belt Local Plans,* Oxford Working Paper No. 38, Department of Town Planning, Oxford Polytechnic.

Healey, P. 1979c. Networking as a Normative Principle. *Local Government Studies*, Vol 5 (1).

Healey, P. 1982a. *British Planning Education in the 1970s and 1980s.* Social Science Research Council, London.

Healey, P. 1982b. *The Implementation of Development Plans: Background Paper 1: Context and Method.* Paper for DoE-financed project, Oxford Polytechnic.

Healey, P. 1982c. Local Planning in Practice: Hampshire. In ed Fudge, C. and Healey, P., *Local Planning in Practice 4.* School of Advanced Urban Studies Working Paper. SAUS, Bristol.

Healey, P. 1982d. Local Planning in Practice: Manchester. In ed Fudge, C. and Healey, P., *Local Planning in Practice 3.* School of Advanced Studies Working Paper. SAUS, Bristol.

Healey, P. 1982e. Understanding Land Use Planning. In ed Healey, McDougall and Thomas, *Planning Theory, Prospects for the 1980s.* Pergamon, Oxford.

Healey, P. and Elson, M. 1981. Development Plans and Development Investment. Paper for *PTRC Summer Meeting 1981.* PTRC, London.

Healey, P. and Underwood, J. 1977a. The types of service which planning departments provide. In ed Healey and Underwood, *The Organization and Work of London Borough Planning Departments.* CES CP 18, Centre for Environmental Studies, London.

Healey, P. (ed) and Underwood, J. 1977b. *The Organization and Work of London Borough Planning Departments.* CES CP 18, Centre for Environmental Studies, London.

Healey, P. and Underwood, J. 1979. *Professional Ideals and Planning Practice.* Progress in Planning Vol 9 (2). Pergamon, Oxford.

Healey, P., Davis, J., Wood, M. and Elson, M. 1982a. *The Implementation of Development Plans.* Report for the DoE. Oxford Polytechnic, Department of Town Planning.

Healey, P., McDougall, G. and Thomas, M.J. 1982b. Theoretical debates in planning: towards a coherent dialogue. In ed Healey, McDougall and Thomas, *Planning Theory: Prospects for the 1980s.* Pergamon, Oxford.

Healey, P., Terry, S. and Evans, S. 1980. *The Implementation of Restraint Policy.* Oxford Working Paper No. 45. Department of Town Planning, Oxford Polytechnic.

Heap, D. 1965. Exit the Development Plan: or The Shape of Planning Things to Come. *Journal of Planning and Property Law,* pp.591-611.

Hebbert, M.J. 1977. *The Evolution of British Town and Country Planning.* University of Reading PhD, unpublished.

Hebbert, M.J. 1980. Viewpoint 1: The Words and Deeds of Michael Heseltine. *Town and Country Planning,* Vol 49 (11).

Hebbert, M.J. 1981. The Land Debate. *Town and Country Planning,* Vol 50(1).

Hebbert, M.J. and Gault, I. 1978. *Green Belt Issues in Local Plan Preparation: The Report of a Seminar held at Oxford Polytechnic.* Oxford Working Paper No. 34, Department of Town Planning, Oxford Polytechnic.

Henry, D.C. 1982. *Planning by Agreement in a Berkshire District.* Town Planning Department Diploma Dissertation, Oxford Polytechnic.

Hertfordshire County Council 1979. *Countywide Housing Study.* Hertfordshire County Council.

Heseltine, M. 1979. Secretary of State's Address. *Town and Country Planning Summer School Proceedings,* pp.25-30.

Hickling, A., Friend, J. and Luckman, J. 1980. *The Development Plan System and Investment Programmes.* Centre for Organizational and Operational Research. DoE, London.

Hill, D.M. 1980. Values and Judgements: The Case of Planning in England since 1947. *International Policy Science Review,* Vol 1 (2), pp.149-67.

Hill, M. 1976. *The State, Administration and the Individual*. Fontana, Glasgow.

Hill, M. *et al*. 1979. Implementation and the Central-Local Relationship. In Jones *et al*., *Central-Local Government Relationships*. SSRC, London.

Hollingsworth, M.J. and Cuddy, M. 1979. The Land Authority for Wales: its Mediating Role in Planning and Implementation. *Local Planning Practice*, PTRC, London.

Hollox, R. 1978. Local Plan Inquiries: Requirements and Procedures. In ed. Hammersley, R., *Development Plan Inquiries*. Department of Urban and Regional Studies, Sheffield Polytechnic.

Hooper, A. 1979. Land Availability. *Journal Planning and Environment Law* (November).

Hooper, A. 1980. Land for Private House Building. *Journal Planning Environment Law* (December).

House Builders Federation, 1977. *Land for Housing*. HBF, London.

House of Commons Expenditure Committee, 1977. *Eight Report: Planning Procedures*, Vol 1. HMSO, London.

Jones, G.W. 1979. Central-local Relations, Finance and the Law. *Urban Law and Policy*, Vol 2 (1), pp.25-46.

Jowell, J. 1977. Bargaining in Development Control. *Journal of Planning and Environment Law*, July pp.414-33.

Jowell, J. and Noble, D. 1980. Planning as Social Engineering: Notes on the First English Structure Plans. *Urban Law and Policy*, Vol 3, pp.293-317.

Jurue, 1977. *Planning and Land Availability*. JURUE., University of Aston, Birmingham.

Keeble, L. 1969. *Principles and Practice of Town and Country Planning*. Estates Gazette, London. (First published, 1951).

Kingston, M.E. 1981. *Monitoring in town and country planning: a study of planner's views on comparison of action and intended effects of policies*. M Phil thesis, University of Manchester.

Kirk, G. 1980. *Urban Planning in a Capitalist Society*. Croom Helm, London.

Koenigsberger, O.N. and Groak, S. (eds) 1980. *A Review of Land Policies*. Pergamon, Oxford.

Konrad, G. and Szeleny, I. 1977. Social Conflicts of Underurbanization. In ed Harloe, M., *Captive Cities*. Wiley, London.

Lamarche, F. 1976. Property Development and the Economic Foundations of the Urban System. In ed Pickvance, C., *Urban Sociology*. Tavistock, London.

Langley, P. 1979. The social impact of structure planning policies. *Strategic and Structure Planning Practice*. PTRC, London, p.13-23.

Larkin, A. 1978. Rural housing - too Dear, too Few and too Few. *Roof* (January).

Lefcoe, G. 1978. When governments become land developers: Notes on the public-sector experience in the Netherlands and California. *Urban Law and Policy*, Vol 1, pp.103-60.

Leiden-Oxford Comparative Planning Research Project 1978. *Paper V Conclusions*. Department of Town Planning, Oxford Polytechnic and Planning Theory Group, University of Delft.

Lewis, J. and Flynn, R. 1979. The Implementation of Urban and Regional Planning Policies. *Policy and Politics*, Vol 7 (2).

Lichfield, N. 1979. Towards a Comprehension of Land Policy. *Habitat International*, Vol 4, pp.379-95.

Lichfield, N. and Darin-Drabkin, H. 1980. *Land Policy in Planning*. Allen and Unwin, London.

Lindblom, C.E. 1965. *The Intelligence of Democracy*. Free Press, New York.

Loew, S. 1979. *Local Planning*. Pembridge Press, London.

Lojkine, J. 1976. Contribution to a Marxist Theory of Capitalist Urbanization. In ed Cox, K., *Urbanization and Conflict in Market Societies*. Methuen, London.

London Borough of Wandsworth 1976. *Prosperity or Slump*. London Borough of Wandsworth, London.

Loughlin, M. 1980. Planning Control and the Property Market. *Urban Law and Policy*, Vol 3, pp.1-22.

Lowe, P.D. 1977. Environmental Values: Social and Economic Implications of Environmental Lobby Concepts. *Built Environment Quarterly*, Vol 3 (1), pp.79-82.

Lowenberg, P. 1980. State Intervention in Land and the Development Process: British Land and Planning Policies and Contemporary Inner City Applications. *Proceedings of the First Bartlett Summer School 1979*. Bartlett School, University College London, pp.11-20.

Luithlen, L. 1977. Planning Credential. *Built Environment Quarterly*, Vol 3 (3), pp.222-4.

Mabey, R. 1976. Structure Plans: Form and Content. In *Papers from the CES Structure Planning Conference*, CES CP 16. Centre for Environmental Studies, London, pp.13-19.

Mabey, R. and Craig, L. 1976. Development Plan Schemes. *The Planner*, Vol 62 (3), pp.70-72.

MacMurray, T. 1974. Local planning, corporate management and the public: Strengthening our approach. *The Planner*, Vol 60 (1), pp.493-5.

Mandelker, D. 1962. *Green Belts and Urban Growth*. University of Wisconsin Press, Madison.

Marriott, O. 1969. *The Property Boom*. Pan, London.

Marsh, G. 1980. *The Role of the Public Inquiry in Local Plan Preparation*. M Phil Thesis, University College, London.

Martin and Voorhees Associates 1981. *Review of Rural Settlement Policies. 1945-1980*. (Martin and Voorhees Associates, London).

Masser, I. 1980. The Limits to Planning. *Town Planning Review*, Vol 51 (1), pp.39-49.

Massey, D. and Catalano, A. 1978. *Capital and Land: Landownership by Capital in Great Britain*. Edward Arnold, London.

Massey, D and Meegan, R. 1979. *The geography of industrial reorganization*. Progress in Planning Vol 10 (3), Pergamon, Oxford.

McAuslan, P. 1975. *Land, Law and Planning*. Weidenfeld and Nicolson, London.

McAuslan, P. 1980. *The Ideologies of Planning Law*. Pergamon, Oxford.

McAuslan, P. 1981. Local Government and Resource Allocation in England: Changing Ideology, Unchanging Law. *Urban Law and Policy*, Vol 4, pp.215-68.

McBride, D. 1979. Planning Delays and Development Control - A Proposal for Reform. *Urban Law and Policy*, Vol 2 (1), pp.47-64.

McDonald, S.T. 1977. The Regional Report in Scotland: A Study of Change in the Planning Process. *Town Planning Review*, Vol 48 (3), pp.215-32.

McGilp, N. 1981. Success for single sheet plan format. *Planning*, 427, 17 July 1981.

McKay, D.H. and Cox, A.W. 1979. *The Politics of Urban Change*. Croom Helm, London.

McLoughlin, J.B. 1966. The PAG report: background and prospect. *Journal of the Town Planning Institute*, Vol 52 (7), pp.257-61.

McLoughlin, J.B. 1969. *Urban and Regional Planning: A Systems Approach*. Faber, London.

McLoughlin, J.B. 1973a. Structure planning in Britain. *Journal of the Royal Town Planning Institute*, Vol 59 (3), pp.115-21.

McLoughlin, J.B. 1973b. *Control and Urban Planning*. Faber and Faber, London.

McLoughlin, J.B. and Thompson, R. 1975. Structure Planning and other Policy
    Vehicles. In Drake *et al.*, *Aspects of Structure Planning*, CES RP 20.
    Centre for Environmental Studies, London.
McNamara, P. 1982a. *Restrain Policy and Development Interests: Housing in
    Dacorum and North Hertfordshire.* Restraint Policies Project Paper No. 8,
    June 1982.
McNamara, P. 1982b. *The role of estate agents in the residential development
    process* (Unpublished paper, Oxford Polytechnic).
McNamara, P. and Elson, M. 1981. *Local Needs and New Dwellings: a survey of
    Dacorum and North Hertfordshire.* Restraint Policies Project Paper No. 5.
    (Department of Town Planning, Oxford Polytechnic).
Ministry of Housing and Local Government 1955. Circular 42/55, *Green Belts*.
    HMSO, London.
Ministry of Housing and Local Government 1962. *Town Centres: Approach to
    Renewal.* Planning Bulletin No. 1. HMSO, London.
Ministry of Housing and Local Government 1965. *The Future of Development
    Plans.* Report of the Planning Advisory Group. HMSO, London.
Ministry of Housing and Local Government 1969. *People and Planning.* The
    Skeffington Report. HMSO, London.
Ministry of Housing and Local Government 1970. *Development Plans: a Manual
    on Form and Content.* HMSO, London.
Minns, R. and Thornley, J. 1978. *State Shareholding.* Macmillan, London.
Mitnick, B.M. 1976. A typology of conceptions of the public interest.
    Administration and Society, Vol 8 (1), pp.5-28.
Moor, N. and Langton, R. 1978. *Planning for New Homes.* Publication
    sponsored by Fairview, The Tarmac Housing Division, Wates, Heron Homes
    and Rialto.
Munton, R.J.C. 1983. *London's Green Belt: Containment in Practice.*
    Allen and Unwin, London.
Murie, A. and Forrest, R. 1980. Wealth, inheritance and housing policy.
    Policy and Politics, Vol 8 (1), pp.1-19.
Neutze, M. 1975. Urban Land Policy in Five Western Counties. *Journal
    Social Politics*, 4 (3), pp.225-42.
Newby, H. 1979. Urbanization and the rural class structure: reflections on
    a case study. Paper presented to the C.E.S. *Urban Change and Conflict
    Conference* (Nottingham).
Newby, H., Bell, C., Rose, D. and Saunders, P. 1978. *Property, Paternalism
    and Power.* Hutchinson, London.
Nizard, L. 1975. Planning as the Regulatory Reproduction of the Status Quo.
    In ed Hayward and Watson, *Planning, Politics and Public Policy.*
    Cambridge University Press.
O'Connor, J. 1973. *The Fiscal Crisis of the State.* St. Martins Press, New
    York.
Offe, C. 1977. The Theory of the Capitalist State and the Problem of Policy
    Formation. In ed Lindberg, L.N. and Alford, R., *Stress and
    Contradiction in Modern Capitalism.* Lexington, Massachusetts.
O'Riordan, T. 1977. Environmental Ideologies. *Environment and Planning* A.
    Vol 9, pp.3-14.
Owen, S. 1980. *Assessing the effects of local planning.* Gloucestershire
    Papers in Local and Rural Planning Issue No. 9. Department of Town and
    Country Planning, Gloucestershire College of Arts and Technology.
Pahl, R.E. 1975. *Whose City?* (revised edition). Penguin, London.
Pahl, R.E. 1977. Managers, Technical Experts and the State: Forms of
    Mediation, Manipulation and Dominance in Urban and Regional Development.
    In ed Harloe, M., *Captive Cities.* Wiley, London.
Pahl, R.E. and Winkler, J.T. 1974. The Coming Corporatism. *New Society*,
    10th October.
Parker, M.A. 1978. Keeping Structure Plans Relevant. *Paper for CES
    Structure Planning Conference*, Centre for Environmental Studies, London.

Patterson, D. 1978. The Berkshire Development Programme. PTRC Conference, *Structure and Regional Planning Practice and Local Planning Practice.* PTRC, London.

Pearce, G.R. and Tricker, M.J. 1977. Land Availability for Residential Development. In ed Joyce, F., *Metropolitan Development and Change: The West Midlands: A Policy Review.* University of Aston, Birmingham.

Perry, J. 1974. Approaches to Local Planning. Introduction to Special Issue on Local Planning. *The Planner,* Vol 60 (1), p.492.

Perry, J. (ed) 1974. Special Issue: Local Planning. *The Planner,* Vol 60 (1).

Perry, J. 1976. Innovations in local planning: Introduction. *The Planner,* Vol 62 (5), p.139-40.

Pickvance, C.G. 1976. On the Study of Urban Social Movements. In ed Pickvance, *Urban Sociology.* Tavistock, London.

Pickvance, C.G. 1976. *Urban Sociology: Critical Essays.* Tavistock, London.

Pountney, M.T. and Kingsbury, P.W. 1983. "Aspects of Development Control: Part 1: The Relationship with Local Plans". *Town Planning Review,* Vol 54(2), pp.139-154.

Preece, R.A. 1979. *Landscape and Planning: A Study of Designated Areas of Outstanding Natural Beauty, with Particular Reference to the Cotswolds.* D Phil thesis, University of Oxford (unpublished).

Preece, R.A. 1981. *Patterns of Development Control in the Cotswolds Area of Outstanding Natural Beauty.* Oxford School of Geography Research Papers 27, Oxford University.

Purdue, M. 1977. *Cases and Materials in Planning Law.* Sweet and Maxwell, London.

Ratcliffe, J. 1976. *Land Policy.* Hutchinson, London.

Rawson, M. and Rogers, A. 1976. *Rural Housing and Structure Plans* (London University, Wye College, Kent).

Reade, E.J. 1980. *Town Planning and the 'Corporatist Thesis'.* SIP Paper No. 10, Organization of Sociologists in Polytechnics.

Reade, E.J. 1982. Section 52 and Corporatism. *Journal of Planning and Environment Law* (January), pp.8-16.

Real Estate Research Corporation 1975. *The Costs of Urban Sprawl.* 3 Vols. US Government Printing Office, Washington, D.C.

Regan, D.E. 1978. The Pathology of British Land Use Planning. *Local Government Studies,* Vol 4 (2), pp.3-23.

Revell, J. 1973. *The British Financial System.* MacMillan, London.

Roberts, N.A. 1976. *The Reform of Planning Law.* MacMillan, London.

Roberts, N.A. 1977. ed. *The Government Land Developers.* DC Heath, Lexington, Massachusetts.

Roweis, S.T. and Scott, A.J. 1978. The Urban Land Question. In ed Cox, K., *Urbanization and Conflict in Market Societies.* Methuen, London.

Royal Institute of Chartered Surveyors (RICS) 1978. *The Land Problem Reviewed.* RICS, London.

Royal Town Planning Institute 1972. RTPI Memorandum on the Local Government Bill. *Journal of the Royal Town Planning Institute,* Vol 58 (4), pp.151-52.

Royal Town Planning Institute 1976. *Planning and the Future.* RTPI, London.

Royal Town Planning Institute 1979. *Development Control: The Present System and Some Proposals for the Future.* RTPI, London.

Royal Town Planning Institute 1982. *The Public and Planning: Means to Better Participation.* RTPI, London.

Sant, M. 1980. Acquisition, Management and Disposal of Land. *Town and Country Planning,* Vol 49 (5), pp.146-51.

Saunders, D.L. 1977. The Changing Planning Framework. In ed Joyce, F.E., *Metropolitan Development and Change: The West Midlands - A Policy Review.* Teakfield, London, pp.36-49

Saunders, P. 1978. Domestic Property and Social Class. *International Journal of Urban and Regional Research*, Vol 2 (2), pp.231-51.

Saunders, P. 1980. *Urban Politics: a Sociological Interpretation*. Penguin, Harmondsworth.

Saunders, P. 1981. *Social Theory and the Urban Question*. Hutchinson, London.

Schuster, G. 1950. *Report of the Committee on Qualifications of Planners 1950*. HMSO, London.

Scott, A.J. 1980. *The Urban Land Nexus*. Pion, London.

Scott, A.J. and Roweis, S.T. 1977. Urban Planning in Theory and Practice, *Environment and Planning* A, Vol 9, pp.1097-1119.

Scottish Development Department (SDD) 1976. 28/76, *Development Plans*, SDD, Edinburgh.

Shucksmith, M. 1981. *No Homes for Locals*, Gower, Farnborough.

Simmie, J.M. 1981. *Power, Property and Corporatism*. MacMillan, London.

Smart, G. 1977. The future of development plans. *The Planner*, Vol 63, pp.5-7.

Smith, D.L. 1974. The Progress and Style of Structure Planning in England: Some Observations. *Local Government Studies*, October, pp.21-24.

Social Democratic Party (SDP) 1982. *Decentralising Government*, Green Paper No. 3. SDP, London.

Solesbury, W. 1974. *Policy in Urban Planning*. Pergamon, Oxford.

Spinney, R. 1978. Comments. In RTPI/RICS Joint Seminar Report, *Releasing Land for Building Development*. RTPI, London.

South East Joint Planning Team (SEJPT) 1970. *Strategic Plan for the South East*. HMSO, London.

Standing Conference on London and South East Regional Planning (SCLSERP) 1971. *The new development plan system*. LRP 1720, SCLSERP, London.

Standing Conference on London and South East Regional Planning (SCLSERP) 1973. *The new development plan system*, LRP 2125, SCLSERP, London.

Standing Conference on London and South East Regional Planning (SCLSERP) 1976. *The Improvement of London's Green Belt*, SC 620, SCLSERP, London.

Stephens, N. 1981. *The Practice of Estate Agency*. Estates Gazette, London.

Stewart, M. 1977. *Planning Systems Research Project*. DoE, London.

Stretton, H. 1976. *Capitalism, Socialism and the Environment*. Oxford University Press, Oxford.

Struthers, W.A.K. and Williamson, C. 1978. Economic Development - Integrated Policy Planning and Implementation in Merseyside, *Structure and Regional Planning Practice and Local Planning Practice*. PTRC, London, pp.1-10.

Tabb, W.K. and Sawers, L. (ed) 1978. *Marxism and the Metropolis*. Oxford University Press, New York.

Thomas, D. 1970. *London's Green Belt*. Faber and Faber, London.

Thomas, D., Minett, J., Hopkins, S., Hamnett, S., Faludi, A., Barrett, D. 1983. *Flexibility and Commitment in Planning*, Martinies Nijhoft, The Hague

Thomas, M.J. 1979. The procedural planning theory of A. Faludi. *Planning Outlook*, Vol 22 (2), pp.72-76.

Thompson, R. 1975. Linkages between structure planning and other agencies. In Drake *et al*. *Aspects of Structure Planning*. CES RP 20. Centre for Environmental Studies, London.

Thompson, R. 1977a. Camden's local plan: a district-wide approach. *The Planner*, Vol 63 (5), pp.145-7.

Thompson, R. 1977b. Making Local Plans Effective: The Camden Experience, *Structure Planning Practice and Local Planning Practice*. PTRC, London, pp.145-55.

Thompson, R. 1981. An alternative direction. *The Planner*, January/ February, pp.16-18.

Thorburn, A. 1968. The future form of development plans in Counties. *Journal of the Town Planning Institute*, Vol 54 (10), pp.468-72.

Thornley, J. 1975. The scope and content of structure planning. In ed. Drake *et al*. *Aspects of Structure Planning*. CES RP 20. Centre for Environmental Studies, London.

Titmuss, R.M. 1972. *Social Policy*. Allen and Unwin, London.

Town and Country Planning Association 1981. A step backwards: the TCPA's response to the proposed circular on development plans. *Town and Country Planning*, Vol 50 (7 and 8), pp.212-13.

Town Planning Institute 1966. Council's Observations on the Planning Advisory Group Report. *Journal of the Town Planning Institute*, Vol 52 (3), pp.86-87.

Townsend, P. 1975. Sociology and Social Policy. In Townsend, P. *Sociology and Social Policy*, pp.1-26. Allen Lane, Penguin.

Trafford, S.G. 1975. Making Local Planning Work - Case Study of Coventry, *Structure Planning Practice and Local Planning Practice*. PTRC, London, pp.123-31.

Trafford, S.G. and Hanna, B. 1977. The Coventry Experience. *Built Environment Quarterly*, Vol 3 (2), pp.147-50.

Turner, C. 1977. Progress in metropolitan structure planning. *The Planner*, Vo. 63 (6), pp.175-8.

Turton, R. 1979. An approach to local planning. In ed. Fudge, C., *Approaches to Local Planning*. SAUS Working Paper No. 3, SAUS, Bristol.

Underwood, J. 1980. *Town Planners in Search of a Role*. SAUS Occasional Paper No. 6, School of Advanced Urban Studies, Bristol.

United Nations (Department of Economic and Social Affairs) 1973. *Land Policies and Land Use Control Measures*. Vols I-VII, ST/ECA/167, Add 1-7. United Nations, New York.

Unsworth, J. 1977. Structure plans: The East Sussex Approach. *Public Finance and Accountancy*, Vol 4 (5), pp.151-3.

Uthwatt Report 1942. *Report of the Expert Committee on Compensation and Betterment*. Cmd 6386, HMSO, London.

Vielba, C.A. 1976. *A survey of those taking part in two structure plan examinations in public*. Institute of Judicial Administration, University of Birmingham.

Vine, K.M. 1980. *Local Plans in Country Towns: Their Validity and Effectiveness*. Town Planning Diploma Dissertation, Oxford Polytechnic.

Walters, A.A. 1974. Land speculation - creator or creature of inflation. In IEA *Government and the Land*, IEA, London.

Wannop, U. 1980. Scottish planning in practice: 4 distinctive characteristics. *The Planner*, Vol 66 (3), pp.64-65.

Watson, M. 1975. A comparative evaluation of planning practice in the liberal democratic state. In ed. Hayward, J. and Watson, M., *Planning, Politics and Public Policy*. CUP, London, pp.445-83.

Westergaard, J. 1977. Class, Inequality and 'Corporatism'. In ed. Hunt, A., *Class and Class Structure*. Lawrence and Wishart, London.

White, J. 1981. *A review of tourism in structure plans*. Centre for Urban and Regional Studies, University of Birmingham.

Whitehead, P. 1976. Public Participation in Structure Planning: A Review Article. *Town Planning Review*, Vol 47 (4), pp.374-83.

Whitney, D. 1974. Attitudes to the public. *The Planner*, Vol 60 (1), pp.496.

Whitney, D. *et al*. 1976. Experience in a Metropolitan District - Wakefield. *The Planner*, Vol 62 (5), pp.142-4.

Williams, R. 1978. Statutory local plans: progress and problems. *Planning Outlook*, Vol 21 (2), pp.22-27.

Williams, S. 1979. *The Implementation of the Covent Garden Action Area Plan*. MSc/Diploma in Urban Planning Options Project, Oxford Polytechnic.

Wilson, G.H. 1977a. Inflexibility delays progress. *Municipal and Public Services Journal*, 15th July.

Wilson, G.H. 1977b. Not much scope for reducing delays. *Municipal and Public Services Journal*, 12th August.

Wood, M. 1982. *The Implementation of Strategic Planning Policy in a Restraint Area in the South East,* Oxford Working Paper No. 67 Department of Town Planning, Oxford Polytechnic.

Yates, P.J. 1975. Local Planning in practice. *Town and Country Planning.* Vol 43 (11), pp.478-82.

Index

Note: Items addressed throughout the book are omitted (e.g.: local plans; Department of the Environment; planning authorities). Place names are also omitted to avoid swamping the index. Legislation, and special terms in British planning procedures, are in italics.